AMERICA IS BORN

Introducing the

Regulus USA National Horoscope

Also by Regulus Astrology LLC

A RECTIFICATION MANUAL
The American Presidency (2007)

for errata and updates visit
www.regulus-astrology.com

AMERICA IS BORN

Introducing the

Regulus USA National Horoscope

Regulus Astrology LLC

Copyright © Regulus Astrology LLC 2008-2021

First Edition, November 25, 2008
Second Edition, May 28, 2021

All rights reserved. No part of this work may be used or reproduced in any manner whatsoever without written permission from the publisher, except in the case of brief quotations embodied in critical articles or reviews.

Grateful acknowledgement is made for permission to publish software output:

Astrology House: For permission to include astrological charts calculated by Janus 5.5 software and Janus fonts, copyright © 1998-2021.

Dynamic Traders Group, Inc.: For permission to include charts of historical market data created by Dynamic Trader 7.1 software, copyright © 1996-2021.

Grateful acknowledgement is made for permission to reprint previously published material:

The Wessex Astrologer: Excerpts on divination and rectification from *The Moment of Astrology*, by Geoffrey Cornelius, copyright © 2003 by Geoffrey Cornelius. Available from www.wessexastrologer.com.

The Wessex Astrologer: Excerpt on the Sibly USA National Horoscope from The Book of World Horoscopes, by Nicholas Campion, copyright © 2004 by Nicholas Campion.

Benjamin Dykes/Cazimi Press: Excerpt on delineation of Saturn/Libra for mundane figures from *Book of Astronomy*, by Guido Bonatti, translated by Benjamin Dykes, copyright © 2007 by Benjamin Dykes. Available from www.bendykes.com.

ISBN: 978-0-9801856-2-1 (paper)
ISBN: 978-0-9801856-3-8 (electronic)

CONTENTS

Preface ix
Introduction xiii
User's Guide xix

Part I THE SIBLY USA NATIONAL HOROSCOPE

Chapter 1	National Horoscopes in Mundane Astrology	3
Chapter 2	Revisiting the Sibly USA National Horoscope	11
Chapter 3	Divination and Rectification	27

Part II THE REGULUS USA NATIONAL HOROSCOPE

Chapter 4	Abū Ma'shar's System of Distributors and Partners	40
Chapter 5	Calculation: Distributors & Partners	47
Chapter 6	Distributor Results: Directing through the Bounds	89

Mars/Sagittarius: Fight for Religious Freedom, Virginia Statute for Religious Freedom.

Mercury/Capricorn: Reorganization of William & Mary. Noah Webster and Early Elementary Education; Jupiter/Capricorn: United States Constitution; Venus/Capricorn: Trade Treaties and War Profiteering; Saturn/Capricorn: *Marbury v. Madison* and Judicial Review; Mars/Capricorn: First Barbary War. Embargo Acts.

Mercury/Aquarius: Maritime Trade, Maritime Law and the War of 1812; Venus/Aquarius: Delineating Aquarius as Internal Improvements. Wedding of the Waters; Jupiter/Aquarius: Engineering Education. Judicial Support for Internal Improvements; Mars/Aquarius: Rise of Partisan Politics; Saturn/Aquarius: Lyceum Movement. Trade Embargo of John Quincy Adams. Abolition Movement.

Venus/Pisces: Romanticism in Art and the Hudson River School. Blackface Performance and Jump Jim Crow; Jupiter/Pisces: United States Exploration Expedition; Mercury/Pisces: Dance Master Juba and the Evolution of Blackface Performance; Mars/Pisces: New England Whaling Industry; Saturn/Pisces: Establishing Boundaries at the Conclusion of the Mexican War.

Jupiter/Aries: Young America Movement. Phrenology; Venus/Aries: Stephen Douglas, Railroads, and Kansas. *Uncle Tom's Cabin*; Mercury/Aries: Kansas Constitutional Crisis; Mars/Aries: Lincoln's Presidential Nomination and the American Civil War; Saturn/Aries: New York Draft Riots. Gettysburg.

Venus/Taurus: Opera in the Gilded Age; Mercury/Taurus: Metropolitan Museum of Art; Jupiter/Taurus: Robber Baron Capitalism; Saturn/Taurus: Chicago Meatpacking Industry; Mars/Taurus: Haymarket Riot: Fight for the Eight Hour Workday.

Mercury/Gemini: Office Automation. Burroughs Calculating Machine. Hollerith Tabulating Machine; Jupiter/Gemini: Populist-Free Silver Movement. Expansion of Telephone and Print Media Industries; Venus/Gemini: Growth of Corporate Trusts. 5 and 10 cent Stores. Invention of the Phonograph; Mars/Gemini: Muckraker Movement. Reckless Risk Taking. Auto Racing; Saturn/Gemini: Business Regulation and Scientific Management. End of Muckraker Era.

Mars/Cancer: Isolationism. Ku Klux Klan. Prohibition; Venus/Cancer: Rise of Consumerism. Mae West-Sex Symbol. Elsie the Cow; Mercury/Cancer: Popularity of Radio. H. G. Wells' *War of the Worlds*. Political Demagogues: Huey Long and Charles Coughlin; Jupiter/Cancer: Henry Wallace and American Farm Policy. Consumer Banking. Credit Unions; Saturn/Cancer: Hollywood Blacklist. McCarthyism.

Jupiter/Leo: Christianity as a Bulwark against Communism. Religion and Scouting; Venus/Leo: The Kennedy *Camelot* Era. Cocktail Culture, Frank Sinatra, and the Rat Pack. Pop Music and the Beatles; Saturn/Leo: Black Panther Party; Mercury/Leo: *Rocky* and the Blockbuster Film Era; Mars/Leo: Action Heroes and Military Revival.

Mercury/Virgo: Microsoft, Windows, and the World Wide Web; Venus/Virgo: The Sopranos. Poker Craze. *Martha Stewart Living* and the Makeover Craze; Jupiter/Virgo: Craft Beer Popularity. Google and Big Data. Obamacare; Mars/Virgo: Wearable Fitness Trackers. Fitness Training. Natural Resource Extraction.

Chapter 7	Partner Results: Ascendant Directions	139
Chapter 8	Partners: Moon	147

1. Heroines - Sybil Ludington and Molly Pitcher. Heroes - Marquis de Lafayette. 2. Columbia River Basin Exploration. Birth of Kit Carson. Erie Canal. 3. Abolition Movement. Smithsonian Institution Bequest. Elimination of Prison Sentences for Debtors. 4. Abolition. Seneca Falls Convention. Bridges. Panama Canal. 5. Emancipation, Lincoln's assassination, and Lincoln's funeral train. Fisk University. 6. Labor Movements. Edward Bellamy and Nationalist Clubs. 7. Panama Canal Opening. Public Radio. 8. Women's Equal Rights Amendment and Election Victories. Coolidge Radio Broadcast. Birth of Shirley Chisholm. 9. Panama Canal and the Arrest of Manuel Noriega. Civil Rights and Congress. George H. W. Bush's *Thousand Points of Light*. 10. Cornelius Vanderbilt and Grand Central Renovation. Amtrack Problems. Women's Rights.

Chapter 9   Partners: Sun   165

1. Capital Building Groundbreaking Ceremony. Thomas Paine's *The Rights of Man* and *The Age of Reason*. 2. Missionaries: Opposition to Indian Removal. Missionaries: Oregon Territory. 3. Transcendentalism. 4. John Fremont and the Mormon Handcart Pioneers. Explorers: Birth of Robert Perry. 5. Antietam, Clara Barton, and the American Red Cross. Four Great Surveys of the West. Missionaries: Birth of Lydia Lord Davis. 6. Valentine McGillycuddy and the Black Hills Gold Rush. Religion: Christian Science. 7. Controversy over Rockefeller Bequests for Missionary Work. Carnegie Bequests for Superannuated Preachers and Faculty. Missionaries: Death of Hudson Taylor. 8. The New Deal. Federal Home Loan Banking Act. Religion: Dominionism. Monuments. 9. Black Hills Legal Settlement. Harvard Medical Center. Founding of Cabrini Hospice. 10. Mortgage Crisis.

Chapter 10   Partners: Lunar Nodes   179

1. Gradual Emancipation of Slaves enacted by New York State. 2. Hartford Convention. 3. Supreme Court Decision: *Mayor of New York v. Miln*. 4. Dispute over Clayton-Bulwar Treaty. 5. Erie Canal Fraud. 6. Pacific Mail Company Fraud. 7. Deterioration of Gold Supplies. 8. Missionaries: Death of Frank Gamewell. Social Security Legislation. Military Service. 9. Segregation Legislation. Missionaries: Vietnam Kidnapping. French Satellite Launch. Dollar Stabilization Program. Military Draft. 10. End of Net Neutrality.

Chapter 11   Partners: Saturn   197

1. Weights and Measures. Jefferson-Hamilton Feud. 2. Coinage Act of 1792 and creation of the United States Dollar. 3. The Second Bank of the United States and the Panic of 1819. 4. The California Gold Rush, Economic Boom, and the Panic of 1857. 5. Post-Civil War Contraction of Greenbacks. 6. Bimetallism Discredited as a Populist Policy; Gold Standard introduced. Corporations, Merger Mania, and the McKinley Assassination. 7. Devaluation of the Sterling and the U.S. Dollar. 8. Supreme Court Appointment: Robert Jackson. Anti-Japanese WWII Legal Measures. 9. Rise of Inflation and the Collapse of U.S. Dollar under the Nixon Presidency. Failed Supreme Court Nomination of G. Harrold Carswell. 10. The Carter-Reagan Divide: Recovered Confidence in the U.S. Dollar. 11. Recovery of the US Dollar following the Great Financial Crisis.

Chapter 12   Partners: Mars   217

1. Death of Charles Lee. End of Revolutionary War with England. 2. End of the 'Era of Good Feelings.' Congressional Nomination of William Crawford for the Presidency. 3. Oregon Territory. 4. Five Points Riot. Panic of 1857. Death of John McLoughlin. 5. Outbreak of Civil War. 6. Venezuela-British Guiana Border Dispute. 7. Panic of 1907. The Great Auto Race of 1908. 8. Proposed Railroad Reorganization - FDR's 100 Days. 9. Chrysler Bailout. Federal Reserve Targets Money Supply. 10.

Formula One Auto Racing. Grand Theft Auto: San Andreas. Bankruptcy of MG-Rover. 11. End to DACA program and National Antifa Rally.

Chapter 13   Partners: Mercury   231

1. Impeachment of John Pickering. New England-Canadian Smuggling. 2. West Florida Occupation. The Negro Fort at Prospect Bluff. 3. Texas and the Mexican War. California Constitutional Convention. 4. *Uncle Tom's Cabin.* Kansas-Nebraska Act. 5. Emancipation Proclamation. Reconstruction. 6. Pittsburgh Manifesto. Disarray of Labor Movements. 7. Immigration Reform: Creation of Ellis Island. Birth of Princess Stephanie Juliann von Hohenlohe. 8. Detonation of nuclear weapons over Hiroshima and Nagasaki. White-Hiss Congressional Testimony. 9. Bugged American Intelligence Embassy in Moscow. Death Sentence of Mass Murderer Richard Speck. Attack on USS Liberty.

Chapter 14   Partners: Venus   243

1. Newburgh Conspiracy. British Abolitionist Movement. 2. Jump Jim Crow. Veto of the Second Bank of the United States. 3. Muncy Abolition Riot. 4. Missouri Compromise Debate and the Nashville Convention. 5. Race Riots: Pulaski, New Orleans and Camilla, Georgia. 6. Reconstruction. Mining Swindles. 7. Food Scarcity - World War I. 8. Passage of the 19th Amendment - Women's Suffrage. Warren Harding's Anti-Lynching Campaign. 9. The Rodney King Verdict. 10. California Proposition 187. Denny's Restaurant Settlement. Coke vs. Pepsi Ad Campaign addresses Sugar Content.

Chapter 15   Partners: Jupiter   257

1. Shay's Rebellion. 2. Andrew Jackson's Bank War. 3. Aroostook War. 4. Retail Banking. 5. Bank Act of 1870. 6. Banks, Debt, Taxation, and Insolvency. 7. Expansion of Bank Lending on the Outbreak of World War I. 8. Defeat of Branch Banking. 9. Kidder Peabody Reorganization. Savings & Loan Crisis: Loss of Branch Banking and Minority Access. 10. Federal Trade Commission: Formation and Lawsuits against Microsoft and Intel.

Chapter 16   Final Thoughts   271

Appendix A   Event Catalog for Initial Rectification Phase 273
Appendix B   Catalog of Ascendant Directions   279
Appendix C   Supplement: Directing through the Bounds   293
Appendix D   Tests of Egyptian versus Ptolemaic Bounds   339
Appendix E   Solar Arc Directions   359
End Notes   391

PREFACE to the 2nd Edition

Since published twelve years ago, I have tracked the progress of this horoscope's primary directions computed for the Ascendant using Abū Ma'shar's System of Distributors and Partners. As described in Chapter 6, Ascendant Distributor's time social movements which correspond to the Distributor's planet/sign combination. Since 2008, the Venus/Virgo distribution completed, the Jupiter/Virgo distribution came and went, and the Mars/Virgo distribution is ongoing. During the Jupiter/Virgo distribution in 2015 I made the first formal public prediction using this horoscope: that Craft Beer popularity would peak in 2016 and decline after the start of the Mars/Virgo distribution on April 28, 2017. Discussion of this prediction and its outcome is available on www.regulus-astrology.com and may form one of several essays on the Regulus USA National Horoscope to be published at a later date. All books have their purpose. This book is designed to document and support the proposed rectification. Keeping to this objective, this second edition updates events which match the astrological delineation of Ascendant Distributors and Partners; nothing more, nothing less.

In addition to delineation and comments on the two additional Ascendant Distributors, this edition adds events for three participating directions:

Lunar Nodes #10. End of Net Neutrality
Saturn #11. Recovery of the US Dollar following the Great Financial Crisis
Mars #11. End to DACA program and National Antifa Rally

Following Ben Dykes, Abū Mashar's System of Distributors and Participators substitutes the word 'Partners' for 'Participators.' The terms are identical.

Finally, example horoscopes supplied in Appendix C have been given a substantial 'once over' with Zodiacal Releasing from Spirit used as an additional rectification tool. Lorenzo Fowler (Jupiter/Aries), Mae West (Venus/Cancer), and Joseph McCarthy (Saturn/Cancer) now replace George Nicholas Sanders, Calvin Coolidge, and Gregory Peck. Rectification details are available on www.regulus-astrology.com.

Dr. H.
Regulus Astrology LLC
May 21, 2021

PREFACE to the 1st Edition

A word of caution to astrologers who choose to study and comment on this figure, whether for educational or professional purposes. If one studies the history of mundane astrology since the Roman era, one finds the most successful mundane astrologers were those who worked directly for the ruling class during times of economic prosperity. Few leaders can withstand cycles of diminishing fortune, nor can their astrologers who quickly find themselves out of a job or worse.

One of the ways astrologers can protect themselves in these situations is to choose their clients carefully and exercise wise counsel in their astrological practice. Easier said than done. But astrologers have an edge on how to navigate these vicissitudes. The edge is Mercury. In medieval astrology, Mercury signifies astrology and the astrologer. It's a point I return to in Chapter 3 on Divination and Rectification where I emphasize the bias of Mercury on an astrologer's own astrological practice and research.

In the same way that marriage partners take on corresponding roles of the Sun and Moon in each other's charts, so too does the astrologer take on the role of Mercury in a client's chart. Speaking as an astrologer who has worked for a single enterprise for an extended period of time, I can state unambiguously that many of my own actions have been timed by primary directions of Mercury to the angles computed for the company's incorporation chart. By choosing to work for the company, I effectively took on the role of Mercury in the company's horoscope with its own unique zodiacal state.

The ramifications of the Mercury-client impact on an astrologer's professional practice are huge. Ideally astrologers should seek out clients whose Mercury placements are fortunate and strong. Forming relationships with clients who meet this condition will allow the astrologer to improve his practice, and in doing so, attain greater wisdom in meeting whatever challenges arise.

If Mercury signifies the astrologer in a client's figure, then what are the implications for Mercury's position in the chart of a mundane figure? It appears to me that astrologers who study a mundane country chart for an extended period of time effectively create a long-term client relationship with the figure. As with clients, I suggest mundane astrologers take on the role of Mercury in a mundane figure after extended study.

If so, then consider the zodiacal state of Mercury in the Regulus USA National Horoscope.

<u>Mercury:</u> 24CA10'32", *retrograde, under the beams, bound of Jupiter/Cancer, dwad Aries, square Saturn, placed in the 8th, ruled by but in aversion to Moon/Aquarius; rules Mars/Gemini in turn.*

The bottom line is Mercury's condition is unfortunate and functions as an accidental malefic. Mercury is peregrine in Cancer, helped somewhat by placement in the bound of Jupiter but this is only minor assistance. Mercury square Saturn and Mercury in aversion to the Moon are two indications of mental illness, all the worse because the Moon is Mercury's ruler. Retrograde, under the beams, and placement in one of the bad houses are serious debilities. Dwad of Aries adds rashness. Ruled by the humanitarian Aquarian Moon, Mercury means well but he still causes strife through rulership of Mars.

To demonstrate the weakness of Mercury, compare this delineation to actual events timed by Ascendant-Mercury directions presented in Chapter 13:

- Impeachment of Judge John Pickering on insanity charges
- Occupation of West Florida on a 'false flag' pretext prior to annexation
- Propaganda surrounding the annexation of Texas
- Demagoguery of anarchist labor movements
- Removal of swindlers preying on Ellis Island immigrants
- Detonation of nuclear weapons over Hiroshima and Nagasaki
- Spy testimony of Alger Hiss
- Spy testimony of Harry Dexter White and White's death
- Death sentence of mass murderer Richard Speck
- Mistaken attack on USS Liberty in the Six-Day War, single largest loss of life by the U.S. intelligence community.

It's my opinion the weakness of Mercury in the Regulus USA National Horoscope means the call for astrologers to work at the national political level should not be answered. I suggest those who choose to do so will ultimately take on the role of Mercury to the detriment of themselves and the nation. As an advisor to America, an astrologer may ultimately help start a false-flag military operation, be confined in a mental institution, or be identified as the fall-guy. To some, these warnings may appear extreme. If you believe so, then you haven't yet studied this figure or the fate of astrologers during periods of upheavals in world history.

So how do I suggest astrologers use this figure?

First one can recast the delineation of Mercury/Cancer, retrograde, and under the beams as the ability to study mundane USA astrology privately in one's own home. Mercury under the beams is hidden; a match to private study. Cancer is the sign of the home; a match to study in the home. Mercury retrograde is a useful for research; here to revisit historical events in order to practice astrological technique. One still can't escape the weakness of Mercury by taking this option; yet by keeping study private one can keep some of the more dire outcomes of Mercury's delineation at arm's length.

A second tactic is to acknowledge Mercury as an accidental malefic and face its challenges directly by creating an astrological practice which specializes in the study of mental illness and criminal behavior. The prevalence of psychics involved in criminal cases, widely publicized through television series like *America's Most Wanted*, demonstrates public acceptance of alternative investigative methods in the United States, a category to which astrology belongs. Ultimately, creation of an astrological profiling consultancy whose services are available to law enforcement agencies should be considered. Within a few more years, sufficient recapture and testing of both Hellenistic and Medieval astrological systems will make this a feasible option.

What restrictions should be placed on astrologers using this figure?

Ethical standards of most astrological organizations prohibit the prediction of death for a client or any prediction which may cause a client unreasonable fear. What is appropriate for individual forecasts made through natal astrology also holds for mundane astrological forecasts. Unfortunately, the recent behavior of American astrologers belies these guidelines with frequent forecasts ranging from *risk periods* to *death* for public officials, often made by astrologers with opposing political views to the party in power. In my opinion, this behavior needs an urgent smack down by the astrological community if astrology wishes to survive in American society. For nothing could be worse than a successful prediction of harm to or death of public officials. For the astrologer making the prediction, it might result in interrogation by the Secret Service, possible incarceration, and a new public identity as the prophet of misfortune who implicitly facilitated the event through accusation of either direct involvement or passive inaction. This is a lose-lose situation. Any astrologer who believes otherwise is naïve or a fool.

INTRODUCTION

The objective of this book is to document a rectified time for the symbolic moment of the United States Declaration of Independence. Based on a mix of 300+ primary directions, solar arc directions, and transits to the Ascendant; the result is July 4, 1776, 6:17:37 PM, LMT +5:00:40, Ascendant = 26SA54'40", Philadelphia, PA. This new chart is named the ***Regulus USA National Horoscope***. Results of this rectification project make significant steps towards, but fall short of, a full delineation. No predictions are offered.

==============

Medieval mundane astrological methods include Jupiter-Saturn conjunctions, ingresses, and eclipses. What are now referred to as *National Horoscopes* were not used in the medieval era because they did not exist. With no consensus on a valid United States National Horoscope some 232 years into the nation's history, skepticism on the relevance of modern National Horoscopes is warranted because modern mundane astrological methods - mostly psychological - suffer the same weaknesses as modern natal astrology.

But does the revival of medieval mundane astrological methods mean National Horoscopes should be dismissed out of hand because practicing medieval astrologers did not use them? Some say yes. True to the art, my teacher Robert Zoller bases his delineation and prediction of mundane forecasts solely on rules and aphorisms left by authors prior to 1600. After considering what the masters have said, Zoller puts down his pen. By contrast, most modern astrologers have probably never read an astrological text written prior to 1600, consider the ingress approach to mundane astrology as old-fashioned, and are content to interpret modern National Horoscopes using psychological astrology as a prop. In bridging this gap, I have taken a hybrid approach. By avoiding modern planets, maintaining traditional rulerships, and making a good faith effort of approaching National Horoscopes within the medieval astrological tradition, the results of this study represent a middle ground. Successful tests of a National Horoscope cast for the American Declaration of Independence on July 4, 1776 confirm the relevance of medieval methods when applied to the question of National Horoscopes.

To be sure, there was no guarantee at the onset of this research project that I would be successful. I could have as easily determined that a horoscope cast for the Declaration of Independence represented a footnote on the day's activities, perhaps reflecting nothing more than chit chat between delegates that day in Philadelphia. To reach this conclusion would have made my life as a professional mundane astrologer much easier; I could have safely tossed out National Horoscopes and returned exclusively to ingresses and other medieval mundane astrological tools.

But the fact the reader is holding a book of some weight and reading these words gives away the outcome. I cracked the code. The ability of the Regulus USA National Horoscope to delineate and predict events ranging from the origin of the Women's Suffrage movement at Seneca Falls (1848) to the Civil War (1861-1865) to the detonation of nuclear weapons over Hiroshima and Nagasaki (1945) represents tangible evidence of the first successful attempt made to validate a National Horoscope using the tools of medieval predictive astrology.

============

As this book evolved, it became clear the workings of mundane astrology required a connection between National Horoscopes and actual individuals playing out larger mundane roles.

Thesis: The Mundane-Natal Horoscope Connection

Mundane astrology works because planetary configurations in mundane charts sympathetically trigger actions by individuals with similar natal configurations. These individuals are 'lifted up' from the masses to play out events promised by mundane horoscopes.

This thesis has important implications for testing National Horoscopes. Take this challenge: delineate and predict an event using any National Horoscope. Compare the prediction to actual events. Determine if individuals involved in observed mundane events possess planetary configurations in their natal figures which are similar to the National Horoscope under study. Determine if these natal configurations are triggered by relevant dynamic measurements at the time of the observed mundane event. I suggest the ability to make these connections represents the acid test for confirming the validity of any proposed National Horoscope. To this end, readers are invited to study results presented in Chapter 6 and Appendix C in support of the proposed rectification for the Regulus USA National Horoscope.

============

Chapter 1 places the Regulus USA National Horoscope, and National Horoscopes generally, within the context of the history of mundane astrology. How a consensus was reached on the Sibly USA National Horoscope is the focus of the chapter.

In Chapter 2, I take up Nick Campion's challenge to experiment with the Sibly USA National Horoscope using medieval methods. Now in my sixth year of working with this chart (2008), I reconstruct my initial (2002) and final (2004) rectification steps to retool the Sibly USA National Horoscope.

Like many research projects conducted over multi-year periods, methods used at the outset evolved considerably. Significant to my astrological development was completion of Robert Zoller's Diploma Course in Medieval Predictive Astrology in March 2005 and rectification research on the American Presidents, published as my first book *A Rectification Manual: The American Presidency* in December 2007. What this means is initial rectification experiments with the Sibly USA National Horoscope taken in 2002 included using transit hits to the angles; an approach I now disparage. That I was able to achieve a result relatively close to the final rectification result made in 2004 with such a dubious method I attribute to two factors. First is the ability of transits to the angles to function as a 'rectification assist' when working with a chart whose parameters are relatively well known. A second factor behind my near success in 2002 was the role of divination, a topic I take up in Chapter 3.

Between 2002 and 2004, I set aside experiments with the Sibly USA National Horoscope to finish my astrological studies with Robert Zoller. This included instruction on primary directions. By the time I returned to the Sibly USA National Horoscope in December 2004, I had made my crucial discovery of the *primary direction sequence* and was ready to attack the Sibly chart once again. Only with the scalpels of primary directions did a reliable rectification solution prove achievable.

As a point of departure, Chapter 3 compares my findings on choosing magical times for rectification to the work of Geoffrey Cornelius who includes a section on Divination and Rectification in *The Moment of Astrology*. While I share the validity of the role of divination in astrology, I differ with Cornelius who rejects a necessary correspondence between computed horoscopes and actual physical events. As posited in *A Rectification Manual*, magical times conducive to rectification occur when connections to the chart under study are made by the current position of transiting Moon or Mercury. I observed these conditions at the conclusion of both initial and final rectification stages and share horoscopes for these *AHA!* moments of discovery as evidence of divination at work. These horoscopes shed light on the status and accuracy of each rectification stage.

Chapters 4 and 5 present the theory and application of *Abū Ma'shar's System of Distributors and Partners* used to rectify the horoscope. Abū Ma'shar combines primary directions of planets to significators with the specialized technique known as Directing through the Bounds. Chapter 5 includes formulas and fully worked out examples for directing planets, aspects, and bounds to the Ascendant by direct and converse motion.

Chapter 6 presents results of Directing through the Bounds and easily constitutes the most important findings of the entire research project. As a contribution to the field of mass social movements, results of this study reveal that many of America's social movements can be explained by directing the Ascendant of the Regulus USA National Horoscope through the Egyptian bounds by primary motion. Whenever the Ascendant moves from one bound to another, the Ascendant adopts characteristics of the respective bound's planet/sign combination as a theme which is borne out through America's national consciousness. Seemingly unrelated historical episodes such as Robber Baron capitalism (1876-1882), the second Ku Klux Klan (1917-1925), and Microsoft, Windows and the World Wide Web (1990-1999) are fully explained by Directing through the Bounds. Not only does Chapter 6 present what is ostensibly the most comprehensive empirical test of Directing through the Bounds ever attempted, it provides evidence which supports Egyptian over Ptolemaic bounds in most cases, a topic taken up further in Appendix D. Considering the precision of historical events occurring at changeovers from one bound to the next, results of Directing through the Bounds are so compelling I suggest the rectification of the Regulus USA National Horoscope can stand alone on the merits of this technique without recourse to any other predictive method.

Chapter 7 introduces Planet & Lunar Node directions to the Ascendant which follow in Chapters 8-15. For astrologers familiar with primary directions, these chapters represent the meat of the rectification. Assigning the Ascendant to the role of Significator, the complete set of planet-Ascendant directions is presented. There is no cherry picking. Every direction is presented for the Ascendant as significator.

Chapter 8 closes with some final thoughts on ideas for future research. Included are a few observations on mundane methodology.

Appendix A lists an event catalog used for the initial July 2002 rectification. It is indicative of the scope of events considered relevant for testing any USA National Horoscope.

Appendix B lists all Ascendant Distributors and Partners, computed by direct and converse motion, for the Regulus USA National Horoscope. Making a copy of this Appendix is recommended for ease of reference.

In support of **The Mundane-Natal Horoscope Connection**, Appendix C provides supplementary evidence from natal charts of individuals who influenced America's national consciousness as defined by the Directing through the Bounds procedure presented in Chapter 6. In many cases, the natal chart replicates the same planet/sign combination as the Distributor for the National Horoscope.

Appendix D takes a closer look at results of Directing through the Bounds presented in Chapter 6. Researched using Egyptian bounds, results are contrasted with results using Ptolemy's bounds. With the exception for the sign of Pisces where some irregularities in Egyptian bounds were noted, the study concludes Egyptian bounds for Capricorn, Aquarius, Aries, Taurus, Gemini, Cancer, Leo, and early Virgo yield more consistent results than Ptolemy's bounds.

Appendix E includes Solar Arc Directions computed for all planet-Ascendant permutations using Ptolemaic aspects. Though solar arcs are not a medieval technique; I include them because they provide results which are just as consistent as primary directions. In an attempt to identify a Rosetta stone which links effects of both solar arc and primary directions, I restate the Solar Arc - Primary Directions Proposition first made in *A Rectification Manual*. A limited data sample suggests the merits of the proposition are maintained and deserve further study.

=============

Acknowledgements: Special thanks to Chris Brennan for editorial assistance, to Meredith Garstin for graphic design, and to Jonathan Pearl for ongoing discussions on medieval techniques.

=============

Dr. H.
Regulus Astrology LLC
November 4, 2008

USER'S GUIDE

A summary of assumptions, notation, and presentation style.

Prerequisites

Rectification of the Regulus USA National Horoscope is based on primary directions and solar arc directions. For those new to primary directions, take a deep breath. This book is designed for beginners. Terminology, formulas, and examples presented in Chapters 4 and 5 assume no prior knowledge of primary directions. What is required are basic algebra and trigonometry skills.

Solar arc directions are presented in Appendix E as supplementary measurements in support of the rectification. The calculation method for solar arc directions is based on the secondary progressed Sun and is not described in this text. For those new to solar arc directions, Noel Tyl's *Solar Arcs* (Llewellyn, 2001) is recommended. For *America is Born*, the abbreviations 'd.s.a.' and 'c.s.a.' are used when presenting results of 'direct solar arcs' and 'converse solar arcs.'

Though concentrating on primary directions, this book does mention other techniques of medieval predictive astrology including Firdaria and solar returns. Assumptions vary widely for these techniques among practicing astrologers. This text continues to use conventions introduced in my first book *A Rectification Manual: The American Presidency* (Regulus Astrology LLC, 2007). With over two dozen endnote references made to *A Rectification Manual*, hereafter abbreviated as *ARM*, it is highly recommended as a prerequisite for study of the Regulus USA National Horoscope.

As a minor change, I have made two simplifications in terminology for this book. *America is Born* uses 'Prenatal Lunation' instead of 'Syzygy Ante Navitatem' and 'Ruler of the Chart' instead of 'Al-mubtazz Figurae.'

Primary Directions

Events central to the proposed rectification of the Regulus USA National Horoscope are computed with primary directions. As a starting point, the rectification restricts computation of primary directions to the Ascendant. For treatment of latitude, I employ the *primary direction sequence* first introduced in *ARM*. This means two directions are computed for each planet-Ascendant direction; the first with the planet's full latitude, the second with zero latitude.

All primary directions are computed using zodiacal projections of planets and their aspects, a method referred to as *in zodiaco* by some authors. Interplanetary directions presented in Appendix C computed for natal charts of prominent Americans are made using the Regiomontanus under the Pole algorithm as computed by Janus 3.0 software.

Presentation

How we choose to label and speak about primary directions plays an important role in how well primary directions as a methodology is communicated. In *ARM*, I chose to present primary directions results based on report output directly from Janus 3.0 software. As readers will soon learn, recovery of the centrality of bounds to primary directions theory has caused me to revisit the notation question. In making changes to the presentation format of primary directions for *American is Born*, I have considered the work of primary directions specialist Rumen Kolev as a starting point.[1]

Historically there has been confusion among authors on definition of the terms 'significator' and 'promissor.' Formally introduced in Chapter 5, the *significator* is the planet or point which is held fixed on the celestial sphere. The *promissor* is the planet, aspect, or point which moves with the celestial sphere as the sphere rotates on its axis. In presenting notation, the promissor always appears first; the significator, second. This is the convention adopted by Rumen Kolev and the one I have chosen to follow.

For this book, this issue becomes important when considering a variety of Ascendant, Midheaven, and interplanetary primary directions computed for natal charts presented in Appendix C. For directions computed by direct motion, Janus software output follows these conventions. In its primary directions module, Janus software labels the first term 'directed planet' which is equivalent to 'promissor.' The second term 'radix' is equivalent to 'significator.' However for directions computed by converse motion, Janus software *reverses* this convention. For Janus users, please be aware that I have modified Janus software output for converse directions in order to maintain the adopted convention that the promissor be listed first and the significator second. Please note this is an issue of notation and presentation, not a debate over the accuracy of Janus primary direction calculations.

Definitions and Suggested Presentation Format for an Article or Book

D	Mars/Sagittarius	P	dex. sextile Moon (l=0) d. → ASC	22-Jul-1777
D	Mars/Sagittarius	P	dex. sextile Moon (l=MO) d. → ASC	1-Aug-1779

Promissor. This is the planet, aspect, or point which moves with the celestial sphere as the sphere rotates on its axis. For the first example, the promissor is the dexter sextile aspect of the Moon, labeled as 'dex. sextile Moon (l=0).'

Significator. This is the point held fixed on the celestial sphere. Originally, only the Ascendant, Midheaven, Sun, Moon, Lot of Fortune, and Prenatal Lunation were allowable significators. Examples in the main portion of this text adhere to this convention using the Ascendant as significator. For this example "ASC" is the symbol for the Ascendant. Note the significator *always* appears to the *right* of the arrow. Later authors allowed planets to take on the role of the significator. Examples of this variation are found in Appendix C. But no matter what is listed as the promissor or significator, the same principal holds that any planet or point listed to the *right* of the arrow is held fixed on the celestial sphere.

Distributors and Partners. Abū Ma'shar introduces two new words to primary directions vocabulary. Formally presented in Chapter 5, the **Distributor** is the Egyptian bound placement for the promissor. Central to Abū Ma'shar's System of Distributors and Partners, the Distributor contributes roughly half of the effect of the actual direction by effectively setting the stage for actors to play out roles as Partners. The **Partner** is nothing more than a pair of promissors and significators. Compared to the way most traditional astrologers practice primary directions, what is new is Abū Ma'shar's introduction of the term **Distributor** for the Egyptian bound. More about this in Chapter 5. For now, recognize that 'D' stands for Distributor and 'P' stands for Partner. For the first example (top row):

D = Distributor = bound = 'Mars/Sagittarius'
P = Partner = 'dex. sextile Moon (l=0) d. → ASC'

Because bounds function differently across signs, bounds need to be identified beyond the planet itself. Stating 'the bound of Mars' tells us little because 'the bound of Mars in Sagittarius' behaves much differently than 'the bound of Mars in Capricorn.' *Bounds need identification by both planet and sign.*

Aspect. The type of aspect between the promissor and significator. Either conjunction, sextile, square, trine, or opposition. For this example 'sextile' denotes the relevant aspect.

Dexter/Sinister. For sextile, square, and trine aspects, there are two aspects to consider. To specify which aspect, the terms dexter (abbreviated 'dex.') and sinister (abbreviated 'sin.') are used. Dexter aspects are found by beginning at the planet and moving against the order of the signs; sinister aspects, vice versa. See Chapter 5, Example 2 for visual examples of both. For this example, 'dex.' is the abbreviation for the dexter aspect of the Moon. With the Moon's position at 27AQ51, the dexter sextile aspect of the Moon is 27SA51. With the bound of Mars defined to be the four degree range from 26SA00'00" to 29SA59'59", this dexter sextile aspect of the Moon falls within the bound of Mars/Sagittarius. This is why Mars/Sagittarius is designated the Distributor.

Latitude. Janus offers latitude assignments for the directed aspect. There are two latitude conditions: either zero latitude or the planet's full latitude. Latitude is abbreviated as 'l.' For zero latitude directions, the number '0' is either listed or omitted for the Sun and Nodes where latitude is always zero. For full planet latitude directions, the planet's name is abbreviated. For the first row in this example, '(l=0)' denotes the direction is computed with a zero latitude assumption for the Moon. For the second row in this example, '(l=MO)' indicates the Moon's full latitude is used to compute the direction.

Direct or Converse. Whether the celestial sphere is moved by direct motion (abbreviated as 'd.') or by converse motion (abbreviated as 'c.') requires identification. For this example, 'd.' indicates direct motion.

The projected event date is listed last. Ptolemy's Key is used to convert the arc of direction to the projected date when the direction is due.
Ptolemy's Key: 1 degree = 1year = 365.2424 days.

Method - *Mundo* versus *In Zodiaco*. Medieval astrologers relied on zodiacal directions, based on the zodiacal projections of planets and their aspects. All directions presented in *America is Born* are computed *in zodiaco*. Mundo primary directions, sometimes referred to as 'mundane', use the earth as a point of reference and were developed later by Placidus. Kolev uses the abbreviations 'M' for mundane and 'ZOD' for zodiacal directions, a choice I support for those who choose to present results for both systems.

Method - Interplanetary directions. Most commonly used in the medieval era were methods by Ptolemy, Regiomontanus, or Placidus. Whatever computation method used for interplanetary directions requires disclosure. As a simplification for *America is Born*, since all interplanetary directions are computed with Regiomontanus under the Pole, I have chosen to omit this calculation choice for primary direction notation.

D	Changeover	bound Saturn/Aries d. → ASC	9-Jul-1863

Distributor Changeovers. When the directed significator changes from one bound to another, the above format is recommended. Added are the words 'Changeover' and 'bound'. Absent is listing of any participating direction designated by the bold letter **'P'**.

Other Conventions - Houses

As of 2008, the whole sign house - quadrant house debate remains a hot topic. Here is the working model I have used for this project:

- By position: planets operate exclusively by their whole sign placement.

- By rulership: planets operate as rulers of whole sign houses AND as rulers of quadrant house cusps. The addition of quadrant house cusps provides additional information to judge affairs associated with relevant houses.

Though I have not reached a definitive conclusion on the house division debate, so far this working model has proven its merits. For example, consider the following planet/house placements for Venus:

For the Regulus USA National Horoscope, Venus falls in the 7th by quadrant houses but in the 8th by whole sign houses. While there are many events regarding death from race riots, death/illness from tainted consumer goods, and investment fraud; these are all 8th house affairs. I cannot make as strong a case for Venus having influence over 7th house affairs. Yet by rulership, both whole sign and quadrant houses appear to work. By whole signs Venus rules the 6th of slaves which ties Venus' signification as white racism to slavery. But Venus does not have full claim over the 6th. Mercury rules the 6th and 9th quadrant house cusps which match the ability of several Mercury directions to time events dealing with immigrant labor. By quadrant houses, Venus rules the 5th house cusp whose significations include elections. Notable is the ability of Venus to time passage of the 19th Amendment granting women the right to vote. But Mars also has a claim over the 5th house by whole signs. American's preference for auto racing and marathon running as forms of recreation/entertainment match Mars/Gemini's rulership of the 5th by whole sign houses.

<u>House Notation</u>. To properly refer to each house defined as either whole sign or quadrant houses would require the abbreviations (WS) for 'whole sign houses' and (AL) for 'Alchabitius quadrant houses' after every house reference in the text. I take this step on the opening page of Chapters 8-15 as a one-time descriptor of planetary effects on house affairs. But to avoid making the text overly cumbersome, I have chosen to omit house references in the main text. Readers will need to refer directly to the horoscope to determine whether a whole sign or quadrant house reference is intended. While this demands a bit of work, I believe the tradeoffs in improved readability make this convention worthwhile.

House Delineations are defined according to the following list:

1st House: Primary motivation of the nation as a whole, health.
2nd House: Wealth.
3rd House: Communication, primary education, and short-term travel.
4th House: Father, home, family, real estate, end-of-life.
5th House: Children, recreation, entertainment, elections.
6th House: Slaves, labor, illness.
7th House: Marriage, open enemies, business partnerships.
8th House: Death, taxes, pensions, inheritance, traded goods.
9th House: God, religion, higher education, travel/exploration.
10th House: King, government, regulatory bodies, reputation and status.
11th House: Groups, organizations, clubs, currency, Congress, Cabinet.
12th House: Prisons, mental institutions, hospitals, enemies, spies, criminals.

Designation of Public Elections as a Fifth House Affair. Assigning public elections to the 5th house is new which deserves mention, particularly for those astrologers coming from the horary tradition where political contests are usually judged by the 1st and 7th houses. In *ARM*, I presented findings in support of this house assignment based on horoscopes for Richard Nixon (ARM p. 634) and Jimmy Carter (ARM pp. 228-229). It's an assignment that has held up well throughout this project. If elections are a fifth house affair, why might this be? Given the 5th is 8th from the 10th, or death of the career by derived houses, it seems career judgments can be made as easily at the voting booth (for the living) as they can be made by a written obituary (for the dead).

Chart, Figure, Horoscope. Used interchangeably for sake of variety.

Ruler of the Chart. Computed by al-mubtazz dignity scoring table. See *ARM*, pp. 64-65. Same as 'Al-mubtazz Figurae.'

Bounds versus Bound Rulers. Moon 27AQ51 falls in the ***bound*** of Saturn/Aquarius defined as the five degree range from 25AQ00'00" to 29AQ59'59". The Moon's ***bound ruler*** is the planet Saturn/Libra 14LI48.

KEY

♈	AR	Aries
♉	TA	Taurus
♊	GE	Gemini
♋	CA	Cancer
♌	LE	Leo
♍	VI	Virgo
♎	LI	Libra
♏	SC	Scorpio
♐	SA	Sagittarius
♑	CP	Capricorn
♒	AQ	Aquarius
♓	PI	Pisces
♄	SA	Saturn
♃	JU	Jupiter
♂	MA	Mars
☉	SU	Sun
♀	VE	Venus
☿	ME	Mercury
☽	MO	Moon
☊	NN	North Node
☋	SN	South Node
⊗	POF	Lot of Fortune
	SAN	Syzygy Ante Navitatem or Prenatal Lunation
	ASC	Ascendant
	MC	Midheaven
	AL	Alchabitius (Quadrant) Houses
	WS	Whole Sign Houses
	d.	Direct primary direction
	c.	Converse primary direction
	dsa	Direct solar arc direction
	csa	Converse solar arc direction
	lat.	Latitude
	tr.	Transit
	prog.	Progression

Ultima Cumaei venit iam carminis aetas;
magnus ab integro saeclorum nascitur ordo.
Iam redit et Virgo, redeunt Saturnia regna,
iam nova progenies caelo demittitur alto.

Now comes the final era of the Sibyl's song;
the great order of the ages is born afresh.
And now justice returns, honored rules return;
now a new lineage is sent down from high heaven.

from the fourth Eclogue of Virgil

PART ONE

The Sibly USA National Horoscope

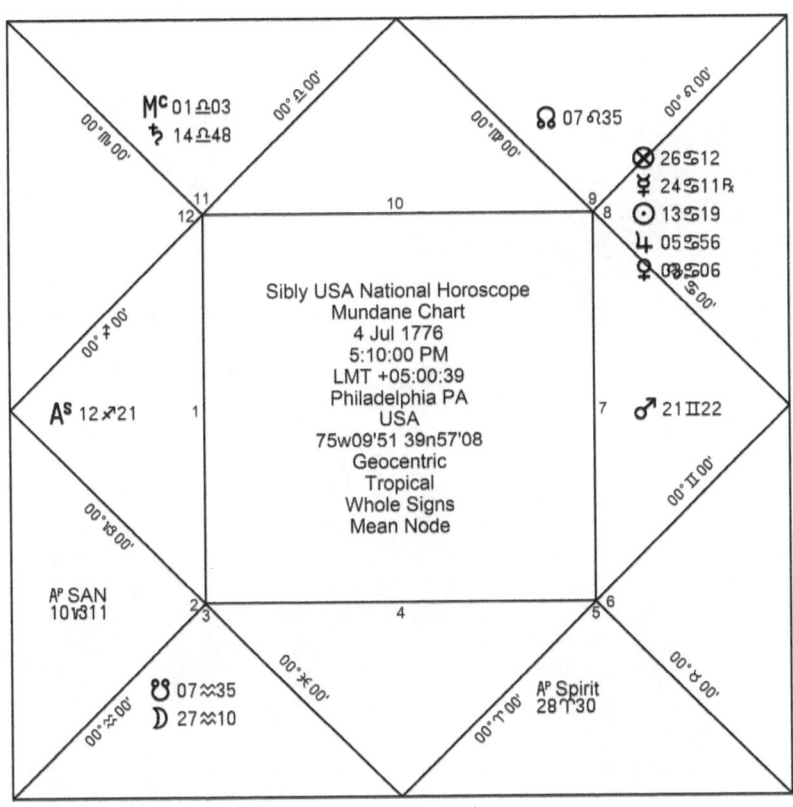

Figure 1. Sibly USA National Horoscope, Alchabitius Houses.

CHAPTER ONE

National Horoscopes in Mundane Astrology

The current preference for National Horoscopes as a mundane analysis tool is placed in historical context. How a consensus was reached on the Sibly USA National Horoscope is the focus of the chapter.

Summary

A Very Brief Introduction to Mundane Astrology. The origins of mundane astrology can be traced to the Babylonian Era. Beginning with records of sky omens, mundane astrology evolved to include a number of disparate threads including the analysis of eclipses, Jupiter-Saturn conjunctions, and ingresses. National horoscopes were not used in the medieval system.

The Rise in Popularity of National Horoscopes. The failed prediction of the outbreak of WWII by leading European astrologers led Charles Carter to largely abandon medieval mundane techniques in favor of National Horoscopes, introduced in his influential text: *An Introduction to Political Astrology*, published in 1951. Since that time, National Horoscopes have grown to dominate the field. Following Robert Zoller's successful prediction of the September 11 attacks using medieval mundane methods, a number of traditional astrologers have revived usage of medieval mundane methods.

United States National Horoscopes and the Sibly Consensus. Unlike countries with reliable historical records, the lack of any unequivocal account for the events of Jul 4, 1776 means mundane astrologers must resort to rectification to recreate a symbolic horoscope for the formation of the United States. Published in 1787, the USA Sibly chart was the first such attempt at creating a National Horoscope. Yet disagreement over its merits has led to the proposal of over a dozen different USA National Horoscopes, some going so far to reject the relevance of Jul 4, 1776 altogether. Despite the methodological problems of using transits for rectification, the transit of Pluto within 17 minutes of the Sibly Ascendant on September 11, 2001 confirmed the Sibly USA National Horoscope for many modern astrologers.

A Very Brief Introduction to Mundane Astrology

Mundane astrology is defined as the application of astrological analysis to world events. The term mundane derives from the Latin word mundus ("the World") and is distinguished from natal astrology where the focus is a single individual. Frequently addressed topics by mundane astrologers are the rise and fall of prophets and religious sects, rise and fall of empires, life and rule of Kings, affairs of the common people, epidemics, natural disasters, meteorology, and financial affairs.

During the heyday of Medieval Predictive Astrology in the 13th Century (using Guido Bonatti's lifetime as a representative gauge), the mundane astrological model comprised a number of disparate threads including omnia, meteors, eclipses, Jupiter-Saturn Conjunctions, ingresses, and lunations. (See opposite page for summary).

As a rule, medieval predictive astrologers did not use country charts nor did they rely heavily on natal charts for Kings. As a practical matter, birth data for Kings (especially enemy Kings) was either unavailable or unreliable. Probably for this reason there are few rules stating how mundane events can be predicted using natal figures for Kings. As one surviving example, Ptolemy instructs that eclipse effects can be tied to a country should the eclipse degree fall in the 10th house of a King's natal chart[1]. But use of natal charts for Kings in this manner is a rarity among medieval mundane astrological practice which was dominated by the quarterly ingress of the Sun into the cardinal signs.

The Rise in Popularity of National Horoscopes

For 21st century students approaching mundane astrology for the first time, ingresses and other medieval mundane predictive tools are often downplayed as outdated procedures. Representative of this movement among practicing mundane astrologers is Nick Campion who advocates the increased relevance of country charts following the rise of nationalism in the 19th century.[2] Providing evidence against ingresses, lunations, and eclipses is Charles Harvey who cited the failed prediction of 'no war' in 1939 made by most European astrologers using these older methods, including the British astrologer Charles Carter[3]. Carter's book: *An Introduction to Political Astrology*, published in 1951, emphasized National Horoscopes for this reason.[4] After publication of Carter's book, the field of mundane astrology gravitated towards country charts and natal charts cast for rulers. My point is students new to mundane astrology are more likely to see National Horoscopes and ruler's nativities emphasized when mundane astrology is discussed. This was not always the case and students need to understand how mundane astrology developed into its present form. Essential references for this purpose

Outline of Medieval Mundane Astrological Methods[1]

Omnia/Sky Omens

- Tabulated by Mesopotamians on clay tables; recorded correspondences between planetary phenomenon and events on earth.

- Included other celestial phenomena including comets.

Eclipses

- Adapted by the Greeks from Mesopotamian sky omens and Egyptian sources. Eclipse rules summarized by Ptolemy in *Tetrabiblos*.

Jupiter-Saturn Conjunctions (JSC)

- Cycles computed based on the conjunctions of Jupiter and Saturn.

- Small, Middle, and Great conjunctions defined by a single JSC (~20 years), a group of JSC's in a single triplicity (~240 years), and a cycle of JSCs through the entire zodiac (~720 years).

- Originally developed by the Persians during the Sassanid Empire (3rd – 7th Centuries AD); reached highest technical form under Abū Ma'shar (9th Century); revived in the Latin West (12th Century).

- Modeled the rise of prophets, religious sects, and their collective influence on people, governments, and civilizations.

Ingresses

- Computed for the Sun's annual entry to the 1st degree of Aries, also known as the Spring Equinox. Some years require additional figures for the Fall Equinox and Summer and Winter Solstices.

- Full or New Moon prior to the annual Aries Ingress was given special attention for specialized topics including epidemics.

- Primary 'bread and butter' tool of mundane astrological analysis. Developed in a similar time frame as Jupiter-Saturn conjunctions.

are Part I of *Mundane Astrology*[5] and the introduction to *The Book of World Horoscopes*[6].

Recent Trends in Mundane Astrology

The second edition of *Mundane Astrology* published in 1992 begins with well-deserved self-recognition by Michael Baigent, Nicholas Campion, and Charles Harvey for their successful forecasts of upheavals in Russia and the fall of the Berlin Wall in the mid to late-1980s based on the horoscope cast for the 1917 Russian Revolution. The accuracy of these predictions mark one of the better recent forecasts made using National Horoscopes as a mundane astrological tool.

Another recent successful mundane forecast was Robert Zoller's prediction of the events of September 11, 2001 several years in advance. As Zoller was the first to introduce medieval astrological techniques for natal chart application in the early 1980s, so too did his interest expand to mundane applications in the 1990s. His mundane prediction for September 2001 was made based on a combination of techniques including eclipses and ingresses. No charts for countries or rulers were used.

For his students, Robert Zoller's prediction triggered a sharp u-turn away from National Horoscopes. In my opinion, Zoller's Intensive on Mundane Astrology, held October 8-11, 2004 in Vancouver, B.C., ranks an important historical event in the revival of medieval mundane astrology in the early 21st century. For the first time, students had access to English translations of selected portions of Bonatti's *Book of Astronomy* relevant to mundane astrology.[7] In addition, Abū Ma'shar's *On Historical Astrology: The Book of Religions and Dynasties* published in 2000 was conveniently on sale at the time of the October 2004 seminar allowing most students to purchase an otherwise prohibitively expensive reference text (US$563.00).[8] This book was the first English translation ever published of the leading mundane astrology text used in the medieval era; together with Bonatti's *Book of Astronomy*, new students of traditional astrology were for the first time equipped to practice mundane astrology with a relatively complete set of medieval texts.

As the astrological scene now stands in 2008, there appears to be a growing trend among practicing medieval astrologers against the use of National Horoscopes in mundane astrology. While medieval astrologers did not use National Horoscopes, it does not necessarily mean they are irrelevant. What is required is testing of these figures to see if they can stand up to the rigors of medieval delineation and predictive methods. As a hybrid product of the modern National Horoscopes and medieval astrological technique, the Regulus USA National Horoscope purports to do just that.

United States National Horoscopes

For modern mundane astrologers covering the United States, there are about a dozen competing figures computed as the 'official' United States National Horoscope to choose from. In addition to the July 4, 1776 date for the Declaration of Independence as one possibility, astrologers have proposed a multitude of other dates including the Declaration of War against Britain (July 6, 1775), signing of the Constitution (September 17, 1787), and ratification of the Articles of Confederation (March 1, 1781). More recently, July 2, 1776 has been added to list based on the account of John Adams; a date revived with the 2001 publication of Adams' biography by historian David McCullough.[9] It is not my intent to rehash arguments for or against a specific figure. For those wishing to review these charts and related arguments, see Campion (2004) and Astrodatabank.[10]

The biggest problem facing astrologers researching any potential USA figure is the unavailability of a definitive timeline of the events of July 4, 1776. Surviving data is scanty and conflicting which means astrologers must resort to rectification in order to reconstruct a theoretical chart. Even the Sibly chart published in 1787 eleven years after the Declaration of Independence has been determined to be a theoretical construct and not based on any first-hand witness of events.[11]

Rectification, or the reverse engineering of birth times based on subsequent events, is a controversial subject. Like many astrologers new to rectification, I started with an approach based on transits, progressions, and solar arc directions of planets to the angles. I also quickly became disillusioned after out-of-sample predictions based on this method failed to demonstrate consistent results. For this reason, I spent over four years applying medieval methods to natal chart rectification in order to develop a methodical approach to rectification. The result is *A Rectification Manual: The American Presidency* published in December 2007. What I discovered was modern methods of rectification relying on transit, progression, and solar arc direction hits to the angles were flawed because the approach makes use of an underspecified predictive model. True, when making minor adjustments to a relatively certain birth time, transits, progressions, and solar arc directions can function as a valuable rectification assist. But only when the full set of predictive tools is put to use can consistent rectification results be achieved - especially when birth data is completely unknown. There are simply too many permutations of seemingly successful rectifications during a 24-hour span for the restricted toolkit of transits, progressions, and solar arc directions to generate consistent results.

Because of the weakness of modern rectification methods, I am in complete agreement with Nick Campion who states the fundamental flaw in the current approach to testing national horoscopes is the procedure of finding dynamic transit hits to the angles for various events without first considering what the planets in the figure might signify.[12] Applied properly, medieval predictive astrology requires delineation proceeds prediction. For transits, this means the zodiacal state of a planet in the natal chart is carried with it as it transits the horoscope. To further specify transit effects, each transit requires filtering the planet and topic in question through as many as five different time lord procedures: Directing by Triplicity, Firdaria, Directing through the Bounds, Lord of the Year, and Lord of the Period.[13] For good reason, medieval predictive astrology considered transits at the bottom of the predictive hierarchy.

This is not to deny the power of transits to time events; only that each event said to correspond to a given transit requires considerably more justification than what is provided by most astrologers who rectify by transits. What is true for transits can also be said for progressions and solar arc directions. The modern rectification approach with its preoccupation on accumulating the highest combination of dynamic hits to the angles deserves a much needed smack down for it epitomizes the 'garbage in => garbage out' lack of specificity from an approach which severs itself from delineation.

In an exercise typical of the modern rectification approach, Astrodatabank compiled a list of U.S. historical events as fodder for rectification testing following the World Trade Center attacks of September 11, 2001. Users were invited to test ten proposed USA National Horoscopes in an effort to reach a consensus on the best USA chart.

And here is where the problems begin:

- Of 49 events listed, 28 involved the start or end of warfare. While I agree that events timed by directions of Mars to the angles are one of the most consistent and successful ways to rectify charts, Mars is still only one of seven traditional planets. A database with over half of its entries related to warfare is so skewed that it is unlikely that directions of other planets (e.g., Sun, Mercury, Jupiter) would time events which populate such a list.

- Properly delineated, the ability of a national horoscope to time international conflict requires that Mars falls in or rules the 9th house of foreign lands. Mars in or ruling other houses sends its effects elsewhere. The possibility that international conflicts are better delineated and predicted using other National Horoscopes or other mundane techniques (e.g., eclipses and ingresses) is implicitly ignored by an approach which force feeds dates of international conflicts into transit hits for National Horoscopes.

CHAPTER 1 - NATIONAL HOROSCOPES IN MUNDANE ASTROLOGY

Table 1. Suggested Events for Testing USA Charts, Astrodatabank[14]

Date	Event
3-Aug-1492	Columbus sailed for the New World.
12-Oct-1492	Columbus landed in the Dominican Republic.
2-Apr-1513	Spanish colony founded at St. Augustine, FL by Juan Ponce DeLeon.
13-May-1607	Jamestown Settlement founded in Virginia.
19-Apr-1775	Revolutionary War: Lexington & Concord.
14-Jun-1775	Washington appointed head of Continental Army.
4-Jul-1776	Declaration of Independence signed.
8-Aug-1786	Dollar defined in terms of gold and silver; decimal system adopted.
21-Feb-1787	Continental Congress resolved in favor of Constitutional Convention.
17-Sep-1787	Constitutional Convention approved final form of Constitution.
28-Sep-1787	Constitution sent to the states for ratification.
30-Apr-1789	George Washington inauguration.
8-May-1846	Mexican War: Battle of Palo Alto.
13-May-1846	US declared war on Mexico.
1-Mar-1861	Abraham Lincoln inauguration.
12-Apr-1861	Civil War Outbreak: Attack on Fort Sumter.
22-Sep-1862	Emancipation Proclamation issued.
9-Apr-1865	Surrender of General Lee to General Grant.
1897-98	Economic rise began that lasted 22 years.
20-Apr-1898	Spanish-American War: U.S. declared war on Spain.
12-Aug-1898	Spanish-American War: U.S. signed armistice with Spain.
10-Dec-1898	Spanish-American War: U.S. and Spain signed Treaty of Paris.
28-Jul-1914	WWI launch: Austria-Hungary declaration of war against Serbia.
6-Apr-1917	WWI: U.S. entry.
11-Nov-1918	World War I armistice signed.
1920s	Boom time, growth and affluence.
25-Oct-1929	Stock market crash. By 1933, ¼ of Americans were unemployed.
7-Dec-1941	WWII: Pearl Harbor and U.S. entry to WWII (following day).
15-May-1942	WWII: Women allowed to serve in all branches of armed services.
30-Apr-1945	WWII: Allied victory in Europe.
6-Aug-1945	WWII: U.S. nuclear attacks against Hiroshima and Nagasaki (Aug 9).
2-Sep-1945	WWII: Japan unconditionally surrendered to US.
4-Oct-1957	Soviets launched of Sputnik.
5-Apr-1961	Alan Shepard first American in space.
1-Nov-1963	Vietnam: American-Vietnamese forces staged coup.
2-Jul-1964	Civil Rights Act of 1964 signed by President Johnson.
7-Aug-1964	Vietnam: Congress passed Gulf of Tonkin Resolution.
27-Jan-1973	Vietnam: Paris Peace Accords signed; 'official' end of war.
29-Mar-1973	Vietnam: Last active duty American forces left Vietnam.
1960s, 70s	Two decades fraught with anti-war sentiment, women's issues and civil rights issues, peace and sexual freedom.
2-Aug-1990	First Gulf War: Iraqi forces invaded Kuwait.
16-Jan-1991	First Gulf War: Operation Desert Storm.
23-Feb-1991	First Gulf War: Desert Storm ended; cease-fire signed 28 Feb 1991.
1-Feb-1992	US and Russia sign treaty officially ending the Cold War.
30-Aug-1995	Operation Deliberate Force, NATO air strikes in Bosnia.
20-Aug-1998	Retaliatory air raids following African embassy bombings.
16-Dec-1998	First of three air strikes targeting Iraq is launched.
23-Mar-1999	NATO begins air strikes against Yugoslavia.
11-Sep-2001	World Trade Center terrorist attacks.

- Worst of all is the emphasis of transits as a predictive tool for rectification. As just stated, any correlation between dynamic hits to the angles and a rectification solution are unreliable unless the zodiacal state of the natal planet and application of the predictive hierarchy is first applied.

The Sibly Consensus

Despite these limitations, Partners in the Astrodatabank exercise voted for the Sibly chart as the best USA National Horoscope. For modern astrologers favoring Pluto as a planet of destruction, no other figure could better time the World Trade Center 9-11 terror attack than the Sibly with transiting Pluto missing the Sibly Ascendant by only 17 minutes of degree. Though there remain proponents of both Gemini and Scorpio rising USA figures cast for July 4, 1776, I agree with Astrodatabank's polling that the 9-11 attacks elevated the Sibly chart as the preferred USA National Horoscope among the majority of American astrologers in the years following 9-11.

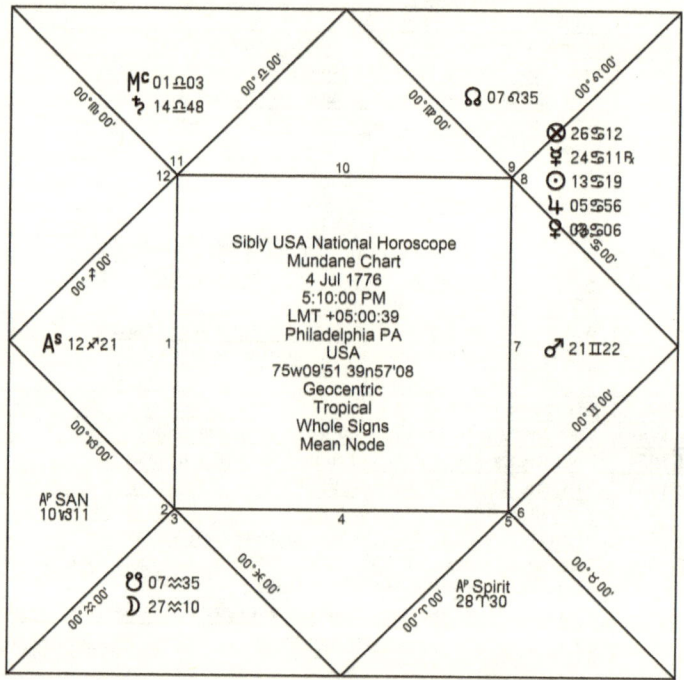

Figure 2. Sibly USA National Horoscope[15]

Transit of Pluto on 11-Sep-2001 = 12SA38

CHAPTER TWO

Revisiting the Sibly USA National Horoscope

In this Chapter, I retrace my steps taken to rectify the Sibly USA National Horoscope.

Summary

<u>Taking up Nick Campion's Rectification Challenge</u>. In *The Book of World Horoscopes*, Campion cites the roots of the Sibly USA National Horoscope in the medieval tradition as a rationale for further investigations using medieval astrological techniques. I take up the challenge.

<u>Initial Rectification Research Phase: July 2002</u>. My first steps to rectify the Sibly chart were taken early in my astrological training. The Medieval techniques of Firdaria and transits of Saturn to the Moon were employed in order to confirm a Sagittarius Ascendant. A 300+ event database was constructed to fine tune the angles through the identification of sensitive degrees by transits. Transit-angle analysis is an approach I no longer use nor recommend, yet the preliminary Ascendant of 26SA33'13 determined by transits was less than twelve minutes of degree from the final rectified Ascendant of 26SA54'40" computed two years later in an approach which relied on primary directions. I attribute this finding to (1) the ability of transits to function as a 'rectification assist' when working with a chart whose parameters are relatively well known and (2) the role of divination explored further in Chapter Three.

<u>Final Rectification Research Phase: December 2004</u>. Having completed my studies in Medieval Predictive Astrology, I reconsidered the Sibly chart with primary directions. With Mars/Gemini angular in the 7th ruling the 4th of homeland delineated a Civil War fought by "brother against brother", I honed in Civil War events to unlock the final degree, minutes, and second of the final rectified chart. In addition to primary directions of planets and their aspects to the angles, the specialized primary directions tool known as Directing through the Bounds was crucial to unlock the rectification.

Taking up Nick Campion's Rectification Challenge

Of potential United States national horoscopes, Campion suggests the viability of the Sibly chart based on its roots in medieval astrology:

> Sibly's horoscope may not be a national horoscope in the modern sense, set for a precisely timed event, but it is entirely consistent with medieval tradition and the chart is therefore presented here not as a horoscope for the Declaration of Independence, but as a horoscope which <u>signifies</u> the Declaration of Independence. Indeed this is the only horoscope we have of this type, so it is therefore THE horoscope which signifies independence and should be experimented with in this context, especially if medieval techniques are being used. Seen from this perspective the Sibly chart therefore emerges from the essentially divinatory perspective of judicial astrology[1].

I take up Campion's rectification challenge by applying medieval techniques for a Sagittarius rising chart. What follows is a discussion of actual rectification steps taken. The initial phase completed in July 2002 confirmed a Sagittarius Ascendant. Coinciding with my early astrology studies, I made the common mistake of overemphasizing transits as a rectification method and left the project incomplete. By the final phase, I had completed my studies in Medieval Predictive Astrology and was prepared to attack the figure with primary directions. Compared to transits which rank at the bottom of the predictive hierarchy, primary directions rank either near or at the top of the hierarchy according to Rhetorius[2] (Hellenstic astrology) and Abū Ma'shar (Arabic/Medieval astrology). Use of Firdaria in the initial phase and primary directions in the final phase meet Campion's requirements.

Initial Rectification Research Phase: July 2002

In what I now call *Stage I Rectification* procedures[3], I took two steps designed to confirm a Sagittarius Ascendant for the Sibly chart. The first was Firdaria analysis which can help determine whether a figure is diurnal or nocturnal. Second is identification of the Moon's degree which also helps to narrow the Ascendant choice. Both are robust rectification techniques which can eliminate large blocks of time from consideration as potential birth times.

Confirming Sect: Firdaria

To confirm the Sibly's diurnal sect, I spot checked a few historical events against the diurnal Firdaria sequence.[4] Because the Nodes produce some of the most unambiguous events using Firdaria, my preference has been to examine Nodal periods for possible event matches. For the three South Node

CHAPTER 2 - REVISITING THE SIBLY USA NATIONAL HOROSCOPE   13

Firdaria periods beginning July 4 for the years 1849, 1924, and 1999; the first thing I noticed was:

- July 7, 1924. Death of Calvin Coolidge Jr.
- July 16, 1999. Death of John F. Kennedy Jr.

Calvin Coolidge Jr. died from blood poisoning contracted through an infected blister on his foot after playing tennis at the White House wearing shoes without socks.[5] John F. Kennedy Jr. died in airplane crash with probable pilot error the cause. JFK Jr. had previously broken his ankle while bungling a paragliding landing. His cast was removed on July 15, 1999 the day before his fatal crash.

As a delineation match to the South Node by sign, Aquarius is assigned to the shanks, or the area from just below the kneecaps down to and including the ankles. An ankle injury matches the account of Calvin Coolidge Jr.'s blister because shoes worn without socks rub against the skin near the ankle. For JFK Jr., the South Node placement suggests his recovering ankle, freshly exposed out of a cast, played a role in his airplane crash.[6]

As a delineation match to the South Node by house, the Sibly South Node falls in the 2nd house, or 5th from the 10th. By derived houses, the 2nd becomes the *President's children*. JFK Jr. was born only 16 days after his father was elected to the Presidency, spent most of his first three years in the White House, and was known as *America's Son*. His death was considered a national tragedy. President Clinton authorized U.S. Navy vessels to assist in the search for the downed plane, an unusual deployment considering JFK Jr.'s civilian status but consistent for an American Son.

Calvin Coolidge Jr. contracted blood poisoning while playing tennis at the White House and died just after his sixteenth birthday. The death of Calvin Coolidge Jr. was a major blow for his father, President Calvin Coolidge. Historians are in general agreement that subsequent to Calvin Jr.'s death, President Coolidge's interest in the Presidency waned. Considering Coolidge remained President for another 4 years 7 months, the death of Calvin Jr. had a material impact on the office of the Presidency.

Both Kennedy and Coolidge deaths were unexpected and traumatic events for their family and friends. But with the South Node/Aquarius activated as time lord by Firdaria, the mundane Sibly USA National Horoscope elevated the deaths of Coolidge and Kennedy to the realm of national tragedy. For an additional link between JFK Jr. and the USA, consider JFK's natal Moon 27AQ25[7] falls very close to the Sibly Moon position of 27AQ10. For JFK Jr.'s 1998 solar return active for the year of death, note the following:

14   AMERICA IS BORN: *Introducing the Regulus USA National Horoscope*

- JFK Jr.'s South Node conjunct the USA Moon within 1 degree.
- JFK Jr.'s Moon conjunct the USA South Node within 7 degrees.

This mundane-natal horoscope connection demonstrates the **Mundane-Natal Horoscope Connection**: planetary configurations in mundane charts sympathetically trigger actions by individuals with similar natal configurations. These individuals are 'lifted up' from the masses to play out events promised by mundane horoscopes. JFK Jr.'s death was both a personal and national tragedy.

As for the first South Node Firdaria period beginning July 4, 1849, Lincoln's son Eddie died on February 1, 1850. But because Lincoln was not President at this time, I do not consider Eddie Lincoln's death as relevant as the other two examples. I am uncertain what the proper event match would be for the South Node period lasting from July 4, 1849 to July 3, 1851.

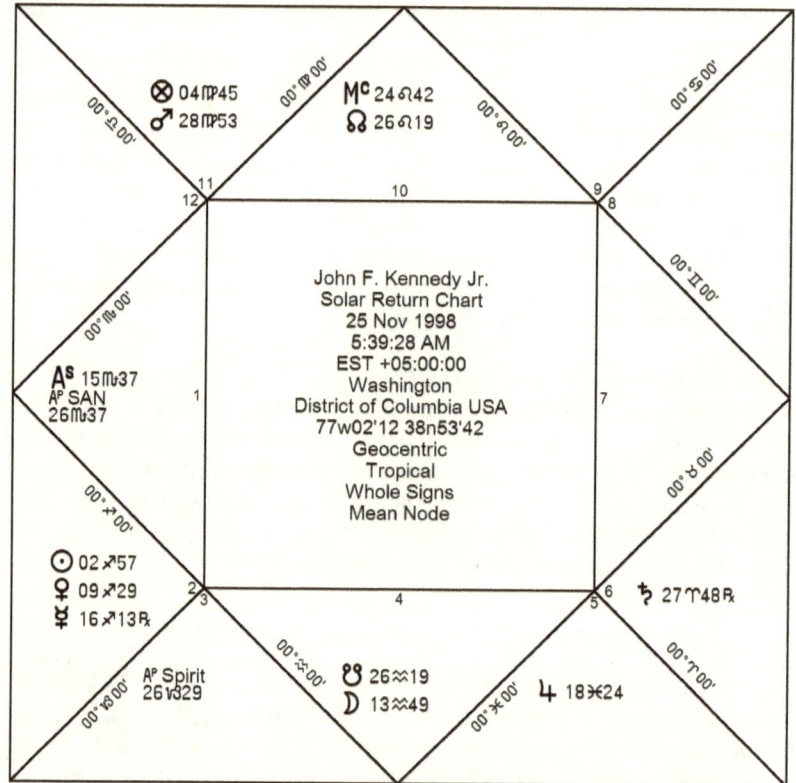

Figure 3. Solar Return for Year of Death, John F. Kennedy, Jr.

Table 2. Diurnal Firdaria Main and Subperiod Rulers, July 4, 1776

Sun	Sun	4-Jul-1776	4-Jul-1851	4-Jul-1926
	Venus	8-Dec-1777	6-Dec-1852	6-Dec-1927
	Mercury	14-May-1779	13-May-1854	13-May-1929
	Moon	16-Oct-1780	16-Oct-1855	16-Oct-1930
	Saturn	22-Mar-1782	21-Mar-1857	21-Mar-1932
	Jupiter	26-Aug-1783	25-Aug-1858	25-Aug-1933
	Mars	28-Jan-1785	29-Jan-1860	29-Jan-1935
Venus	Venus	4-Jul-1786	4-Jul-1861	4-Jul-1936
	Mercury	26-Aug-1787	25-Aug-1862	25-Aug-1937
	Moon	16-Oct-1788	17-Oct-1863	17-Oct-1938
	Saturn	7-Dec-1789	7-Dec-1864	7-Dec-1939
	Jupiter	29-Jan-1791	29-Jan-1866	29-Jan-1941
	Mars	21-Mar-1792	22-Mar-1867	22-Mar-1942
	Sun	12-May-1793	13-May-1868	13-May-1943
Mercury	Mercury	4-Jul-1794	4-Jul-1869	4-Jul-1944
	Moon	13-May-1796	13-May-1871	13-May-1946
	Saturn	21-Mar-1798	22-Mar-1873	22-Mar-1948
	Jupiter	29-Jan-1800	28-Jan-1875	28-Jan-1950
	Mars	8-Dec-1801	8-Dec-1876	8-Dec-1951
	Sun	18-Oct-1803	18-Oct-1878	18-Oct-1953
	Venus	26-Aug-1805	26-Aug-1880	26-Aug-1955
Moon	Moon	4-Jul-1807	4-Jul-1882	4-Jul-1957
	Saturn	15-Oct-1808	15-Oct-1883	15-Oct-1958
	Jupiter	28-Jan-1810	28-Jan-1885	29-Jan-1960
	Mars	13-May-1811	13-May-1886	13-May-1961
	Sun	25-Aug-1812	25-Aug-1887	25-Aug-1962
	Venus	6-Dec-1813	6-Dec-1888	6-Dec-1963
	Mercury	22-Mar-1815	22-Mar-1890	22-Mar-1965
Saturn	Saturn	4-Jul-1816	4-Jul-1891	4-Jul-1966
	Jupiter	29-Jan-1818	29-Jan-1893	29-Jan-1968
	Mars	26-Aug-1819	26-Aug-1894	26-Aug-1969
	Sun	22-Mar-1821	22-Mar-1896	22-Mar-1971
	Venus	17-Oct-1822	17-Oct-1897	17-Oct-1972
	Mercury	12-May-1824	12-May-1899	12-May-1974
	Moon	8-Dec-1825	8-Dec-1900	8-Dec-1975
Jupiter	Jupiter	4-Jul-1827	4-Jul-1902	4-Jul-1977
	Mars	21-Mar-1829	21-Mar-1904	21-Mar-1979
	Sun	7-Dec-1830	7-Dec-1905	7-Dec-1980
	Venus	25-Aug-1832	25-Aug-1907	25-Aug-1982
	Mercury	12-May-1834	12-May-1909	12-May-1984
	Moon	29-Jan-1836	29-Jan-1911	29-Jan-1986
	Saturn	16-Oct-1837	16-Oct-1912	16-Oct-1987
Mars	Mars	4-Jul-1839	4-Jul-1914	4-Jul-1989
	Sun	4-Jul-1840	4-Jul-1915	4-Jul-1990
	Venus	4-Jul-1841	4-Jul-1916	4-Jul-1991
	Mercury	4-Jul-1842	4-Jul-1917	4-Jul-1992
	Moon	4-Jul-1843	4-Jul-1918	4-Jul-1993
	Saturn	4-Jul-1844	4-Jul-1919	4-Jul-1994
	Jupiter	4-Jul-1845	4-Jul-1920	4-Jul-1995
N Node	N Node	4-Jul-1846	4-Jul-1921	4-Jul-1996
S Node	S Node	4-Jul-1849	4-Jul-1924	4-Jul-1999

Confirming the Sibly Moon: Saturn Transits

Moon Sign. For Jul 4, 1776, the Moon transits Aquarius until 9:52 PM when it makes its Pisces ingress. Moon in Aquarius signifies fair treatment of all humans. Falling in the sign opposed to Leo which signifies Kings, Moon in Aquarius matches the elevation of the common man in the social order, a major philosophical tenet of the Age of Enlightenment.

Moon's Bound. The application of science to human reasoning and society was another premise of the Enlightenment and matches the Moon's bound as Saturn/Aquarius (25AQ00' – 29AQ59'). If correct, this bound placement limits the time to between 1:34 PM and 9:52 PM. Times before 1:34 PM place the Moon in the bound of Mars/Aquarius which as a significator of discrimination[8] would seriously degrade the Moon. I rule out this possibility because discrimination can be shown by other factors in the chart, including the fact that the Moon is void of course and has difficulty in fulfilling her need to treat all humans equally.

Confirming the Moon's degree. Seldom do transits of Saturn to the Moon fail to produce meaningful effects. For the Sibly chart, this tendency should be ameliorated because Saturn is dignified in Libra and receives the Moon by sign. So what kind of effects should we expect for Saturn-Moon transits? Saturn is placed in the 11th of political organizations which for a nation signifies legislative bodies (e.g., Congress) and the President's Cabinet. More generally, Saturn/Libra signifies legal precepts and organizational structures which achieve the highest possible balance between competing forces because Libra is the sign of the scales and Saturn is in his exaltation. As I will demonstrate later, Saturn/Libra also signifies the U.S. Dollar (because the 11th is the King's money - 2nd from the 10th) and the Supreme Court because Saturn is placed in the bound of Jupiter/Libra.

With Saturn-Moon transits, there should be legal precepts or rules instigated by Congress, the Cabinet, the Supreme Court, and/or other American political alliances which impact the people. Also note because transits fall at the bottom of the predictive hierarchy, at this stage it cannot be stated unambiguously whether Saturn-Moon transits may time events which *aid* or *harm* the Aquarian Moon. For now, we can only expect a mixing of effects for events timed by Saturn's transit to the Moon.

CHAPTER 2 - REVISITING THE SIBLY USA NATIONAL HOROSCOPE   17

Transit 1: Constitutional Convention

23-Apr-1787 25-Jul-1787 15-Jan-1788	On 4-May-1787, James Madison arrived in Philadelphia for the Constitutional Convention. A quorum was reached on 25-May-1787 and the meeting officially convened. The **Constitutional Convention adopted the Great Compromise** on 16-Jul-1787, approved the document in its final form on 17-Sep-1787, and voted to send the Constitution to the states for ratification on 28-Sep-1787. Delineation match: Saturn/Libra in the 11th of political groups including Congress signifies the system of checks and balances between the Executive, Legislative, and Judicial branches embodied by the Great Compromise. Transit to the Moon indicates bringing the system of checks and balances to the people in order to guarantee equality and fair treatment of the populace. Error: 2nd transit to Great Compromise = 9 days

Transit 2: Veto of Bonus Bill

20-Feb-1817	On 3-Mar-1817, **President Madison vetoed the Bonus Bill** for road and canal construction because he believed it to be unconstitutional. Delineation match: One Saturn cycle later, James Madison still plays out the transit. The issue of constitutionality (Saturn/Libra) is brought to local transportation (Moon/Aquarius/3rd). Error: transit to veto of Bonus Bill = 11 days

Transit 3: Dred Scott Case and Wilmot Proviso

2-Apr-1846 24-Aug-1846 20-Dec-1846	While the well-known Dred Scott v. Sandford case was not decided in the Supreme Court until 3-Mar-1857, **Dred Scott made his first legal appeal** during April 1846 coinciding with the first pass of Saturn over the Moon. Delineation match: Courts (Saturn/Libra) are asked to intervene in order to restore freedom of all people including slaves (Moon).

	David Wilmot (PA) attached the **Wilmot Proviso** to President Polk's request for funds to purchase land from Mexico after the Mexican-American War on 8-Aug-1846. The measure proposed that slavery be banned from all territories acquired from Mexico. It passed the House but not in the Senate. Delineation match: Congress (Saturn/Libra) attempts to ban slavery in order to restore freedom to all people (Moon/Aquarius). Error: 2nd transit to Wilmot Proviso = 16 days

Transit 4: Grant's Message to Congress

6-Feb-1876	In his final Annual Message to Congress on 7-Dec-1875, **President Grant called for mandatory public education, separation of church and state, elimination of polygamy, and enactment of stable currency laws**. Note this message appearing in a lame duck period appears to have minimized this transit's impact. Delineation match: Mandatory (Saturn/Libra) public education (Moon/Aquarius/3rd) and stable currency laws (Saturn/Libra) match the tone of Grant's remarks. Error: transit to Grant's address = 61 days

Transit 5: Lochner Era and Railroad Rate Regulation

16-Mar-1905 26-Sep-1905 3-Dec-1905	On 17-Apr-1905, in **Lochner v. New York**, the Supreme Court ruled that a New York state law limiting the number of hours for bakers was illegal because it interfered with the 'right to contract' implicit in the Due Process Clause of the 14th Amendment. This controversial decision opened what has been termed the *Lochner Era* when many laws designed to protect workers' rights passed during the Progressive Era were modified or overturned. Delineation match: Supreme Court (Saturn/Libra) overturned the bakers law which was designed to provide fairness and equal treatment (Moon/Aquarius) of baking personnel relative to workers in other industries. Error: 1st transit to Lochner decision = 21 days

CHAPTER 2 - REVISITING THE SIBLY USA NATIONAL HOROSCOPE   19

	On 5-Dec-1905, President Roosevelt called for **government regulation to prevent unjust or unreasonable railroad rates**.
	Delineation match: Calls for government regulation (Saturn/Libra) were made to ensure fair prices (Moon/Aquarius).
	Error: 3rd transit to Roosevelt's address = 2 days

Transit 6: West Coast Waterfront Strike

| 4-May-1934
14-Jul-1934
21-Jan-1935 | The **1934 West Coast waterfront strike** was a milestone in the evolution of trade unionism. The strike was started on 9-May-1934; in part to demand a closed shop in order to strengthen the union's position in hiring and other decisions. On 5-Jul-1934, a confrontation erupted in San Francisco later known as "Bloody Thursday", leaving two dead. The San Francisco Labor Council voted for a general strike on 14-Jul-1934. The strike was broken in 4 days after intervention by the California National Guard which allowed company owners and anti-Communist vigilantes relative free reign to destroy local offices of strikers. Though seen as an initial victory by the company owners, the later imposition of arbitration gave unions considerable power over dealings with owners.

Delineation match: Saturn/Libra signifies arbitration and Moon/Aquarius signifies the longshoremen. Note one signification of Aquarius is waterworks and the Moon is placed in the 3rd house of short-term transportation. This delineation fully specifies longshoremen to the Moon/Aquarius/3rd.

Error: 1st transit to strike outbreak = 5 days
Error: 2nd transit to Bloody Thursday = 9 days

On 20-Jan-1935, the **Senate voted down the World Court proposal**. In this example, the Senate plays the role of Saturn/Libra.

Error: 3rd transit to World Court veto = 1 day |

Transit 7: Supreme Court 'One Person One Vote' ruling

28-Feb-1964	On 17-Feb-1964, in **Wesberry v. Sanders**, the Supreme Court ruled that congressional districts in Georgia had to be approximately equal in population. Known as the 'one person, one vote' rule, it had the practical effect of diminishing the power of sparsely populated rural districts to the benefit of urban voters. This decision also played a key role in launching the political career of Jimmy Carter. Delineation match: Supreme Court (Saturn/Libra) made a judgment to balance Congressional representation (Saturn in 11th) in order to guarantee equality and fair treatment of the populace (Moon/Aquarius) in electoral procedures (Moon exalted ruler of 5th). Error: transit to Sanders decision = 11 days

Transit 8: Dollar Peak and Whitewater Special Prosecutor

6-Apr-1993 16-Aug-1993 2-Jan-1994	The dollar turned in a mixed performance in 1993, holding up despite low to negative real interest rates which prompted the first major gold rally in many years. Gold bottomed on 30-Mar-1993, peaked on 2-Aug-1993, and made a retest high on 5-Jan-1994 which coincided with a **significant high in the Dollar Index** on 4-Jan-1994. These turning points in the currency markets paralleled events in the Justice Department with Janet Reno's confirmation on 10-Mar-1993 one day after the gold low, increasing scrutiny of the Clinton Administration following Travelgate (employees fired May 19), Waco (April 19), Vince Foster's suicide (July 20), and calls for Reno to appoint a special prosecutor to investigate Whitewater on January 5, 1994 coinciding with the Dollar's peak. **Reno appointed Robert B. Fiske Whitewater special prosecutor** on 12-Jan-1994. Delineation match: Saturn/Libra raised the dollar to an exalted level by the last transit after which it collapsed. From its high on 5-Jan-1994 to its low on 19-Apr-1995, the Dollar Index declined 18% in a virtual straight line. Appointment of the Whitewater special prosecutor by Attorney General Janet Reno triggered efforts by Congress and the Courts (Saturn/Libra) to judge the Clintons for past financial speculations and romantic affairs (Moon/Aquarius falls 5

	signs from the MC/Libra = King's speculations and love life) which would result in significant distraction to the first Clinton administration. Error: 1st transit to Gold low = 27 days Error: 1st transit to Reno confirmation = 26 days Error: 3rd transit to Dollar high = 2 days Error: 3rd transit to Appointment of Fiske = 10 days

Conclusion on Saturn-Moon Transits. I believe this evidence overwhelming supports the ability of Saturn-Moon transits to time *legal precepts or rules instigated by Congress, the Cabinet, the Supreme Court, and/or other American political alliances which impact the people.* What level of accuracy is implied by these transits? Recall this exercise is designed to confirm the Sibly chart with Sagittarius rising. For an Ascendant computed for 0 degrees Sagittarius, the Moon's position is 26AQ33'51"; for the final degree and minute of Sagittarius, 27AQ59'25". Transits of Saturn to this Moon range of 1deg25'34" produces a difference of dates ranging from one to two weeks. This means IF the events cited match the dates of Saturn-Moon transits within an average error of two weeks or less THEN the Ascendant should be Sagittarius.[9] For most events this test is met.

Winding up the 2002 trial Rectification. After confirming a Sagittarius Ascendant for the Sibly USA National Horoscope, I proceeded to fine tune the angles by transits. Selecting a larger event sample than suggested by Astrodatabank (see Appendix A for the complete event list), I performed several mathematical optimizations to determine the most frequently observed degree which fell closest to the Sibly Ascendant. Based on this approach, I determined a trial Ascendant of 26SA33'13" on July 20, 2002. Compared to the final rectified Ascendant of 26SA54'40" made on December 3, 2004, this trial Ascendant erred less than 15 minutes of degree. The fact that I was able to get so close to the final result with an approach I now disparage speaks to the ability of transits to help fine tune the angles for horoscopes with well-defined parameters.

But does this method work consistently or was I just lucky?

Faced with these results, my teacher Robert Zoller reminded me of his mantra *delineation precedes prediction* and any attempt to determine the Ascendant based on optimized degrees computed by transit-angle analysis was a waste of time. Zoller often made the point that no better technique demonstrated the zodiacal state of a planet than primary directions of said planet to the angles. Failing to take this crucial delineation step prior to transit analysis meant statistical artifacts uncovered through optimization represented nothing more than a stupendous feat of mathematical fantasy. Considering that tests I made during 2003-2004 for other natal charts rectified in this manner showed sloppy results in out-of-sample performance, I concluded in 2004 that *yes*, I was lucky.

A review of my working papers made in preparation for writing this book in 2008 revealed another factor at work. That 'something else' was the power of the moment in a divinatory sense for the trial rectification made on July 20, 2002. I revisit this divination-rectification link in Chapter 3.

Final Rectification Research Phase: December 2004

After the 2002 trial rectification, I wisely put the chart aside and awaited completion of my astrological studies before making any attempt to revisit the figure. By late 2004 I decided to return to the trial rectification. This was a purposeful revisiting of the 2002 figure based on Mercury's November 30, 2004 retrograde station at 26SA44 falling on the Ascendant of the 2002 trial horoscope. I explore the divinatory effect of this choice further in Chapter 3.

During the interval between the 2002 trial and the 2004 final rectification, I completed my studies under Robert Zoller. I also started work on a rectification project for the American Presidents and had made my crucial discovery of the *primary direction sequence*[10] by late 2004. As it turned out both primary directions and its specialized application known as Directing through the Bounds were required to reach a final rectification solution.

Civil War Focus

<u>Civil War Outbreak</u>. In *ARM*, I express my agreement with Alfred Pearce and W.J. Simmonite that directions of Mars, Saturn and the Sun to the angles are the most reliable rectification measurements.[11] Accordingly, the Sibly Mars caught my attention for its angularity in the 7th of conflict ruling the 4th of homeland. This configuration can be delineated as Civil War. The Mars/Gemini - Civil War delineation match makes even more sense if one considers that Gemini is the sign of the twins and the Civil War garnered a reputation as a war fought 'brother against brother.' With this delineation, it seemed reasonable that directions of Mars to the angles (or perhaps Mars to the Moon) should time key events related to the Civil War.

<u>Lincoln Assassination</u>. In the Sibly chart, I note the Sun (signifier of the President) applies by square to Saturn, without reception; and Saturn rules the 8th position from the Sun (13AQ19). I posit that a Saturn-Sun direction might signify Lincoln's death and found this sequence in support:

D	Jupiter/Capricorn	P	opp. Sun (l=SA) d. → Saturn	13-May-1865
D	Jupiter/Capricorn	P	opp. Sun (l=0) d. → Saturn	3-Jul-1865

CHAPTER 2 - REVISITING THE SIBLY USA NATIONAL HOROSCOPE

Compared to Lincoln's assassination of April 15, 1865, this is reasonably close. And if not assassination, then his stress in the last days of the War.

Social Mood. In the specialized primary directions technique known as Directing through the Bounds, each significator (Ascendant, Midheaven, Sun, Moon, Prenatal Lunation) is directed through the Egyptian bounds. The active bound is named the *Distributor* in a system developed by Abū Ma'shar formally introduced in Chapter 4. Focusing on the Ascendant, my findings suggest the Ascendant's Distributor predisposes the native to behavior consistent with the Distributor's planet and sign. When considering the social mood of the United States during the Civil War, the implication of this system means America should become more warlike whenever the directed Ascendant or Moon falls in the bound of Mars. With this delineation in mind, I was interested to see the position of the directed Ascendant in the bound of Mars/Aries near the outbreak of the Civil War. In fact both malefics were Distributors during the entire 1861-1865 Civil War era. This is a delineation match for a citizenry interested in war.

D	Mars/Aries	ASC-Changeover	2-Nov-1860
D	Saturn/Aries	ASC-Changeover	4-Dec-1863
D	Venus/Taurus	ASC-Changeover	6-Feb-1867

With delineation of Mars/Gemini as Civil War, a set of Saturn-Sun primary direction sequences near Lincoln's assassination, and both malefics functioning as Distributors during the Civil War, I felt ready to attempt a final rectification solution.

Saturn in Aries, Gettysburg, and the New York Draft Riots. One of the things that Abū Ma'shar says about Directing through the Bounds is the severity of events when the directed Ascendant moves from the bound of one malefic to another, especially if directions of other malefics to the Ascendant participate. For these cases, Abū Ma'shar predicts death for an individual.[12] With this in mind, I kept staring at the position of the directed Ascendant and its passage through the malefics and asked:

Was there anything especially warlike about November 2, 1860 when the directed Ascendant moved to the bound of Mars/Aries? Yes, this was Lincoln's election which was the final trigger for the South to secede, but there are many other precipitating events of anger among the populace which might work as well. One could make a good case that the American population was sufficiently agitated (e.g., fit to be described by Mars/Aries) long before November 1860.

Did anything happen when the bound changed from Mars/Aries to Saturn/Aries on December 4, 1863 and what should that transition mean anyway - besides being very dangerous according to Abū Ma'shar? Having seen Saturn/Aries signify defensive guerilla warfare for George Washington and as bombing halts for LBJ during Vietnam led me to delineate Saturn/Aries as the frustration/halt (Saturn) of war (Aries). And this was the key delineation step which allowed me to restate the question:

Q. When did the American populace (Directed Ascendant) become frustrated (Saturn) with the Civil War (Aries)? Were such feelings of frustration accompanied by a large loss of life (which might be expected at the changeover from one malefic to another)?

A. Following the Battle of Gettysburg fought July 1-3, 1863, the conduct of the Civil War changed to feature defensive tactics. Gettysburg was followed by the new military draft on July 11, 1863 which triggered the New York Draft Riots on July 11-16, 1863.

The directed Ascendant's shift from the bound of Mars/Aries to Saturn/Aries is a perfect delineation match for timing both Gettysburg and the New York Draft Riots. First, Gettysburg was the battle with the largest number of casualties during the Civil War. This finding is in line with Abū Ma'shar's warnings about the changeover from the bound of one malefic to another. Second, after Gettysburg, Confederate General Robert E. Lee did not attempt any other major offensives for the balance of the war. Defensive fighting, including the use of sieges, was more frequent after Gettysburg and is a better match to Saturn/Aries delineated as guerilla warfare. Finally, frustration about fighting matches the mood of the populace during the New York Draft Riots. This is another delineation match to Saturn/Aries.

With this realization, I adjusted the Ascendant so the changeover from Mars/Aries to Saturn/Aries corresponded to the period between Gettysburg and the Draft Riots. Here are the results:

D	Saturn/Aries		ASC-Changeover	9-Jul-1863

D	Mars/Aries	P	dex. sextile Mars (l=MA) d. → ASC	4-Nov-1860
D	Mars/Aries	P	dex. sextile Mars (l=0) d. → ASC	18-Apr-1861

D	Jupiter/Capricorn	P	opp. Sun (l=SA) d. → Saturn	4-Apr-1865
D	Jupiter/Capricorn	P	opp. Sun (l=0) d. → Saturn	19-May-1865

What is remarkable about the Ascendant-Mars sequence is that it times Lincoln's election on November 6, 1860 (the final signal for the South to secede) and the first casualties after Fort Sumter on April 19, 1861. For the Sun-Saturn direction, Lincoln's death on April 15, 1865 falls within the date range established by the primary direction sequence.

At this point I felt I had reached the *AHA!* moment of rectification but wished to check a few other Ascendant directions.

| D | Jupiter/Capricorn | P | sin. square Saturn (l=SA) d. → ASC | 5-Apr-1792 |

George Washington signed the Coinage Act of 1792 into law on April 2, 1792 which created the United States dollar. Saturn/Libra in the 11th house of the king's money (or currency) is a delineation match to the moniker for America's currency as 'the Almighty Dollar' because the word *almighty* matches the character of Saturn when *exalted* in Libra.

| D | Mars/Gemini | P | conj. Mars (l=MA) d. → ASC | 9-Oct-1907 |

This direction timed the famous stock market panic of 1907 which led to the creation of the Federal Reserve. In addition to ruling the 4th by sign, Mars/Gemini rules the 2nd of wealth by exaltation. Mars in the 7th ruling the 2nd of wealth signifies excessive risk taking in business partnerships which harms wealth. This is a perfect delineation match to speculative excesses of the Knickerbocker Trust Company whose demise triggered the panic.

| D | Mars/Cancer | P | conj. Venus (l=VE) d. → ASC | 22-Aug-1920 |

On August 19, 1920, the 19th amendment to the Constitution granting women the right to vote was ratified. Venus is a significator for women and ruling the 5th house of elections ties her effects to the voting booth.

| D | Mercury/Cancer | P | conj. Sun (l=0) d. → ASC | 30-Jun-1932 |

This direction preceded FDR's famous July 2, 1932 *New Deal* speech at the Democratic National convention by two days and is a perfect delineation match to the Sun (President) in Cancer (caring) in the 8th house (government debt) ruling the 4th (end-of-life) who would later institute the modern welfare state on a massive scale with Social Security and Medicare two of its greatest lasting components.

I find enough other primary direction delineation matches that I declared the rectification *locked down* on December 3, 2004.

CHAPTER THREE

Divination and Rectification

In response to Geoffrey Cornelius' divinatory approach to astrology, this Chapter presents the author's own findings on Divination and Rectification.

Divination Defined. For purposes of this chapter, divination is defined as astrological delineations and predictions made using preternatural methods.

Summary

Divination and Rectification. In *The Moment of Astrology*, Cornelius includes an insightful passage on rectification where he observes accurate results after anchoring a rectification on a few events which match the precise delineation found through horoscope symbolism. Yet this observation was not consistent. The inability of a 'right' horoscope cast with official birth certificate data to properly delineate and forecast life affairs as well as the opposite situation - the ability of a 'wrong' horoscope to function correctly - raises significant questions for Cornelius on the validity of rectification. He concludes that a single natal figure may have more than one correct rectified solution.

Mercury and the Moon as significators for Astrology and Divination. Traditional authors assign the signification of astrology to Mercury and divination to the Moon. What is missing from Cornelius' perspective is the bias of every astrologer based on the unique configuration of the astrologer's own natal Mercury and Moon. I suggest astrologers with an afflicted Mercury and strong Moon are more likely to take a divinatory approach to prediction; those with a strong Mercury and afflicted Moon, vice versa.

Capturing *The Moment of Astrology* in Rectification. When completing successful rectification exercises, I noted close synastry between transiting Mercury and the Moon to planets, angles, and points for the chart under the rectification microscope. As a contribution to the divination literature, I suggest transits of Mercury and the Moon effectively load the figure under study into a data cache which facilitates its study.

Divination and Rectification

Given the current vogue of recasting astrology as a divinatory practice in U.K. academic circles, I thought it would be of interest to comment on my own experience with divination in rectifying the Regulus USA National Horoscope. In *ARM*, I included the following comments on selecting *magical times* when conducting rectification projects, crediting the role of divination in the rectification process:

> *Are astrologers driven to study and research certain figures, be they clients or historical personages, based on the position of currently transiting planets? I answer in the affirmative. This from the experience of comparing times when I locked down a rectification to the natal figure studied at that time. The most common connections I witnessed were between transiting planets and the figure's Moon or Mercury* [1].

As I make clear, what I describe appears a form of 'divination assist' in contrast to a pure form of divination. I have never heard voices, experienced prophecy through dreams, or otherwise acknowledged an intuitive response to the question of computing a rectified birth time for a natal horoscope. Yet in line with my above statements, I indeed *have* found the task of rectification much easier during times when dynamic connections are present between the figure under study and transiting planets.

In tackling this subject, I first turn to the findings of Geoffrey Cornelius on the topic of divination and rectification. After contrasting my own experience with Cornelius on the accuracy of astrology, I present two horoscopes computed for key moments during the rectification project. Connections made between the chart cast for moments of discovery and the horoscope under study confirm the process I refer to as 'divination assist.'

The Moment of Astrology

Originally published by the British astrologer Geoffrey Cornelius in 1994, *The Moment of Astrology*[2] has produced a large following among advocates of divination. Among the many subjects Cornelius considers is rectification. Included in his own section entitled *Divination and Rectification*, Cornelius states:

> *The definitive direction is usually discovered in rectification where the astrologer has to choose between different directions testifying to several different possible birth times . . . It will often be found, though not always, that the solution is not to average out a moderate fit for several of the major directions. The more effective*

CHAPTER 3 - DIVINATION AND RECTIFICATION

solution is to choose one direction which is highly revealing for a significant event and produce an exact rectification from this alone, even if this means sacrificing altogether several other possibly relevant directions which now fall out of acceptable orb for their supposed events. The frequent result is that this decisive and singular rectification is later found to yield equally decisive measures to certain other events, past or future, where the 'averaged out' rectification, true to its origin, continues to give soggy results.[3]

In these comments, I am in complete agreement with Cornelius and believe he captures what I have described as the *AHA!* moment of rectification. For me, use of the *primary direction sequence*[4] which matches pairs of events to pairs of dates computed by primary directions matches the spirit of Cornelius' observation that some astrologers *choose one direction which is highly revealing for a significant event*. I push things further than Cornelius by requiring at least two primary direction sequences; together with a few other single direction hits. I prefer at least eight or nine *revealing* directions; the more the better.

And here is where I differ with Geoffrey Cornelius on rectification. For in the immediately preceding pages he demonstrates the ability of four different natal figures for Princess Diana to time events in her life including her royal wedding and death. Cornelius proceeds to state that

Rectification is likely to yield variants of the horoscope, each of which work, and are therefore 'right.'[5]

Which brings him back to his central thesis that

. . . the coming-to-pass of astrological effects or showings is not founded in a coincidence in objective time of heavens above and event below.[6]

Working in the context of an astrological model appended by trans-Saturnian planets and other modernisms, it is not surprising that Cornelius reached the conclusion that he did. As I make the case in *ARM*, a weakness of modern astrology is its underspecified predictive model. Relying primarily on transits, progressions, and solar arc directions, modern astrology has failed to demonstrate consistent rectification results. For some astrologers, rectification is so discredited few bother to consider anything other than the official birth certificate time. Of course, the official birth certificate time *is*, *should be*, and *remains* the starting point for natal astrology. But there are exceptions to the reliability of birth certificate times; and of course, cases where no birth time has been recorded.[7] What I am saying is with an underspecified predictive model, it is quite easy to produce multiple charts which purport to be the *correct* figure. Especially when the addition of Uranus, Neptune, and Pluto adds another three variables to the interpretation scheme. With medieval predictive astrology, mistakes can still be made in rectification; however, if the full gamut of medieval predictive methods is deployed, mistakes are much less likely.

Though I have been referencing Cornelius' comments on rectification, the same can be said for his approach to astrology in general. Cornelius' rejection that a horoscope necessarily links planetary positions computed for that moment to actual physical manifestation appears to stem from a number of personal events. They include his own disappointment as a customer of inaccurate horary readings and disillusionment following the failure of astrology to stand up to scientific testing in the 1970s and 1980s. And what appears to be a pivotal moment in Cornelius' development was his discovery that the randomly selected horoscope by Humanistic scientists in their famous 1975 attack against astrology cast in 1907 actually proved radical in judging the Humanist attack 68 years later even though there was no astrological reason why such a random chart, e.g., the 'wrong chart', should shed light on the 1975 attack.[8]

True, Cornelius allows for the possibility that scientific tests of modern astrology have failed because –

> . . . some other element is involved in the practice of astrology[9]

or

> . . . the nature and function of 'technique' have been completely misunderstood in astrological theory[10]

but in choosing to recast astrology as primarily a divinatory practice Cornelius tacitly falls in line with scientific skeptics who deny the merits of horoscopic astrology. Divination becomes a fallback position for astrology's justification.

Mercury and the Moon as significators for Astrology and Divination

In my opinion, there is an important point which Cornelius misses. A fundamental principle of natal astrology is pure planetary influences are never perceived directly. Instead individual perception is based on planets filtered through an array of signs, aspects, and house positions uniquely defined for the person at birth. An individual with Mars in the Ascendant may experience the Martian quality of strife directly through a military career. Another with Mars in the sixth house may experience the Martian quality of heat through sunburn as an illness.

These same arguments apply for an individual's approach to astrology and divination. For traditional authors, Mercury is the significator of astrology; the Moon – in certain signs and configurations with Mercury – signifies divination.[11] Each individual – including every astrologer – approaches astrology and divination differently through the lens of their own Mercury and Moon uniquely constructed in their own natal figure.

For Geoffrey Cornelius, his divinatory use of horoscopes as quasi-tarot decks may tell us more about how Cornelius approaches astrology and divination through the lens of his own natal Moon and Mercury. *Which may not be applicable to the entire art of astrology as a discipline.* Not privy to the complete details of Cornelius' own natal chart – a self-described 'reserved 8th house Sun in Capricorn with Saturn rising'[12] – this line of reasoning cannot be pursued. But Cornelius's approach to astrology is consistent with afflicted Mercury (which can subvert astrological practice) and a strong Moon (which can produce powerful insights from divination).

I do agree wholeheartedly with Cornelius that divination plays a role in astrological practice and historically some astrologers have swept these *moments of astrology* under the rug for various reasons – perhaps to avoid scathing attacks from scientific skeptics. However I disagree with the central premise that astrology should be recast as divination because the negative findings Cornelius presents. Just because Cornelius can't make contemporary astrology work consistently doesn't mean the rest of us needs to replace the rules of horoscopic astrology with a divinatory framework.

Perhaps we should use a different system; medieval astrology, anyone?

Mercury and the Author

If Mercury signifies astrology and each person views Mercury differently through the lens of their unique natal figure, then Mercury is a source of bias in the astrologer's practice. Compared to Cornelius, my experience with astrology has been much different. For instance, I have paid for a dozen or so horary readings in the last ten years. The accuracy rate was 100%, a tribute to the methods of William Lilly preserved by a growing number of contemporary students and teachers. As far as my own success in medieval predictive astrology, I can say that I learn something from every chart judgment, every refinement of technique, and have improved in accuracy each year.

Consequently, the zodiacal state of my own natal Mercury is relevant to my astrological practice generally and the validity of the Regulus USA National Horoscope as a research product. While at this point I have chosen not to release the entire details of my own natal figure, I will state the following: Moon/Virgo, 2nd quarter, sect leader, angular, in hayz, applies within a degree to Mercury/Taurus by trine, with both Moon and Mercury in mutual reception by exaltation. Mercury/Taurus is at his second station and applies within a degree to the square of Saturn at his first station. For this combination, Ptolemy states the Virgo Moon, waxing and together with Mercury, produces 'magicians, astrologers, and oracular persons, possessing prescience.' He also states that when Saturn testifies to Mercury, individuals are 'managers of the affairs of others, or interpreters of dreams, or will be engaged in temples for the purpose of divination, and for the sake of their fanaticism'.[13] True, Mercury applying to the square of Saturn can produce roadblocks and mistakes; yet Saturn at his first station means these periodic hindrances eventually give way like a crumbling rooftop which allows a full unencumbered view of the sky.

In general, I agree that Ptolemy's assessment of the Moon-Mercury-Saturn configuration matches my employment situation quite accurately. Where Ptolemy's delineation falls short is on the topic of having second sight. Indeed I would self-describe my talents in divination in a psychic sense as absolutely zero. I have never had the slightest intuition about how a particular astrological configuration might be delineated and predicted for any individual without first applying the rules of medieval predictive astrology. And any attempt to delude myself in thinking I had such intuitive or psychic insight on a standalone basis has proven ruinous.

I attribute my own lack of intuition due to the absence of any traditional planet in water signs in my own figure; further polarized by an emphasis of planets in earth signs which are by definition opposed to water signs. My personal opinion is that divinatory power of a psychic nature is associated with the three water signs of Cancer, Scorpio, and Pisces. I have no traditional planets in those signs; therefore I am not psychic. Yet I am an astrologer.

I engage in this self-analysis so others can see the stage I have erected. Imagine this author sitting in front of multiple computer screens in an office with a well-stocked reference library and internet access to virtually any public database through a local university connection. This is all well and good but something remains missing.

Divination and the Author

In theory, I can sit down at my desk any day at any time and work through the three stages of rectification[14] and complete a rectification project as quickly as 30 minutes. Yet some days the process is more difficult. What is missing is *the moment*.

As I stated in the opening of this section, I observed a relationship between transits of Mercury or the Moon computed for the *AHA!* moments of rectification and the position of planets, points, or angles for the figure under study. Why should such a correspondence aid the rectification process?

Using computer vocabulary to aid the analogy, it seems whenever transits of Mercury or the Moon highlight natal horoscope planets, angles, or points, the horoscope is loaded into a memory cache. Just as data loaded into a memory cache is faster for computer users to retrieve, so does a natal figure become easier to interpret when Mercury and the Moon are available to guide reason and intuition.

Exactly where this cache is located or how it operates is beyond the scope of my investigations. It may lie within my own brain or it may exist elsewhere with Mercury and the Moon acting as some kind of gateway. But I wish to be clear the effect I describe appears to be a form of *divination assistance* rather than a pure form of divination in what is typically associated with psychic ability. If it is something else, I will leave it to the experts on divination to sort out. Perhaps I am too close to the situation to be objective.

Capturing the 'Moment of Astrology'

During rectification projects, whenever I reached the *AHA!* moment and locked down the rectified time, I pressed the election button on my astrological software program and created a new horoscope for the *AHA!* moment of discovery. I printed and saved these charts with my working papers for the project.

For the 2002 trial rectification made July 20, I did not consciously choose this date as a *magical time* for rectification work on the USA Sibly National Horoscope. In contrast, for the final rectification made December 3, 2004, I deliberately chose the time period to complete the rectification. As it turned out, there was a tight synastry link between transiting Mercury and both trial and final rectified figures.

Before continuing, remember what you are about to see are snapshots of the *AHA!* moment of rectification computed for the exact time when I completed a trial rectification on July 20, 2002 and a final rectification on December 3, 2004. In other words, when I said to myself *THIS IS IT!* I clicked on a button on my astrological software and captured the moment.

A triple Mercury-Jupiter-Sun conjunction in Cancer dominates Figure 4. This marks a Mercury return, Jupiter return, and Sun return for the USA figure. I consider the Mercury return the most significant feature. Note the rare cazimi Jupiter.

What makes this figure radical to the USA National Horoscope? The figure's Ascendant is partile conjunct the USA Mars. The figure's Midheaven is partile conjunct the USA Moon. I judge that any one of these conditions is sufficient for radicality. But the combined effect of a Mercury return and two incidences of transit-angle synastry appears very powerful.

Yet Mercury is combust. This is one of the greatest debilities according to medieval authors.[15] How does it spoil the trial rectification? As stated earlier, I employed the transit-angle 'hit' approach, a method today I disparage as faulty for its assumption which severs the connection between the delineation and prediction.

Yet despite the weakness of this approach, the trial rectification made in 2002 proved only 15 minutes of degree in error from the final rectified time computed in 2004. Considering the weakness of Mercury, I suggest *the power of this moment on July 20, 2002 in a divinatory sense* helped facilitate a close approximation of the final result.

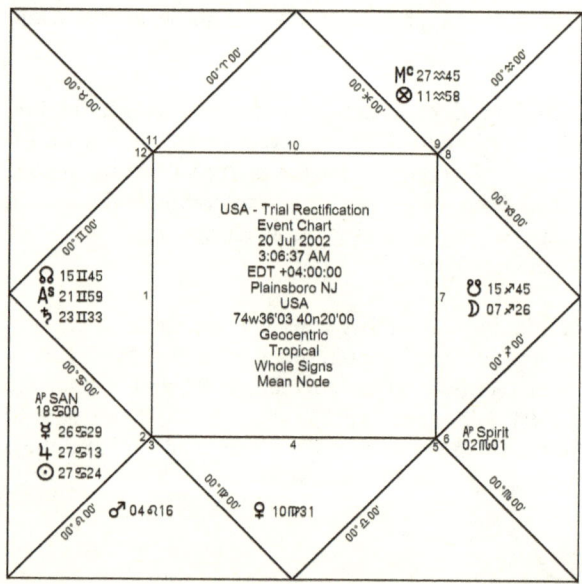

Figure 4. Regulus USA National Horoscope, Rectification July 20, 2002.

As stated earlier, I purposely revisited the initial 2002 rectification later in 2004 based on the proximity of Mercury's retrograde station on November 30, 2004 to the trial USA Ascendant computed in 2002. In my opinion, this deliberate choice elected the *moment of astrology* for the rectification project. On December 3, 2004 at 8:11:17 AM, I reached the *AHA!* moment of rectification, recording 26SA54'40" as the final Ascendant for the USA figure. The Regulus USA National Horoscope was born.

Consider Figure 5 on a standalone basis. If judged as a natal figure, the 9th house offers evidence of the efficacy behind the final rectified product. Quoting Abū 'Ali, Bonatti states:

If the Lord of the ninth (or third) were in the Ascendant or in the Midheaven, free from the malefics, it signifies the rulership of the native over his partners, and he will be of good sense and the best morals, and complete in faith, especially if Jupiter were the Lord of the ninth, or the Lord of the ninth were in the Ascendant, in the aspect of Jupiter.[16]

Sun rules the 9th and falls in the 1st. Sun is free of both malefics and is in sextile aspect with Jupiter who is oriental, angular in the 10th by quadrant

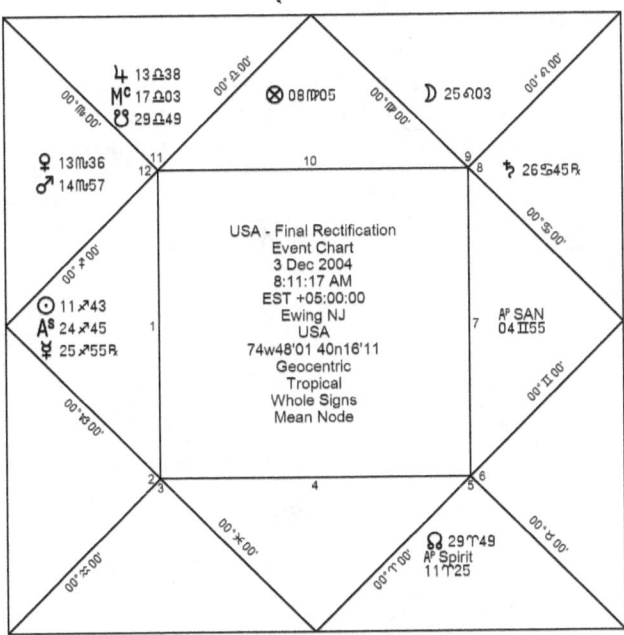

Figure 5. Regulus USA National Horoscope, Rectification December 3, 2004.

signs, and placed in the 11th house of his joy. Though Mercury-retrograde is a debility, the Moon's application to Mercury by trine and Jupiter's reception of Mercury help Mercury to complete the project. Jupiter is the Ruler of the Chart. I said earlier my own natal Mercury may prove the best judge of the success of the Regulus USA National Horoscope. In all likelihood, this December 3, 2004 chart should also have some bearing on the future of this figure because arguably it represents its *birth*.

Already I have seen some evidence of the predictive power of the figure. The recent solar arc direction of *d. Jupiter conj. MC* exact on April 14, 2008 timed writing efforts for this paper designed to document events timed by Ascendant directions. In the final editing phase of this book in the fall of 2008, transiting Mercury passed over the MC three times. Consider the Libra MC in this figure also matches the Libra MC of the Regulus USA National Horoscope itself, as does the Sagittarius Ascendant.

If this figure's Firdaria sequence offers any predictive ability, then the Regulus USA National Horoscope should reach its high point of influence through the astrological community during the Sun-Jupiter subperiod January 24, 2012 to June 29, 2013.

Update for 2nd edition

The Firdaria prediction failed to generate any effect. However the following primary direction timed the first public presentation made on the horoscope to the Astrological Society of Princeton on March 8, 2020 within 3 days:

| D | Saturn/Sagittarius | P | ASC d. Sun | 5-Mar-2020 |

Note: Method of Regiomontanus

PART TWO

The Regulus USA National Horoscope

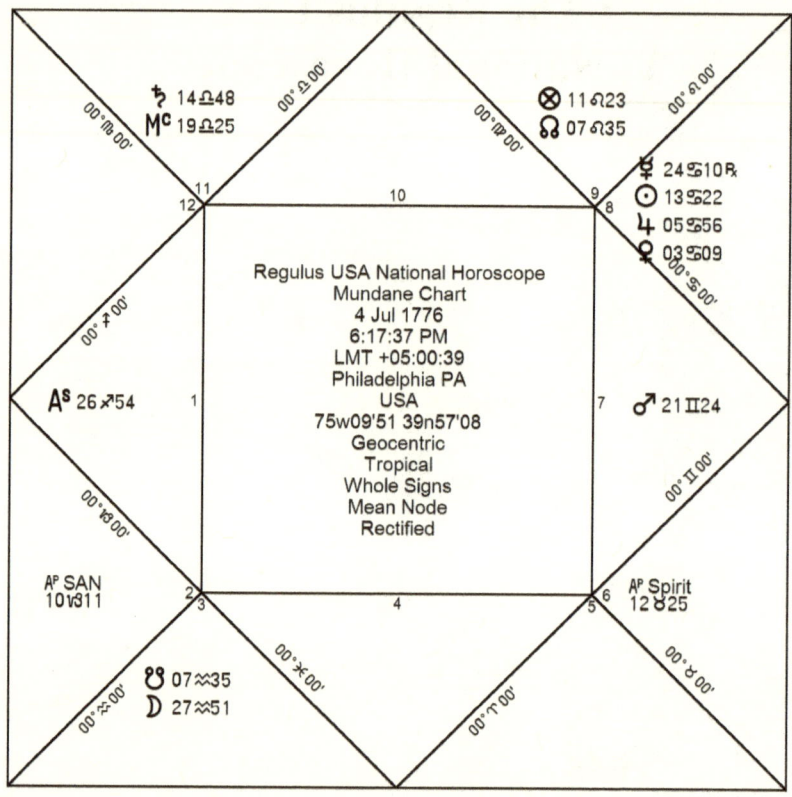

Figure 6. Regulus USA National Horoscope, Whole Sign Houses.

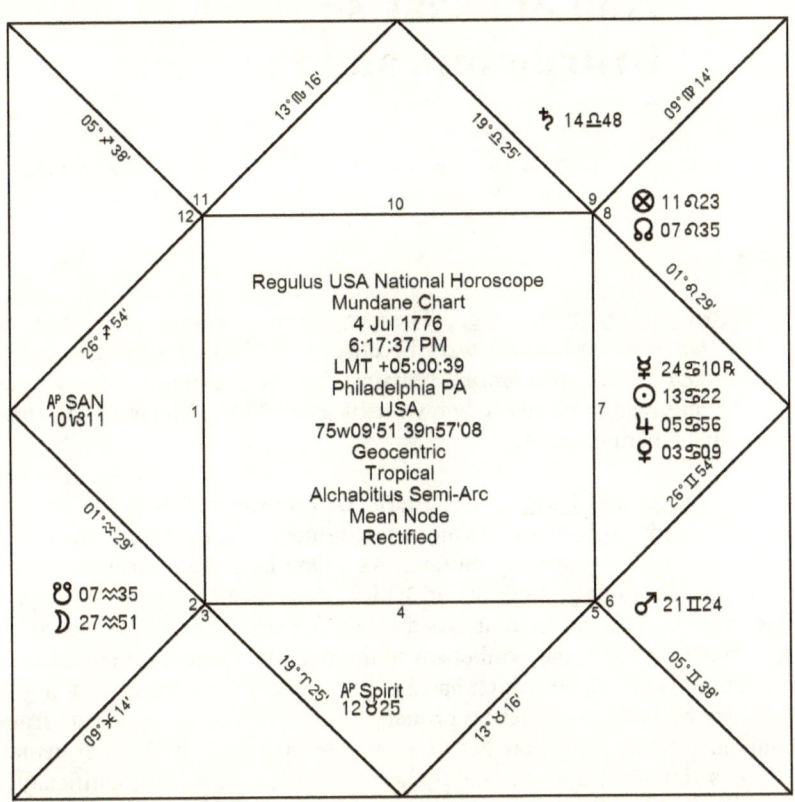

Figure 7. Regulus USA National Horoscope, Alchabitius Houses.

CHAPTER FOUR

Abū Ma'shar's System of Distributors and Partners

This chapter introduces the theory of *Abū Ma'shar's System of Distributors and Partners*.

Summary

History and Nomenclature. The procedure is named *Abū Ma'shar's System of Distributors and Partners* because Abū Ma'shar's treatment of the method in *On Solar Revolutions* remains the most extensive commentary which has survived in currently known texts as of 2008. The method dates to the Hellenistic period.

Distributors and Partners. The term **Distributor** refers to the currently active bound for a given significator, determined by moving the significator through the bounds by primary motion. As a time lord, the Distributor adds its intrinsic nature to any significator which dynamically passes through its degree range by primary motion. As a result, the significator is predisposed to actions consistent with the symbolism of the bound's planet/sign combination. The **Partner** is the planet which has most recently made contact with a given significator by body or aspect by primary motion. Its meaning differs from a standalone primary direction because the planet named as Partner remains active as a time-lord until the next planet or aspect meets the significator by primary motion.

Integration of Distributors and Partners. Because the Distributor predisposes the Significator to specific types of actions, the Distributor can be considered a stage set for a play whose plot lines are acted out by Partners who take their turn in the spotlight. Partners should be evaluated by the zodiacal state of the promissor involved in the direction, whether the aspect is dexter or sinister, and what type of Ptolemaic aspect joins promissor and significator. A relative 50-50 weighting of Distributor and Partner is recommended for judging the overall effect of the event timed by the Partner's direction.

CHAPTER 4 - ABŪ MA'SHAR'S SYSTEM OF DISTRIBUTORS AND PARTNERS

Overview

When stepping back from primary direction mathematics employed by this technique, it is apparent *Abū Ma'shar's System of Distributors and Partners* belongs to a set of predictive techniques properly classified as time lord methods. Compared to modern predictive methods which yield only discrete days for events to occur, time lord methods effectively divide the native's entire life into chapters which offer a complete cradle-to-grave predictive system. Examples include the Dasha system (Indian), Firdaria (Medieval), Directing by Triplicity (Hellenistic/Medieval), and the Hellenistic system currently referred to as Zodiacal Releasing from Spirit ('ZRS') by Project Hindsight.[1] As of 2008, one of the hot topics in astrological research is how these techniques interact with each other and which ones may carve out a higher position on the predictive hierarchy.

At this point, my findings suggest that *Abū Ma'shar's System of Distributors and Partners* works as advertised and ranks at or near the top of the predictive hierarchy. Whether or not it takes the #1 spot I cannot say at this time. But it is certainly close, if not actually taking the highest spot.

History and Nomenclature of the Technique

As an astrologer, my interests and expertise lie in the testing and practical application of astrological technique. I am not a translator nor do I claim any expertise in the history or transmission of these methods. I present this disclaimer because the name I present for the method - *Abū Ma'shar's System of Distributors and Partners* - represents a convenient moniker which may not prove historically accurate.[2] What we know is Abū Ma'shar writing in his treatise *On Solar Returns*[3] left behind the most complete treatment of this method in surviving texts translated as of 2008.

Distributors

Abū Ma'shar's System of Distributors and Partners integrates two separate techniques into a single predictive method. The first technique applies Directing through the Bounds[4] to each significator, yielding a set of Distributors. The word Distributor is simply the active bound computed for a given significator by primary direction. Since there are six significators[5], there are six active Distributors at any given time.

Example: The Ascendant of the Regulus USA National Horoscope is 26SA54'40". This falls in the bound of Mars/Sagittarius which is defined as the four degree range between 26SA00'00" to 29SA59'59". On July 4, 1776, the Ascendant's Distributor was Mars/Sagittarius. Mars remained the Ascendant Distributor until the Ascendant reached 0CP00'00" by primary motion, about three years later. At that time, the Ascendant Distributor changed to Mercury/Capricorn because the first six degrees of Capricorn are assigned to the bound of Mercury.

Table 3. Regulus USA National Horoscope: Distributors for 4-July-1776.

Significator	Zodiacal Position	Distributor
Ascendant	26SA54	Mars/Sagittarius
Midheaven	19LI25	Jupiter/Libra
Moon	27AQ51	Saturn/Aquarius
Sun	13CA22	Mercury/Cancer
Lot of Fortune	11LE28	Saturn/Leo
Prenatal Lunation	10CP11	Jupiter/Capricorn

Note: I identify each Distributor not just by the planet assigned to the bound, e.g., 'Mars', but by both planet's name and the zodiac sign the bound is assigned to, e.g., 'Mars/Sagittarius.' This is a conscious decision because the behavior of the bound's assigned planet varies considerably from sign to sign. Simply saying the current Distributor is 'Mars' without specifying its sign position is an incomplete way to describe the Distributor.

Bounds - Definition. Bounds are defined as unequal five-fold divisions of each zodiacal sign. Subdivisions range from two to twelve degrees. Only the five visible planets are assigned to these subdivisions (e.g., Saturn, Jupiter, Mars, Venus, Mercury); luminaries are not. Ptolemy considered the quantitative power of bounds on par with rulership and exaltation. He assigned each dignity the numeric quantity of +1 in a scoring system. By the medieval era, bounds had been downgraded to occupying the fourth place on a five level hierarchy of essential dignities: sign (+5); exaltation (+4); triplicity (+3); bound (+2); and decan (+1).

How are the subdivisions determined? Their apparent random design has left many astrologers haggling over their relevance; some like Jean Baptiste-Morin simply threw them out. However there is one pattern which helps explain their design: the number of degrees assigned to each planet, when summed across all signs, equals the major years[6] of each planet. While this rule does not provide the complete formula, it does demonstrate bound assignment is not random. Unfortunately at this point, we know nothing more about their construction. There are also several competing sets of bounds. For *America is Born*, Egyptian bounds are assumed. See Appendix D for tests of this system.

Table 4. Egyptian Bounds

♈	0–Jupiter	6–Venus	12–Mercury	20–Mars	25-Saturn
♉	0-Venus	8-Mercury	14-Jupiter	22-Saturn	27-Mars
♊	0-Mercury	6-Jupiter	12-Venus	17-Mars	24-Saturn
♋	0-Mars	7-Venus	13-Mercury	19-Jupiter	26-Saturn
♌	0-Jupiter	6-Venus	11-Saturn	18-Mercury	24-Mars
♍	0-Mercury	7-Venus	17-Jupiter	21-Mars	28-Saturn
♎	0-Saturn	6-Mercury	14-Jupiter	21-Venus	28-Mars
♏	0-Mars	7-Venus	11-Mercury	19-Jupiter	24-Saturn
♐	0-Jupiter	12-Venus	17-Mercury	21-Saturn	26-Mars
♑	0-Mercury	7-Jupiter	14-Venus	22-Saturn	26-Mars
♒	0-Mercury	7-Venus	13-Jupiter	20-Mars	25-Saturn
♓	0-Venus	12-Jupiter	16-Mercury	19-Mars	28-Saturn

How to read: Each zodiacal sign of 30 degrees is subdivided into five unequal divisions. Each division is known as a 'bound.' Examining bounds for the sign of Aries, see the first 6 degrees assigned to Jupiter; next 6, Venus; next 8, Mercury; next 5, Mars; last 5, Saturn.

Table 5. Allocation of Egyptian Bound Degrees to Major Years

	Mercury	Venus	Mars	Jupiter	Saturn	Total
Aries	8	6	5	6	5	30
Taurus	6	8	3	8	5	30
Gemini	6	5	7	6	6	30
Cancer	6	6	7	7	4	30
Leo	6	5	6	6	7	30
Virgo	7	10	7	4	2	30
Libra	8	7	2	7	6	30
Scorpio	8	4	7	5	6	30
Sagittarius	4	5	4	12	5	30
Capricorn	7	8	4	7	4	30
Aquarius	7	6	5	7	5	30
Pisces	3	12	9	4	2	30
Major Years	**76**	**82**	**66**	**79**	**57**	**360**

How to read: The bound of Mercury falls from 12AR00'00" to 19AR59'59". This eight degree range in Aries is listed under row 'Aries' and column 'Mercury.' Aggregated across all twelve signs, Mercury fills out 76 degrees of the entire 360 degree zodiac. The quantity 76 is the number of Mercury's major years.

Bounds - Application. Now we know how bounds are defined and that a bound is renamed 'Distributor' when a directed significator moves to its location, what next? Consider first how bounds actually function in natal astrology. Based on the Presidential database, I concluded bounds impart their intrinsic quality to any planet, point, or aspect placed within their specific degree range.[7] A planet, point, or aspect falling in a bound functions like it is conjunct the planet/sign combination defined for that bound. This is the static relationship. But the same principle works dynamically: *a bound also adds its intrinsic nature to any significator which passes through its degree range by primary motion*. Now we can start to apply the method.

Consider the Ascendant which signifies the nation as a whole. In Chapter 2, I stated the Directed Ascendant of the Regulus USA National Horoscope placed in a specific bound predisposed America to certain types of activities. When the Ascendant passed through the bound of Mars/Aries by primary motion, the Civil War broke out as Americans became warlike. When the Distributor changed from Mars/Aries to Saturn/Aries after Gettysburg, Americans became frustrated with war, protested against the draft, and engaged in defensive guerilla tactics for the balance of the war. These are the kind of effects we should expect to see if Mars/Aries and Saturn/Aries were active time lords for the early and latter stages of the Civil War. Ascendant Distributors appear to set a stage for the nation consistent with the delineation of the bound. Once the stage is set, the actors can perform.

Partners

For *Abū Ma'shar's System of Distributors and Partners*, those *actors* are nothing more than horoscope planets who contact the Ascendant by body or aspect by primary motion. These actors are formally named *Partners* in Abū Ma'shar's system. This sounds like the definition of a planet involved in any type of primary direction. Which it is. Except in this case the primary direction is not treated as the timer of a standalone event to be discarded once the event has passed. In Abū Ma'shar's system, the Partner remains active as a time lord until the next planet or aspect meets the significator. For horoscopes with aspects which are fairly wide, this means a Partner could conceivably function as a time lord for five to ten years before another planet takes over as its body or aspect meets the Ascendant by primary motion.

Nomenclature. Outside of Abū Ma'shar's System of Distributors and Partners, we usually run into the terms *Significator* and *Promissor* when speaking about primary directions. Continue to use these terms. Significators are defined as the six points known as the Ascendant, Midheaven, Moon, Sun, Lot of Fortune, and Prenatal Lunation because each significator 'signifies' something. For example, the Ascendant *signifies* the physical body for an individual in natal astrology. Significators differ from Promissors because the planets (as Promissors) *promise* some type of accident - good or bad. Mars in the 6th house of illness might promise a fever. This means when Mars contacts the Ascendant, the individual has a fever. In considering the terms Significator and Promissor within Abū Ma'shar's System of Distributors and Partners, there is really no difference between the words Promissor and Partner. Only when the roles of Significator and Promissor are flip-flopped in primary direction calculations does the Significator take on the role of the Partner. Also be aware there is no relation between Promissors and Distributors. They are separate concepts.

Integration of Distributors and Partners

Evaluating the combined effects of Distributors and Partners requires astrologers to consider the joint effect of an active bound and the Promissor of a recent primary direction as time lords. Based on this study, here are my findings on how the system works in practice:

Distributor. The active bound as time lord predisposes the Significator to committing actions consistent with the bound's delineation. Judge the Distributor before the Partner. Consider the Distributor as a time lord who sets the stage for a play whose plot lines are acted out by Partners who take the spotlight.

Partner - Zodiacal state. Delineate the Partner. Include the Partner's sign, bound, and dwad; its ruler, aspects, and house position.

Partner - Dexter or Sinister aspect. Consider whether the direction's aspect is dexter or sinister as one way to judge the level of intensity for the direction. I have mentioned the dexter sextile aspect of Mars which triggered the Civil War as one example of the relative power of dexter aspects. Dexter aspects, formed against the order of the astrological signs, are said to be more forceful than sinister aspects formed in the order of the signs.[8] A careful study of Mars-Ascendant directions for the Regulus USA National Horoscope confirms the consistency of this finding.

Partner - Ptolemaic aspect. Consider whether the significator and promissor meet by conjunction, sextile, square, trine, or opposition. If by conjunction, give the body with the higher latitude more weight in the outcome. If by sextile or trine, judge the event to occur effortlessly. If by square or opposition, judge the event occur with strife or difficulty. Consider an *effortless* sextile/trine which includes a malefic may not be pleasant.

Relative Weighting of Distributor and Partner. Treat Distributor and Partner as co-equals in judging the overall effect; e.g., 50-50.

Summary

Compared to the standalone practice of primary directions, *Abū Ma'shar's System of Distributors and Partners* has added three things:

1. <u>Nomenclature</u>: The words *Distributor* and *Partner*.

2. <u>Distributors</u>: Direct each significator through the bounds as a first step before considering primary directions of planets and their aspects.

3. <u>Partners</u>: Consider the most recent planet which contacted the significator by body or aspect as a time lord until the next planet takes over.

Given the ability of the Distributor to modify the effect of the primary direction by as much as 50%, the addition of Distributors is the most significant change to primary directions as currently practiced.

CHAPTER FIVE

Calculation: Distributors and Partners

In this second of two chapters on Abū Ma'shar's System of Distributors and Partners, the mathematics of the system are explained and illustrated with example calculations. Full treatment of the system means applying its rules for each significator: Ascendant, Midheaven, Moon, Sun, Lot of Fortune, and Prenatal Lunation. As a starting point, Abū Ma'shar's system is applied to the Ascendant of the Regulus USA National Horoscope.

Summary

<u>Introducing Primary Directions</u>. The basis of primary directions is the apparent clockwise motion of planets rising in the Eastern sky and setting in the Western sky. This is known as *diurnal motion*. Additional concepts are introduced including the three types of primary directions, direct vs. converse motion, latitude, Significators vs. Promissors, the celestial sphere, the zodiacal coordinate system, and the equatorial coordinate system.

<u>Mathematics of Ascendant Directions</u>. Choosing the Ascendant as significator, mathematics of Ascendant primary directions are outlined. Computed for both direct and converse motion, examples are presented for directing the Ascendant through the bounds and directing a planet or its aspect to the Ascendant with and without latitude.

Introducing Primary Directions

<u>You are there</u>. It is early evening, July 4, 1776, 6:17:37 PM to be exact. On this day, the Second Continental Congress signed the Declaration of Independence and sent the document to the printer. Exactly what time these events occurred, nobody knows. Accordingly the proposed time is nothing more than a symbolic moment of importance for that date. A horoscope cast for 6:17:37 PM has proven to consistently time events which match the figure's delineation by the technique of primary directions. What is this technique? And how do we make sense of it?

Pennsylvania State House, c. 1770s (now 'Independence Hall').[1]

<u>View 1</u>. You are standing on the other side of Chestnut Street facing the Pennsylvania State House. As you look directly at the building, you face South. East is to your left and West is to your right. For the time 6:17:37 PM it is early evening and the Sun, just above the western sky to your right, is getting ready to set. Venus has just finished up her stint as a morning star and is no longer visible. It hides under the sunbeams with Jupiter and Mercury. Saturn is directly overhead, still invisible at this hour. The Moon is below the horizon and will not rise until for a few more hours.

<u>View 2</u>. The horoscope, pictured below, captures this moment. The horizon is represented by the horizontal line starting at 26SA54 on the left and moving across the page to 26GE54. The Moon 27AQ51 pictured in the lower left quadrant of the figure is invisible to the human eye. Everything above the horizon is visible. See the Sun 13CA22 just above the western horizon on the right side of the chart. Now imagine the entire horoscope rotating clockwise. Spin it just a little bit and the Sun, now just above the western horizon, will move exactly to the western horizon where it will set and become invisible to the human eye. Keep rotating the horoscope and eventually the Moon will rise to the left on the eastern horizon. If you had a few hours to spare, you could stand across Chestnut Street facing the State House and see it yourself.

The motion just described, planets rising in the east, culminating overhead, and setting in the west, is called **diurnal motion**. It is the basis of primary directions. The inventors of this predictive technique surmised that actions like the ones just described, e.g., the Sun setting or Moon rising, must have significance for someone born that day. An elaborate system of mathematics was created to define these events of significance. To tackle primary directions, let's divide primary directions into three categories: Ascendant directions, Midheaven directions, and interplanetary directions.

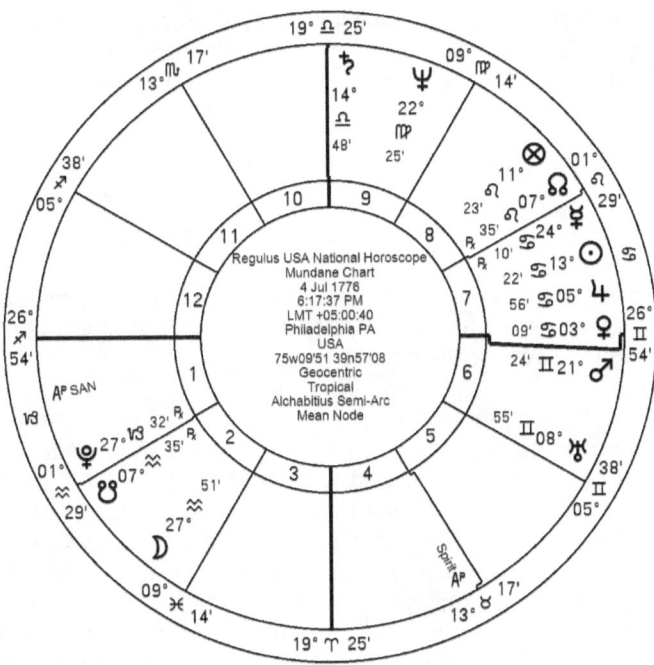

Figure 8. Regulus USA National Horoscope, Alchabitius House Cusps.

Ascendant directions

Return to the image of the Moon rising on the eastern horizon a few hours after sunset. Ask this question:

Q. Exactly when will the Moon rise, and when it does, what astrological event might be signified by the Moon's rising? Asking this type of question puts us in the category known as Ascendant directions. We are concerned with planets making contact with the Ascendant by body or aspect.

A. The Moon rose at 9:53 p.m. that night. The Moon traced out an arc from its starting position under the horizon at 27AQ51 computed at 6:17:37 PM to its position exactly on the eastern horizon at 9:53 p.m. In that space of time the Moon moved from 27AQ51 to 00PI01. That's an interesting fact, but for purposes we care only about the Moon's actual position of 27AQ51 computed for the horoscope time of 6:17:35 PM.

What events did the Moon signify when it rose to meet the Ascendant? Computed two ways, with and without the Moon's latitude, yields two projections: 52.58 and 54.85 years which when added to July 4, 1776 projected February 2, 1829 and May 10, 1831. What happened at that time? The Aquarius Moon signifies a humanitarian philosophy manifesting through publications because of her placement in the 3rd house of communications. The origin of William Lloyd Garrison's abolitionist newspaper *The Liberator* first published in 1831 is one such delineation match.

Midheaven Directions

Consider the Sun's position just above the Western horizon.

Q. Earlier in the day, the Sun was directly overhead. How many hours have transpired since the Sun's culmination and what astrological event might be signified by the Sun's culmination?

A. The Sun culminated earlier at 12:04 PM. This type of motion, imagining the Sun moving backwards in the sky, is known as converse motion. Its arc was 93.40 years and projected to November 25, 1869. What happened on that date? Following the breakup of Jay Gould's infamous gold corner on September 24, 1869, legal proceedings reached a crescendo with judges battling over the right to access and examine Gould's books. Sun falls in the 8th house of debt and bankruptcy; Sun ruling the POF in Leo, sign of gold, ties debt/bankruptcy to gold. Sun also rules the 4th house by exaltation which signifies the end of the matter. This is a delineation match to what today would be called a forensic financial investigation. An investigation of Gould's business affairs revealed one of the largest financial frauds uncovered in the 19th century.

Interplanetary Directions

Reconsider the Sun's position just above the Western horizon.

Q. See the Sun above the western horizon about to set. Now imagine its position frozen while everything else in the sky continues to rotate clockwise from left to right. When would Saturn, currently overhead, meet the Sun's position, and what astrological event might be signified by Saturn's conjunction to the Sun?

A. Saturn met the Sun's frozen position about 6 hours later. This corresponded to an arc of 64.65 years which projected a date of February 25, 1841. What happened? One month later President William Henry Harrison caught a cold which quickly developed into pneumonia. He died on April 4, 1841. This direction timed the death of a President. Why? Saturn rules the 8th sign from the Sun's position in Cancer which is one indication that Saturn is the killing planet of the Sun.

This type of direction involves two planets and is the third type known as **interplanetary directions**. Unlike Ascendant and Midheaven directions, for which there is no disagreement by authorities on their computation, there are a number of competing methods of computing interplanetary directions. This is an advanced topic which I am reserving for another text. For now, be aware that three most common types of interplanetary directions computed by traditional astrologers were based on methods by **Ptolemy**, **Regiomontanus**, and **Placidus**.

Focus on Ascendant Directions

When one considers all permutations of Ascendant, Midheaven, and Interplanetary directions, at least 2,000 directions can be computed for the Regulus USA National Horoscope. In keeping with the stated goal of this text, I am interested in presenting a sufficient number of directions to confirm the rectification, nothing more. In the following chapters, approximately 200 events timed by primary directions are presented.

Because the Ascendant is the most important significator, I have chosen to focus exclusively on Ascendant directions. I have also found it easier to choose the Ascendant in my first application of Directing through the Bounds for this figure. As explored in Chapter 6, this method demonstrates strong explanatory power for America's social movements. As a member of the U.S.

citizenry, I have found it relatively easy to study the history of social movements because I have lived through some of them myself.

Some Definitions and Clarifications

Points, Planets, and Aspects. The three examples so far have included the Ascendant, Midheaven, Moon, Sun, and Saturn. The first two are mathematical calculations, or points. The Moon, Sun, and Saturn are planets. Aspects of planets and other objects like Arabic Parts and fixed stars can also be directed. Chapter 5 will direct planets, aspects of planets, and bounds.

Significators and Promissors. In each primary direction there are two points involved. In the third Saturn-Sun direction recall the Sun was fixed in its position calculated at the time the horoscope was set for. Saturn was moved by its diurnal motion to meet the Sun by conjunction. Likewise, both Ascendant and Midheaven were essentially held fixed as the Moon and Sun traveled by diurnal motion to meet those points. Points fixed are named **Significators** because they *signify* one element of the native's being. The principal significators are the Ascendant, Midheaven, Moon, Sun, Lot of Fortune, and the Prenatal Lunation. For example, the Ascendant signifies the physical body of the native; the Midheaven, the native's career and social status. The second of two points involved in a primary direction is named the **Promissor** because it indicates, or *promises*, some type of accident, good or bad, lying dormant until the promissor or its aspect meets the significator by primary motion.

Latitude. In the Moon-Ascendant direction just mentioned, I listed two dates computed with and without latitude. It turns out the choice of latitude has been one of the hairier problems in the history of primary directions. Fortunately, it's a problem that I have tackled and proposed a solution to with the discovery of the **Primary Direction Sequence** first introduced in *ARM*. Instead of haggling with latitude adjustments, the primary direction sequence leapfrogs the question of a single optimal latitude by computing a set of dates with all latitude combinations between significator and promissor. For Ascendant-planet and Midheaven-planet directions, a pair of dates is computed. The first direction is computed with the full latitude of the planet. The second direction assumes the planet has zero latitude. As with the Moon-Ascendant direction, the interval between February 2, 1829 and May 10, 1831 timed a number of events consistent with the Moon's delineation.

Converse Motion. In the Sun-Midheaven direction just mentioned, recall the direction was computed as if the diurnal motion went from right to left, as if we were watching the picture in a time machine set to go backwards in time. This type of direction is known as a **converse direction**. Few medieval astrologers endorsed them and they remain controversial today. Why?

Chapter 5 - Calculation: Distributors and Partners

Consider that in the second Sun-Midheaven direction, the Sun culminated at 12:04 PM on July 4, 1776. Now think about this statement carefully. The chart for the Regulus USA National Horoscope was not cast until 6:17:37 PM. The Sun-Midheaven direction is based on an astronomical event which occurred more than six hours earlier! What is implied by converse directions is a relationship between astronomical events *before* horoscopes are cast and physical events occurring *after* horoscopes are cast. Simply stated, converse directions imply a cosmos with premeditated intent. While modern astrologers may find this stark deterministic philosophy difficult to swallow, the ability of converse directions to reliably time events for the Regulus USA National Horoscope confirms their validity.

Technical Section: Computing Ascendant Primary Directions

Welcome beginners! What follows are six examples for computation of Ascendant primary directions. They are fully worked out, skip no steps, cover all latitude permutations, and present solutions for both direct and converse motion. Except for learning a few new terms, there are no prerequisites.

Nomenclature for Coordinate Systems

Properly taught, primary directions require a comprehensive treatment of spherical geometry. Presentation of three-dimensional graphs showing projections of various coordinate systems is helpful in this regard. My current plans are to save a full treatment of spherical geometry and primary directions for a future book.[2] For now, I present the barest bones of spherical geometry in order to facilitate learning Ascendant primary directions.

Ascendant directions are a bit tricky because planets, and aspects, and points being directed are defined relative to the *ecliptic*, but the arc of direction is measured on the *equator*. The ecliptic belongs to the Zodiacal coordinate system; the equator; the equator, the Equatorial coordinate system.

Points from *both* **Zodiacal** *and* **Equatorial coordinate systems** are projected against the **Celestial Sphere**, an imaginary sphere at the limit of the universe. All objects in the sky can be considered lying on the inside of this sphere. Each object on the celestial sphere can be measured by either system.

The **Zodiacal coordinate system** is most familiar to astrologers. When astrologers speak of Saturn at 14 degrees of Libra, the Zodiacal coordinate system is being used. Points on the celestial sphere can be identified by **celestial longitude** and **celestial latitude**. The prefix word *celestial* is used to differentiate points on the celestial sphere from points on earth which are also defined by the words longitude and latitude. Sometimes the word prefix *terrestrial* is used to distinguish longitude/latitude on earth from longitude/latitude on the celestial sphere; e.g., as in *terrestrial longitude* or *terrestrial latitude*. However in common practice, since the terrestrial latitude of the birthplace is one of the few earth-based measurements used in mathematical astrology, most authors drop the prefix word *celestial* from *celestial longitude* and *celestial latitude*, saying **longitude** and **latitude** only, and assume the reader knows they are speaking of coordinates on the celestial sphere. That's the practice I will use here: unless the word prefix *terrestrial* is used, assume the words **longitude** and **latitude** refer to the celestial sphere.

The **Equatorial coordinate system** is less familiar to beginning astrologers. Its units are **right ascension** and **declination**. There are no word prefixes to worry about here.

The reason we need two different systems occurs because the earth's axis tilts at an angle relative to the Sun's axis of rotation. This angle is called the **obliquity of the ecliptic**. It's a little over 23 degrees. The effect gives the earth its seasons. It also forces astrologers to convert back and forth between Zodiacal and Equatorial coordinate systems when computing primary directions. This is necessary because all points, planets, and aspects are computed under the Zodiacal coordinate system. However, these same planets, aspects, and points are then rotated on the celestial sphere where they trace out their arcs of directions. Because of the obliquity of the ecliptic, the celestial sphere has a *different* axis of rotation. Visualization of these spheres is helpful to understand what is happening with the interactive 3-D celestial sphere of Rumen Kolev's software Placidus Version NK 4.1 one of the best currently available software programs for this purpose. For now, just learn the calculations, remembering that we use trigonometry formulas to convert between systems.

Helpful Hints for Microsoft Excel users

Decimal Format. Please note that all computations are presented in decimal format. This presentation style differs from many primary directions textbooks which show computations in degrees, minutes, and seconds.

Hint! Here is the correct Excel formula to convert degrees to decimal format:

21AR24'28" => decimal format: $= (21 + ((24 + 28/60)/60)) = 21.407778$.

Hint! If using Microsoft Excel, it is necessary to convert degrees to radians before using trig functions. Multiply degrees by PI/180 to convert to radians.

Chapter 5 - Calculation: Distributors and Partners

Mathematical Outline:

Ascendant Directions computed by Oblique Ascension[3]

Starting with the longitude and latitude of the point, planet, or aspect directed to the Ascendant, here is the formula outline:

(1) Compute **Declination** based on *longitude* and *latitude*.

(2) Compute **Right Ascension** based on *longitude* and *declination*.

(3) Compute **Ascensional Difference** from *declination* and *terrestrial latitude*.

(4) Compute **Oblique Ascension** from *right ascension* and the *ascensional difference*. Repeat steps (1) – (4) for the Ascendant.

(5) Compute the **difference** between oblique ascensions computed for the Ascendant and the Promissor.

(6) Convert the difference from degrees to years. Name this quantity measured in years the **Arc of Direction**.

(7) Compute the **projected date** by adding the arc of direction to the birth date.

Notation/Abbreviations

ASC	= Ascendant
OA	= Oblique Ascension
RA	= Right Ascension
RAMC	= Right Ascension of the Midheaven
OBL	= Obliquity of Ecliptic
LONG	= Longitude
LAT	= Latitude
LAT-BP	= Terrestrial Latitude of Birthplace
AD	= Ascensional Difference
DEC	= Declination
sin	= sine
cos	= cosine
tan	= tangent
asin	= arcsine
acos	= arccosine
atan	= arctangent
sgn	= sign of number, +1 if positive; -1 if negative

Preliminary Step: Compute Oblique Ascension of the Ascendant

In the seven step outline just presented, recall the arc of direction requires computing the difference between the oblique ascension of the Ascendant and the oblique ascension of the planet, aspect, or point directed. Since the oblique ascension of the Ascendant is used in all six examples, let's compute it first.

Shortcut Formula

There is a shortcut to computing the Ascendant's Oblique Ascension. It is:

OA(ASC) = RAMC + 90

where RAMC = 197° 55'17" = 197.921389

OA(ASC) = 197.921389 + 90 = **287.921389**

Full Formula

If instead we perform steps (1) - (4) in the Mathematical Outline, a slightly different number is generated. For our purposes the difference is trivial. Yet for accuracy and for those readers who compare these computations with the Excel spreadsheet available for download from www.regulus-astrology.com which *does* takes these steps in computing the OA(ASC), here they are:

Required Inputs

Obliquity of the Ecliptic (OBL)	= 23° 28' 6"	= 23.468333
Terrestrial latitude of Birthplace (Lat-BP)	= 39° 57' 8"N	= 39.952222N
Right Ascension of Midheaven (RAMC)	= 197° 55' 17"	= 197.921389
Longitude (LONG)	= 266° 54' 40"	= 266.911111
Latitude (LAT)	= 0° 0' 0"	= 0.000000

Some helpful Intermediate Calculations

sin(LONG)	= -0.998547
cos(LONG)	= -0.053885
tan(LONG)	= 18.531019
sin(LAT)	= 0.000000
cos(LAT)	= 1.000000
sin(OBL)	= 0.398242
cos(OBL)	= 0.917280
tan(LAT-BP)	= 0.837680
tan(DEC)	= -0.433406

CHAPTER 5 - CALCULATION: DISTRIBUTORS AND PARTNERS   57

LET'S GO!

(1) Compute *Declination* based on *longitude* and *latitude*.

DEC = Arcsin [cos(OBL) * sin(LAT) + sin(OBL) * cos(LAT) * sin(LONG)]

Note: At this stage because LAT=0 and sin(LAT)=0, the first term drops out. Here is the simplified declination formula for points with zero latitude:

DEC = Arcsin [sin(OBL) * cos(LAT) *sin(LONG)]

DEC = Arcsin [0.398242 * 1.000000 * -0.998547]

DEC = **-23.432198**

---

(2) Compute *Right Ascension* based on *longitude* and *declination*.

Computation of Right Ascension depends on what quadrant the longitude of the planet, aspect, or point falls in.

If 0 ≤ LONG < 90	RA = X
If LONG = 90	RA = 90
If 90 < LONG < 270	RA = X + 180
If LONG = 270	RA = 270
If 270 < LONG < 360	RA = X + 360

Where

$$X = \arctan\frac{\tan(LONG)}{\cos(OBL)} - \text{sgn}[\cos(LONG)] * \arcsin\frac{\tan(DEC) * \sin(OBL)}{\sqrt{\tan(LONG)^2 + \cos(OBL)^2}}$$

and the function sgn[ ] means 'sign' and returns either +1 or -1.

Step 1. *Compare the longitude to the table and determine the required formula*

To compute the right ascension of 26SA54'40", see that 266 degrees longitude is between 90 and 270, therefore according to the table **RA = X + 180**.

Step 2. *Compute 1st term of 'X'*

$$\arctan \frac{\tan(LONG)}{\cos(OBL)} =$$

$$\arctan \frac{18.531019}{0.917280} = \underline{\mathbf{87.166188}}$$

Step 3. *Compute sign of cos(LONG)*

cos(LONG) = -0.053885. It's sign is negative; therefore, sgn[cos(LONG)]= **-1**

Step 4. *Compute 2nd term of 'X'*

$$\arcsin \frac{\tan(DEC) * \sin(OBL)}{\sqrt{\tan(LONG)^2 + \cos(OBL)^2}} =$$

$$= \arcsin \frac{-0.433406 * 0.398242}{\sqrt{18.531019^2 + 0.917280^2}} = \underline{\mathbf{-0.533016}}$$

Step 5. *Compute 'X'*

X = 87.166188 - [(-1) * -0.533016] = **86.633172**

Step 6. Compute Right Ascension

As identified in Step 1, since the longitude of the promissor falls between 0 and 90, the Right Ascension of the promissor is identical to

X + 180 or

86.633172 + 180 = **266.633172**

---

(3) Compute *Ascensional Difference* from *declination* and *birthplace latitude*.

AD = arcsin [tan(DEC) * tan(terrestrial birthplace latitude)]

AD = arcsin [-0.433406 * 0.837680]

AD = **-21.287956**

CHAPTER 5 - CALCULATION: DISTRIBUTORS AND PARTNERS 59

(4) Compute *Oblique Ascension* from *right ascension* and *ascensional difference*.

OA = RA − AD

OA = 266.633172 − (−21.287956)

OA(ASC) = 287.921128

Finished.

Compare this number to **287.921389** computed by the shortcut method.

As I said at the outset, for our purposes the difference is trivial.

How trivial?

Compare the recent d. Sun sextile Ascendant computed for October 1, 2007.

	Oblique Ascension	Projected Direction
Shortcut Method	287.921389	1-Oct-2007 3:23 AM
Full Method	287.921128	1-Oct-2007 5:41 AM

The difference is just over 2 hours. And this for a direction projected 231 years into the future. As I said, for our purposes the difference is trivial.

Nevertheless the following calculations present the OA(ASC) computed using the full method for consistency with spreadsheet computations.

Example 1: Directing the Ascendant through the Bound, direct motion

In this example we will direct the bound of Saturn/Aries to the Ascendant.

Required Inputs (single)

Obliquity of the Ecliptic (OBL)	= 23° 28' 6"	= 23.468333
Terrestrial latitude of Birthplace (Lat-BP)	= 39° 57' 8"N	= 39.952222N
Right Ascension of Midheaven (RAMC)	= 197° 55' 17"	= 197.921389

Required Inputs (for Ascendant and point, planet, or aspect directed)

Longitude (LONG) 25AR0' 0"	= 25.000000
Latitude (LAT) 0° 0' 0"	= 0.000000

Some helpful Intermediate Calculations

sin(LONG)	= 0.422618
cos(LONG)	= 0.906308
tan(LONG)	= 0.466308
sin(LAT)	= 0.000000
cos(LAT)	= 1.000000
sin(OBL)	= 0.398242
cos(OBL)	= 0.917280
tan(LAT-BP)	= 0.837680
tan(DEC)	= 0.170740

CHAPTER 5 - CALCULATION: DISTRIBUTORS AND PARTNERS

What's going on?

The bound of Saturn/Aries begins at 25AR00'00". As an overlay on the Regulus USA National Horoscope [here with planets omitted], see the bound near the 4th house cusp at the bottom of the figure.

By direct primary motion, imagine the zodiac wheel spinning clockwise. The symbol for Saturn/Aries follows the path marked the arrow and rises to meet the Ascendant. This path is the arc of direction. It is measured in degrees and converted at the rate of one degree per one year. The projection is July 6, 1863; a few days after Gettysburg.

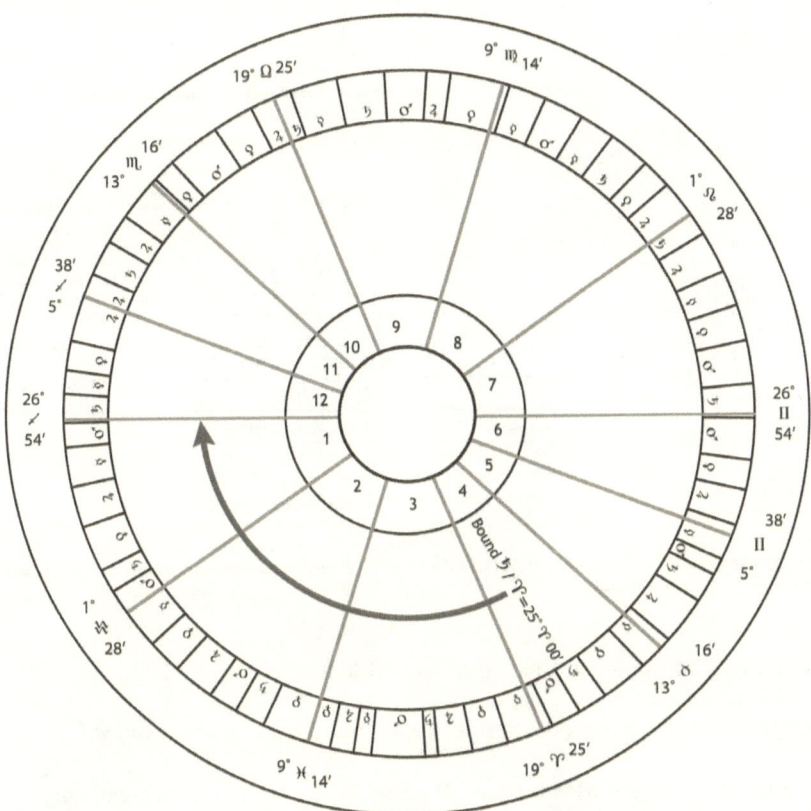

Figure 9. Regulus USA National Horoscope with Egyptian Bounds. Directing the Bound of Saturn/Aries to the Ascendant, direct motion.

LET'S GO!

(1) Compute *Declination* based on *longitude* and *latitude*.

DEC = Arcsin [cos(OBL) * sin(LAT) + sin(OBL) * cos(LAT) * sin(LONG)]

Note: At this stage because LAT=0 and sin(LAT)=0, the first term drops out. Here is the simplified declination formula for points with zero latitude:

DEC = Arcsin [sin(OBL) * cos(LAT) *sin(LONG)]

DEC = Arcsin [0.398242 * 1.000000 * 0.422618]

DEC = **9.689248**

---

(2) Compute *Right Ascension* based on *longitude* and *declination*.

Computation of Right Ascension depends on what quadrant the longitude of the point, planet, or aspect falls in.

If $0 \leq LONG < 90$	RA = X
If LONG = 90	RA = 90
If $90 < LONG < 270$	RA = X + 180
If LONG = 270	RA = 270
If $270 < LONG < 360$	RA = X + 360

Where

$$X = \arctan\frac{\tan(LONG)}{\cos(OBL)} - \text{sgn}[\cos(LONG)] * \arcsin\frac{\tan(DEC)*\sin(OBL)}{\sqrt{\tan(LONG)^2 + \cos(OBL)^2}}$$

and the function sgn[ ] means 'sign' and returns either +1 or -1.

<u>Step 1.</u> *Compare the longitude to the table and determine the required formula*

To compute the right ascension of 25AR00'00", see that 25 degrees longitude is between 0 and 90, therefore according to the table **RA = X**.

CHAPTER 5 - CALCULATION: DISTRIBUTORS AND PARTNERS   63

Step 2. *Compute 1st term of 'X'*

$$\arctan \frac{\tan(LONG)}{\cos(OBL)} =$$

$$\arctan \frac{0.466308}{0.917280} = \mathbf{26.946915}$$

Step 3. *Compute sign of cos(LONG)*

cos(LONG) = 0.9063. It's sign is positive; therefore, sgn[cos(LONG)] = **+1**

Step 4. *Compute 2nd term of 'X'*

$$\arcsin \frac{\tan(DEC) * \sin(OBL)}{\sqrt{\tan(LONG)^2 + \cos(OBL)^2}} =$$

$$= \arcsin \frac{0.170740 * 0.398242}{\sqrt{0.466308^2 + 0.917280^2}} = \mathbf{3.788832}$$

Step 5. *Compute 'X'*

X = 26.9469 - [(+1) * 3.7888] = **23.158083**

Step 6. Compute Right Ascension

As identified in Step 1, since the longitude of the promissor falls between 0 and 90, the Right Ascension of the promissor is identical to 'X' or **23.158083**

---

(3) Compute *Ascensional Difference* from *declination* and *birthplace latitude*.

AD = arcsin [tan(DEC) * tan(terrestrial birthplace latitude)]

AD = arcsin [0.170740 * 0.837680]

AD = **8.222952**

(4) Compute *Oblique Ascension* from *right ascension* and *ascensional difference.*

OA = RA – AD

OA = 23.158083 – 8.222952

OA = **14.935131**

---

(5) Compute the *difference* between oblique ascensions computed for the Ascendant and the Promissor.

If we try to compute

OA(25AR00'00") – OA(ASC) = 14.935131 - 287.921128 = **- 272.985997** = ?

we get a negative number which is puzzling. Here is where some common sense is required. Refer to Figure 9 and see that the arc of direction passes over 0 degrees of Aries. At this point the zodiacal degree counting system moved from 359°59'00" to 0°00'00". This fact needs to be taken into account. To do so, we add 360 degrees to the Oblique Ascension of the bound of Saturn/Aries and recompute the formula:

(14.935131 + *360.000000*) - 287.921128 = **87.014003**

---

(6) Convert the difference from degrees to years for the *Arc of Direction.*

A search of the primary directions literature reveals many different keys used to convert the Arc of Direction to a time measure. Ptolemy's key of 1 degree = 1 year is the most common and is the key I use exclusively for natal figures.

Apply Ptolemy's key => 1 degree = 1 year

87.014003 degrees = **87.014003 years**

(7) Compute the *projected date* by adding the arc of direction to the birth date.

87.014003 years = 87 years 5 days

July 4, 1776 + 87 years 5 days = **July 9, 1863**

Wrap-up: Example One

| D | Changeover | bound Saturn/Aries d. → ASC | 9-Jul-1863 |

Stepping back from the world of mathematics, here is a reminder to what we have just done. In computing the Arc of Direction for the first minute, degree, and second of the bound of Saturn/Aries directed to the Ascendant, the date of July 9, 1863 was projected. This is the date Saturn/Aries replaced Mars/Aries as Ascendant Distributor. This is also when the Civil War battle strategies changed from overt frontal assaults to guerilla-style battle tactics. It also timed the population's increasing frustration with the war, manifesting in the bloody New York Draft Riot.

Next I will fill out the Civil War measurements described in Chapter 2 with the direction of the sextile of Mars to the Ascendant, with and without latitude, a.k.a. the Mars-Ascendant *Primary Direction Sequence* that timed the Civil War's outbreak.

Note that I will direct not Mars itself, but its aspect. The calculations are the same and if you have mastered the last six pages, there is nothing new in the pages to follow.

Example 2:

Directing a Planet's Aspect to the Ascendant; with latitude, direct motion

In this example we will direct the dexter sextile of Mars to the Ascendant.

Required Inputs (single)

Obliquity of the Ecliptic (OBL)	= 23° 28' 6"	= 23.468333
Terrestrial latitude of Birthplace (Lat-BP)	= 39° 57' 8"N	= 39.952222N
Right Ascension of Midheaven (RAMC)	= 197° 55' 17"	= 197.921389

Required Inputs (for Ascendant and point, planet, or aspect directed)

Longitude (LONG) 21AR24'28"	= 21.407778
Latitude (LAT) 0N22'56"	= 0.382222

<u>NOTE: If Latitude were **SOUTH** then **LATITUDE** is **NEGATIVE**.</u>

Intermediate Calculations

sin(LONG)	= 0.365003
cos(LONG)	= 0.931006
tan(LONG)	= 0.392052
sin(LAT)	= 0.006671
cos(LAT)	= 0.999978
sin(OBL)	= 0.398242
cos(OBL)	= 0.917280
tan(LAT-BP)	= 0.837680
tan(DEC)	= 0.153244

What's going on?

Mars falls at 21GE24. We are directing not Mars, but the sextile of Mars. There are two: 21AR24 and 21LE24. Which one do we want? *The dexter sextile.* Start at the position of Mars itself and move against the order of the signs. Since the order of the signs is counterclockwise, and we the opposite, we move *clockwise* to find the dexter sextile of Mars and choose 21AR24. Mars' sextile aspect is carried to the Ascendant by direct motion. The projection is November 4, 1860, two days before Lincoln's election.

This sextile aspect of Mars is computed with latitude. Latitude cannot be displayed in the standard horoscope wheel. This means I won't show this chart again in Example #3 for the direction of the sextile aspect of Mars without latitude. Rest assured latitude will be reflected in the calculations.

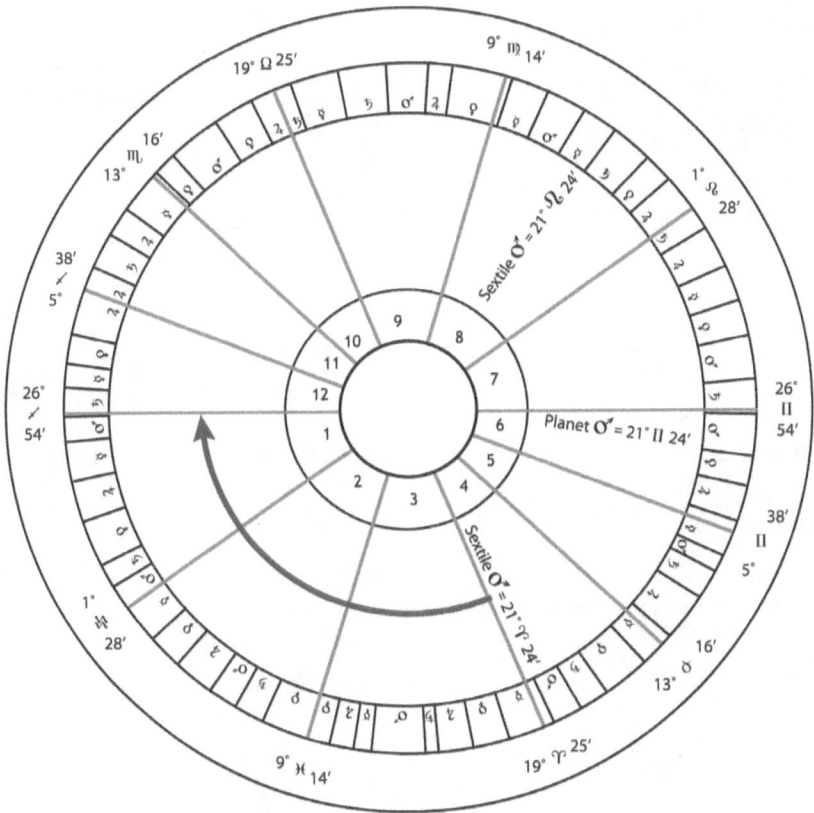

Figure 10. Regulus USA National Horoscope with Egyptian Bounds. Directing the dexter sextile of Mars to the Ascendant, direct motion.

68 AMERICA IS BORN: Introducing the Regulus USA National Horoscope

LET'S GO!

---

(1) Compute **Declination** based on *longitude* and *latitude*.

DEC = Arcsin [cos(OBL) * sin(LAT) + sin(OBL) * cos(LAT) * sin(LONG)]

DEC = Arcsin [0.917280 * 0.006671 + 0.398242 * 0.999978 * 0.365003]

DEC = **8.712448**

---

(2) Compute **Right Ascension** based on *longitude* and *declination*.

Computation of Right Ascension depends on what quadrant the longitude of the point, planet, or aspect falls in.

If 0 ≤ LONG < 90	RA = X
If LONG = 90	RA = 90
If 90 < LONG < 270	RA = X + 180
If LONG = 270	RA = 270
If 270 < LONG < 360	RA = X + 360

Where

$$X = \arctan\frac{\tan(LONG)}{\cos(OBL)} - \text{sgn}[\cos(LONG)] * \arcsin\frac{\tan(DEC)*\sin(OBL)}{\sqrt{\tan(LONG)^2 + \cos(OBL)^2}}$$

and the function sgn means 'sign' and returns either +1 or -1.

<u>Step 1.</u> *Compare the longitude to the table and determine the required formula*

To compute the right ascension of 21AR24'28", see that 21 degrees longitude is between 0 and 90, therefore according to the table **RA = X**.

<u>Step 2.</u> *Compute 1ˢᵗ term of 'X'*

$$\arctan\frac{\tan(LONG)}{\cos(OBL)} =$$

$$\arctan\frac{0.392052}{0.917280} = \mathbf{23.142218}$$

CHAPTER 5 - CALCULATION: DISTRIBUTORS AND PARTNERS

Step 3. *Compute sign of cos(LONG)*

cos(LONG) = 0.931006. It's sign is positive; therefore, sgn[cos(LONG)] = **+1**

Step 4. *Compute 2nd term of 'X'*

$$\operatorname{asin} \frac{\tan(DEC) * \sin(OBL)}{\sqrt{\tan(LONG)^2 + \cos(OBL)^2}} =$$

$$= \operatorname{arcsin} \frac{0.153244 * 0.398242}{\sqrt{0.392052^2 + 0.917280^2}} = \mathbf{3.507431}$$

Step 5. *Compute 'X'*

X = 23.142218 - [(+1) * 3.507431] = **19.634787**

Step 6. Compute Right Ascension

As identified in Step 1, since the longitude of the promissor falls between 0 and 90, the Right Ascension of the promissor is identical to 'X' or **19.634787**

---

(3) Compute *Ascensional Difference* from *declination* and *terrestrial latitude*.

AD = arcsin [tan(DEC) * tan(terrestrial birthplace latitude)]

AD = arcsin [0.153244 * 0.837680]

AD = **7.375368**

---

(4) Compute *Oblique Ascension* from *right ascension* and *ascensional difference*.

OA = RA – AD

OA = 19.634787 – 7.375368

OA = **12.259419**

(5) Compute the *difference* between oblique ascensions computed for the Ascendant and the Promissor.

(12.259419 + *360.000000*) - 287.921128 = **84.338291**

---

(6) Convert the difference from degrees to years for the *Arc of Direction.*

Apply Ptolemy's key

1 degree = 1 year

84.338291 degrees = **84.338291 years**

---

(7) Compute the *projected date* by adding the arc of direction to the birth date.

84.338291 years = 84 years 124 days

July 4, 1776 + 84 years 124 days = **November 4, 1860**

Wrap-up: Example Two

| D | Mars/Aries | P | dex. sextile Mars (l=MA) d. → ASC | 4-Nov-1860 |

In this case, we directed a planet's aspect, not the planet itself. We used the concept of dexter and sinister aspects to distinguish between two different sextile aspects of Mars to the Ascendant.

The example required the use of latitude. As I noted, be aware if latitude is *South* instead of North, for mathematical purposes latitude is *negative*.

CHAPTER 5 - CALCULATION: DISTRIBUTORS AND PARTNERS   71

Example 3:

Directing a Planet's Aspect to the Ascendant; zero latitude, direct motion

In this example we will direct the dexter sextile of Mars to the Ascendant.

Required Inputs (single)

Obliquity of the Ecliptic (OBL)	= 23° 28' 6" =	23.468333
Terrestrial latitude of Birthplace (Lat-BP)	= 39° 57' 8"N =	39.952222N
Right Ascension of Midheaven (RAMC)	= 197° 55' 17" =	197.921389

Required Inputs (for Ascendant and point, planet, or aspect directed)

Longitude (LONG) 21AR24'28"   = 21.407778
Latitude (LAT) 0°00'00"   = 0.000000

Intermediate Calculations

sin(LONG)   = 0.365003
cos(LONG)   = 0.931006
tan(LONG)   = 0.392052
sin(LAT)   = 0.000000
cos(LAT)   = 1.000000
sin(OBL)   = 0.398242
cos(OBL)   = 0.917280
tan(LAT-BP)   = 0.837680
tan(DEC)   = 0.146920

LET'S GO!

(1) Compute **Declination** based on *longitude* and *latitude*.

DEC = Arcsin [cos(OBL) * sin(LAT) + sin(OBL) * cos(LAT) * sin(LONG)]

Note: At this stage because LAT=0 and sin(LAT)=0, the first term drops out. Here is the simplified declination formula for points with zero latitude.

DEC = Arcsin [sin(OBL) * cos(LAT) *sin(LONG)]

DEC = Arcsin [0.398242 * 1.000000 * 0.365003]

DEC = **8.358106**

---

(2) Compute **Right Ascension** based on *longitude* and *declination*.

Computation of Right Ascension depends on what quadrant the longitude of the point, planet, or aspect falls in.

If 0 ≤ LONG < 90	RA = X
If LONG = 90	RA = 90
If 90 < LONG < 270	RA = X + 180
If LONG = 270	RA = 270
If 270 < LONG < 360	RA = X + 360

Where

$$X = \arctan\frac{\tan(LONG)}{\cos(OBL)} - \text{sgn}[\cos(LONG)] * \arcsin\frac{\tan(DEC)*\sin(OBL)}{\sqrt{\tan(LONG)^2 + \cos(OBL)^2}}$$

and the function sgn means 'sign' and returns either +1 or -1.

Step 1. *Compare the longitude to the table and determine the required formula*

To compute the right ascension of 21AR24'28", see that 21 degrees longitude is between 0 and 90, therefore according to the table **RA = X**.

Step 2. *Compute 1st term of 'X'*

CHAPTER 5 - CALCULATION: DISTRIBUTORS AND PARTNERS

$$\arctan \frac{\tan(LONG)}{\cos(OBL)} =$$

$$\arctan \frac{0.392052}{0.917280} = \mathbf{23.142218}$$

Step 3. *Compute sign of cos(LONG)*

$\cos(LONG) = 0.931006$. It's sign is positive; therefore, $\text{sgn}[\cos(LONG)] = \underline{+1}$

Step 4. *Compute 2nd term of 'X'*

$$a\sin \frac{\tan(DEC) * \sin(OBL)}{\sqrt{\tan(LONG)^2 + \cos(OBL)^2}} =$$

$$= \arcsin \frac{0.146920 * 0.398242}{\sqrt{0.392052^2 + 0.917280^2}} = \mathbf{3.362523}$$

Step 5. *Compute 'X'*

$X = 23.142218 - [(+1) * 3.362523] = \underline{\mathbf{19.779695}}$

Step 6. Compute Right Ascension

As identified in Step 1, since the longitude of the promissor falls between 0 and 90, the Right Ascension of the promissor is identical to 'X' or **19.779695**

---

(3) Compute *Ascensional Difference* from *declination* and *terrestrial latitude*.

AD = arcsin [tan(DEC) * tan(terrestrial birthplace latitude)]

AD = arcsin [0.146920 * 0.837680]

AD = **7.069429**

---

(4) Compute *Oblique Ascension* from *right ascension* and *ascensional difference*.

OA = RA − AD

OA = 19.779695 − 7.069429

OA = **12.710266**

---

(5) Compute the *difference* between oblique ascensions computed for the Ascendant and the Promissor.

(12.710266 + *360.000000*) − 287.921128 = **84.789139**

---

(6) Convert the difference from degrees to years for the *Arc of Direction*.

Apply Ptolemy's key

1 degree = 1 year

84.789139 degrees = **84.789139 years**

---

(7) Compute the *projected date* by adding the arc of direction to the birth date.

84.789139 years = 84 years 209 days

July 4, 1776 + 84 years 209 days = **April 18, 1861**

Wrap-up: Example Three

D	Mars/Aries	P	dex. sextile Mars (l=MA) d. → ASC	4-Nov-1860
D	Mars/Aries	P	dex. sextile Mars (l=0) d. → ASC	18-Apr-1861

The sequence concludes. This primary direction sequence is an excellent example which demonstrates the power of the beginning of a sequence to set off a series of events which culminate as the sequence ends.

4-Nov-1860	**Mars-Ascendant sequence begins**
6-Nov-1860	Lincoln elected President
10-Nov-1860	South Carolina calls State convention in December
6-Dec-1860	South Carolina met to consider secession
20-Dec-1860	South Carolina seceded from the Union
12-Apr-1861	Hostilities began at Fort Sumter
18-Apr-1861	**Mars-Ascendant sequence ends**
19-Apr-1861	First casualties reported: 6th Massachusetts Infantry.

CHAPTER 5 - CALCULATION: DISTRIBUTORS AND PARTNERS   75

Example 4:

Directing the Ascendant through the Bounds, converse motion.

In this example we will direct the bound of Mars/Cancer to the Ascendant by converse motion. Other than a small change in Step (7), the math is the same.

Required Inputs (single)

Obliquity of the Ecliptic (OBL)	= 23° 28' 6"	= 23.468333
Terrestrial latitude of Birthplace (Lat-BP)	= 39° 57' 8"N	=39.952222N
Right Ascension of Midheaven (RAMC)	= 197° 55' 17"	=197.921389

Required Inputs (for Ascendant and point, planet, or aspect directed)

Longitude (LONG) 00CA00'00	= 90.000000
Latitude (LAT) 0°00'00"	= 0.000000

Intermediate Calculations

sin(LONG)	= 1.000000
cos(LONG)	= 0.000000
tan(LONG)	= undefined
sin(LAT)	= 0.000000
cos(LAT)	= 1.000000
sin(OBL)	= 0.398242
cos(OBL)	= 0.917280
tan(LAT-BP)	= 0.837680
tan(DEC)	= 0.434155

What's going on?

The bound of Mars/Cancer is defined as the seven degree range from 0CA00'00" to 6CA59'59". In this example, we are concerned with the beginning of this bound, or 0CA00'00" which is identical to 90 degrees of longitude. The symbol for this bound appears just above the 7th house cusp.

The big difference between direct and converse directions is the celestial sphere's direction of movement. For converse directions, the celestial sphere moves from right to left, as if time is moving backwards. Planets, aspects, and points appear to rise in the west (Descendant), culminate above (Midheaven), and set in the eastern sky (Ascendant). In this example the arrow's direction moves counterclockwise in order to carry the bound of Mars/Cancer to the Ascendant by converse motion.

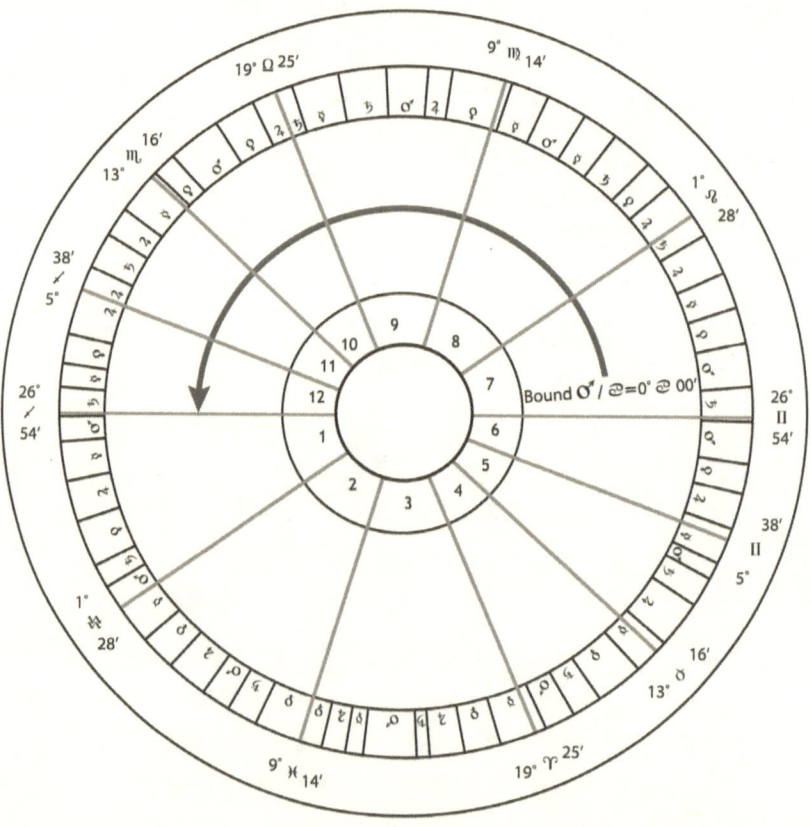

Figure 11. Regulus USA National Horoscope with Egyptian Bounds. Directing the bound of Mars/Cancer to the Ascendant, converse motion.

CHAPTER 5 - CALCULATION: DISTRIBUTORS AND PARTNERS

LET'S GO!

---

(1) Compute ***Declination*** based on *longitude* and *latitude*.

DEC = Arcsin [cos(OBL) * sin(LAT) + sin(OBL) * cos(LAT) * sin(LONG)]

Note: At this stage because LAT=0 and sin(LAT)=0, the first term drops out.

DEC = Arcsin [sin(OBL) * cos(LAT) *sin(LONG)]

DEC = Arcsin [0.398242 * 1.000000 * 1.000000]

DEC = **23.468333**

---

(2) Compute ***Right Ascension*** based on *longitude* and *declination*.

Computation of Right Ascension depends on what quadrant the longitude of the point, planet, or aspect falls in.

If 0 ≤ LONG < 90	RA = X
If LONG = 90	RA = 90
If 90 < LONG < 270	RA = X + 180
If LONG = 270	RA = 270
If 270 < LONG < 360	RA = X + 360

Where

$$X = \arctan \frac{\tan(LONG)}{\cos(OBL)} - \text{sgn}[\cos(LONG)] * \arcsin \frac{\tan(DEC)*\sin(OBL)}{\sqrt{\tan(LONG)^2 + \cos(OBL)^2}}$$

and the function sgn means 'sign' and returns either +1 or -1.

<u>Step 1.</u> *Compare the longitude to the table and determine the required formula*

To compute the right ascension of 90CA00'00", see that 90 degrees longitude is equal to 90, therefore RA = 90. We luck out and get to skip some calcs.

RA = **90.000000**

(3) Compute *Ascensional Difference* from *declination* and *terrestrial latitude*.

AD = arcsin [tan(DEC) * tan(terrestrial birthplace latitude)]

AD = arcsin [0.434155 * 0.837680]

AD = **21.326560**

---

(4) Compute *Oblique Ascension* from *right ascension* and *ascensional difference*. Repeat steps (1) – (4) for the Ascendant or use the shortcut formula: OA(ASC) = RAMC + 90.

OA = RA – AD

OA = 90.000000 – 21.326560

OA = **68.673440**

---

(5) Compute the *difference* between oblique ascensions computed for the Ascendant and the Promissor.

NOTE: Because we are computing this direction by converse motion, in this case we **DO** want a **NEGATIVE NUMBER** which lets us know we are moving **BACKWARDS** in time.

68.673440 - 287.921128 = **-219.247688**

---

(6) Convert the difference from degrees to years for the *Arc of Direction*.

Apply Ptolemy's key

1 degree = 1 year

-219.247688 degrees = **-219.247688 years**

CHAPTER 5 - CALCULATION: DISTRIBUTORS AND PARTNERS   79

(7) Compute the *projected date* by adding the *absolute value* of the arc of direction to the birth date.

For converse directions, there is a change in Step (7). If we were to subtract 219.247688 years from July 4, 1776, the projection is April 5, 1557. This doesn't get us anywhere. So instead we essentially *transpose* the negative arc computed by converse motion to a positive number and revert to the same procedure used to compute arcs by direct motion.

219.247688 years = 219 years 91 days

July 4, 1776 + 219 years 91 days = **October 3, 1995**

Wrap-up: Example Four

| D | Changeover | bound Mars/Cancer c. → ASC | 3-Oct-1995 |

Event: Acquittal of O. J. Simpson on murder charges of Nicole Brown and Ronald Goldman, October 3, 1995. This is an exact date hit.

I will have more to say on this after examples 5 and 6.

Example 5:

Directing a Planet to the Ascendant; with latitude, converse motion

In this example we will direct Venus to the Ascendant by converse motion.

Required Inputs (single)

Obliquity of the Ecliptic (OBL) = 23° 28' 6" = 23.468333
Terrestrial latitude of Birthplace (Lat-BP) = 39° 57' 8"N = 39.952222N
Right Ascension of Midheaven (RAMC) = 197° 55' 17" = 197.921389

Required Inputs (for Ascendant and point, planet, or aspect directed)

Longitude (LONG) 3CA09'45" = 93.162500
Latitude (LAT) 0°06'04" = 0.101111

Intermediate Calculations

sin(LONG) = 0.998477
cos(LONG) = -0.055168
tan(LONG) = -18.098840
sin(LAT) = 0.001765
cos(LAT) = 0.999998
sin(OBL) = 0.398242
cos(OBL) = 0.917280
tan(LAT-BP) = 0.837680
tan(DEC) = 0.435467

What's going on?

As in Example 4, for any direction computed by converse motion, the celestial sphere rotates counterclockwise. Since we are directing the planet Venus herself, see Venus about to set in the western sky in Figure 12 and stop the clock. Now let the clock move backwards in time, imagining Venus retracing her steps as culminates at the Midheaven and rises at the Ascendant earlier on July 4, 1776. It is the rise of Venus on the eastern horizon which is computed by this converse direction.

As before, latitude can't be depicted on a zodiac wheel. Accordingly I omit a diagram for Example 6, computed for Venus with zero latitude.

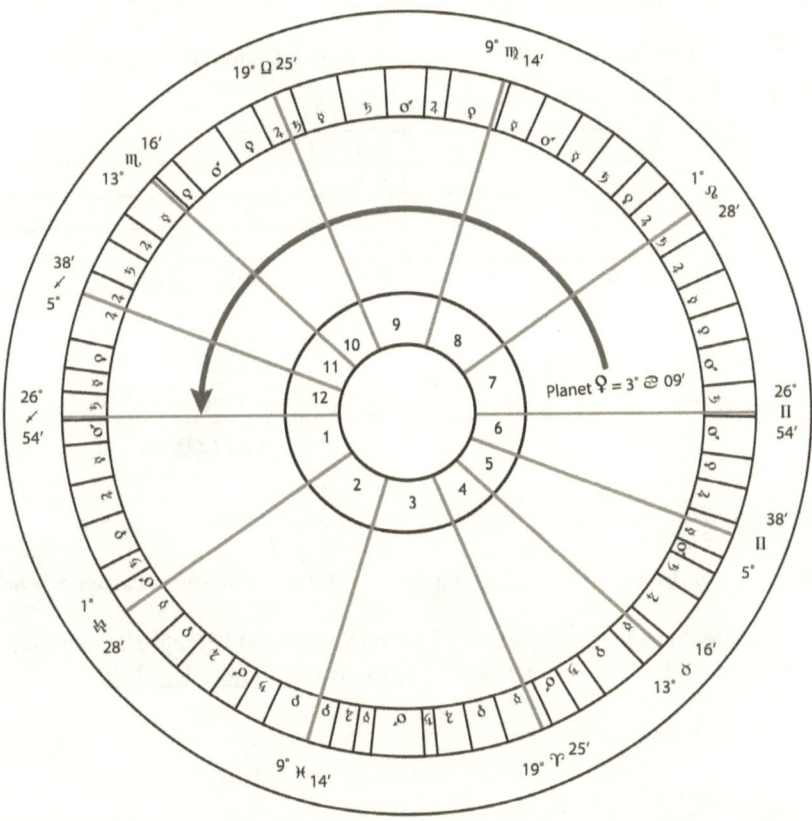

Figure 12. Regulus USA National Horoscope with Egyptian Bounds. Directing the planet Venus to the Ascendant, converse motion.

LET'S GO!

---

(1) Compute ***Declination*** based on *longitude* and *latitude*.

DEC = Arcsin [cos(OBL) * sin(LAT) + sin(OBL) * cos(LAT) * sin(LONG)]

DEC = Arcsin [0.917280 * 0.001765 + 0.398242 * 0.999998 * 0.998477]

DEC = **23.531538**

---

(2) Compute ***Right Ascension*** based on *longitude* and *declination*.

Computation of Right Ascension depends on what quadrant the longitude of the point, planet, or aspect falls in.

If 0 ≤ LONG < 90	RA = X
If LONG = 90	RA = 90
If 90 < LONG < 270	RA = X + 180
If LONG = 270	RA = 270
If 270 < LONG < 360	RA = X + 360

Where

$$X = \arctan\frac{\tan(LONG)}{\cos(OBL)} - \text{sgn}[\cos(LONG)] * \arcsin\frac{\tan(DEC) * \sin(OBL)}{\sqrt{\tan(LONG)^2 + \cos(OBL)^2}}$$

and the function sgn means 'sign' and returns either +1 or -1.

Step 1. *Compare the longitude to the table and determine the required formula*

To compute the right ascension of 3CA09'45", see that 93 degrees longitude is between 90 and 270, therefore according to the table **RA = X + 180**.

Step 2. *Compute 1st term of 'X'*

$$\arctan\frac{\tan(LONG)}{\cos(OBL)} =$$

$$\arctan\frac{-18.098840}{0.917280} = \textbf{-87.098634}$$

Step 3. *Compute sign of cos(LONG)*

cos(LONG) = -0.055168. It's sign is negative; sgn[cos(LONG)] = **-1**

Step 4. *Compute 2nd term of 'X'*

$$a\sin \frac{\tan(DEC) * \sin(OBL)}{\sqrt{\tan(LONG)^2 + \cos(OBL)^2}} =$$

$$= \arcsin \frac{0.435467 * 0.398242}{\sqrt{-18.098840^2 + 0.917280^2}} = \mathbf{0.548307}$$

Step 5. *Compute 'X'*

X = -87.098634 - [(-1) * 0.548307] = **-86.550327**

Step 6. *Compute Right Ascension*

As identified in Step 1, since the longitude of the promissor falls between 90 and 270, the Right Ascension of the promissor is identical to X + 180:

RA = X + 180 = -86.550327 + 180 = **93.449673**

---

(3) Compute *Ascensional Difference* from *declination* and *terrestrial latitude*.

AD = arcsin [tan(DEC) * tan(terrestrial birthplace latitude)]

AD = arcsin [0.435467 * 0.837680]

AD = **21.394159**

---

(4) Compute *Oblique Ascension* from *right ascension* and *ascensional difference*. Repeat steps (1) – (4) for the Ascendant or use the shortcut formula: OA(ASC) = RAMC + 90.

OA = RA – AD

OA = 93.449673 – 21.394159

OA = **72.055514**

(5) Compute the *difference* between oblique ascensions computed for the Ascendant and the Promissor.

NOTE: Because we are computing this direction by converse motion, in this case we *DO* want a *NEGATIVE NUMBER* which lets us know we are moving *BACKWARDS* in time.

72.055514 - 287.921128 = **-215.865613**

---

(6) Convert the difference from degrees to years for the *Arc of Direction.*

Applying Ptolemy's key

1 degree = 1 year

-215.865613 degrees = **-215.865613 years**

---

(7) Compute the *projected date* by adding the *absolute value* of the arc of direction to the birth date. (See Example Four for discussion)

-215.865613 years = 215 years 316 days

July 4, 1776 +215 years 316 days = **May 16, 1992**

Wrap-up: Example Five

| D | Mars/Cancer | P | conjunction Venus (l=VE) c. → ASC | 16-May-1992 |

In this example, the planet Venus was directed by converse motion to the Ascendant. The full latitude of Venus was used in the calculation.

CHAPTER 5 - CALCULATION: DISTRIBUTORS AND PARTNERS   85

Example 6:

**Directing a Planet to the Ascendant;
zero latitude, converse motion**

In this example we will direct Venus to the Ascendant by converse motion.

Required Inputs (single)

Obliquity of the Ecliptic (OBL)   = 23° 28' 6" = 23.468333
Terrestrial latitude of Birthplace (Lat-BP) = 39° 57' 8"N = 39.952222N
Right Ascension of Midheaven (RAMC)   = 197° 55' 17" = 197.921389

Required Inputs (for Ascendant and point, planet, or aspect directed)

Longitude (LONG) 3CA09'45"   = 93.162500
Latitude (LAT) 0°0'0"   = 0.000000

Intermediate Calculations

sin(LONG)   = 0.998477
cos(LONG)   = -0.055168
tan(LONG)   = -18.098840
sin(LAT) = 0.000000
cos(LAT) = 1.000000
sin(OBL) = 0.398242
cos(OBL) = 0.917280
tan(LAT-BP)   = 0.837680
tan(DEC) = 0.433370

LET'S GO!

---

(1) Compute *Declination* based on *longitude* and *latitude*.

DEC = Arcsin [cos(OBL) * sin(LAT) + sin(OBL) * cos(LAT) * sin(LONG)]

Note: At this stage because LAT=0 and sin(LAT)=0, the first term drops out.

DEC = Arcsin [sin(OBL) * cos(LAT) *sin(LONG)]

DEC = Arcsin [0.398242 * 1.000000 * 0.998477]

DEC = **23.430456**

(2) Compute *Right Ascension* based on *longitude* and *declination*.

Computation of Right Ascension depends on what quadrant the longitude of the point, planet, or aspect falls in.

If 0 ≤ LONG < 90	RA = X
If LONG = 90	RA = 90
If 90 < LONG < 270	RA = X + 180
If LONG = 270	RA = 270
If 270 < LONG < 360	RA = X + 360

Where

$$X = \arctan\frac{\tan(LONG)}{\cos(OBL)} - \text{sgn}[\cos(LONG)] * \arcsin\frac{\tan(DEC)*\sin(OBL)}{\sqrt{\tan(LONG)^2 + \cos(OBL)^2}}$$

and the function sgn means 'sign' and returns either +1 or -1.

Step 1. Compare the longitude to the table and determine the required formula

To compute the right ascension of 3CA09'45", see that 93 degrees longitude is between 90 and 270, therefore according to the table **RA = X + 180**.

Step 2. Compute 1ˢᵗ term of 'X'

$$\arctan\frac{\tan(LONG)}{\cos(OBL)} =$$

$$\arctan\frac{-18.098840}{0.917280} = \underline{\mathbf{-87.098634}}$$

Step 3. Compute sign of cos(LONG)

cos(LONG) = -0.055168. It's sign is negative; sgn[cos(LONG)] = **-1**

Step 4. Compute 2ⁿᵈ term of 'X'

$$a\sin\frac{\tan(DEC)*\sin(OBL)}{\sqrt{\tan(LONG)^2 + \cos(OBL)^2}} =$$

$$= \arcsin \frac{0.433370 * 0.398242}{\sqrt{-18.098840^2 + 0.917280^2}} = \underline{\mathbf{0.545667}}$$

Step 5. *Compute 'X'*

X = -87.098634 - [(-1) * 0.545667] = **-86.552967**

Step 6. *Compute Right Ascension*

As identified in Step 1, since the longitude of the promissor falls between 90 and 270, the Right Ascension of the promissor is identical to X + 180:

RA = X + 180 = -86.552967 + 180 = **93.447033**

---

(3) Compute *Ascensional Difference* from *declination* and *terrestrial latitude*.

AD = arcsin [tan(DEC) * tan(terrestrial birthplace latitude)]

AD = arcsin [0.433370 * 0.837680]

AD = **21.286096**

---

(4) Compute *Oblique Ascension* from *right ascension* and *ascensional difference*. Repeat steps (1) – (4) for the Ascendant or use the shortcut formula: OA(ASC) = RAMC + 90.

OA = RA – AD

OA = 93.447033 – 21.286096

OA = **72.160937**

(5) Compute the *difference* between oblique ascensions computed for the Ascendant and the Promissor.

NOTE: Because we are computing this direction by converse motion, in this case we *DO* want a *NEGATIVE NUMBER* which lets us know we are moving *BACKWARDS* in time.

72.160937 - 287.921128 = **-215.760191**

---

(6) Convert the difference from degrees to years for the *Arc of Direction.*

Applying Ptolemy's key

1 degree = 1 year

-215.760191 degrees = **-215.760191 years**

---

(7) Compute the *projected date* by adding the *absolute value* of the arc of direction to the birth date. (See Example Four for discussion)

-215.865613 years = 215 years 278 days

July 4, 1776 +215 years 278 days = **April 7, 1992**

Wrap-up: Examples 4-6

D	Mars/Cancer	P	conjunction Venus (l=0) c. → ASC	7-Apr-1992
D	Mars/Cancer	P	conjunction Venus (l=VE) c. → ASC	16-May-1992

The primary direction sequence of Venus directed to the Ascendant by converse motion was computed as April 7, 1992 to May 16, 1992. What happened? On April 29, 1992 the acquittal of Los Angeles police officers involved in the beating of Rodney King triggered the Los Angeles Riots. The riots peaked on April 30/May 1 and ran their course by May 4. In Chapter 14, the delineation of Venus/Cancer as white racism is borne out by events of this direction. As Distributor, Mars/Cancer set the stage of extreme defensiveness which exploded into cruelty as the actress Venus/Cancer entered the spotlight.

CHAPTER SIX

Distributor Results: Directing through the Bounds

What follows are empirical findings for directing the Ascendant through the bounds for the Regulus USA National Horoscope. A total of forty-three Egyptian bounds are delineated and compared to the nation's first two hundred thirty two years of history.

Summary

Ability to observe the true function of Planets in Signs. Directing through the Bounds offers a unique laboratory to observe effects of planetary behavior in various zodiac signs. Freed from the necessity to consider rulership, aspect, speed, position relative to the Sun, house position, and other conditions; bounds manifest events which are consistent with the purest form of their planet/sign combination.

Power of Directing through the Bounds in Rectification. Any evaluation of primary directions is complicated by the necessity of untangling myriad projections computed by direct and converse motion, varying latitude assumptions, and calculation method - not to mention the validity of solar arc directions as a completely separate predictive methodology. In contrast, there is no uncertainty on mathematics for directing the Ascendant through the bounds. Only the choice of bound systems is disputed; a debate which largely supports Egyptian bounds (see Appendix D.) Considering the precision of historical events observed at each changeover, Directing through the Bounds yields compelling results which are capable of supporting the rectification on a standalone basis without recourse to any other predictive technique.

Ability to Delineate and Predict the National Consciousness. Results demonstrate that major social movements in American history, hereafter referred to as the *national consciousness*, can be delineated by the planet/sign combination for each Egyptian bound and timed by primary directions of the Ascendant through the bounds.

Jumping In

The Ascendant of the Regulus USA National Horoscope is 26SA54'40". This falls in the bound of Mars/Sagittarius. This means at the outbreak of the Revolutionary War, Americans were militant in their righteous indignation against abuse of their rights by the British government. This lasted a few years until the directed Ascendant moved to the bound of Mercury/Capricorn. After this time, Americans settled down, counted their gains & losses, and established a methodical system of education as a structural foundation for the new Republic. On and on through the rest of the bounds.

Remember this analysis does *not* include any planets in the horoscope. This means the same analysis conceivably applies to *any* horoscope with an Ascendant of 26SA54'50". Only the difference in terrestrial latitude from Philadelphia, Pennsylvania would alter the primary direction calculations, making differences in timing of changeovers commensurate with latitude differences.

Ability to observe the true function of Planets in Signs

Essential dignities are the principal method used to describe how planets function when placed in zodiacal signs. Central to the concept is the ability of a planet to function in accordance with its nature when the planet has some dignity. Rulership is best and produces effects which are in harmony with a planet's nature; effects are also long-lasting. As planets step down the dignity ladder, they produce effects which are not as strong or stable. By the time a planet has no essential dignity, it must rely on its ruler for guidance. And when a planet is in the sign of his detriment or fall, the planet acts in a way that is opposite to its nature.

Essential dignities are a valuable model and form the backbone of medieval delineation and prediction. Yet as useful as essential dignities are, they nevertheless leave the beginning student unprepared for a horoscope reading which is practical and understandable to clients in simple English. Consider Mercury in Capricorn. Except for the first seven degrees where Mercury has dignity by bound, Mercury has zero dignity in the rest of Capricorn. Planets with no dignity are named *peregrine*. Effects of peregrine planets are judged primarily by their rulers and are likened to travelers in a foreign country dependent on their host. Besides evaluating the ruler of Mercury/Capricorn, there are a few other delineation steps including evaluating Mercury/Capricorn's speed, proximity to the Sun, and influences from other aspecting planets. These are all important steps to be taken and I in no way denigrate them; I only suggest these theoretical steps fall short of what is required for a delineation which is accurate and practical.

Taking a step away from essential dignities, consider instead combining key words for the planet Mercury and the sign Capricorn:

Mercury	**Capricorn**	= ?
communication	structure	= methodical
words	structure	= grammar
business	wealth	= mercantilism

What I present here is by no means complete, but paradigmatic of how descriptors for planets and signs can be combined for delineation purposes. As I will demonstrate when discussing Mercury/Capricorn as Ascendant Distributor from November 30, 1779 to May 4, 1787, the delineation of Mercury/Capricorn as a methodical approach to communication (e.g., grammar) comes alive when it is learned Noah Webster published his grammar textbooks during the Mercury/Capricorn Distribution. They were instant best sellers and ubiquitous in American households for the next one hundred years.

I suggest this style of delineation based on key words is more appropriate for analyzing effects of bounds as Distributors. Why? Because bounds are not planets. Each bound is based on a fixed division of the zodiac unencumbered by conditions used to delineate planets in the heavens. Concepts such as rulership, aspect, speed, position relative to the Sun, and house position do not apply to bounds. Accordingly, analyzing effects of active Distributors is one of the best laboratories for observing the purest form of planetary behavior. Want to know how Mercury/Capricorn behaves? Look to the actions of Americans during the Mercury/Capricorn Distribution to see effects of the Distributor in action. Still unsure how to proceed? Then identify prominent national figures active at the time *with Mercury/Capricorn placements in their own natal figures* and observe the impact of *their* actions on the nation.

Power of Directing through the Bounds in Rectification

In *ARM* Chapter 8, I suggest Directing through the Bounds as a rectification tool is limited in natal astrology because observable effects of the Distributor rarely occur at the precise changeover. Not so for mundane astrology if the results of the Regulus USA National Horoscope prove any guide. With millions of American citizens, there appear to be a sufficient number of individuals who *do* engage in activities which *are* observable at changeovers to make Directing through the Bounds a viable rectification tool for National Horoscopes in mundane astrology.

What does the Ascendant Signify?

In modern mundane astrology, the public is usually assigned to the Moon and the King or President to the Sun. This is a watered down version of medieval mundane methods advocated by Abū Ma'shar and Bonatti who approached mundane figures through identification of the Lord of the Year and Significator of the King. In this medieval method, planets in strong condition either placed near or ruling the Ascendant were favored as the Lord of the Year; planets near the Midheaven, Significator of the King.[1]

Since the Ascendant is the basis of computing the Lord of the Year in medieval mundane methods, and the Lord of the Year was designed to signify the common people, my expectation was application of Directing through the Bounds to the Ascendant would yield events for the American people. Actual findings differ. Though directing the Ascendant through the Bounds often defines popular social movements, the populace does not hold exclusivity over the technique's domain. At times, directing the Ascendant through the Bounds finds the President, members of Congress, the Judiciary, or leading businessmen playing out the symbolism delineated by Egyptian bounds. Given these observations, the Ascendant appears to represent the national consciousness as a whole. A summary of these themes follows in Table 6.

Human Agents as Partners

In Chapter 2, I used the death of John F. Kennedy Jr. as an example of how individuals can be raised to national prominence. **The Mundane-Natal Horoscope Connection** is explored further in a two-step process. *Step One* delineates the national consciousness according to the planet/sign symbolism for each bound. These results are presented in the remaining pages of Chapter 6. *Step Two* identifies prominent individuals who influenced the national consciousness during each Distribution. These results are presented as supplementary material in Appendix C. For many Distributors, I was able to find a prominent individual whose own natal chart recapitulated the same natal planet/sign combination as the Distributor. One of the best examples is Mercury/Leo in the natal figure for Sylvester Stallone. Significator of an optimistic spirit, a Mercury-Ascendant direction in Stallone's natal figure timed writing of the film script for *Rocky* at the same time the directed Ascendant of the Regulus USA National Horoscope entered the bound of Mercury/Leo.

The journey begins with the bound of Mars/Sagittarius. The stage is set with righteous indignation against colonial rule by the British. You are seated in the congregation of Virginia preacher Peter Muhlenberg as he approaches the pulpit and begins his sermon. Welcome to America.

CHAPTER 6 - DISTRIBUTOR RESULTS: DIRECTING THROUGH THE BOUNDS

Table 6. Ascendant Distributors and the National Consciousness.

Date	Planet	Sign	National Consciousness
4-Jul-1776	Mars	Sagittarius	Fight for Religious Freedom
30-Nov-1779	Mercury	Capricorn	Early and Collegiate Education
5-May-1787	Jupiter	Capricorn	Federalism/Constitution Convention
4-May-1794	Venus	Capricorn	Trade Treaties
19-Oct-1801	Saturn	Capricorn	Judicial Review: Marbury v. Madison
26-Apr-1805	Mars	Capricorn	First Barbary War
12-Sep-1808	Mercury	Aquarius	Maritime Law and the War of 1812
24-Apr-1814	Venus	Aquarius	Internal Improvements: Social Aspects
1-Nov-1818	Jupiter	Aquarius	Internal Improvements: Financing
26-Oct-1823	Mars	Aquarius	Rise of Partisan Politics
18-Mar-1827	Saturn	Aquarius	Lyceum and Abolition Movements
25-Jun-1830	Venus	Pisces	Hudson River School; Blackface Acting
14-Dec-1837	Jupiter	Pisces	U. S. Exploration Expedition
9-May-1840	Mercury	Pisces	Dance in Blackface Performance
19-Feb-1842	Mars	Pisces	New England Whaling Industry
2-Jun-1847	Saturn	Pisces	Boundaries after Mexican War
2-Aug-1848	Jupiter	Aries	Young America Movement; Phrenology
3-Feb-1852	Venus	Aries	Uncle Tom's Cabin; Railroad Greed
18-Aug-1855	Mercury	Aries	Kansas Constitutional Crisis
7-Jun-1860	Mars	Aries	Lincoln Nomination and the Civil War
9-Jul-1863	Saturn	Aries	Gettysburg and the New York Draft Riots
9-Sep-1866	Venus	Taurus	Opera in the Gilded Age
25-Dec-1871	Mercury	Taurus	Art History/Metropolitan Museum of Art
1-Mar-1876	Jupiter	Taurus	Robber Baron Capitalism
2-Feb-1882	Saturn	Taurus	Chicago Meatpacking Industry
8-Jan-1886	Mars	Taurus	Labor Protests and Haymarket Riot
21-Jun-1888	Mercury	Gemini	Office Automation
6-Aug-1893	Jupiter	Gemini	Populist Movement; Telephone Industry
12-Jan-1899	Venus	Gemini	Corporate Trusts; 5 and 10 cent stores
23-Oct-1903	Mars	Gemini	Muckrakers, Risk Taking, Auto Racing
14-Nov-1910	Saturn	Gemini	Business Regulation; Scientific Mgmt.
5-Apr-1917	Mars	Cancer	Isolationism, Ku Klux Klan, Prohibition
30-Jan-1925	Venus	Cancer	Consumerism, Mae West, Elsie the Cow
23-Jan-1932	Mercury	Cancer	Radio and Political Demagogues
4-Apr-1939	Jupiter	Cancer	Farm Policy; Consumer Banking
9-Nov-1947	Saturn	Cancer	Hollywood Blacklist; McCarthyism
5-Nov-1952	Jupiter	Leo	Christianity: Bulwark against Communism
27-May-1960	Venus	Leo	Camelot, Cocktail Culture, Rat Pack
28-Sep-1966	Saturn	Leo	Black Panther Party
22-Aug-1975	Mercury	Leo	Blockbuster Film Era
9-Apr-1983	Mars	Leo	Action Heroes and Military Revival
19-Nov-1990	Mercury	Virgo	Microsoft, Windows, and the Internet
24-Sep-1999	Venus	Virgo	Poker Craze, the Sopranos, and Makeovers
23-Apr-2012	Jupiter	Virgo	Craft Beer, Big Data, and Obamacare
28-Apr-2017	Mars	Virgo	Fitness Trackers and Nat Resource Dev.

Mars/Sagittarius: July 4, 1776 - November 29, 1779

Mars	+ Sagittarius	= ?
aggression	+ philosophy	= blusterous intimidation
force	+ belief	= fanaticism
war	+ justice	= righteousness
fighting	+ horses	= cavalry
cutting	+ leg	= leg injury from knife or gunshot

Fight for Religious Freedom

Though largely characterized as a rebellion against taxation without representation, religion was also an issue for the American Revolution. Fears that Britain's Anglican Church would be forced on colonists were fanned by rumors that Britain was prepared to send Anglican Bishops to America. In addition, the relatively staid and conservative practices of the Anglican Church (compared to the livelier Baptist and Methodist sects which flourished since the Great Awakening of the 1730s-1740s) made the Anglican Church another easy target for the colonists to direct their rage.

Priests themselves played an important role in Revolutionary activities. James Caldwell, known as the 'soldier parson,' represents another variation on the Mars/Sagittarius theme (soldier=Mars; parson=Sagittarius). Caldwell served as a military Chaplain; a type of war service encouraged by President George Washington. Another was Peter Muhlenberg who after preaching a sermon removed his robes to reveal a uniformed Virginia militia officer. The following day, Muhlenberg departed with a newly formed militia unit. He later served with distinction at Yorktown.

If not in the battlefield, religious leaders favorable to the colonial rebellion offered fodder for resistance when speaking from the pulpit. John Witherspoon; Presbyterian minister, Princeton University President, and a signer of the Declaration of Independence, was one of the most powerful colonial preachers who argued for religious freedom.[2] The British named Witherspoon a 'firebrand' and considered him a serious political risk.

Virginia Statute for Religious Freedom

Thomas Jefferson submitted the *Statute for Religious Freedom* to the Virginia General Assembly on **June 18, 1779**. Though it did not pass until January 16, 1786, its sentiments arguably capture the culmination of the Distribution's demand for religious freedom.

Supplement: *Benjamin Franklin ~ Benedict Arnold and the French Alliance.*

Mercury/Capricorn: November 30, 1779 – May 4, 1787

Mercury	+ Capricorn	= ?
communication	+ structure	= methodical
words	+ structure	= grammar
business	+ wealth	= mercantilism

Reorganization of William & Mary

As visitors of William & Mary, Thomas Jefferson and James Madison successfully usurped the Virginia Legislature with a curriculum overhaul in 1779 designed to diminish the influence of explicit religious instruction. As a result, George Wythe occupied the chair of law; the first such law chair established in the United States. Wythe's personality appears one of the purest examples of Mercury/Capricorn active during the Federal Era. Biographer Marie Kimball describes Wythe as methodical, learned, logical, profound, and sound; all characteristics consistent with Mercury/Capricorn.[3]

Noah Webster and Early Elementary Education

Still in print today, Webster's Dictionary dates from the 1806 edition of Webster's *A Compendious Dictionary of the English Language.* Predating this work was his three volume *A Grammatical Institute of the English Language*, published in the years 1783 (speller), 1784 (grammar), and 1785 (reader). Webster's education system began with sounds and vowels and progressed to words and sentences in a methodical manner. Under various editions, Webster's spelling book stayed in print for a hundred years and posted annual sales of 1 million copies by the Civil War.[4]

Noah Webster's speller was so popular that the Distributor's theme of a methodical approach to learning language was copied by other printers. Isaiah Thomas competed with Webster's books by publishing and promoting the works of the Scottish grammarian William Perry. Thomas was America's leading printer during the Federalist Era. He is also of interest to American astrologers for publication of an annual astrological ephemeris.

<u>Supplement</u>: *Isaiah Thomas ~ The Massachusetts Spy*

Jupiter/Capricorn: May 5, 1787 – May 3, 1794

Jupiter + Capricorn = ?
philosophy + centralized control = Federalism

United States Constitution

The original Articles of Confederation provided very limited Federal authority over the new American nation. Its weakness was quickly evident as deterioration in debt and currency markets caused numerous economic disruptions. A weak system of tax collection compounded the Federal Government's financial problems. Though many historians cite risks posed by the Whiskey Rebellion to the wealthy class as the immediate precursor to the Constitutional Convention, arguably the Whiskey Rebellion was indicative of disorder in the capital markets as the true underlying cause.

By far, Alexander Hamilton was the most important advocate of a strong central government backed by well-established capital markets. Capricorn is the sign of accumulated wealth and status. As universal significator of philosophy and expansion, Jupiter brought to focus Capricorn traits for a nation as a whole. The Jupiter/Capricorn Distribution defined Hamilton's peak era of influence over the nation's development.

The thesis that economic interests were dominant among the Constitution's signers was promoted by historian Charles A. Beard in *An Economic Interpretation of the Constitution* published in 1913.[5] Beard's thesis fell out of favor among American historians after the mid-1940s but appears relevant based on Jupiter/Capricorn as Distributor.

Constitution Timeline

3-May-1787   James Madison arrived in Philadelphia
13-May-1787   George Washington arrived in Philadelphia
14-May-1787   Originally planned opening of convention - postponed
25-May-1787   Constitutional Convention opened
16-Jul-1787   Convention adopted 'Great Compromise'
17-Sep-1787   Final draft of Constitution signed
28-Sep-1787   Congress sent Constitution to states for ratification
27-Oct-1787   First of Federalist Papers appeared
28-May-1788   Federalist Papers 1-85 published in book form
16-Aug-1788   Last of Federalist Papers appeared
29-May-1790   Rhode Island ratified Constitution

<u>Supplement</u>: *Alexander Hamilton ~ The Federalist Papers*

Venus/Capricorn: May 4, 1794 – October 18, 1801

Venus	+ Capricorn	= ?
love	+ status	= heraldry
money	+ old	= established economic interests
harmony	+ accumulated wealth	= peace treaty with senior partner

Choreography Note: Capricorn = London

Though empirical tests confirm the assignment of Aries to England; evidence suggests the City of London (and to a lesser extent London as representative of England) is better signified by Capricorn. London has long been known as a financial center which is consistent with Capricorn's signification as accumulated wealth. Capricorn planets are heavily emphasized in nativities of the major pro- and anti-Federalist factions during the Federal Era. With these observations, it is not surprising that pro-Federalists favored relations with England and anti-Federalists did not (usually favoring France). James Madison (Mars/Capricorn), leader of the anti-Federalist faction, was one of the most outspoken English-haters of his era, fearing that adoption of Hamilton's mercantilism and renewed ties with England would invariably lead the United States back to a governmental system and philosophy it had just overthrown.

Trade Treaties and War Profiteering

Washington's appointment of John Jay as envoy to England on *April 16, 1794* and Washington's *May 27, 1794* appointments of James Monroe and John Quincy Adams to France and the Netherlands respectively straddle the kickoff of Venus/Capricorn as Distributor on May 3, 1794. Most important was the Jay Treaty, negotiated on November 19, 1794; ratified by the Senate on June 24, 1795; and signed by Washington on August 14, 1795. James Madison would be forever upset by the failure of John Jay to tackle the issue of impressments of American citizens by the English navy; an unsettled issue which would be one catalyst for the War of 1812 launched under James Madison's Presidency. Yet Jay's Treaty did normalize trading relations with Britain. The result was a trade and economic boom for the United States. As a neutral country supplying both France and England (mostly England) during the French-English war, United States economic agents were essentially war profiteers. War profiteering is a delineation match to the lusty reputation of Venus/Capricorn. In the sign of Capricorn where Mars is in his exaltation, Venus salivates over the prospect of booty obtained through military conquest.

Supplement: *John Jay ~ The Jay Treaty*

Saturn/Capricorn: October 19, 1801 – April 25, 1805

Saturn	+ Capricorn	= ?
enforcement	+ accumulated status	= legal maneuvers
containment	+ accumulated wealth	= bond investments

Marbury v. Madison and Judicial Review

The changeover from Venus to Saturn marked the political transition from Hamilton's Federalists to Jefferson's Republicans. It also marked the elevation of John Marshall to Chief Justice of the Supreme Court. The Marshall Court convened on *August 4, 1801*; the event which best signified the changeover from Venus to Saturn. Marshall is tied to the Distribution by placement of his own natal Saturn in Capricorn (b. 24-Sep-1755).

If Capricorn signifies accumulated wealth and status, then Saturn in Capricorn builds walls in order to maintain wealth and status once acquired. Bond market investments, typically marketed to risk averse investors desirous of maintaining investment capital once acquired, are one delineation match to Saturn/Capricorn. Another is legal maneuvers designed for maintaining accumulated social status. Given the Marshall Court's reputation as the Court which defended and secured the Judiciary's independence, Saturn/Capricorn is a delineation match to legal maneuvers designed to maintain social status of Federalists embodied by the Constitution. By defining the Constitution as essentially a Federalist doctrine, I give credence to the Beard thesis that the Constitution was largely an economic tool designed to protect wealthy creditor classes in the wake of Shay's Rebellion.

Created during the Jupiter/Capricorn Distribution, the Constitution is reinforced during Saturn/Capricorn's Distribution by the legal maneuver known as judicial review; the lasting legacy of *Marbury v. Madison*. Judicial review asserts the right of the Supreme Court to strike down any law deemed unconstitutional. It remains one of the most important tools used by the Supreme Court to maintain its independence.

As Distributor for roughly two-thirds of Jefferson's administration, Saturn/Capricorn underscored the ongoing Federalist-Republican power struggle following Jefferson's inauguration. Relevant to the power struggle over Court independence are the following events:

3-Feb-1802	Repeal of the Judiciary Act of 1801.
24-Feb-1803	Marbury v. Madison.
1-Mar-1805	Impeachment trial of Justice Samuel Chase (acquitted).

Supplement: *John Marshall ~ The Nationalist Supreme Court*

CHAPTER 6 - DISTRIBUTOR RESULTS: DIRECTING THROUGH THE BOUNDS   99

Mars/Capricorn: April 26, 1805 – September 11, 1808

Mars	+ Capricorn	= ?
drive	+ status	= ambition
war	+ status	= fighting over tribute
fighting	+ wealth	= trade war

First Barbary War

The First Barbary War (1801-1805) originated from Jefferson's unwillingness to pay tribute to the Pasha of Tripoli in exchange for safe ocean passage. Under the Pasha's control, the Mediterranean Ocean was patrolled by the Barbary Pirates who routinely extracted bribes for safe passage from neutral vessels. Following defeat of the 14-gun corsair vessel Tripoli by the USS Enterprise on August 1, 1801, the United States had several naval engagements with forces under the Pasha's control. Beginning *April 27, 1805*, a single day after the start of the Mars/Capricorn Distribution, was the Battle of Derne which lasted to May 13, 1805. A decisive victory for America, the Battle of Derne was the first official battle fought by the United States on foreign soil. The successful Marine attack on Derne was immortalized by the lyrics 'to the shores of Tripoli' written for the Marine hymn.

Embargo Acts

Jefferson's second Presidential term was marred by British harassment of American ships and impressment of American seamen. Fighting the French during the Napoleonic Wars, Britain revived enforcement of its Rule of 1756 which operated from the premise that neutral nations trading with the enemy were implicitly aiding the enemy. Under this principle, all American vessels trading with France were subject to seizure. This period of American hostility towards the British flew out of control when the British warship HMS Leopard fired on, boarded, and impressed four Royal Navy deserters from the USS Chesapeake. The so-called 'Chesapeake Incident' of June 22, 1807 outraged Americans who clamored for war against Britain. Jefferson responded with a series of Embargo Acts which halted all U.S. shipping from December 22, 1807 to March 1, 1809.

Besides the Marine victory, a trade war against the British appears a second signification of Mars/Capricorn as Distributor. Compare the difference between Venus and Mars as Distributors considering that Mars and Venus as planets are enemies. Under the Distribution of Venus/Capricorn, John Jay traveled to England to negotiate a trade treaty. Under Mars/Capricorn, America fought a trade war against Britain.

<u>Supplement</u>: *James Madison ~ Opposition to British Trade*

Mercury/Aquarius: September 12, 1808 – April 23, 1814

Mercury	+ Aquarius	= ?
writing	+ old knowledge	= history
writing	+ fixed knowledge	= mathematical axioms
recording	+ fixed lines	= cartography
measuring	+ fixed lines	= surveying
recording	+ fixed knowledge	= codification of laws
writing	+ waterways	= maritime law
business	+ waterways	= maritime trade

Maritime Trade, Maritime Law and the War of 1812

As an outsider to the Napoleonic Wars (1803-1815), America attempted to maintain neutrality with both France and England. With France and England playing America's trading interests against one another, the ability of America to maintain neutrality proved impossible. At issue were disputes with France and England over maritime trade laws, a delineation match to Mercury/Aquarius as Distributor. America's desire for fair maritime trade law was a consistent philosophical principle underlying many of America's actions during the War of 1812.

The transition between the Jefferson and Madison administrations brought the repeal of Jefferson's unsuccessful Embargo Acts on *March 2, 1809* which had halted all foreign trade and sent the United States into an economic recession. Though the Embargo Acts were soon replaced by various Non-Intercourse Acts, the new laws were designed to restrict shipping to England and France, somewhat less restrictive than Jefferson's complete ban on foreign trade. In the period 1809-1812 leading up to the War of 1812, both France and England engaged America with diplomatic efforts in order to lift trade restrictions in a manner which was either unauthorized or deceitful. America's desire for fair maritime law, so egregiously violated by both France and England, explains why America who had suffered similar abuses for well over a decade finally decided to engage in war. Under any other Distributor, Americans might not have deemed impressments and cargo seizures sufficient cause to go to war. But with Mercury/Aquarius as Distributor the need for fair maritime law was elevated as a national priority, making continued violation of maritime law an affront to the national consciousness.

The repeal of all embargo and non-importation laws as of *April 14, 1814* signaled the end of fair maritime law as an American priority and coincides with the end of Mercury/Aquarius as Distributor on April 23, 1814.

Supplement: *John Elihu Hall ~ American Law Journal*

Venus/Aquarius: April 24, 1814 – October 31, 1818

Delineating Aquarius as Internal Improvements

As early as Manilius (c. 10 AD), Aquarius has been associated with canals and waterworks of all types.[6] Assigning Aquarius to waterworks is the key delineation step required to unlock many of the Aquarius Distributions. If Aquarius = canals, then Mercury/Aquarius = surveys for canals; Venus/Aquarius = pleasant social intercourse achieved through canal transportation which reduces isolation between groups of people; Jupiter/Aquarius = teaching of, judicial support for, and investor/magnate support for canal construction; Mars/Aquarius = partisan reaction against internal improvements; Saturn/Aquarius = canal engineering.

Wedding of the Waters

Beginning on July 4, 1817, construction of the Erie Canal culminated on November 4, 1825 when New York Governor and canal supporter DeWitt Clinton poured water from Lake Erie into the Hudson River after traversing the Erie Canal for the first time. Named the 'Wedding of the Waters,' the ceremony was a perfect delineation match to Venus (love/wedding) + waterworks/canals (Aquarius).

In the early days of the American Republic, George Washington expressed concern that westward migration of citizens beyond the Appalachian Mountains would engender an eventual breakup of America should citizens be diverted by the French, Spanish, or other some other cause. Washington envisioned canal construction as a solution because improved transportation and faster communication would eliminate geographic barriers between citizens on both sides of the Appalachian Mountains. Unfortunately for Washington, the Potomac's geology proved too difficult to overcome.[7]

Following the War of 1812, Americans returned to canal construction as one of three elements of Henry Clay's *American System* designed to stimulate economic growth.[8] Treasury Secretary Albert Gallatin's earlier April 1808 report *On the Subject of Public Roads and Canals* was taken up by South Carolina Congressman John Calhoun, who on February 4, 1817 echoed Washington's earlier sentiments on the benefic effect that a transportation network would have on the political health of America. Calhoun feared America's expansiveness and isolated pockets of citizenry would lead to sectional conflict and the risk of disunion.[9] Calhoun's remarks reflect the absence of partisan strife in the early days of James Monroe's administration known as the 'Era of Good Feeling,' a phrase first coined on July 12, 1817.[10]

Supplement: *John C. Calhoun ~ Bonus Bill of 1817*

Jupiter/Aquarius: November 1, 1818 – October 25, 1823

Jupiter	+ Aquarius	= ?
teaching	+ waterways	= civil engineering education
justice	+ waterways	= judicial support for canals

Engineering Education

Prior to the Erie Canal, the pool of engineering talent in America was virtually nil. True there were individuals who had interests in engineering subjects, but the lack of any available engineering schools limited the knowledge base required for executing designs for internal improvements.

Canvass White was one such individual with engineering interests. Recognizing his lack of engineering education as a professional impediment, White traveled to Europe where he made an extensive survey of canal designs. Upon his return to America, his knowledge proved helpful in designing the Erie Canal. But it was his accidental discovery of limestone deposits in close proximity to the planned canal route which proved to be White's lasting legacy. Requiring little processing, limestone mixed with water created hydraulic cement (e.g., cement which cures when submerged in water.)[11] Manufacture of onsite hydraulic cement allowed successful completion of the Erie Canal at a reasonable cost, not to mention the launch of the nation's cement industry. White's innovations, and other techniques learned from Erie Canal construction, provided the genesis for professional engineering education in America.[12] Even the site of Elisha Carey's barroom near Syracuse, New York; where White first demonstrated the stability of hydraulic cement in *1818*, is now an engineering school.[13]

Judicial Support for Internal Improvements

Supreme Court Justice William Johnson's 1822 advisory opinion to President James Monroe is a rare exception to the constitutionally designed separation of powers between the Executive and Judicial branches. Following Monroe's May 4, 1822 veto of internal improvements, Johnson responded with an advisory letter to Monroe in which Johnson cited *McCulloch v. Maryland* as justification for Congressional funding of internal improvements. As a member of the judicial branch of government, Johnson's actions demonstrate delineation of 'Jupiter = judge' for this Jupiter/Aquarius Distribution.

Supplement: *DeWitt Clinton ~ Erie Canal*

Mars/Aquarius: October 26, 1823 – March 17, 1827

Mars	+ Aquarius	= ?
fighting	+ old knowledge	= anti-intellectualism
fighting	+ common man	= partisan politics
fighting	+ waterways	= revolt against infrastructure

Rise of Partisan Politics

In his book *Internal Improvement: National Public Works and the Promise of Popular Government in the Early United States*, John Lauritz Larson[14] writes a chapter entitled 'Spoiling Internal Improvements' as a descriptor for the reaction against intellectualism and internal improvements which took place after the Distributor changeover to Mars/Aquarius in the fall of 1833. In short, the effect of Mars/Aquarius was to upset gains made by Mercury/Aquarius, Venus/Aquarius, and Jupiter/Aquarius under prior Distributions.

The most famous Martian reaction was the public reception to John Quincy Adams' December 6, 1825 State of the Union speech which called for an expansion of internal improvements to be funded at the Federal level, construction of a national university, and funding for other institutions designed for scientific research including observatories. The public reaction to Adams' proposals was so caustic that some historians have gone so far to label him a lame duck President following this speech. None of his proposals were enacted.

Preceding Adams' State of the Union speech was *The Letters of Wyoming*, written and published by Andrew Jackson political operative John Henry Eaton in *1823*. This anti-establishment message was based on anti-intellectualism designed to promote the political fortune of Andrew Jackson. Jackson defeated John Quincy Adams in the Presidential Election of 1828.

Mars/Aquarius signifies partisan politics for the willingness of Mars to fight against the humanitarian principle of equality espoused by Aquarius. What this meant for the *General Survey Act*, passed earlier with the intent of gathering information through surveys in preparation for further construction of internal improvements, was the award of survey contracts based on partisan lobbying. The 'road to nowhere' was not built, but plenty of surveys outlining 'roads to nowhere' were made instead.

Supplement: *William Crawford ~ Election of 1824*

Saturn/Aquarius: March 18, 1827 – June 24, 1830

Saturn	+ Aquarius	= ?
old	+ knowledge	= science
binding/control	+ ankles	= leg shackles for slaves
black	+ fairness	= abolition movement

Lyceum Movement

After studying with Benjamin Silliman at Yale, Josiah Holbrook developed an interest in scientific education. A culmination of his endeavors as an itinerant teacher, Holbrook developed a unique forum for adult education: the Lyceum. Named for the Athens gymnasium where Aristotle taught, the Lyceum was designed as a system whereby the public could attend lectures and demonstrations on topics including science. In an 1826 article "The Lyceum" published in the *American Journal of Education*, Holbrook included a recommended list of discussion topics:

> *The several branches of Natural Philosophy, viz, Mechanics, Hydrostatics, Pneumatics, Chemistry, Mineralogy, Botany, and branch of the Mathematics, History, Political Economy, or any political, intellectual, or moral subject, may be examined and discussed by the society.*[15]

Holbrook held the first Lyceum session during November 1826 in Millbury, Massachusetts. The movement quickly gained hold with the first Lyceum cooperative formed in Worcester, Massachusetts in **early 1827**. Holbrook eventually formed a national organization of his Lyceum concept which maintained its popularity well beyond the end of the Saturn/Aquarius Distribution in 1830. In later years, Lyceums functioned as a communications infrastructure used by the Transcendentalist and Abolitionist Movements.[16]

Trade Embargo of John Quincy Adams

In response to Britain closing West Indies ports to American ships, Adams ordered all American ports closed to British goods on **March 17, 1827**. Matches Saturn/Aquarius as the restriction (Saturn) of waterways (Aquarius).

Abolition Movement

The first issue of *Freedom's Journal* appeared on **March 16, 1827**. It was the first African American newspaper published in America. Delineation match to Saturn/Aquarius as black (Saturn) equality/freedom (Aquarius).

Supplement: *Benjamin Silliman ~ Scientific Education in America*

CHAPTER 6 - DISTRIBUTOR RESULTS: DIRECTING THROUGH THE BOUNDS   105

Venus/Pisces: June 25, 1830 – December 13, 1837

Venus	+ Pisces	= ?
love	+ sacrifice	= forgiveness
love	+ sacrifice	= melodrama
love	+ sublime	= romanticism
art	+ water	= river painting
entertainment	+ feet	= dance

Romanticism in Art and the Hudson River School

Founded by Thomas Cole, the Hudson River School was the closest American artistic movement linked to European romantics such as Goethe and Beethoven. By the time the Ascendant Distributor moved to Venus/Pisces in 1830, the Erie Canal had been open for five years. Completion of the Erie Canal facilitated population expansion west of the Appalachian Mountains and a corresponding increase in economic activity. A central theme of Thomas Cole was the exaltation of untamed wilderness in the wake of America's largest economic boom to date. With this perspective, Cole's portrayal of Hudson Valley landscapes can be interpreted as a reaction to untrammeled economic development. Cole died on February 11, 1848 towards the end of the Saturn/Pisces Distribution. His death, a few weeks after the January 24, 1848 gold discovery at Sutter's Mill marked a symbolic end for the entire Pisces Distribution.

Blackface Performance and Jump Jim Crow[17]

A boom in cotton prices (until the Panic of 1837), the accompanying growth in plantation investment, and the popularity of dance as a social activity fused to create blackface as a unique form of American comedy. First performed in 1828 by Thomas Dartmouth (T.D.) "Daddy" Rice, the song and dance routine *Jump Jim Crow* became so popular that sheet music with its tune circulated widely in the early 1830s. A reworded version appeared as an 1832 campaign song performed at the time of the Democratic National Convention.

We are so far removed from the 1830s it is difficult to create a mental picture of *Jump Jim Crow* in performance or the popularity it enjoyed. Venus/Pisces as Distributor offers a clue. Often the exaltation of Venus/Pisces comes at the expense of another party who requires demotion in order for Venus/Pisces to emerge as the pinnacle of the artistic hierarchy. I suggest the stereotyped caricature of a black person in the form of Jim Crow fulfilled that function for Venus/Pisces. *Jump Jim Crow* quickly became a staple of the minstrel tradition which emerged in the 1840s.[18]

Supplement: *Thomas Cole ~ Hudson River School*

Jupiter/Pisces: December 14, 1837 – May 8, 1840

| Jupiter | + Pisces | = ? |
| exploration | + water | = maritime expedition |

United States Exploration Expedition

Less well known than the Lewis & Clark Expedition (1804-1806) is the U.S. Exploring Expedition (1838-1842). First proposed by President John Quincy Adams and approved by Congress in May 1828, the U.S. Exploring Expedition was intended to gather scientific information with the ultimate objective of supporting commerce and existing investment in the whale and seal hunting industries. Congress eventually funded the plan on May 18, 1836 and a group of six sailing vessels departed on August 18, 1838 under the command of U.S. Navy Lieutenant Charles Wilkes.

Perhaps no better significator can describe the U.S. Exploring Expedition than Jupiter/Pisces for its delineation as a maritime expedition. Jupiter also signifies things which are 'large.' Consider the large quantity of specimens returned to the United States (later displayed in the Smithsonian Institution):

ethnographic objects: 4,000
pressed plants: 50,000 specimens of 10,000 species
living plants: 1,000+
plant seeds: 638
birds: 2,150
mammals: 134
fish: 588
fossils: 300
coral: 400
crustacean: 1,000
smaller insects/specimens: 208
larger insects/specimens: 5,100

In addition, 241 surveying maps were drawn with details on 280 Pacific Islands, 800 miles of the Oregon coast, 100 miles of the Columbia River, the overland route from Oregon to San Francisco, and 1,500 miles of the Antarctic coastline. Charles Wilkes spent most of his remaining life documenting the scientific findings of the U.S. Exploring Expedition.

Supplement: *Charles Wilkes ~ The United States Exploring Expedition*

CHAPTER 6 - DISTRIBUTOR RESULTS: DIRECTING THROUGH THE BOUNDS   107

Mercury/Pisces: May 9, 1840 – February 18, 1842

In the sign of his detriment and fall, Mercury/Pisces functions as humor, with comedic talent a common manifestation. With the feet assigned to Pisces, Mercury/Pisces in the sign of his astrological fall also signifies a physical fall; usually because the feet are unstable and slip.

Dance Master Juba and the Evolution of Blackface Performance

In the spring of 1841, P. T. Barnum presented the dancer 'Juba.'[19] A review from a later performance demonstrates Mercury/Pisces in action:

> . . . there never was such a laugh as the laugh of Juba–there is in it the concentrated laugh of fifty comic pantomimes; it has no relation to the chuckle, and, least of all, to the famous horse laugh; not a bit of it–it is a laugh distinct, a laugh apart, a laugh by itself–clear, ringing, echoing, resonant, harmonious, full of rejoicing and mighty mirth, and fervent fun; you may hear it like the continuous humming sound of nature, permeating everywhere; it enters into your heart and you laugh sympathetically–it creeps into your ear, and clings to it, and all the subsequent sounds seem to be endued with the cachinnatory quality.
>
> Well, though the laugh of Juba be wondrous, what may be said of Juba's dancing? . . . Such mobility of muscles, such flexibility of joints, such boundings, such slidings, such gyrations, such toes and such heelings, such backwardings and forwardings, such posturings, such firmness of foot, such elasticity of tendon, such mutation of movement, such vigour, such variety, such natural grace, such powers of endurance, such potency of pastern, were never combined in one nigger. Juba is to Vauxhall what the Lind is to the Opera House. We hear that Juba has been commanded to Buckingham Palace.[20]

The Legacy of Master Juba: from Minstrelsy to Break Dancing

Viewed within the development of the minstrelsy tradition, Master Juba's debut occupies a spot between *Jump Jim Crow* (Venus/Pisces Distribution) and the first full evening entertainment of blackface minstrelsy performed by the Virginia Minstrels (following the Mercury/Pisces Distribution) on January 31, 1843.[21] Worth further investigation is whether *Jump Jim Crow* introduced the basic song & dance format to minstrelsy (1830-1837), was further modified by comedic elements of Master Juba (1840-1842), and finally emerged as a standardized routine in 1843 with the Virginia Minstrels.

Dance and popular culture historian Marian Hannah Winter revived Juba's reputation in a 1947 article.[22] Winter described Juba as 'the most single influential performer of nineteenth-century American dance.' Tap, step, and ultimately contemporary break dancing (my opinion) can be traced to Juba.

Mars/Pisces: February 19, 1842 – June 1, 1847

Mars	+ Pisces	= ?
killing	+ fish	= whaling

New England Whaling Industry

Following the War of 1812, America's whaling industry entered its Golden Age which lasted until the late 1850s.[23] Perhaps no geographic location embodied the age more than Nantucket Island, whose isolation from the mainland has helped maintain its historical character for tourists to the present day.

By 1842, the Nantucket whaling industry was suffering growing pains. Ships were so loaded with whale oil that Nantucket's relatively shallow channels proved a problem: returning vessels could no longer reach the island and unload their cargo. The solution was provided by Peter Folger Ewer who designed hollow wooden pontoons (known as 'camels') which elevated whaling vessels a sufficient vertical distance that they could successfully traverse shallow waters. The first unsuccessful trial was held September 4, 1842; the second successful trial, September 21, 1842.[24]

As the Mars/Pisces Distribution culminated, by 1846 the American whaling industry had grown to the point where its 735 ships constituted 81% of the world's 900 whaleships.[25] The year 1846 was important in another respect. For Nantucket Island, a major fire on July 13, 1846 destroyed most of the town's whaling infrastructure. Shortly thereafter, the California Gold Rush of 1848 lured many adventurous men to 'Go West!' With this demographic staple of the whaling industry employment now departing in large numbers for California, the whaling industry suffered a labor shortage. With Nantucket's fire, overhunting of sperm whales, and a growing labor shortage, the Golden Age of Whaling soon came to an end.

Supplement: *The Folgers of Nantucket ~ A Whaling Family Dynasty*

Saturn/Pisces: June 2, 1847 – August 1, 1848

Saturn	+ Pisces	= ?
control	+ water	= barricade

With Saturn's dryness, placement of Saturn in any water sign is problematic. Though Saturn in water signs shares coldness as an intrinsic quality, the dry/wet mismatch creates a polarizing effect. Saturn placed in Cancer, ruled by the Moon significator of the people, places controls on the public in response to a witch-hunt mentality. Saturn placed in Scorpio, ruled by Mars significator of the military, creates paranoia and responds by erecting security structures for protection. Saturn placed in Pisces, ruled by Jupiter, places restraints on the free flow of wisdom through the erection of barricades. The image of a castle surrounded by a moat is apropos.

Establishing Boundaries at the Conclusion of the Mexican War

Of all American Presidents, only two have Saturn/Pisces placed in their natal figures: James Monroe and John Tyler. For Monroe, Saturn/Pisces signified a 'hands-off' foreign policy towards Central and South America culminating with the Monroe Doctrine of December 2, 1823 timed by a Saturn/Pisces-Ascendant primary direction for his natal figure.[26] Returning to the castle imagery, replace 'castle' with 'Central and South America' and 'moat' with 'Pacific Ocean' and the isolationist image of Saturn/Pisces is complete.

Given this backdrop, it is not surprising to find President Polk using the Monroe Doctrine as partial justification for the Mexican War in his Annual Message to Congress on December 6, 1847. Polk stated Mexico's inability to control its northern territory left a power vacuum which some other country might take advantage of should the United States not demand Mexico's northern territory as a part of a settlement.[27] With victory at Vera Cruz in October 1847, America had won the Mexican War. In Polk's mind, securing northern Mexican territory would maintain American hegemony by shoring up America's Southern border. I suggest the Texas-Mexican border demarcated by the Rio Grande functions as the moat in the Saturn/Pisces castle analogy.

Supplement: *Nicholas Trist ~ Treaty of Guadalupe Hidalgo*

Jupiter/Aries: August 2, 1848 – February 2, 1852

Jupiter	+ Aries	= ?
expansion	+ fighting	= philosophy of war
teaching	+ head	= phrenology

Young America Movement

The year 1848 was a pivotal year for America in the 19th Century. Famous for the year of European revolutions and the gold discovery at Sutter's Mill which heralded the California Gold Rush, 1848 is the year that Americans cast aside the relative passivity of the early antebellum era for a more aggressive philosophy of western expansion under the banner of *Manifest Destiny*.

Founded in 1845 by Edwin de Leon and George H. Evans, the Young America Movement was a faction of the Democratic Party which sought territorial expansion through military means. The Mexican War (1846-1848) conducted under the Polk Presidency was one objective of the group. Others included conquest of Mexico, Central America, and Cuba for the purpose of expanding slavery.[28] George Nicholas Sanders became the chief spokesman for the movement, taking on the post of editor for the *Democratic Review* in 1851. The Sanders-Polk connection merits attention. Sanders organized an 1843 political caucus which helped bring James Polk's name to national attention for Polk's aggressive stance towards Texas. Shortly thereafter, Polk was elected to the Presidency on December 4, 1844 on a platform which favored acquisition of Texas and Oregon. Separately, Stephen Douglas later played a prominent role in the Young America Movement.

Phrenology

Widely popular in America during the mid-19th century, phrenology is the study of determining personality traits by analyzing the shape of the human head. Certain regions of the head were thought to correspond to aspects of human behavior. Orson Squire Fowler and his brother Lorenzo Niles Fowler were the top phrenologists of the day.[29] Together with Samuel Wells and Nelson Sizer, the Fowler brothers operated the publishing house Fowler & Wells in New York City from 1846 to 1854, overlapping the period defined by Jupiter/Aries as Distributor. As a connection to the upcoming Mercury/Aries Distribution when Walt Whitman influenced the national consciousness, note that Whitman briefly worked as an editor for Fowler during the Jupiter/Aries Distribution and Fowler later funded publication of the second edition of Whitman's *Leaves of Grass* during the Mercury/Aries Distribution.

Supplement: *Lorenzo Fowler ~ Phrenology*

Venus/Aries: February 3, 1852 – August 17, 1855

Venus	+ Aries	= ?
love	+ fighting	= bloodlust
love	+ blood	= sadism
money	+ action	= greed

Stephen Douglas, Railroads, and Kansas

The Distribution of Venus/Aries is sandwiched between the 1848 California Gold Rush and the 1857 financial panic. This period was an economic boom marked by an explosion in railroad construction. Stephen Douglas is tied to the Distribution with Venus/Aries placed in his natal figure (b. 23-Apr-1813). Like many, Douglas attempted to cash in on the railroad boom. As significator of greed, Venus/Aries is consistent with Douglas' motivation behind his introduction of the Kansas-Nebraska Act on January 4, 1854. The original intent of the Kansas-Nebraska Act was to facilitate a Midwestern Transcontinental Railroad. Passage would personally benefit Douglas through anticipated gains on his private real estate interests held in the vicinity of the proposed railroad line.[30]

Signed into law on May 30, 1854, the final version of the Kansas-Nebraska Act invalidated the Compromise of 1850 with its doctrine of *popular sovereignty* which allowed each state to vote on the legality of slavery within its borders. The result was migration of pro and anti-slavery constituents to Kansas which triggered widespread violence in 1855 ('Bleeding Kansas') as the Distribution culminated.

Uncle Tom's Cabin

Published in book form on **March 20, 1852**, *Uncle Tom's Cabin* described many sadistic practices forced on slaves. The book was an immediate best seller, with 300,000 copies sold in the first year after publication. Eventually *Uncle Tom's Cabin* ranked as the best-selling novel of the 19th century, second only to the Bible.[31] Graphic details of the cruelty of slavery emboldened the abolitionist movement in Northern States. Published just two years after passage of the Fugitive Slave Act on September 18, 1850, the increased agitation of Northern abolitionists brought on by *Uncle Tom's Cabin* led to violent protests against the return of captured slaves to Southern states. Capture of Anthony Burns in Boston on May 24, 1854 was perhaps the most famous incident. Burns' capture loomed large in the mind of many Northerners, including Walt Whitman in the year before he published the first edition of *Leaves of Grass*.[32]

Supplement: *Harriet Beecher Stowe ~ Uncle Tom's Cabin*

Mercury/Aries: August 18, 1855 – June 6, 1860

Mercury	+ Aries	= ?
writing	+ war	= military constitution
communication	+ action	= troop mobilization
communication	+ war	= military strategy
communication	+ rash	= lying, deceit

Kansas Constitutional Crisis

Concurrent to acts of violence during Bleeding Kansas was an attempt to enact a constitution for the proposed state of Kansas. In opposition to the pro-slavery Territorial legislature, a group of Free-State voters coalesced to hold the Topeka Constitutional Convention during October 1855. The Free-Staters' anti-slavery candidates and platform were accepted in an election held January 15, 1856 boycotted by most pro-slavery voters. On January 24, 1856, President Franklin Pierce declared the group revolutionary and ordered the arrest of its leaders. In response, the Territorial legislature met during September 1857 to produce a pro-slavery document known as the *Lecompton Constitution*. In a series of elections held from late 1857 to mid-1858 marked by violence and ballot box irregularities, the Lecompton Constitution was finally rejected. President Buchanan, who had recommended passage of the Lecompton Constitution, stumbled badly by attempting to manage the Kansas Constitutional crisis through an overly legalistic approach which ignored the larger issues at stake.[33] Significations of Mercury/Aries ranging from troop mobilization to a military constitution are exemplified by the Kansas Constitutional Crisis.

Walt Whitman: *Leaves of Grass*

The start and finish of the Mercury/Aries Distribution brackets the peak popularity of Walt Whitman's poetry. The first edition of *Leaves of Grass* was published on **July 4, 1855** as the sequence opened. On **June 14, 1860**, one week after the Distribution ended, Whitman's publishers informed him the first printing of the third edition had sold out.[34]

At its simplest Mercury/Aries signifies writing about war; a theme fully embodied by the poet Walt Whitman. His famous Civil War patriotic poem *Beat! Beat! Drums!* (1862) was preceded by a more militant patriotic tone in the poem cluster *Chants Democratic and Native American* from the third edition of *Leaves of Grass*.[35]

Supplement: *Walt Whitman ~ Leaves of Grass*

CHAPTER 6 - DISTRIBUTOR RESULTS: DIRECTING THROUGH THE BOUNDS   113

Mars/Aries: June 7, 1860 – July 8, 1863

| Mars | + Aries | = ? |
| fighting | + action | = offensive war |

Lincoln's Presidential Nomination and the American Civil War

Three weeks prior to the start of the Mars/Aries Distribution, Lincoln received the Presidential nomination on ***May 18, 1860***. For many Southerners, Lincoln's November 8, 1860 election to the Presidency sealed the decision to secede from the Union.

The purest mundane delineation of Mars/Aries is offensive warfare. Not much more can be said about this period except for the nation's tremendous leap to war in accordance with the willingness of Mars/Aries to fight. Arguably the culminating moment of Mars/Aries as Distributor was Pickett's Charge on July 3, 1863 during the Battle of Gettysburg. The location of Pickett's Charge on what is now known as Cemetery Ridge is widely considered the high-water mark of the Confederacy.

Supplement: *Alexander Stephens ~ Launch of Civil War*

Saturn/Aries: July 9, 1863 – September 8, 1866

Saturn	+ Aries	= ?
stop	+ fighting	= anti-war
wall	+ fighting	= siege

The Distributor changeover from Mars to Saturn on July 9, 1863 is discussed in detail in Chapter 2. To review, delineation of Saturn/Aries as anti-war sentiment is consistent with anti-war protests during the New York Draft Riots of July 1863. Saturn/Aries is also a delineation match to the increased use of defensive battlefield tactics after Gettysburg.

New York Draft Riots

Following Congressional passage of America's first conscription act on March 3, 1863, the first drawing of names for Union Civil War service occurred on *July 11, 1863*. Among those opposed to the military draft were the Copperheads, a name given to a faction of Northern Democrats who favored immediate settlement with the Confederacy on the slavery issue (maintaining slavery as an institution). The first fighting broke out in New York on *July 13, 1863* and by the time Federal troops restored order on *July 16, 1863* the casualty list was 100+ dead and 2000+ injured.

Another visible symbol of the changeover to Saturn/Aries was Ohio Congressman Clement Vallandigham, considered the unofficial leader of the Copperheads. He spoke out against President Lincoln and was jailed in response (see supplement). His problems with Lincoln paralleled the time of the New York Draft Riots.

Gettysburg

After Confederate General Robert E. Lee's disastrous offensive at Gettysburg, the Civil War became a war of attrition. Union General Ulysses S. Grant used defensive tactics against Lee in the 1864 Richmond campaign. The Siege of Petersburg followed, lasting from June 1864 to March 1865. Daily desertions of Lee's Confederate troops sealed the fate of the Confederate Army.

Supplement: *Clement Vallandigham ~ General Order Number 38*

CHAPTER 6 - DISTRIBUTOR RESULTS: DIRECTING THROUGH THE BOUNDS   115

Venus/Taurus: September 9, 1866 – December 24, 1871

Venus	+ Taurus	= ?
Music	+ throat	= opera singing

Opera in the Gilded Age

    With the opening of the Academy of Music on October 2, 1854, opera arrived in New York City. Despite a reputation for excellent acoustics, a poor architectural design limited stage views in the original building. As the Venus/Taurus Distribution started, a fire destroyed the auditorium in 1866 which was rebuilt and reopened in March 1867. The new Academy of Music prospered so much that by the time of the Jupiter/Taurus Distribution, the nouveau riche of the Gilded Age constructed the Metropolitan Opera House in 1883 in order to guarantee themselves seats. By the Mars/Taurus Distribution of 1866, the struggling Academy of Music closed its doors.[36]

    In the Gilded Age, opera was used as a backdrop by leading figures of the era. Speculators Jim Fisk and Jay Gould rose to national prominence following their attempts to corner the gold market which culminated in the first 'Black Friday' gold and stock market crash of September 24, 1869. Controlled by Fisk and Gould, the Erie Railway's corporate offices were housed above the stage of the Grand Opera House on West 23rd Street, one of several theatres purchased by Fisk who was also a prolific opera producer.[37]

    The accuracy of the changeover is suggested by the debut of opera diva Minnie Hauk on ***October 13, 1866.***

<u>Supplement</u>: *Minnie Hauk ~ America's First Opera Diva*

Mercury/Taurus: December 25, 1871 – February 28, 1876

Mercury	+ Taurus	= ?
history	+ beauty	= art history
study	+ business	= stock market analyst

Metropolitan Museum of Art

On July 4, 1866, John Jay - grandson of the first U. S. Chief Justice of the same name - informally proposed that America create its first national art museum. A group of New Yorkers in earshot agreed and plans were started to construct what eventually became the Metropolitan Museum of Art.[38] Included in the Museum's April 13, 1870 charter is the mission statement:

> . . . *to be located in the City of New York, for the purpose of establishing and maintaining in said city a Museum and library of art, of encouraging and developing the study of the fine arts, and the application of arts to manufacture and practical life, of advancing the general knowledge of kindred subjects, and, to that end, of furnishing popular instruction.*[39]

The Museum opened its doors on ***February 20, 1872*** at 681 Fifth Avenue.

Consider that objects of art are Venus and the Museum concept was first proposed on July 4, 1866 three months prior to the Venus/Taurus Distribution on September 9, 1866. Yet the Museum did not open its doors until the Mercury/Taurus Distribution. The Metropolitan Museum is not simply a 'picture gallery' or 'house of objects' which would fit the nature of Venus/Taurus; it is a full-fledged educational facility which exemplifies the nature of Mercury to speak, walk, draw, and study. The mission statement phrase *application of arts to manufacture and practical life* echoes the practicality of Taurus as an earth sign.

<u>Supplement</u>: *J. P. Morgan ~ Patron of Metropolitan Museum of Art*

CHAPTER 6 - DISTRIBUTOR RESULTS: DIRECTING THROUGH THE BOUNDS 117

Jupiter/Taurus: March 1, 1876 – February 1, 1882

Jupiter	+ Taurus	= ?
expansion	+ business	= magnate

Robber Baron Capitalism

Started by the failure of railroad financier Jay Cooke & Company on September 18, 1873, the Panic of 1873 ushered in a deflationary depression which lasted until 1879. This period of economic decline allowed surviving investors to increase business operations through mergers and acquisitions.

In a position to capitalize on economic turmoil was Jay Gould, a speculator/financier who pioneered the use of legal maneuvers and bankruptcy to profit from an otherwise poor business environment. Gould allegedly made $500,000 during the Panic of 1873 in a single day. By spring 1874, Gould acquired enough shares of the railroad Union Pacific that he became a Director.

Union Pacific Timeline

1-Jul-1862	Pacific Railway Act of 1862: "An Act to aid in the construction of a railroad and telegraph line from the Missouri river to the Pacific Ocean, and to secure to the government the use of the same for postal, military, and other purposes."
1-Jul-1862	Incorporation of Union Pacific Railroad.
10-May-1869	Joined with Central Pacific Railroad to complete the United States Transcontinental Railroad. Ceremony at Promontory Point, Utah.
1872	Union Pacific involved in Crédit Mobilier scandal.
24-Jan-1880	Emerged from bankruptcy reorganization as Union Pacific Railway (name change); Jay Gould, President.
1893	Union Pacific Railway declared bankruptcy.
1-Jul-1897	Emerged from bankruptcy reorganization as Union Pacific Railroad (original name).

Supplement: *Jay Gould ~ Union Pacific Railroad*

Saturn/Taurus: February 2, 1882 – January 7, 1886

Saturn	+ Taurus	= ?
partition	+ cattle	= meatpacking

On first glance, slaughterhouse operations might appear a better delineation match to Mars/Taurus because Mars' nature is to cut. But meat must be stored and shipped after slaughter. After cutting, each individual piece of meat is further wrapped and packaged for consumer distribution. Partition, wrapping, and storage are Saturnine methods.

Chicago Meatpacking Industry

Chicago's Union Stockyards ('The Yards') were created in 1864 by a railroad consortium. With growth in railroad construction following the Civil War, Chicago quickly became a major railway distribution center. Cheaper transportation facilitated shipment of cattle to a central location for slaughter.

While *The Yards* enjoyed steady growth through the early 1920s, the introduction of refrigerated rail cars by Gustavus Franklin Smith (1880-The Peninsular Car Company) and Philip Danforth Amour (1883-Armour Refrigerator Line) created significant growth in the early 1880s.

Introduction of refrigerated rail cars in the early 1880s is the key event which ties the meatpacking industry to the Saturn/Taurus Distribution. Saturn's cold and dry elemental qualities match conditions inside refrigeration units where meat is stored and aged.

Supplement: *Philip Armour ~ Chicago Meatpacking Industry*

CHAPTER 6 - DISTRIBUTOR RESULTS: DIRECTING THROUGH THE BOUNDS   119

Mars/Taurus: January 8, 1886 – June 20, 1888

Mars	+ Taurus	= ?
Fighting	+ capitalism	= labor protests

Haymarket Riot: Fight for the Eight Hour Workday

As a primary objective of newly organized labor movements, the Federation of Organized Trades and Labor Unions established the eight-hour work day by May 1, 1886. A general strike in support of this goal was held on May 1, 1886 as planned.

In Chicago, a conflict between strikers and strikebreakers at the McCormick Harvesting Machine Co. plant led to violent protests and multiple deaths from gunfire on May 3 - 4, 1886. The culminating event was a pipe bomb thrown into the crowd on May 4, 1886 which killed police officer Mathias J. Degan and triggered a melee. This incident was later known as the Haymarket Riot, known as most widely remembered 19th century American labor protest, despite the fact that its financial losses paled in comparison to the May 11, 1894 Pullman Strike and other larger labor protests.

What made Haymarket memorable was the legal treatment of seven men accused of instigating the rally and charged with Degan's murder. Like the highly publicized Sacco and Vanzetti case of the 1920s, the trial of Haymarket 'anarchists' was marred by poor legal jurisprudence, starting with the fact that none of the accused could be directly tied to throwing the pipe bomb which killed Degan. The accused:

August Spies
Albert Parsons
Adolph Fisher
George Engel
Louis Lingg
Michael Schwab
Samuel Fielden
Oscar Neebe

Neebe was sentenced to 15 years in prison; all others were sentenced to death. Fielden's and Schwab's sentences were later commuted to life in prison; Lingg committed suicide before his scheduled execution; Spies, Parsons, Fischer, and Engel were executed by hanging on November 11, 1887.

Supplement: *Louis Lingg ~ Haymarket Riot and Suicide*

Mercury/Gemini: June 21, 1888 – August 5, 1893

Mercury   + Gemini   = ?
communicate   + information   = data organization

Office Automation

The modern business corporation dates from the 1880s when America's Industrial Revolution gained traction following the Civil War. An indirect result of the growth of business culture was an increased need for clerical workers to accommodate increased levels of business activity. It is estimated between 1880 and 1910 the number of clerical workers increased from 1.1% to 5.1% of the population.[40] As number crunching grew, so did the need for accuracy. These business requirements proved fertile ground for the development of an array of office equipment including calculators, typewriters, and other mechanized devices.

Burroughs Calculating Machine

On *August 21, 1888*, a patent was granted for the 'W. S. Burroughs Calculating Machine,' two months after the start of Mercury/Gemini as Distributor. This was one of the first adding machines ever developed and was used extensively by banking institutions.

Hollerith Tabulating Machine

Developed in order to speed the tabulation of the 1890 Census, Herman Hollerith developed a punch card system whose data entries could be counted or sorted by machines. Hollerith was issued U.S. Patent 395,782 on *January 8, 1889* for his tabulating machine. In 1911, Hollerith's company was merged into Computing Tabulating Recording Corporation (CTR), renamed International Business Machines Corporation (IBM) in 1924.

Supplement: *William S. Burroughs I ~ Patent for a 'Calculating-machine'*

CHAPTER 6 - DISTRIBUTOR RESULTS: DIRECTING THROUGH THE BOUNDS

Jupiter/Gemini: August 6, 1893 – January 11, 1899

The phrase 'making a mountain out of a molehill' is an apt description for Jupiter/Gemini's ability to blow facts out of proportion relative to their actual importance. For this reason, Jupiter/Gemini signifies a style of rhetoric commonly found in stump speeches of populist political candidates for its appeal to a low level of intellectual sophistication.

Populist-Free Silver Movement

Price deflation was a dominant feature of the post-Civil War economic era. As weak agricultural prices failed to maintain real income of the farm sector, farmers (and others suffering effects from weak commodity prices) rallied around the strictness of the gold standard as the cause of their problems. Both the diagnosis of the problem - the gold standard - and the proposed solution - minting of silver - were overly simplistic yet appealed to the logic of Jupiter/Gemini as Distributor. Consider also that Gemini is a double-bodied sign, a match to the dual nature of gold and silver as monetary instruments, formally referred to as bimetallism. As Jupiter/Gemini's Distribution wound up in 1899, economic fundamentals had changed. New gold discoveries from the Klondike Gold Rush of 1896 made their way into the nation's money supply, ending the post-Civil War deflationary era. With easier credit, the economic basis for populist political movements dried up after 1896. For further details on populism, see Saturn-Ascendant Direction #6.

Expansion of Telephone and Print Media Industries

Another delineation of Jupiter/Gemini is an expansion (Jupiter) of communication methods (Gemini). Expiration of Bell Telephone Company patents in 1893 and 1894 set the stage for an explosion in new telephone companies and service.

A similar expansion occurred in print media with magazines taking the lead. *McClure's Magazine*, which featured so strongly in the following Mars/Gemini Distribution, was founded in June 1893 near the start of the Jupiter/Gemini Distribution. *McClure's* was paradigmatic of a new wave of magazine publishing which benefited from decreased postal rates, rural mail delivery, and innovations in printing processes including halftone photoengraving presses which allowed illustrations to be printed at inexpensive prices for the first time. Magazines also caught the wave of emerging consumerism as the preferred vehicle for consumer advertising.[41]

Supplement: *Alexander Graham Bell ~ Growth of Telephone Industry*

Venus/Gemini: January 12, 1899 – October 22, 1903

Venus	+ Gemini	= ?
beauty	+ business	= sale of adornments
money	+ mutable (business) sign	= high transaction turnover
music	+ business	= music in advertising
music	+ speaking	= song/phonographs
love	+ talk	= popularity of telephones

Growth of Corporate Trusts

With gold entering the money supply following the 1896 Klondike Gold Rush, the lengthy deflationary period following the Panic of 1893 ended. Easy credit facilitated business expansion and combinations through financial engineering. Business operations based on high transaction turnover embodied one Venus/Gemini theme (See Saturn-Ascendant Direction #6). The period between January 1898 and January 1904 marked the birth of 75 per cent of American trusts, whose capital increased seven-fold.[42]

5 and 10 cent Stores

A bustling economy and increased immigrant arrivals were two conditions favorable to growth of 5 and 10 cent stores. S. S. Kresge founded his dime store *S. S. Kresge* in 1899 and grew to 85 stores by 1912 (later renamed Kmart Corporation in 1977). Woolworth's, the leader in the 5 and 10 cent store business, grew its stores from 54 to 76 between 1899 and 1903, an increase of 41%.[43][44] Hair pins, hat pins, feathers, shoelaces, knitting needles, yarn, combs, brushes, and dishpans were representative items purchased for adornment and other functional uses by immigrants and the lower class.[45]

Invention of the Phonograph

The Victor Talking Machine Company was incorporated in October 1901 by Eldridge R. Johnson. It became one of the world's largest manufacturers of phonographs and phonograph records.

Supplement: *Frank Woolworth ~ the Five and Dime Store*

Mars/Gemini: October 23, 1903 – November 13, 1910

Mars	+ Gemini	= ?
fighting	+ trickster	= lawlessness
fighting	+ information	= muckraker
aggression	+ business	= high risk taking, financial volatility
aggression	+ communication	= legal maneuver, lawsuit
aggression	+ information	= controversy
war	+ information	= lying, misrepresentation
steal	+ information	= identity theft
speed	+ transportation	= racing cars
speed	+ transportation	= railroads

Muckraker Movement

Formed in response to reckless and illegal dealings of business and government, the Muckraker movement gained traction in *January 1903* with a special issue of *McClure's Magazine*.[46] Included were articles by Ida Tarbell, Lincoln Steffans, and Ray Stannard Baker on corrupt practices by Standard Oil, local politicians, and union officials. Editor C. C. McClure defined the common theme of all articles as lawlessness, an explicit observation he made in the opening pages. By the time Theodore Roosevelt officially coined the movement as 'muckraking' in his April 14, 1906 speech, the public's taste for controversial reporting had largely run its course. The movement would continue at lower levels of agitation for several more years.

Reckless Risk Taking

The failure of the Knickerbocker Trust Company in the fall of 1907 triggered the Panic of 1907 which ultimately led to formation of the Federal Reserve System in 1912. See Mars-Ascendant Direction #5

Auto Racing

The newness of automobiles led to a craze in auto racing as a way to test durability and reliability of automobile engineering. Interest in racing culminated with *The Great Auto Race of 1908*. See Mars-Ascendant Direction #5.

Supplement: *John D. Rockefeller ~ Standard Oil*

Saturn/Gemini: November 14, 1910 – April 4, 1917

Saturn	+ Gemini	= ?
control	+ business	= regulation
science	+ business	= scientific management, 'Taylorism'

Business Regulation and Scientific Management

The unbridled risk taking era of the early 1900s came to a screeching halt in the fall of 1910. The philosophy behind government regulation was outlined by former President Theodore Roosevelt in his ***August 27, 1910*** Osawatomie speech. Roosevelt preached a New Nationalism was required to free the government from control of special interests. The New Nationalism

> *...implies far more governmental interference with social and economic conditions than we have yet had, but I think we have got to face the fact that such increase is now necessary...The man who wrongly holds that every human right is secondary to his profit must now give way to the advocate of human welfare, who rightly maintains that every man holds his property subject to the general right of the community to regulate its use to whatever degree the public welfare may require it.* [47]

In short, America had grown tired of the excesses of the robber baron era. As a result, business practices came under increased government scrutiny and regulation. The most cited example of regulation during this era is the Supreme Court's May 15, 1911 order to breakup monopoly practices of Standard Oil. But it was not the first. On ***November 10, 1910***, Boston lawyer Louis Brandeis denied railroads a rate increase because Brandeis claimed that *Scientific Management* would instead allow railroads to cut costs in order to maintain profit margins. With this statement four days before the Distributor changeover to Saturn/Gemini, Brandeis propelled *Scientific Management* promoter Frederick Winslow Taylor to national attention.

End of Muckraker Era

Besides triggering regulation, Saturn/Gemini was also inimical to muckraker efforts which brought many ethical and financial abuses to light. *McClure's Magazine*, most closely associated with leading muckraker journalists, went into bankruptcy during August 1911. Journalist David Graham Phillips, whose reports exposed influence peddling in the Senate, was shot and killed on January 24, 1911. Saturn/Gemini can also be delineated as a journalist's (Gemini) death (Saturn).

Supplement: *Frederick Taylor ~ Principles of Scientific Management*

CHAPTER 6 - DISTRIBUTOR RESULTS: DIRECTING THROUGH THE BOUNDS 125

Mars/Cancer: April 5, 1917 – January 29, 1925

Mars/Cancer is placed in the sign of his fall. Instead of forthright martial actions, Mars/Cancer acts defensively and reacts violently when threatened. All significations of Cancer are defended; they include home, family, women, milk, and nurture. The style of force used by Mars/Cancer to defend itself is brutal and cruel; often unspeakable.

Isolationism

Though historians largely associate American isolationism with the period immediately following World War I, the start of Mars/Cancer as Distributor three days after President Woodrow Wilson's April 2, 1917 war message suggest otherwise. For a President who had just won re-election on the slogan "He kept us out of the war" to reverse course and declare war a few months later must have riled many. I suggest the seeds for America's post-WWI isolationism were sown by Wilson's reversal on WWI.

Ku Klux Klan

In what historians have labeled the Second Ku Klux Klan, the 1915 revival by William J. Simmons at Stone Mountain reached its peak in 1924 with the Indiana Grand Dragon D. C. Stephenson a key figurehead. In the wake of WWI, increased migration of African Americans to cities (some of whom returning from WWI service), increased immigration, and the growing status of Jews and Catholics threatened white middle class culture, largely in Midwestern and Southern states. America's worst period of white racism, lynchings, and race riots occurred under this distribution. More than 20 race riots occurred during the summer of 1919.

Many race riots were instigated on accusations of interracial sex/rape between black men and white women. The most sensational cases of mob violence against black men reveal Mars/Cancer at its most cruel. Prior to lynching, some men were beaten, tortured, castrated, and burned.[48]

Prohibition

Support by the KKK for prohibition is one of those puzzling cases of strange bedfellows until one considers that alcohol represents a threat to Cancerian issues of home, family, women, milk, and nurture. KKK members were one of the strongest supporters of the 18th Amendment passed on December 18, 1917.[49]

Supplement: *D. C. Stephenson ~ Grand Dragon of the Indiana Ku Klux Klan*

Venus/Cancer: January 30, 1925 – January 22, 1932

Venus/Cancer combines Venusian significations of harmony, beauty, food, and romance with the care and comfort of Cancer. Because Cancer's signification of care and comfort also translates to the home; Venus/Cancer also signifies consumer and home products. Other significations include love of the color white, dairy products, and female breasts as a preferred sexual erogenous zone.

Rise of Consumerism

The 1920s are remembered for the rise of consumerism. For an excellent summary of consumerism as a social movement, refer to the research collection made available by the Library of Congress: *Prosperity and Thrift: The Coolidge Era and the Consumer Economy, 1921-1929.*[50]

Mae West - Sex Symbol

Following the October 1929 stock market crash and onset of the Great Depression, Venus/Cancer remained active as a time lord. No longer able to afford consumer goods, Americans turned to the actress Mae West as an alternative outlet for Venus/Cancer themes for the remaining 28 months of the Distribution.

Her voluptuous figure epitomized female breasts as American's preferred sexual erogenous zone. Mae West's signature Broadway role as Diamond Lil first ran between April and September 1928. Mae West garnered such popularity she accepted a film contract with Paramount Pictures in *October 1932* nine months after the end of the Distribution.[51]

Elsie the Cow

As significator of dairy products, the Distribution of Venus/Cancer may be related to the birth of the dairy industry's advertising icon Elsie the Cow in *1932* (no exact date given).[52]

Supplement: *Mae West ~ Diamond Lil as Female Sex Icon*

CHAPTER 6 - DISTRIBUTOR RESULTS: DIRECTING THROUGH THE BOUNDS   127

Mercury/Cancer: January 23, 1932 – April 3, 1939

Mercury in the cardinal water sign Cancer is noted for sensitivity to the immediate environment because the Moon rules Cancer and the Moon governs instinct and sensory perception. Though Mercury is not technically in detriment, his manifestation as fleeting sensitivity underlies problems faced by Mercury in all water signs where the facts Mercury tries to communicate can be clouded or dissolved by the water element.

Because Cancer is ruled by the Moon - a common significator for the public in mundane astrology - Mercury/Cancer has an affinity for both reading and swaying the public's mood. As a communications medium, radio works particularly well for Mercury/Cancer because the lack of direct imagery allows the radio broadcast greater influence over the brain's information processing.

Popularity of Radio - War of the Worlds

Commercial radio broadcasts began in 1920 and by 1928 the United States had two working national radio networks owned by NBC and CBS. Radio was wildly popular during the 1930s, occupying a unique sweet spot on the evolutionary path of media between newsprint and television. The dominance of radio in the 1930s matches the influence of Mercury/Cancer as Distributor for the period. By 1939, the majority of American households owned a radio. The ability of radio to exert a sensational impact on listeners was epitomized by public panic after broadcast of H. G. Wells' *War of the Worlds* on **October 30, 1938**.

The success of Franklin Roosevelt's first Fireside Chat on March 12, 1933 and the popularity of Charles Coughlin's radio broadcasts (first FDR's ally, later his nemesis), exemplifies the importance of radio's impact on politics during the 1930s.

Political Demagogues: Huey Long and Charles Coughlin

Named one of the most dangerous men in America by President Franklin Roosevelt, Huey Long and his *Share the Wealth* program was a populist political movement which threatened success of FDR's New Deal program. The Catholic priest Charles Coughlin also rose to popularity through radio and was one of the era's most notorious demagogues.

Supplement: *Charles Coughlin ~ Radio Demagogue*

Jupiter/Cancer: April 4, 1939 – November 8, 1947

Jupiter	+ Cancer	= ?
wealth	+ consumers	= consumer banking
growth	+ nourishment	= farming
philanthropy	+ consumers	= food stamps

Henry Wallace and American Farm Policy

As Secretary of Agriculture, Henry Wallace inherited a farm economy with surplus production and low product prices. One step taken to combat low prices was creation of the nation's first Food Stamp Program which operated from *May 16, 1939* to early 1943. The program was designed to transfer surplus agricultural goods to the neediest citizens. As to the precision of the changeover, consider that a non-partisan group of Mid-Western Senators met on *April 1, 1939* in an effort to create a unified national farm program with Wallace taking a leading role.[53] In addition, the NYT published a special report by Henry Wallace on *April 2, 1939* explaining problems in the farming sector, existing programs such as the Agricultural Adjustment Act of 1938, and future plans including the Food Stamp Program.[54] Wallace's popularity peaked with his acceptance of nominee for President by the Progressive Citizens of America party on *December 2, 1947* as the Distribution ended.[55]

Consumer Banking

Consumer banking took a step forward with the recognition that surplus funds in the banking system could be loaned to consumers. This was the opinion of John Paddi of Manufacturers Trust Company of New York in a *June 6, 1939* speech made to the American Institute of Banking.[56] Paddi and others spoke again on *June 24-25, 1939* on consumer credit at the first conference of the Bankers Association for Consumer Credit, recently organized on *June 5, 1939*.[57]

Credit Unions

In 1934, President Roosevelt signed the Federal Credit Union Act into law authorizing formation of federally chartered credit unions in all states. The purpose of the federal law was to make credit available and promote thrift through a national system of nonprofit, cooperative credit unions. Credit Union membership grew steadily during the 1940s. The initial assignment of the Farm Credit Administration as lead oversight agency for the Federal Credit Union Act demonstrates the significations of Jupiter/Cancer as consumer banking and farming combined in a single organizational structure.

<u>Supplement</u>: *Henry A. Wallace ~ Secretary of Agriculture*

Saturn/Cancer: November 9, 1947 – November 4, 1952

Saturn	+ Cancer	= ?
control	+ people	= homeland security
polarization	+ people	= witch-hunt

In the sign of his detriment, Saturn in Cancer acts as a polarizing influence between Saturn's need for structure/control and Cancer's sphere of nurture/mother/home. For an individual, Saturn/Cancer produces effects ranging from the denial of comfort/nurture to an overbearing attempt to provide comfort/nurture through harsh measures. At the mundane level, the polarizing effect of Saturn/Cancer against the Moon-signified populace yields a witch-hunt mentality.

Hollywood Blacklist

Following WWII, the onset of the Cold War brought with it a new enemy in the form of Russian Communism. Many liberals, including Hollywood figures, had joined the American Communist Party in earlier years when Russia was still considered an ally against the fascism of Hitler. America's friendship with Russia changed abruptly after WWII and the status of Americans who sympathized with the Communist Party changed accordingly. This reversal of attitude towards the Communist Party was epitomized by the House Committee on Un-American Activities (HUAC). The onset of Saturn/Cancer as Distributor coincides with HUAC's investigation and censure of Hollywood figures, arguably the kickoff event for McCarthyism.

23-Oct-1947. Ronald Reagan testified before HUAC (one of many).
17-Nov-1947. Screen Actors Guild voted to make officers swear to non-Communist pledge.
24-Nov-1947. HUAC voted citations against ten Hollywood figures for contempt of Congress; thereafter known as the 'Hollywood Ten.'

McCarthyism

Wisconsin Republican Senator Joseph McCarthy rose to political attention on February 9, 1950 in his Lincoln Day speech were he cited a list of 205 known individuals who worked in the State Department he believed were members of the Communist Party. His initial investigations were conducted by the Tydings subcommittee under the auspices of the Senate Foreign Relations Committee. McCarthy's prominence lasted into 1953 and did not suffer a fall from grace until the start of his Army hearings in the fall of 1953. His political career ended with censure by the Senate on December 2, 1954.

Supplement: *Joseph McCarthy – Communist Witch Hunt*

Jupiter/Leo: November 5, 1952 to May 26, 1960

Jupiter	+ Leo	= ?
religion	+ King	= King's religion

Christianity as a Bulwark against Communism

Jupiter/Leo as the significator of unification of church and state has its origins in Constantine the Great (b. 27-Feb-272) who established Christianity as Rome's officially sanctioned religion. More recently, Southern Baptist minister and former Arkansas Governor Mike Huckabee (b. 24-Aug-1955) aligned his 2008 Presidential bid with Christian conservatives seeking the increased stamp of Christianity on American government. Both Constantine and Huckabee have Jupiter/Leo placements in their natal charts.

If Saturn/Cancer generated the McCarthy witch-hunts in reaction to fear against Communist infiltration, then Jupiter/Leo allowed Americans to raise the bulwark of Christianity as a defense against 'Godless Communists'. Think of Jupiter/Leo and Saturn/Cancer as the respective 'carrot' and 'stick' anti-communist strategies practiced during the Cold War.

Religious personalities including Reinhold Niebuhr, Fulton J. Sheen, Billy Graham, and Norman Vincent Peale were the leaders of this era which saw church membership grow from 64.5 to 114.6 million between 1940 and 1960.[58] At the national level, the phrase *under God* was added to the Pledge of Allegiance with President Eisenhower's approval on June 14, 1954. As to the accuracy of the changeover, consider the Knights of Columbus, a Catholic fraternal service organization, adopted resolutions that *under God* be recited in the Pledge of Allegiance by their members on meetings held **August 21, 1952** and **September 24, 1952**. Subsequently the Knights called for this change to be made at the national level.[59] Separately the national motto *In God We Trust* was made official in 1956 and appeared on paper currency on October 1, 1957.

Religion and Scouting

The same trends which favored growth of church membership in the 1950s also swelled the ranks of the Boy Scouts and Girl Scouts. Though nondenominational, the Boy Scouts discriminate against atheism in their Scout Law whose 12th point calls for reverence to God. Founded in 1910, the Boy Scouts of America added religious awards in 1948 which became a popular program in the 1950s. Embracement of God and Country awards and other concepts including honor, loyalty, and reverence made the Scouts an ideal foil against 'Godless Communists' during the Cold War era.[60]

Supplement: *Fulton Sheen ~ Life is Worth Living*

CHAPTER 6 - DISTRIBUTOR RESULTS: DIRECTING THROUGH THE BOUNDS   131

Venus/Leo: May 27, 1960 – September 27, 1966

Venus	+ Leo	= ?
adornment	+ France	= French fashion
food	+ France	= French cooking
money	+ yellow	= gold
pleasure	+ flamboyant	= cocktail culture
music	+ flashy	= pop music
love	+ Kings	= Camelot

The Kennedy *Camelot* Era

Among females, no single individual better personified the era than Jackie Kennedy with her love of French culture, fashion, and cooking. For this reason, nomination of her husband John F. Kennedy as Democratic Presidential candidate on ***July 13, 1960*** is a logical kickoff for the Venus/Leo Distribution. Reaching beyond the fare of White House state dinners, the popularity of French cooking powered the launch of Julia Child's 1961 *Mastering the Art of French Cooking* and her television show *The French Chef* (1963) which continued well after Kennedy's 1963 assassination.

Cocktail Culture, Frank Sinatra, and the Rat Pack

The early 1960s male embodiment of Venus/Leo lubricated himself with cocktails, preferably martinis, and in the case of the first James Bond film *Goldfinger* – 'shaken not stirred.' For males, Venus/Leo signifies a flamboyant partier exemplified by the carefree antics of Frank Sinatra's Rat Pack in their first hit film *Ocean's Eleven* which made its debut on ***August 10, 1960***. President John F. Kennedy's acceptance of the Rat Pack style, including a relatively brief association with Frank Sinatra as cohort, filled out the spirit of Venus/Leo in America's first family.

Pop Music and the Beatles

Though Kennedy's assassination ended the Camelot era, the Distribution of Venus/Leo was far from over. As if on cue, the first television story on *Beatlemania* appeared on CBS Morning News on November 22, 1963 (day of the Kennedy assassination) and paved the way for the Beatles' February 7, 1964 American television debut on the Ed Sullivan show. Beyond the Beatles, pop music was used as a prop for many other performances with a Venus/Leo theme. Consider the December 22, 1964 premiere of *Goldfinger* was the first Bond film to feature the theme song performed by a pop music artist. The film's title song was performed by the British vocalist Shirley Bassey.

<u>Supplement:</u> *Frank Sinatra ~ The Rat Pack*

Saturn/Leo: September 28, 1966 – August 21, 1975

Saturn	+ Leo	= ?
destruction	+ celebrity	= fall of celebrity culture
black	+ king	= Black Power movement
black	+ lion	= Black Panther movement

Black Panther Party

Though the term *Black Power* was used as early as 1954 by author Richard Wright, it is Stokely Carmichael's use of *Black Power* in a political context on **June 16, 1966** during the James Meredith-inspired *March Against Fear* which is relevant to Saturn/Leo as Distributor. Official creation of the Black Panther Party on **October 15, 1966** by Huey P. Newton and Bobby Seale accurately timed the changeover. The Panthers were the most well-known counter-culture group during the Saturn/Leo Distribution.

Compared to Thomas Jefferson's laundry list of nineteen complaints against King George III which I suggest is the best list of Saturn/Leo abuses of political power ever compiled[61], The Black Panther Party's Ten Point Program shares common ground with Jefferson for its demands for an end to police brutality, an end of wars of aggression, freedom for the imprisoned, and impartial jury trials.

Transition from Venus/Leo to Saturn/Leo

According to Abū Ma'shar, Distributor changeovers from benefics to malefics are difficult. With Saturn/Leo in detriment, this changeover was quite bad. The April 8, 1966 *Time* magazine cover "Is God Dead?" was one symbol of the approaching nihilism which would overtake the go-go spirit of the early 1960s. Another was Frank Sinatra's marriage to Mia Farrow on July 19, 1966 which ushered in one of his most difficult life episodes. Sinatra separated from Farrow after she refused to abandon her 1967 filming schedule for *Rosemary's Baby* whose plot featured birth of a devil child on June 6, 1966. Joseph Lanza details the allusions to cocktail culture in the film (one of the most salient aspects of the prior Venus/Leo period) and concluded *Rosemary's Baby* signified the 'end-of-the-sixties millennia' event.[62]

One can also argue that creation of Timothy Leary's *League for Spiritual Discovery* on **September 19, 1966** marked the culmination of the early 1960s go-go era. The U.S. government's classification of LSD as an illegal substance on **October 6, 1966** was another event which marked the changeover to from the hard partying Venus/Leo era to the dictatorial style of Saturn/Leo.

Supplement: *Robert F. Williams ~ Negroes with Guns*

CHAPTER 6 - DISTRIBUTOR RESULTS: DIRECTING THROUGH THE BOUNDS

Mercury/Leo: August 22, 1975 – April 8, 1983

Mercury	+ Leo	= ?
reason	+ splendor	= optimistic spirit
writing	+ dramatic	= blockbuster entertainment

Rocky and the Blockbuster Film Era

Though most Americans associate the late 1970s with the economic gloom of stagflation and the U.S. Embassy hostage crisis in the wake of the Iranian Revolution, American society never devolved into widespread civil disorder which necessitated a government-imposed state of emergency. True, crime did increase in line with the 'Misery Index' – the sum of inflation and unemployment rates, but the country survived without anarchy.

Arguably, Mercury/Leo as Distributor explains how Americans were able to get through the late 1970s without unbearable angst. Mercury signifies communications and all things written; placed in Leo ruled by the life-giving Sun yields an optimistic spirit declared in an unabashed flamboyant manner. By far, Sylvester Stallone's portrayal of Rocky Balboa defined the era's optimistic spirit as an underdog who exceeded expectations against all odds. Stallone wrote the film script during the summer of 1975 as the Mercury/Leo Distribution started; *Rocky* was released on November 21, 1976.

Rocky was one of many Hollywood blockbuster films which defined the Mercury/Leo Distribution. Released ***June 20, 1975***, *Jaws* was the first film to exceed $100 million in theatre sales. With *Jaws*, MCA, Inc. President and CEO Sidney Sheinberg changed standard industry practices by instituting a simultaneous release across hundreds of screens. *Jaws* was also accompanied by a nation-wide marketing campaign. The success of Jaws made the 'wide release' style of marketing standard protocol for Hollywood film production and marketing.

Chronology of Blockbuster films (US Release dates)

20-June-1975	*Jaws*
21-Nov-1976	*Rocky*
25-May-1977	*Star Wars*
15-June-1979	*Rocky II*
21-May-1980	*The Empire Strikes Back*
12-June-1981	*Raiders of the Lost Arc*
28-May-1982	*Rocky III*
25-May-1983	*Return of the Jedi*

<u>Supplement</u>: *Sylvester Stallone ~ Rocky Balboa*

Mars/Leo: April 9, 1983 – November 18, 1990

Mars	+ Leo	= ?
action	+ fame	= action hero
fighting	+ fire	= firemen, rescue workers
fighting	+ King	= rebels
fighting	+ honor	= defense of honor

Action Heroes and Military Revival

Though Sylvester Stallone continued to reprise the character of Rocky Balboa in the 1980s, during this period Stallone was better known for his portrayal of the character John J. Rambo.

22-Oct-1982	*First Blood.*
22-May-1985	*First Blood. Part II.*
25-May-1988	*Rambo III.*

Rambo is a heroic figure who defends the honor of American POWs by staging a successful hostage rescue as a rebellious act in defiance of a disinterested government. The character Rambo embodies all major themes of the Mars/Leo profile.

Other POW rescue films made during this period:

16-Dec-1983	*Uncommon Valor*
16-Nov-1984	*Missing in Action*
2-Mar-1985	*Missing in Action II*
22-Jan-1988	*Braddock: Missing in Action III*

Susan Jeffords makes the case that male action figures like Sylvester Stallone (*First Blood*) and Chuck Norris (*Missing in Action*) functioned to revitalize the nation's sense of masculinity.[63] Jeffords develops the theme that the 1980s genre of action films reflected favorably on President Ronald Reagan's efforts to help Americans restore confidence following Vietnam and the weakness of the Carter era. Reagan's **October 25, 1983** invasion of Grenada, named Operation Urgent Fury, paralleled the heroics of action heroes on the screen. Grenada was the first military operation launched since the Vietnam War. Though small in scope, the operation's success provided a boost to military morale.

Supplement: *Mr. T. ~ the A-Team*

CHAPTER 6 - DISTRIBUTOR RESULTS: DIRECTING THROUGH THE BOUNDS   135

Mercury/Virgo: November 19, 1990 – September 23, 1999

Mercury	+ Virgo	= ?
information	+ detail	= information stored on computer chip
information	+ business	= business software programs

Microsoft, Windows, and the World Wide Web

Compared to Mercury/Gemini which organizes information in bits and bytes, the sign Virgo's penchant for detail makes Mercury/Virgo gather and store information in a hierarchical manner. Besides *detail*, the sign Virgo is also associated with *small*. Transferring this analogy to the technology world makes Mercury/Virgo the logical significator for computer chips whose increased storage capacity developed during the 1990s was a large factor behind the rise of the PC-Internet world. The word 'Micro' in the name 'Microsoft' is another hint Microsoft's products are a key to unlocking the events of the Mercury/Virgo Distributor because 'Micro' = 'small'.

As to the precision of the changeover, consider on *November 12, 1990* at the Comdex/Fall trade show, Bill Gates promoted the concept of 'instantly accessible data' as a new way to use computers.[64] This is a delineation match to the hierarchical data structure consistent with Mercury/Virgo's orientation to detail.

Microsoft Chronology

22-May-1990	Microsoft launched Windows 3.0.
6-Aug-1991	Debut of World Wide Web (Tim Berners-Lee).
24-Aug-1995	Microsoft launched Windows 95 and MSN.
18-May-1998	FTC antitrust suit launched.
25-Jun-1998	Launch of Windows 98, criticized for unreliability.
19-Oct-1998	Antitrust trial began.
24-Mar-1999	Bill Gates published Business @ the Speed of Thought.
5-Nov-1999	Microsoft is ruled a monopoly by the FTC.

Note Microsoft's anti-monopoly FTC ruling did not occur until after the Mercury/Virgo Distribution had finished.

Supplement: *Bill Gates ~ Microsoft, Windows, and the World Wide Web*

Venus/Virgo: September 24, 1999 – April 22, 2012

Venus in the sign of her fall means Venus-signified objects and actions like food, clothing, adornment, love, and financial matters are compromised. Instead of women with attractive clothing and adornment, Venus/Virgo signifies homely women who are drastically in need of a makeover. Instead of lawful investments, Venus/Virgo turns to gambling and illicit financial activities common to mafia and other criminal organizations.

Martha Stewart Living and the Makeover Craze

For women in need of a makeover, Martha Stewart provided a total solution for the Venusian realms of clothing, adornment, food, and decoration. The initial public offering of Martha Stewart Living Omnimedia on **October 19, 1999** is the logical kickoff for the Venus/Virgo Distribution. Stewart's 2004 conviction on insider trading charges demonstrates illicit financial activities also common to Venus/Virgo. Note that just a month after Stewart's June 4, 2003 indictment the makeover show *Queer Eye for the Straight Guy* was launched on July 15, 2003. This demonstrates the steady influence of Venus/Virgo as Distributor despite the fall of her most prominent icon.

15-Jul-2003 – 30-Oct-2007	*Queer Eye for the Straight Guy*
18-Jan-2003 – present	*What Not to Wear*
4-Mar-2004 – 24-May-2007	*Pimp My Ride*
2003-2005	*Ambush Makeover*
22-Apr-2002 – present	*MADE*
2002 – 15-May-2007	*Extreme Makeover*
15-Feb-2004 – present	*Extreme Makeover: Home Edition*

The Sopranos

Originally broadcast from January 10, 1999 to June 10, 2007, the HBO cable television series *The Sopranos* was the most successful cable television series in American history. *Vanity Fair* named it the 'greatest pop-culture masterpiece of its day.'[65] *The Sopranos'* portrayals of mafia activities are consistent with Distributor Venus/Virgo.

Gambling – the Poker Craze

The poker game *Texas Hold'em* first reached the nation's consciousness with the September 11, 1998 release of the film *Rounders*. The unexpected victory of Chris Moneymaker in ESPN's 2003 World Series of Poker further added to the popularity of *Texas Hold'em* as a national craze.

<u>Supplement</u>: *Martha Stewart ~ Makeovers and Insider Trading*

CHAPTER 6 - DISTRIBUTOR RESULTS: DIRECTING THROUGH THE BOUNDS   137

Jupiter/Virgo: April 23, 2012 – April 27, 2017

Jupiter	+ Virgo	= ?
heat/moisture	+ grains	= beer
large	+ business metrics	= "big data"
expansion	+ health	= Obamacare

Craft Beer Popularity

Two months after the start of the Jupiter/Virgo distribution, Anheuser-Busch InBev announced its bid to buy Grupo Modelo, maker of Corona Beer, on *June 29, 2012*.[66] While this specific merger was later blocked, it did ignite a wave of investor interest in the beer industry. From 1988 to 2011, Global Beer Trekking reports an annual average of 1.6 brewery-to-brewery mergers and acquisitions in the US craft beer industry. With the changeover of distributor to Jupiter/Virgo, the average number of corporate transactions jumped to 18 between 2012/2017 with 2015 the peak year of 22 deals. After 2017, annual deals fell below 10.[67] Googletrends search results for 'craft beer' show similar findings, peaking in *May 2015*. As of this writing (March 2021), reported interest in craft beer has fallen over 50% to 39.[68] Similar metrics include the price of hops which peaked in *2016*[69] and the annual growth rate of barrels brewed which peaked at 42% in *2014* before falling to between 0-3% in the years *2016-2018*.[70] On *May 3, 2017*, Anheuser-Busch InBev announced its purchase of *Wicked Weed*, its 10th and final purchase for its craft beer portfolio six days after the end of the distribution.

Google and Big Data

"Big Data" refers to any large collection of business information whose granularity limits its usefulness when considered on a standalone basis. Only when granular data is collected on a large scale are insights for decision making possible. Googletrends search results for 'big data' peaked *October 2014* during this distribution.

Obamacare

Effective March 23, 2010, the Affordable Care Act, a.k.a. Obamacare, was reaffirmed by the *June 28, 2012* Supreme Court decision which upheld the constitutionality of the individual mandate. For the years *2013-2017*, CSR cost sharing subsidies were paid to insurance companies. On *October 12, 2017*, the Trump administration ended CSR subsidy payments 6 months after the Ascendant Distributor changed from Jupiter/Virgo to Mars/Virgo.

Supplement: *Google Initial Public Offering*

Mars/Virgo: April 28, 2017 – January 30, 2026

Mars	+ Virgo	= ?
Action	+ data	= fitness trackers
Action	+ health	= fitness training
Cutting	+ earth	= natural resource extraction
Fighting	+ ground	= army
Fire	+ earth	= land mines

Wearable Fitness Trackers

Six weeks after the start of the Mars/Virgo distribution on *June 8, 2017*, Apple hired Dr. Sumbul Desai, the executive director of Stanford Medicine's Center for Digital Health, to be Apple's VP of health.[71] This followed Apple's creation of its in-house fitness lab in 2015 and preceded Apple's launch of its Watch Series 6 on *September 14, 2020* with fitness tracking capabilities.[72]

Fitness Training

As the US fitness industry is dominated by disbursed private business interests with few large corporate publicly traded investment vehicles, finding a fitness industry metric which can be easily tracked and linked to the Mars/Virgo Distributor is difficult. An exception can be found in fitness equipment distributed nationally through gym purchases and direct sales to individuals. One example is Peloton which launched its Initial Public Offering on *September 26, 2019* with Mars/Virgo placed in its own bound (25VI07). Peloton produces stationary bikes with added video/sound equipment to allow owners to participate in group rides while staying at home. From its IPO price of $29, Peloton stock reached $166.10 on January 14, 2021, making it one of the most popular pandemic stocks tracked by Wall Street during 2020.

Natural Resource Extraction

On *August 17, 2020*, the Trump administration announced plans for an oil and gas leasing program in the Artic National Wildlife Refuge.[73] Leases were auctioned on *January 6, 2021*. Oil drilling in the ANWF has been a high-profile issue of national controversy ever since the Trans-Alaska Pipeline System was completed in the late 1970s.

Supplement: *Peloton Initial Public Offering*

CHAPTER SEVEN

Partner Results: Ascendant Directions

What follows is the complete set of planet-Ascendant directions computed for the Regulus USA National Horoscope. There is no cherry picking. Every direction is presented for the Ascendant as significator.

Summary

The Limits of Traditional Aphorisms in Mundane Rectification. Surviving mundane aphorisms for ingresses can be adapted for interpreting National Horoscopes. Though a good place to start, these rules are rarely comprehensive. A reversion to delineation methods used in natal astrology is recommended to fill out a complete delineation.

Rectification Expectations by Planetary Condition. Beginning with the zodiacal state of Mercury, which as significator of communications has some bearing on the accuracy of the recorded birth time itself, each planet needs investigation prior to rectification. At issue is whether a planet's condition can impede or aid the rectification. Planets which are malefic, angular, or fall in cardinal signs produce effects which are more readily identifiable when researching a figure. Planets which are combust or fall in the 12th prove more complicated when attempting to match events to direction timing.

Impact of Distributors. In *Abū Ma'shar's System of Distributors and Partners*, the Distributor contributes approximately 50% of the nature of the event timed by the Partner's direction. The Distributor's effect should be considered prior to examining event matches to Partner directions.

Scope and Limits of Ascendant Directions. In a departure from most traditional authors, the position of promissors and significators can be reversed when computing directions. These permutations dramatically increase the number of possible directions. Though this step was not taken, the existence of a large number of unidentified directions means some events may be incorrectly attributed to directions by this study.

The Limits of Traditional Aphorisms in Mundane Rectification

How does a traditional astrologer approach rectification of planets in a mundane figure? Because delineation precedes prediction, any successful rectification requires delineation of each planet and house before proceeding. To do this, one of the first tools available to traditional astrologers are mundane aphorisms left for delineating ingresses. For literature prior to 1600, the two most complete sets of mundane aphorisms (available in English translations as of January 2008) are by Abū Ma'shar[1] and Bonatti[2].

Taking Saturn/Libra as an example, we can pretend the Regulus USA National Horoscope is actually an ingress figure and reference Bonatti:

Abū Ma'shar said if Saturn were in Libra, and his latitude were northern, it signifies the heat of the air and its dryness; and it signifies few rains in that revolution, and the wasting of waters. And if his latitude were southern, it signifies the goodness of the air, and its sweetness; nor will there be harmful winds.

And if he were oriental, it signifies the desire of shameful, criminal men. But if he were occidental it signifies infamy is going to fall upon fornicators, and those abusing shameful sexual intercourse.

If however he were retrograde, it signifies the infirmities of male and female slaves, and of low-class people. And if he were direct, it signifies the middling quality of supplies, and particularly of barley.

And Abū Ma'shar said it signifies the rupturing of the census upon the king.[3]

The first step in applying this aphorism is to cut out irrelevant sections based on Saturn's actual condition. Saturn's latitude is northern, motion is direct, and position relative to the Sun is occidental. Those conditions eliminate roughly half of Bonatti's statements.

<u>Weather</u>. Many surviving mundane aphorisms detail weather conditions. For Saturn/Libra with northern latitude, Bonatti indicates weather which is hot and dry, few rains, and wastes water, presumably from excess evaporation. Given Saturn rules the Moon/Aquarius/3rd whose significations include waterworks, irrigation systems, and canals; a reasonable delineation is open water irrigation systems will face reduced capacity from excess water evaporation. The type of canals which connect the Colorado River to California agricultural districts come to mind, but this is an issue which did not surface when researching actual Saturn-Ascendant directions. But it is a legitimate delineation and speaks to the difficulty of maintaining a sustainable

human population in the western United States. Migration to the arid west was facilitated by the 1862 Homestead Act. Dams and irrigation systems created largely under Franklin Roosevelt's New Deal programs helped to sustain human settlements in the west. Environmentalists have questioned the long-term sustainability of western population settlements given the increasing artificial nature of water management programs.[4] Abū Ma'shar would agree.

Bonatti's aphorisms draw extensively from Abū Ma'shar whose translations sometimes yield different results. Returning to a direct translation of Abū Ma'shar's original text, he says Saturn in Libra with northerly latitude yields blowing and raging winds.[5] The significance of this weather condition to the destiny of America appears questionable until one discovers the solar arc direction of Saturn conjunct Ascendant computed for August 15, 1851 timed America's victory at a sailing race later known as America's Cup, the most prestigious sailing race in the world. Needless to say, frequent blowing winds are a highly useful condition for winning sailing races. Note also Mars/Gemini signifies speed and forms a trine to Saturn. The aspect between Mars and Saturn means Mars assists Saturn with high speed. Mars also rules the 5th house of recreational sports.

Infamous sex scandals. Saturn/Libra is occidental; Bonatti says this condition results in shameful sexual behavior and infamy from sex scandals. Drawing from natal aphorisms which state an elevated Saturn square Venus signifies a 'shameful handler of women,'[6] there is additional testimony for Bonatti's aphorism. True to form, Saturn-Ascendant Direction #2 culminated with Alexander Hamilton's resignation, due in part because his scandalous affair with Maria Reynolds was being circulated among Washington power circles. Though a comprehensive review of sex scandals involving Treasury Secretaries and other heads of post-WWII supranational organizations was not made for this study, recent scandals involving World Bank President Paul Wolfowitz[7] and International Monetary Fund Managing Director Dominique Strauss-Kahn[8] suggest the continuing relevance of this delineation.

Other. Saturn in direct motion signifies a middling of supplies, especially of barley. I don't know what to make of this aphorism nor Bonatti's last comment that Saturn/Libra signifies the rupturing of the census upon the King. Discarding these two last aphorisms means that Bonatti has provided us with two mundane aphorisms for Saturn/Libra which were confirmed by actual directions of Saturn to the Ascendant. As for the last two, either I don't understand their relevance ("rupturing of the census upon the King?") or I can't see a legitimate way to test their accuracy (e.g., data for "middling of supplies, especially of barley?").

Reversion to natal methods. In general, delineation rules for natal astrology are more comprehensive than for mundane astrology. After considering mundane aphorisms first, the next logical step is to apply natal rules for mundane horoscopes. Here follows the basic steps of the author's natal delineation process adapted to delineation of National Horoscopes:

- Analyze a planet's essential dignities, emphasizing sign, bound, and dwad.

- Determine how a planet is modified by its sect, position relative to the Sun, by aspects from other planets, and from other special configurations with planets (e.g., antiscia, application/separation, etc.)

- Follow the energy flow through the figure by identifying sign rulers as the source and cause of events signified by planets they rule. Consider also the Moon's separation and application as a measure of energy flow.

- Specify planetary effects to country affairs through house positions. Consider a planet's position and rulership by whole signs as a first order condition. Consider a planet's rulership of a quadrant-style house cusp provides supplementary testimony to affairs of that house.

Rectification Expectations by Planetary Condition

Mercury as astrology. As significator of astrology, Mercury is the first planet that requires scrutiny. Because Mercury signifies communications and all things written, an afflicted Mercury at birth interferes with proper recording of the birth time and makes the rectification exercise more challenging for astrologers.

Implication. In the Preface I examined the zodiacal state of Mercury in the Regulus USA National Horoscope and concluded Mercury functions as an accidental malefic. When one considers that there remains significant debate on the USA birth time some 232 years after the Declaration of Independence, I suggest that as astrologers we look no further than the weakness of Mercury itself as the cause of the current dispute over the 'correct' USA National Horoscope. Moreover, the justification of various birth times by American astrologers based on a fleeting, emotional, and rash argumentative style of communication – personally witnessed by the author on numerous occasions – conforms to some of Mercury's worst effects including demagoguery, propaganda, and faulty intelligence. As a first order condition, Mercury's weakness makes the rectification job a challenging exercise.

Planets which are difficult to test. When conducting rectification projects, some planets are easier to research than others. Effects of planets are often hidden when combust or placed in the 12th house. Planets meeting this condition are more likely to pose problems when attempting rectification because they generate events which are hard to fathom (when delineating) and hard to uncover (when researching actual events).

Implication. Venus/Jupiter/Mercury//Cancer/8th. With Jupiter combust and both Venus & Mercury under the sunbeams, these three planets should prove more difficult to successfully delineate and match to actual events. Compared to initial expectations, I expect surprises for these planets.

<u>Planets which are easy to test</u>. If hidden planets are difficult to judge, then the opposite conclusion should be reached for angular planets whose effects are more overt. In addition, malefic planets – no matter what house position – reliably generate effects which are memorable and long-lasting. Finally, planets in cardinal signs are generally easier to study because their indefatigable nature produces multiple effects which are more easily observed because of their quantity.

Implication: Mars/Gemini/7th and Saturn/Libra/10th. Both malefics on the angles should produce effects which are evident and easy to track. This is one reason why I chose to focus on Civil War events to time directions of Mars to the Ascendant in Chapter 2.

Implication: Moon/Aquarius/3rd. Moon in her 3rd house of joy should yield many events relatively easy to uncover and study. Placement in Aquarius facilitates research on Moon directions because Aquarius in the fixed air sign likes to hoard information. Placed in the 3rd house of communications which for a mundane figure include the press, ample news of Moon-Aquarius timed events should be available for study.

Implication: Sun/Cancer/8th. According to guidelines just presented the feminine Sun in a cardinal sign and succedent house is in mixed condition. Sun's rulership of the 4th house end-of-the-matter means some records of the Sun's events should be left behind for future reference.

Impact of Distributors

Presenting results of Ascendant Distributors before Partners is a deliberate choice I made in structuring this book. As it will become evident when studying Partners, the nature of the event predicted by each direction requires delineating the Distributor for a full account of the event. To repeat a point made in Chapter 4, the Distributor as a time lord sets the stage for a play whose plot lines are acted out by Partners who take the spotlight. In my opinion, it appears that fully 50% of the quality of the event predicted depends on the stage set by the Distributor. This is exactly the kind of results we should expect if Abū Ma'shar's model is correct. Wherever possible, each direction includes comments which demonstrate the impact of the Distributor. In some cases, I was not able to make this connection.

Chapter 6 presented analysis of Distributors computed by direct motion. Though I did not complete a study of Distributors computed by converse motion, the ability of the bound of Mars/Cancer to time the O. J. Simpson trial verdict by converse motion (presented as Chapter 5, example 4) gives credence to a second set of converse Distributors operating in tandem with direct Distributors. Without a detailed study of converse Distributors, discussion of Distributors for converse participating directions is more limited in scope for Chapters 8-15.

Scope and Limits of Participating Ascendant Directions

As a first step in tackling the Regulus USA National Horoscope, Ascendant directions are considered because the Ascendant is universally recognized as the focus of the entire horoscope. In meeting my stated goal of justifying the rectification, I consider a catalog of 200+ events which match the delineation of Distributors and Partners sufficient evidence to support the rectification.

Though the following chapters present a complete discussion of all Planet-Ascendant primary directions computed by oblique ascension, this set of directions does not exhaust all possible permutations of Ascendant directions. In what follows, planets and their aspects are assigned the role of promissor; the Ascendant, significator. This means when the celestial sphere moves, the Ascendant is held fixed and planets and their aspects are moved until they meet the Ascendant. This is the purist form of Ascendant primary directions adhered to by most traditional authors.

Some authors since 1600 have suggested allowing the promissor – significator relationship to be reversed; in effect, allowing significators like the Ascendant to be moved with the celestial sphere as planets are held fixed. Taking this approach significantly expands the number of Participating directions. Why? Because when planets are held fixed, the mathematics of primary directions require use of interplanetary directions[9]. Considering interplanetary directions computed by methods of Ptolemy, Placidus under the Pole, and Regiomontanus – together with their latitude permutations – there are easily another 300 Ascendant directions to consider. And taking a step beyond Ascendant directions to include directions of the Midheaven, Sun, Moon, and Lot of Fortune; in all there are realistically 2,000+ primary directions which can be computed for the Regulus USA National Horoscope.

What this means is the following catalog of Ascendant directions represents approximately 10% of the primary directions available for study.

CHAPTER 7 - PARTICIPATOR RESULTS: ASCENDANT DIRECTIONS   145

The chance that a cited event in support of a given direction may be incorrectly assigned to the direction is an important limitation of the sample. An event may be more accurately attributed to some other primary direction, solar arc direction, or other predictive technique such as Firdaria, profections, or secondary progressions. Attribution becomes more debatable the more distant an event moves from the proximity of the computed direction by date and time. In all likelihood, further investigation will require reclassification of some of the events matches presented here. Still, I believe there are a sufficient number of event-direction matches support the accuracy of the rectification. Not to mention the results of Directing through Bounds presented in Chapter 6, for which the precision of Distributor changeovers demonstrates compelling evidence for the rectification.

Human Agents as Partners

In discussing the connection between JFK Jr. and the Sibly chart which elevated JFK Jr.'s death to that of a national tragedy (Chapter 2, pp. 13-14), I stated the validity of mundane astrology is demonstrated by connections made between mundane horoscopes and natal horoscopes for individuals who act out mundane planetary configurations. Taken to the extreme, this relationship between natal and mundane horoscopes suggests for every direction in a mundane horoscope, a similar direction (or other predictive technique) should be active for natal horoscopes of individuals involved in mundane affairs. This complex analytical step was taken for Distributors identified in Chapter 6 and presented in Appendix C.

For results of Partners presented in Chapters 8-15, a slightly different variation of the Mundane-Natal Horoscope Connection was uncovered. Table 7 lists individuals who are born or die when a planet in the Regulus USA National Horoscope is directed to the Ascendant. The connection between directions in the National Horoscope and the following

Table 7. Birth or Death of Individuals timed by Participating Directions

Individual	Event	Direction
Kit Carson	Birth	Moon-Ascendant #2
Jeremiah Evarts	Death	Moon-Ascendant #3
Shirley Chisholm	Birth	Moon-Ascendant #8
Robert Peary	Birth	Sun-Ascendant #4
Lydia Lord Davis	Birth	Sun-Ascendant #5
Hudson Taylor	Death	Sun-Ascendant #7
John McLoughlin	Death	Mars-Ascendant #4
Princess Hohenlohe	Birth	Mercury-Ascendant #7
Harry Dexter White	Death	Mercury-Ascendant #8
Miles Kirkpatrick	Death	Jupiter-Ascendant #10

individuals occurs because the delineation of the respective planet in the National Horoscope manifests as a major life theme.

Consider the life of Lydia Lord Davis. She was born on August 31, 1867, nine days from Sun-Ascendant Direction #5 computed for September 9, 1867. One signification of the Sun is religious missionaries who risk their lives in overseas service. As one of America's most well-known female missionaries of the 19th Century, Lydia Lord Davis did just that. Yet this direction times her birth and not her actual missionary service which did not happen until years later. It appears that planet-Ascendant directions for a mundane figure open some kind of portal whereby individuals whose activities conform to specific planet's delineation are either born or die. Since this finding is new, it must be treated as tentative.

Other Time Mismatches

The case of John Fremont in Sun-Ascendant Direction #4 offers another type of time mismatch between actual events and a direction's timing. Besides missionaries, Sun/Cancer/8th ruling the 9th also signifies explorers willing risk death for scientific expeditions. Such is the case for John Fremont who nearly died from exposure during the winter of 1843/1844 while on a western land survey. Among his discoveries was the first sighting of the Great Salt Lake on September 6, 1843. After hearing of Fremont's discovery, the Mormons selected Utah as their homeland.

Fast forward to June 17, 1856 when John Fremont was nominated for President. His nomination coincided with Sun-Ascendant Direction #4 computed for June 9, 1856. Sun signifies the President; Fremont, an explorer who previously risked death while on a scientific expedition, is nominated for President. In addition, the first wave of Mormon 'Handcart Pioneers' left Iowa City on June 9, 1856 for Utah. What is interesting is this Sun-Ascendant Direction did not time Fremont's near death from exposure during the winter of 1843/1844 (arguably the better delineation); yet timed his nomination for President by the Republican Party.

What this suggests is directions time events lived out by individuals which may not be synchronous with the direction itself. True, Fremont's near death from exposure during the winter of 1843/1844 may be timed by some other Sun direction not yet uncovered. Yet the possibility that time mismatches may distort the process of matching events to directions needs to be considered as a proposition.

CHAPTER EIGHT

Partners: Moon

Longitude	27AQ51'14"
Latitude	1s53'16"
Speed	14deg31'41" (fast)
Sign	Aquarius
Bound	Saturn/Aquarius
Dwad	Capricorn
Houses	<u>Occupies</u> 3rd
	<u>Rules</u> 6th, 8th (WS), 5th (AL)[1]
Rulers	<u>Ruled</u> by Saturn/Libra
	<u>Rules</u> Venus, Jupiter, Sun, Mercury
Other	3rd Quarter waning
	Placed in 3rd house of joy (WS)
	Separates from Mars and is Void of Course

<u>Planet</u>: Moon signifies the public-at-large and their instinctual needs. Moon also signifies women.

<u>Sign</u>: The symbol of Aquarius often shows a man pouring water from an urn. In some depictions, the water forms a river shown as the constellation Eridanus. As early as Manilius (c. 10 AD), Aquarius has been associated with canals and waterworks of all types.[2] Canals are signified because Aquarius is a fixed sign, whose nature is to contain, control, and hoard. Placement in an air sign adds an intellectual bent to water control through engineering.

Aquarius is also associated with a humanitarian philosophy which seeks fair and equal treatment of humans. Why? Consider the scientific fact that poured water seeks the lowest possible space before pooling. Once water is settled, the result is a smooth surface which makes no distinction where it travels and what it covers. An analogy can be made to the humanitarian spirit which includes the lowest participants of the social order in the fair and equal treatment of all social classes. Aquarius is also the sign opposed to Leo, the sign of Kings and concentrated power. Aquarius signifies the opposite.

Bound: As the Moon's bound, Saturn/Aquarius combines the Saturnian principle of control with the Aquarian characteristic of information which is codified, fixed, stored, or hoarded. This combination produces scientists, mathematicians, and engineers. Given the ability of the Saturn/Aquarius Distributor to time the rise of the abolition movement (See Chapter 6, p. 106), another delineation of Saturn/Aquarius appears to be black (Saturn) equality (Aquarius). Yet no malefic is entirely friendly. Because Saturn also signifies control and Aquarius the lower part of the legs, Saturn/Aquarius is also consistent with slavery because slaves brought to America were chained at the ankles (Aquarius) with iron shackles (Saturn).

Dwad: Moon in Capricorn signifies the need for status; as an economic indicator, a high price.

Separation from trine of Mars/Gemini/7th: Moon's separation from Mars means the Moon carries with it results of a prior Martian event. Significations of Mars/Gemini include incendiary forms of firepower, reckless business affairs, identity theft, and slander. Placed in the 7th house of open enemies, business partners, and marriage ruling the 4th of the homeland, the delineation of Mars includes Civil War, property theft, and disputes over real estate ownership which harms marriages.

Void of course: Void of course means the Moon is incapable of perfecting her interests unless the Moon's ruler assists it. Moon's ruler is Saturn whose significations include Congress, the Supreme Court, and supranational organizations which promote export of U.S. traded goods. With the U.S. Dollar another Saturn/Libra signification, financial health of the Treasury appears another precondition for Saturn to assist the Moon's goals.

Ruled by Saturn/Libra: Signifies Congress, the Supreme Court, and supranational organizations, and the U.S. Dollar. These significations of Saturn will be the source and outcome of the Moon's effects.

Rules – Venus/Cancer: Signifies both committal and judgment of financial scandal, consumer bankruptcy, and white racism. These significations of Venus will be the result of the Moon's actions.

Rules – Jupiter/Cancer. Signifies indebted farmers, consumer banking, and legal protection for consumers. These significations of Jupiter will be the result of the Moon's actions.

Rules – Sun/Cancer. Signifies the President, missionaries, and explorers willing to sacrifice their lives for the export of American democratic principles, scientific expeditions, and foreign trade. These significations of the Sun will be the result of the Moon's actions.

Rules Mercury/Cancer: Signifies incoherent emotional reasoning common to demagoguery and media sensationalism. These significations of Mercury will be the result of the Moon's actions.

Synthesis – The Moon

John Locke's political philosophy based on equality and fair treatment of all humans empowered by dispassionate scientific reasoning is embraced by the American public. Principles of equality primarily manifest through the abolition movement, women's suffrage, canal construction, public transportation, public education, and public radio. Though vitally interested in these activities, the public requires assistance from Congress and the Supreme Court for legal and institutional support to fulfill the Lockean promise.

Canal and transportation construction increases availability of consumer goods for purchase. The integration of minorities (including freed slaves) into the consuming public triggers white racism from established white social classes who feel threatened by minority advancement.

The principle for equality and fair treatment of all humans extends to the banking system. Bank capital is no longer restricted to the wealthy, yet access does not extend to minority consumers who still suffer the effects of white racism. A provincial attitude among states derails the uniformity of a national branch banking system.

Democracy as America's fundamental philosophy is exported through missionaries and military personnel while on overseas pilgrimages and deployments.

The need for scientific exploration causes the President to fund expeditions in foreign lands which help support foreign trade or result in gold discoveries. Results of scientific expeditions are reflected through the public education system and institutions designed to display trip artifacts (e.g., Smithsonian).

The need for fair treatment of all people causes the President to create a welfare system designed to provide care and comfort for the elderly.

Fair treatment of all people as a political philosophy attracts immigrant workers who find it difficult to integrate into American society without taking full advantage of access to public education, transport, and voting rights.

Moon-Ascendant Direction #1

D	Mars/Sagittarius	P	dex. sextile Moon (l=0) d. → ASC	20-Jul-1777
D	Mars/Sagittarius	P	dex. sextile Moon (l=MO) d. → ASC	8-Aug-1779

Heroines – Sybil Ludington and Molly Pitcher

On *April 26, 1777*, the sixteen year old Sybil Ludington convinced her father to allow her to make an all-night horseback ride to warn American militia of British forces in nearby Danbury, Connecticut. She summoned several hundred militiamen in a futile attempt to save Danbury which was burned by the British; however, the men were successful in a later engagement against General William Tryon at the Battle of Ridgefield.

At the Battle of Monmouth on *June 28, 1778*, Molly Pitcher took over her husband's position by his cannon after he was injured. 'Molly' was a common nickname for 'Mary.' 'Pitcher' originates from the practice of women aiding their husbands on the battlefield by bringing them pitchers of water in order for them to swab their cannons.[3]

Partner. With the symbol of Aquarius showing a man pouring water from a pitcher, the image of women bringing pitchers of water to men on the battlefield is a delineation match. With the Moon a feminine planet, these events concern women not men. In fact the feminine Moon in the masculine sign of Aquarius introduces a sexual androgyny to the delineation. There are several historical accounts of women dressed as men in order to serve alongside men in the American Revolution.[4]

Moon falling in the bound of Saturn/Aquarius is a match to cannons and cannonballs because both are black (Saturn), heavy (Saturn), and are intended to shoot projectiles on a fixed path in the air (Aquarius = fixed air sign) with the help of engineering (Saturn/Aquarius).

Distributor. These events occur during wartime (Mars). Ludington's horseback ride is consistent with Sagittarius whose symbol features a centaur, half-horse. Mars/Sagittarius also appears an astrometerological influence. Mars (hot/dry) in Sagittarius (hot/dry) indicates extreme heat. The Battle of Monmouth was a draw; in part, because hot summer weather induced heatstroke for both American and British forces.

Moon-Ascendant Direction #1 – Continued

Heroes – Marquis de Lafayette

The Marquis de Lafayette, later known as Gilbert du Motier after he renounced his title of *Marquis*, was an ambitious Frenchman seeking military glory who took up the cause of freedom by serving under George Washington. He arrived in South Carolina on June 13, 1777; spent the next month traveling by horseback arriving in Philadelphia on July 27, 1777; and met with George Washington for the first time on ***July 31, 1777***. In his first deployment at Brandywine on September 11, 1777, Lafayette suffered a leg injury. Later, Lafayette rounded out his military service by functioning as a diplomatic liaison between the American colonies and France. Lafayette was in France during the first half of 1779 and returned to the American colonies in ***July 1779*** as the sequence closed. He borrowed money on his own account to pay for supplies for soldiers who were poorly equipped.

Partner: Lafayette's willingness to fight on the side of the common man against the English crown is a match to the Moon in Aquarius which opposes the royal sign of Leo. Bound Saturn/Aquarius matches Lafayette's leg injury at Brandywine on September 11, 1777, a planet/sign combination recapitulated in Lafayette's natal figure (b. 6-Sep-1757). Lafayette's contributions to military supplies demonstrate the power of the Moon's placement in the dwad of Capricorn to signify the scarcity of sustenance which drives up its price. Separately, this incident links to George Washington's own natal Moon in Capricorn in the 6th ruling the 12th – delineated as soldier rebellion on account of insufficient supplies and salaries.[5]

The weakness of the void-of-course Moon is evident with Lafayette's projected expedition against Canada aborted, his retreat at Barren Hill, and his participation in the Battle of Monmouth which was a tactical draw (though strategic victory). Note also the Molly Pitcher legend is tied to the Battle of Monmouth.

Distributor: Lafayette was 'brave to rashness; and he never shrank from danger or responsibility if he saw the way open to spare life or suffering, to protect the dead, to sustain the law and preserve order.'[6] This character profile is delineation match to the aggressive, blusterous, and fearless nature of Mars/Sagittarius.

Moon-Ascendant Direction #2

D	Saturn/Scorpio	P	dex. square Moon (l=MO) c. → ASC	23-Dec-1809
D	Saturn/Scorpio	P	dex. square Moon (l=0) c. → ASC	22-May-1811

Columbia River Basin Exploration

Working as a surveyor, mapmaker, and fur trapper for the Hudson Bay Company, David Thompson achieved a reputation as one of the greatest cartographers in world history. During his career, he mapped 3.9 million kilometers of North America; some of his maps were used well into the mid-20th century for their accuracy[7]. As the sequence opened, he established Saleesh House during *November 1809*, the first trading post established west of the Rocky Mountains in Montana. As the sequence closed, he reached Fort Astoria at the mouth of the Columbia River Basin on *July 11, 1811* on the heels of John Jacob Astor's fur-trading expedition which landed in Astoria on *March 22, 1811*.

Partner: Though manmade canals and waterworks were not the objective of these explorations; waterworks made by beavers were. Thompson's objective was mapping territory to facilitate the catching and skinning of beavers. Bound Saturn/Aquarius signifies a beaver trap because traps (Saturn) kill (Saturn) beavers in waterways (Aquarius). The Capricorn dwad adds an expensive price; beaver pelts were luxury goods sold for hat making on the East Coast. There is also a correspondence between the Moon's rulership of Venus to Thompson's surveys (Moon) facilitating sale of consumer goods (Venus).

The inability of the void of course Moon to perfect matters appears remedied by the Moon's ruler Saturn/Libra. Saturn/Libra signifies wealthy magnates including John Jacob Astor and the owners of the Hudson Bay Company who facilitated Thompson's mapping expedition with extensive financial support.

Birth of Kit Carson

The frontiersman Kit Carson was born on *December 24, 1809*. He would later work for the Hudson Bay Company as a trapper. Together with John Fremont, Carson would help map the second section of the Oregon Trail to the Columbia River, used extensively by settlers to travel west after the 1848 California gold discovery at Sutter's Mill.

Moon-Ascendant Direction #2 – Continued

Erie Canal

Following the Revolutionary War, New York's DeWitt Clinton expressed renewed interest in canal construction. Clinton's motivation was improved transport of goods and economic benefits to New York City. At the time of Clinton's proposal, the fastest method of transporting goods to the western interior of the United States was carts pulled by draft animals. The first canal feasibility study was presented on ***January 20, 1809***; Clinton was appointed one of Commissioners to study Erie Canal construction during ***March 1810***; yet was unsuccessful in his proposal for construction in ***1811***. After his election to Governor of New York in 1817 he was instrumental in pushing through the canal program. First date of construction was ***July 4, 1817***[8]. The Erie Canal officially opened October 26, 1825.

Distributor: Need for canals and waterworks as a method of short-term transportation to facilitate investment activity is a delineation match to Moon/Aquarius in the 3rd ruling the 8th. Bound of Saturn/Aquarius adds engineering ability. There were a number of engineering feats involved in the canal's construction, including development of hydraulic cement by the engineer Canvass White who traveled to England in 1817 to study English engineering methods.[9] Moon in the dwad of Capricorn signifies a high price. The Erie Canal was considered expensive because 50 locks were required for its construction.

The inability of Clinton to secure passage of the proposed Erie Canal during the years 1809-1811 matches the weakness of the void-of-course Moon to perfect events. This changed once he became Governor and garnered greater influence over the legislature. Both Clinton's position as Governor (Sun) and his relationship with the legislature (Saturn) were necessary to perfect the Moon's promise for canal construction.

Moon-Ascendant Direction #3

D	Saturn/Aquarius	P	conjunction Moon (l=0) d. → ASC	1-Feb-1829
D	Changeover		bound Venus/Pisces d. → ASC	25-Jun-1830
D	Venus/Pisces	P	conjunction Moon (l=MO) d. → ASC	18-May-1831

Abolition Movement

Settling in Boston, the free slave David Walker worked as distribution agent for *Freedom's Journal*, the first African American newspaper published in America. Its first issue published on March 16, 1827 fell just two days before the start of the Saturn/Aquarius distribution on March 18, 1827. Separately from his position as *Freedom's Journal* distributor, Walker published the pamphlet *Walker's Appeal* on **September 28, 1829**. Walker called for immediate, universal, and unconditional emancipation, condemned colonization of freed slaves, and urged violent uprisings against slave owners. Walker was widely criticized for his activities with several bounties offered for his capture. He was found dead on ***June 28, 1830*** for reasons unknown.

Abolitionist William Lloyd Garrison founded his newspaper *The Liberator* on ***January 1, 1831*** and edited its last edition on December 29, 1865, two days prior to Lincoln's Emancipation Proclamation went into force.

Death of the Christian missionary Jeremiah Evarts on ***May 10, 1831*** closed this sequence. He died from exhaustion following his advocacy for the Cherokee Indian tribe against Andrew Jackson's plans for Indian Removal. [For more on Evarts, see Sun-Ascendant Direction #2]. Public revulsion over Indian removal was another organizing factor behind the rise of the Abolitionist movement.

<u>Partner</u>: Moon/Aquarius signifies equal treatment of all humans, including slaves. Bound of Saturn/Aquarius adds control (Saturn) of the legs (Aquarius) through iron shackles which are black (Saturn) and heavy (Saturn).

<u>Distributors</u>. The effect of Saturn/Aquarius on David Walker's pamphleteering and Venus/Pisces on Garrison's activities is striking. Saturn/Aquarius is consistent with violent uprisings because Saturn is a destroyer and Aquarius is a human sign. Incredibly, Walker was found dead on ***June 28, 1830***, just three days after the directed Ascendant changed from Saturn/Aquarius to Venus/Pisces. Garrison's public abolitionist tactics avoided calls for violence because of Garrison's religious pacifism, consistent with the forgiving spirit of Venus/Pisces.

Smithsonian Institution Bequest

The Englishman James Smithson was a member of the Royal Society in London, conducted scientific research, and published papers on chemistry, geology, and mineralogy during his lifetime. Smithson wrote an unusual bequest in his will dated October 23, 1826. He stated that should his nephew, James Henry Dickinson die without children, his estate should be given "to the United States of America, to found at Washington an establishment for the increase and diffusion of knowledge among men."[10]

Smithson died on *June 27, 1829*. His will passed through the UK probate system on November 4, 1829 and was published in the London Times on December 10, 1829. The New-York American paper picked up the London Times article and published Smithson's bequest on January 26, 1830.[11] His nephew, without heirs, lived to 1835. In *1836*, Congress accepted the bequest worth just over $500,000, a large sum for the time. There was considerable debate among Congress over whether the bequest should be accepted, and once so, how the funds should be spent. Initially the proceeds were invested in Arkansas and Michigan state bonds which soon defaulted. After more debate, Congress agreed to refund the bequest with legislation passed on August 10, 1846. The first building was completed in 1855.

Partner: Moon's separation from Mars signifies reckless investment management of Smithson's bequest which precedes construction of the Smithsonian Museum. The Moon itself is a delineation match to the need for sharing (Aquarius) knowledge (air sign) through public education (3rd house). Moon's rulership of the 8th house of investments, debt, and bequests all apply here. Moon's Capricorn dwad matches the Smithsonian building's stone edifice and Dinosaur bones which would later grace its collection. The weakness of the void of course Moon is demonstrated by the failure of the initial bequest to fund the institution specified by Smithson's will. Willingness of Congress to refund the bequest shows the ability of Saturn (as the Moon's ruler) to perfect the Moon's objective.

Distributor: Saturn/Aquarius signifies science and further specifies the bequest to scientific education. Because the Moon falls in the bound of Saturn/Aquarius, the Distributor is reinforced by the bound of the Moon itself.

Elimination of Prison Sentences for Debtors

On *April 25, 1831*, New York State abolished prison terms for debtors. As Distributor, Moon/Aquarius ruling the 8th is a delineation match to fair treatment of debts. As Partner, Venus/Pisces signifies a forgiving style of love which matches the tenor of this direction.

Moon-Ascendant Direction #4

D	Mars/Libra	P	dex. trine Moon (l=MO) c. → ASC	25-Jul-1848
D	Changeover		bound Venus/Libra c. → ASC	2-Aug-1848
D	Venus/Libra	P	dex. trine Moon (l=0) c. → ASC	11-Jun-1849

Abolition

Harriet Tubman's escape from slavery on **September 17, 1849** falls ten weeks past the end of the sequence, yet evidence shows she was planning the escape months prior to the actual escape.[12] She is known for facilitating freedom for slaves using the Underground Railroad during the Civil War and for fighting for women's suffrage in its wake.

Seneca Falls Convention

The first major women's rights conference was held in Seneca Falls, New York, on **July 19-20, 1848**. Written by Elizabeth Cady Stanton, a Declaration of Sentiments was written and issued on **July 20, 1848**.

Partner: Moon in Aquarius demands equal treatment for all humans, women as well as men. Moon's separation from Mars/Gemini/7th ruling the 4th is consistent with disputes between women and their husbands over property rights; one motivation for the Conference. Moon in the 3rd of communications matches the publicity the Declaration intended to garner. Ineffectiveness of the void of course Moon is evident as the Equal Rights Amendment remains unfinished legislation some 150 years later. As a subtle connection to the Moon's signification as canal transportation, note that Seneca Falls is located on the Erie Canal, a location which presumably facilitated transportation to the event.

Bridges

On **August 1, 1848**, the Niagara Falls Suspension Bridge Company opened a 770 foot suspension bridge for foot traffic between the United States and Canada. The bridge was an early example of suspension bridges, matching the Moon's placement in the bound of Saturn/Aquarius delineated as engineering. The same company opened a double decker bridge on March 18, 1855, later used by Vanderbilt's New York Central Railroad. (See Moon-Ascendant Direction #10 for more examples of Cornelius Vanderbilt's connections to transportation development.)

Panama Canal

The origins of the Panama Canal can be traced to this sequence which timed the California Gold Rush and western migration, the start of both Atlantic and Pacific Mail Steamship Companies, and the Panama Railroad Company.

Gold was first discovered at Sutter's Mill, California, on January 24, 1848. The *New York Herald* published the first major story on the gold rush on the East Coast on **August 19, 1848**, later confirmed by President James Polk in his Annual Message to Congress on December 5, 1848.

A treaty with New Granada (Columbia) on **June 10, 1848** allowed for the formation of the Panama Railroad Company on **April 7, 1849** in the state of New York. Construction began in 1850, was marred by problems including illness of workers, and was not completed until January 28, 1855. These assets would eventually be purchased by the United States Government on **April 23, 1904**[13]. Steamship company operations proved a more immediate success, with the Pacific founded during April 1848.

As the sequence ended, there was movement towards canal construction in Nicaragua with U.S. diplomat Ephraim George Squier's arrival in Nicaragua on **June 22, 1849**. Shortly thereafter an agreement between the Nicaraguan government and Cornelius Vanderbilt was signed granting Vanderbilt exclusive rights to build a canal within twelve years and a land-and-water transit route during canal construction. This venture would not be successful.

Distributor: Venus/Libra can be delineated as a diplomatic measures designed to find balance among competing interests. Squier plays the role of the Distributor for this Panama Canal direction.

Moon-Ascendant Direction #5

D	Saturn/Aries	P	sin. sextile Moon (l=0) d. → ASC	25-Apr-1865
D	Changeover		bound Venus/Taurus d. → ASC	9-Sep-1866
D	Venus/Taurus	P	sin. sextile Moon (l=MO) d. → ASC	25-Jul-1867

Emancipation, Lincoln's assassination, and Lincoln's funeral train.

Following Lincoln's assassination on April 15, 1865, Lincoln's funeral train departed Washington on *April 21, 1865* and arrived in Springfield, Illinois on *May 3, 1865*. A Pullman railcar used in the funeral train proved valuable advertising fodder for the launch of the Pullman Palace Car Company on *February 22, 1867*.

Partner: Moon/Aquarius is placed in the 3rd house whose significations include short-term travel. As cause, Saturn signifies Lincoln's death[14]. The Moon in turn provides publicity for Lincoln's death (Sun/Cancer/8th = famous death of President), a new style of consumerism (Venus/Cancer/8th = plush style of Pullman Palace Cars), and fake news/sensationalism (Mercury/Cancer/8th). Though George Pullman advertised that its *Pioneer* car carried Mary Lincoln in the funeral train, Mary Lincoln did not leave the White House until May 23, 1865 and the *Pioneer* car was not in service until May 26, 1865, three weeks after Lincoln's funeral train had passed through Chicago. Nevertheless, the *story* of Mary Lincoln's occupancy of a Pullman Palace Car in her husband's funeral train for promotional purposes by the Pullman Company has been kept alive for many years.[15]

Distributors: Saturn/Aries signifies obstructions to fighting. Lincoln was assassinated at the Civil War's end. Venus/Taurus signifies capitalism and matches the post-Civil War period of economic revival which enabled companies like the Pullman Palace Car Company to vigorously expand.

Fisk University

Fisk University is one of America's earliest black colleges. First classes were taught on January 8, 1886 and the University was officially incorporated *August 22, 1867*, five weeks after the sequence completed.

Partner: Given the Moon's delineation as the abolition movement in earlier sequences, education for freed slaves is a logical extension of the Moon's placement in the 3rd of education.

Moon-Ascendant Direction #6

D	Mars/Taurus	P	sin. square Moon (l=0) d. → ASC	16-Sep-1886
D	Changeover		bound Mercury/Gemini d. → ASC	21-Jun-1888
D	Mercury/Gemini	P	sin. square Moon (l=MO) d. → ASC	21-Dec-1888

Labor Movements

Formation of the United Labor party on *September 23, 1886* and the American Federation of Labor on *December 8-11, 1886* under Samuel Gompers kick off the sequence.

Partner: Gompers' interest in obtaining fair and equitable wages for workers matches the delineation of the Aquarian Moon as a fair price.

Distributor: As a fighting style, Mars/Taurus signifies explosive shows of force. As a social indicator, Mars/Taurus signifies fights (Mars) against capitalists (Taurus). These two themes culminated in the Haymarket Riot of May 4, 1886, labeled as an attack by anarchist labor leaders against the citizenry. The subsequent national anti-labor attitude provided the opportunity for Gompers to start a more conservative type of labor organization with his AFL which opposed anarchist tactics.

Edward Bellamy and Nationalist Clubs

In January 1888, Edward Bellamy published his novel *Looking Backward*[16] which described a socialist utopia set in 2000. *Looking Backward* became such a best-seller it spawned formation of groups interested in discussing the book's utopian philosophy. Initially named Bellamy Clubs, they were later renamed Nationalist Clubs. An organizational meeting for creating the club structure occurred during *December 1888*. On *January 9, 1889*, Boston Nationalist Club #1 had its inaugural meeting.

Distributor: Mercury/Gemini signifies curiosity (Gemini) about books (Mercury). As the Distributor changed from Mars/Taurus to Mercury/Gemini in June 1888, a cheaper edition was published which helped increase sales.[17]

Partner: Fair treatment of humans in a utopian community matches the idealism of the Aquarian Moon.

Moon-Ascendant Direction #7

D	Saturn/Gemini	P	sin. trine Moon (l=0) d. → ASC	8-Dec-1914
D	Saturn/Gemini	P	sin. trine Moon (l=MO) d. → ASC	18-Dec-1916

Panama Canal Opening

The Panama Canal opened for business on August 15, 1914. The following events are relevant to the sequence:

6-Dec-1914. Russian exports started to clear the Canal.[18]

9-Dec-1914. The Panamanian President signed a boundary convention between the United States and Panama.[19]

9-Dec-1914. Canal Governor Goethals asked for Navy Destroyers to police foreign warships in Panama Canal.[20]

11-Dec-1916. Goethals called for abrogation of the Taft agreement and unilateral control over the Canal Zone by the United States.[21]

Partner: Panama Canal is a delineation match to the need for canal transportation in order to facilitate foreign trade.

Distributor: Saturn/Gemini matches Goethal's 1914 request for enforcement (Saturn) of commerce (Gemini). His 1916 call for abrogation of the Taft agreement was an attempt to control (Saturn) commerce (Gemini).

Public Radio

American Public Radio dates from the first broadcast of WHA-AM Wisconsin Public Radio on ***December 4, 1916***, 11:00 AM, Madison, WI.[22]

Partner: Moon/Aquarius/3rd signifies public/fair communications.

Distributor: Saturn/Gemini can be delineated as scientific research (Saturn) of communications technology (Gemini). This is a delineation match to the radio research of University of Wisconsin physicists Edward Bennett and Earle M. Terry which spawned WHA-AM. Note that Gemini is a double-bodied sign and there were two scientists involved in the radio startup.

Moon-Ascendant Direction #8

D	Mars/Leo	P	opposition Moon (l=MO) c. → ASC	11-Dec-1923
D	Mars/Leo	P	opposition Moon (l=0) c. → ASC	9-Nov-1924

Women's Equal Rights Amendment and Election Victories

Following successful passage of the 19th Amendment guaranteeing women the right to vote, suffragist Alice Paul argued that remaining discrimination based on gender required passage of an Equal Rights Amendment. This legislation was introduced in the Senate and House on *December 10* and *December 13, 1923*, respectively, by Kansas Republicans Charles Curtis and Daniel R. Anthony, Jr.[23]

Women made strong inroads as candidates in the fall elections held *November 4, 1924*. Women took spots as Governors (2), state legislators (88), and a seat in the House of Representatives (1).[24]

Coolidge Radio Broadcast

President Calvin Coolidge made the first Presidential Broadcast via radio on *December 6, 1923*. This radio message was delivered to a joint session of Congress. This event shows the influence of the Moon's rulership over the Sun (President Coolidge). As ruler of the Moon, Saturn (Congress) shows the cause of the Moon's effects (radio address).

Birth of Shirley Chisholm

Shirley Chisholm was born on *November 30, 1924*, twenty two days after the conclusion of the sequence. She was the first African American woman elected to Congress and served in the House of Representatives from 1968 to 1983. She entered the 1972 Presidential race, received 152 delegates, but lost the nomination to George McGovern.[25]

Moon-Ascendant Direction #9

D	Mars/Leo	P	opposition Moon (l=0) d. → ASC	26-Feb-1988
D	Mars/Leo	P	opposition Moon (l=MO) d. → ASC	24-Jan-1989

Panama Canal and the Arrest of Manuel Noriega

On February 5, 1988, Panamanian military ruler Manuel Noriega was indicted by the DEA on drug charges. Noriega was dismissed as commander of Panama's Defense Forces on *February 25, 1988*.

By definition, this direction is identical to the direction of the Moon to the 7th house cusp which signifies legal disputes. Delineation match: a police action (Distributor = Mars/Leo) regarding the Panama Canal (Partner = Moon/Aquarius) to enforce a legal indictment (7th cusp).

Civil Rights and Congress

As the sequence opened, the House passed a bill on *March 3, 1988* to overturn a 1984 Supreme Court decision that limited application of Civil Rights laws.[26] Republicans feared a backlash against Reagan's veto of this legislation which they voted to override with the Senate on March 23, 1988.[27] As the sequence ended, on *January 25, 1989* the House was rated the most liberal in 40 years.[28] This after ERA Legislation was re-introduced by 129 House members on January 4, 1989.[29]

George H. W. Bush's *Thousand Points of Light*

Culminating with the Inauguration of George H. W. Bush on *January 20, 1989*, the sequence captures the humanitarian spirit of the Aquarian Moon with Bush's *Thousand Points of Light* speech given at the Republican National Convention on August 18, 1988; a theme encored at a special reception the eve before his Presidential inauguration. Delivered on the stage set by Mars/Leo as Distributor, Bush affirmed America's diversity against a backdrop of law enforcement (supporting capital punishment for killers of police), defense of honor (in favor of guns to protect one's home), and tales of heroism (presenting himself as an accomplished fighter pilot).[30]

Moon-Ascendant Direction #10

D	Saturn/Gemini	P	sin. trine Moon (l=MO) c. → ASC	19-Jan-1996
D	Saturn/Gemini	P	sin. trine Moon (l=0) c. → ASC	29-Jan-1998

Cornelius Vanderbilt and Grand Central Renovation

Moon/Aquarius/3rd signifies the need for public transportation because the Moon in the 3rd house of joy likes to take short-term trips and Aquarius signifies the non-exclusivity inherent to public transportation. A key figure in the history of America's transportation network was Cornelius Vanderbilt. He started by running a steamship service on the Hudson River in 1829 (sequence #3), transported California Gold Rush 49ers via rail in Nicaragua in 1849 (sequence #4), and purchased the Hudson River Railroad in 1864 and the New York Central Railroad in 1867 (sequence #5). Metro-North commissioned a Grand Central renovation plan during 1988 (sequence #9) which started in late *January 1996* and concluded with a rededication on *October 1, 1998* (sequence #10). Grand Central's renovation is one of the better examples of the Moon's Capricorn dwad on architecture. Grand Central's elaborate Beaux-Arts style matches the delineation of Moon in Capricorn as the need for expensive items as a way to demonstrate high social status. Use of stone as a building material also matches the Capricorn dwad because Capricorn signifies mountain rocks.

Amtrak Problems

The influence of Saturn/Gemini as bound is evident with a major New Jersey Transit train crash on *February 9, 1996*[31] as the sequence opened and a debate over Amtrak funding on *January 17, 1998*[32] as the sequence closed. The train accident, subsequent accident investigation, and threats to reduce Amtrak funding are a delineation match to Saturn/Gemini as government regulation and investigation.

Women's Rights

The goal of the Feminist Expo '96 held *February 3-5, 1998* was to reinvigorate the women's rights movement which some participants felt had stalled.[33] Gloria Steinem attended, herself the subject of a recent *January 25, 1998* biographical review.[34] Continuing discrimination felt by women attending the Expo is a delineation match to the tactic of scrutiny often employed by Distributor Saturn/Gemini.

CHAPTER NINE

Partners: Sun

Longitude	13CA22'03"
Speed	00deg57'12" (slow)
Sign	Cancer
Bound	Mercury/Cancer
Dwad	Sagittarius
Houses	<u>Occupies</u> 8th
	<u>Rules</u> 5th, 9th (WS), 4th, 8th (AL)
Rulers	<u>Ruled</u> by Moon/Aquarius
	<u>Rules</u> North Node/Leo, Lot of Fortune/Leo
Additional	Though not positioned in the 9th house of his joy, the Sun does *rule* the 9th house.
	Member of Venus-Jupiter-Sun-Mercury stellium.
	Sun placed in 12th sign from sign he rules (Leo).

<u>Planet – Sun</u>: Leadership, fame, and authority. National leaders including the President and/or Prime Minister. Men.

<u>Sign – Cancer</u>: Sun in the cardinal water sign of Cancer combines the Sun's leadership/fame/authority with Cancer's outgoing nurturing character.

<u>Bound – Mercury/Cancer</u>: Mercury/Cancer is noted for sensitivity to the immediate environment because the Moon rules Cancer and the Moon governs instinct and sensory perception. Though Mercury/Cancer is not technically in detriment, his manifestation as 'fleeting sensitivity' underlies problems faced by Mercury in all water signs. Here the facts Mercury tries to communicate can be clouded or dissolved by the water element. With Moon-ruled Cancer assigned to the public in mundane astrology, Mercury/Cancer's better application is found in deciphering and manipulating crowd behavior. Stump speaking and demagoguery are common Mercury/Cancer communication styles.

Dwad: Sun in the dwad of Sagittarius adds optimism. Sagittarius is also associated with travel by horseback and airplanes.

Ruled by Moon/Aquarius: The demand for equal treatment of humans in matters of free speech, public education, and local transportation is the primary signification of the Aquarian Moon. All of these effects will prove the source and result of the Sun's actions.

Rules North Node/Leo: North Node/Leo in the 9th house of God, religion, higher education, and travel/exploration increases those affairs. Sun is the cause of the North Node's expansion of 9th house activities.

Rules Lot of Fortune/Leo: POF/Leo in the 9th is best delineated as monetary gain from foreign affairs with ruler Sun in 8th showing the President's involvement in foreign trade agreements as the cause.

Synthesis – The Sun

Religion. An important theme of the Sun is his influence on the 9th house of God, religion, higher education, and travel/exploration because he rules the North Node/Leo in the 9th. By rulership, the Sun is the source of the North Node's increase of 9th house affairs.

The Sun signifies the willingness to die (Sun in 8th) overseas (Sun ruling 9th) while providing care and comfort (Sun in Cancer). The most straightforward delineation of the Cancer Sun is overseas humanitarian relief performed by religious missionaries. The willingness to sacrifice is marred by the Sun's placement in the bound of Mercury/Cancer, a placement recapitulated by the planet Mercury/Cancer approaching combustion. What this means is the Sun's philosophy is degraded by an emotional style of reasoning which does not lend itself well to discussions with the dispassionate Aquarian Moon.

As the Sun's ruler, the Aquarian Moon is the primary significator for John Locke's philosophy of government by the consent of the people. Other Lockean tenets include religious tolerance and scientific rationalism.

The emotionalism of the Sun and the dispassionate scientific approach of the Moon establish a polarity central to many American religious debates. They include the 1830s conflict between the Transcendentalists (Sun) and Unitarians (Moon), the conflict between faith healing in the Christian Science movement (Sun) and modern medicine (Moon), and the ongoing conflict between creation science (Sun) and evolution (Moon).

Perhaps the most famous example of the Sun-Moon polarity in popular culture can be read through the science fiction franchise Star Trek. Conflict between the emotionalism of Captain James T. Kirk (Sun) and the logic of Mr. Spock (Moon) is a recurring theme which is fundamental to the series' drama.

Expeditions. The need for scientific exploration causes the President to fund expeditions in foreign lands which help support foreign trade or result in gold discoveries. Christian missionaries are often indirect participants of scientific expeditions, either as guides or as beneficiaries of pathways opened by explorers. Results of scientific expeditions are housed in institutions designed to display trip artifacts (e.g., Smithsonian) and incorporated in public school primary education curriculum.

Welfare State. The need for fair treatment of all people causes the President to create a welfare state whose focus is subsidized housing and guaranteed retirement income. (Sun in 8th ruling 4th signifies transfer payments for real estate and retiree pensions). Establishment of the welfare state brings the President in conflict with Congress, his Cabinet, the Supreme Court, and other supranational organizations (Sun applies to square of Saturn).

Overseas Service. Providing care and comfort in foreign lands draws missionaries, medical volunteers, and military personnel to participate in overseas pilgrimages and military missions designed to provide care and comfort in an outgoing and nurturing manner. Examples include the Red Cross, CARE, Doctors without Borders, and periodic relief missions supervised by the military.

Other Sun Delineations

- Monuments in honor of Presidents, military heroes, and military battles.

- Missionary service on Indian Reservations.

- Charitable bequests for hospitals and hospice care administered by religious organizations.

Sun-Ascendant Direction #1

| D | Jupiter/Capricorn | P | opposition Sun d. → ASC | 21-Sep-1793 |

Capital Building Groundbreaking Ceremony

On *September 18, 1793*, George Washington laid the cornerstone for the United State Capital Building in a Masonic ceremony. Sun rules the 4th of real estate, buildings, and their foundations. An event involving Washington (Sun) and a building foundation (4th) is a delineation match.

Distributor: The changeover to Jupiter/Capricorn on May 4, 1787 coincided with the start of the Constitutional Convention. A significator of Federalism, Jupiter/Capricorn facilitated efforts to centralize government control of American political life in the early days of the Republic's history. The 1793 Capital groundbreaking ceremony, occurring near the end of Jupiter/Capricorn's Distribution, can be directly traced to the 1787 Constitutional Convention. Among the Convention's achievements was creation of the Executive, Legislative, and Judicial branches. As the legislative branch, Congress would be housed in the Capital building.

Thomas Paine's *The Rights of Man* and *The Age of Reason*

Today, most Americans associate social welfare programs with Roosevelt's New Deal (see Sun-Ascendant Direction #8). But the philosophy of the welfare state predates Roosevelt. In his *1791-1792* work *The Rights of Man,* Thomas Paine proposed both progressive income and inheritance taxes in addition to public assistance to the poor, public works projects, free elementary education, pensions for the aged, marriage bonuses and maternity benefits, and provision for funerals for the poor[1]. Immediately after the timing of Direction #1, Paine was imprisoned in France and started work on the *Age of Reason* (Part I finished *December 28, 1793* and published *January 28, 1794*[2]). This was a work which attacked the literal interpretation of the Christian Bible through the use of objective rational thought. Paine's rejection of the Bible in the *Age of Reason* conforms to the dispassionate scientific delineation of the Aquarian Moon; his philosophy of progressive taxation of the ruling class to support a welfare state in *The Rights of Man* matches the caring Cancer Sun. Direction #1 falls at the midpoint of Paine's most important writings on these topics.

Sun-Ascendant Direction #2

| D | Mercury/Scorpio | P | sin. trine Sun c. → ASC | 29-Sep-1829 |

Missionaries: Opposition to Indian Removal

Until Andrew Jackson's Inauguration in March 1829, American Missionaries were purposely encouraged and funded by the Federal Government (from George Washington on) to assist Indian assimilation into American society through education and religious training. This changed under Jackson whose hatred for Indians was notorious. Under his administration, Jackson instituted the most racist policies against Indians since the Declaration of Independence was signed in 1776. The main battleground was the Southeast; the primary target, the Cherokee nation. Ironically, the Cherokee had shown great progress in assimilating American culture under the influence of American Missionaries. Leading the opposition to Jackson's plans for Indian removal was Jeremiah F. Evarts, a Christian missionary and advocate for American Indians. Evarts also served as Treasurer and Secretary of the Boston-based American Board of Commissioners for Foreign Missions (ABCFM) which was opposed to Indian removal. Under the nom de plum 'William Penn,' Evarts published articles in the *National Intelligencer*[3] in addition to a pamphlet which was read by an estimated 500,000 people by the ***end of summer 1829***, matching the time period for this Sun-Ascendant Direction. Evarts' pamphlet was the most widely read work since Thomas Paine's Common Sense published in 1776.[4]

Partner: As a missionary, Evarts plays the role of the caring Cancer Sun in his efforts to treat Indians with fairness.

Distributor. Active from August 2, 1822 to October 2, 1832, Mercury/Scorpio signifies the deceit, trickery, and incensed speech emanating from anti-Indian forces. With this backdrop, Evarts appeals were unsuccessful and Jackson's Indian Removal Act was signed into law on ***May 28, 1830***.

Missionaries: Oregon Territory

In 1829 (a possible match which requires further research to confirm the precise event timing), the ABCFM learned the existence of unconverted Indians living on the West Coast. This report would set into motion missionary Jason Lee's 1834 trek to Oregon. Lee was an important figure in the history of Oregon pioneers.

Sun-Ascendant Direction #3

| D | Jupiter/Pisces | P | dex. trine Sun d. → ASC | 11-Oct-1838 |

Transcendentalism

Following publication of *Nature* in 1837, widely considered the manifesto of Transcendentalism, Ralph Waldo Emerson addressed Harvard's Divinity School on graduation day on July 15, 1838, taking aim at his opponents. The address was reviewed in print on August 27, August 30, and ***October 1, 1838*** which corresponds to the timing for Sun-Ascendant Direction #3.[5] Transcendentalism was a reaction against the Lockean notion that the human mind is a blank slate at birth, filled with facts and observations made according to the scientific method.[6] Emerson and others thought otherwise; essentially the human mind was smart enough to discern truth through its own methods of sensory perception. Essentially, transcendentalism was a reaction against logic in favor of a more emotional spiritual path.

<u>Partner</u>: Sun/Cancer signifies Emerson. The Sun's bound – Mercury/Cancer – is a perfect match to the sensory and fleeting mental style which makes transcendentalism so difficult to describe.

<u>Distributor</u>: Jupiter/Pisces combines philosophy (Jupiter) and Christianity (Pisces). Pisces is associated with Christianity because (1) Jesus of Nazareth was born after the Jupiter/Saturn conjunction in Pisces and (2) the two fish symbol of Pisces is associated with Christianity. Emerson's Divinity School Address was controversial because Emerson presented Jesus as a man, not God. Emerson also discounted the need to believe in his historical miracles.

Sun-Ascendant Direction #4

| D | Mercury/Aries | P | dex. square Sun d. → ASC | 9-Jun-1856 |

John Fremont and the Mormon Handcart Pioneers

It is fitting that one of America's greatest 19th century explorers was nominated for President on *June 17, 1856*. John Fremont undertook five major surveys of the American West, in part aided by his father-in-law Thomas Benton, who as Senator was one of the strongest proponents of the Manifest Destiny doctrine. Like all of America's 19th century surveys, Fremont's expeditions had a scientific component; his contribution was botany. The primary function of Fremont's surveys was to facilitate western land settlement through survey and mapping of trails and mountain passages. How does Fremont play the role of the Cancer Sun in the 8th ruling the 9th? As Sun positioned in the 8th of death ruling the 9th of exploration, Fremont nearly died during the winter of 1843/1844 from exposure during his second expedition. Significant to the story is Fremont's sighting of the Great Salt Lake on September 6, 1843. After hearing of Fremont's discovery, the Mormons selected Utah as their homeland. Though Fremont did not sacrifice himself as a missionary per se; he risked death during an expedition whose discoveries triggered Mormon migration.

The first group of Mormon 'handcart' Emigrants left Iowa City, Iowa on *June 8, 1856* and reached Utah on *September 26, 1856*.[7] There were ten companies who made the 1,030 mile trek from Iowa City to Salt Lake City between 1856 and 1860. Though a minority of the total number of Mormons who migrated West during the years 1848-1868, Mormons who traveled with handcarts are recognized because of the hardships required for the journey. Two companies suffered major loss of life from exposure.

Distributor: Mercury placed in the Mars-ruled sign of Aries adds force and produces a runner with powerful hands. Arguably as a time lord, Mercury/Aries supplied the physical fortitude for Mormons to migrate with hand carts instead of oxen.

Explorers: Birth of Robert Peary

Robert Peary, an American explorer who claimed he was the first to reach the geographic North Pole, was born on *May 6, 1856*, a month before this direction. His first arctic trip departed on *July 16, 1905*, three months after the April 8, 1905 Sun-Ascendant Direction #7.

Sun-Ascendant Direction #5

| D | Mercury/Libra | P | sin. square Sun c. → ASC | 9-Sep-1867 |

Antietam, Clara Barton, and the American Red Cross

Though a tactical draw, the Battle of Antietam of September 17, 1862 was considered enough of a strategic victory for Lincoln to unveil his Emancipation Proclamation on September 22, 1862. Antietam was the single bloodiest day in American history with approximately 23,000 casualties. Antietam National Cemetery was dedicated on *September 17, 1867*.

Clara Barton first provided medical supplies at the Battle of Bull Run on July 21, 1861. By 1862 she received formal permission for battlefield access. At the Battle of Antietam, she received recognition for her tireless and fearless feats of medical care which earned her the nickname 'Angel of the Battlefield.' At the time of the *1867* direction, she was in the midst of making 300+ speeches on the lecture circuit. Barton became so exhausted she traveled overseas to recuperate where she learned about the Red Cross.[8] She later established the American Red Cross on May 21, 1881. Barton's foreign trip matches the caring Cancer Sun in the 8th of death (here extreme fatigue) ruling the 9th of foreign travel.

Four Great Surveys of the West

Of the 'Four Great Surveys of the West' begun in *1867*[9], the best fit appears John Wesley Powell's expedition. Though Powell was made famous by his Colorado River ride of 1869, his first explorations were during 1867. During his second 1871/1872 expedition, he was led by the Mormon Missionary Jacob Hamblin. Powell developed his philosophy of water conservation (the water sign Cancer ruling the 9th) from scientific observations on water made during his Colorado River expeditions.

Missionaries: Birth of Lydia Lord Davis

Born on *August 31, 1867*, Lydia Lord Davis was a prominent missionary to China. After her return to the United States, she worked as Assistant Secretary and later as Executive Secretary for the American Board of Commissioners for Foreign Missions (ABCFM). She is considered one of the most well-known and influential female missionaries.[10]

Sun-Ascendant Direction #6

| D | Mercury/Taurus | P | dex. sextile Sun d. → ASC | 18-Sep-1875 |

Valentine McGillycuddy and the Black Hills Gold Rush

The discovery of gold on *November 13, 1875* in Deadwood Gulch officially triggered the Black Hills Gold Rush of 1875. Predating this discovery were Black Hills Expeditions led by Custer during July-August 1874[11] and by the Newton-Jenney party in 1875. Both ventures had a scientific information-gathering focus which exemplifies the Aquarian Moon's influence as ruler, or cause of the Sun's actions.

Partner: This direction shows evidence of the Sun's rulership of the Lot of Fortune in Leo, assigned to gold. Placer gold discovered in Deadwood Gulch was traced back to the mother lode discovery at Lead, South Dakota on April 9, 1876. Later known as the Homestake Mine, the operation produced over $1 billion in gold in its 126 years of operation.[12] Consider that the POF falls 11 signs from Saturn/Libra, significator of the U.S. Dollar. In Hellenistic astrology, the 11th place from the POF is named the place of acquisition and provides secondary testimony for delineating wealth.[13] I suggest this configuration signifies the original gold underpinnings of America's currency.

A member of the U.S. Geologic Survey-sponsored Newton-Jenny Party, the surveyor Valentine McGillycuddy plays the role of the Sun. Following the Black Hills survey, he was a contract surgeon for the U.S. Army during the Indian Wars. He was later recognized for maintaining favorable relations with Indians while Indian Agent for the Red Cloud Agency. McGillycuddy's role as a physician conforms to the Cancer Sun's caring nature shared by missionary activities timed by other Sun-Ascendant directions.[14]

Religion: Christian Science

On *October 30, 1875* Mary Baker Eddy published *Science and Health with Key to the Scriptures*. The Bible of the Christian Science movement, *Science and Health* shows the influence of Aquarian Moon's quest for scientific knowledge as the cause of the Sun-signified religious sect. Sun/Cancer signifies a practice which is devotional, outgoing, and focused on care. Mary Baker Eddy (b. 16-Jul-1821) recapitulates both Sun/Cancer and Moon/Aquarius placements in her natal figure.

Sun-Ascendant Direction #7

| D | Venus/Virgo | P | sin. sextile Sun c. → ASC | 8-Apr-1905 |

Controversy over Rockefeller Bequests for Missionary Work

The New York Times reported on *April 9, 1905* protests by the Baptist Preacher Francis Rowley against John D. Rockefeller's recent gift to the Baptists for missionary work. The point of contention stems from ethics of accepting a gift derived from prior illicit business practices in contrary of Church doctrine, e.g., 'dirty money.' Rockefeller's gift matches delineation of the Sun as a bequest for missionary work. Instead of the Sun's 8th house placement manifesting as fame from the willingness to risk death, in this case 8th house affairs pertaining to investments and inheritance apply.

<u>Distributor</u>: Venus/Virgo signifies fraudulent business practices including money laundering common to mafia enterprises; here 'dirty money.' This placement is recapitulated in Rockefeller's nativity (see Appendix C, p. 320).

Carnegie Bequests for Superannuated Preachers and Faculty

Best known for gifts to libraries, Carnegie was involved in a number of other charitable ventures. On *April 8, 1905*, the New England Methodist Conference announced on 'Missionary Day' that Carnegie agreed to provide the last $1 million for a $25 million fund for superannuated[15] preachers. On *April 28, 1905,* Carnegie established *The Carnegie Foundation* to provide pensions for superannuated teachers in colleges[16]. In the latter bequest, Carnegie specifically disallowed applicants from schools which imposed a theological test for enrollment or who were sectarian in any other way. Sun in the 8th of investments ruling the 4th can be delineated as old-age pensions because the 4th signifies end-of-life. Moon's rulership of the Sun signifies fair treatment of applicants.

Missionaries: Death of Hudson Taylor

The British native Hudson Taylor made his last trip to China, departing San Francisco on March 23, 1905 and arriving in Shanghai on *April 17, 1905*. He died on June 3, 1905. His China Inland Mission was later rated the largest Protestant mission agency in the world. Missionaries relied on faith, prayer, and acceptance by local populations where they traveled. They were not paid.

Sun-Ascendant Direction #8

| D | Mercury/Cancer | P | conjunction Sun d. → ASC | 30-Jun-1932 |

The New Deal

I pledge you, I pledge myself, to a new deal for the American people.

--Franklin Roosevelt, Democratic National Convention, *July 2, 1932*.[17]

FDR created the modern welfare state with New Deal Programs. Sun/Cancer can be delineated as a 'President who cares.' Sun is placed in the 8th of investments and rules the 4th of end-of-life. Social Security is a match.

Federal Home Loan Banking Act

President Herbert Hoover signed the Federal Home Loan Banking Act into law on *July 22, 1932*. This Act created the Federal Home Loan Banks whose primary task was facilitating consumer mortgage loans. Financing real estate transactions is another delineation of Sun in 8th ruling the 4th.

Religion: Dominionism

The American Evangelical Christian theologian, philosopher, and Presbyterian pastor Francis Schaeffer met his future wife Edith Seville on *June 26, 1932* at a meeting where both defended the Bible against attacks by a Unitarian.[18] They married in 1935. Schaeffer strongly influenced the entry of Evangelicals into 1980s politics based on dominionism, or the influence/control of secular political institutions by religious activists. Here, Francis and Edith Schaeffer play the role of the Sun; the Unitarian, the Moon.
As a subtle connection to Sun-Ascendant Direction #7, note Edith Seville was the daughter of missionary parents who served with the China Inland Mission under Hudson Taylor.

Monuments

Fort Necessity, the site of George Washington's battle loss during the French & Indian Wars, was dedicated on its entry to the National Park Service *July 4, 1932*. Washington's willingness to risk death (Sun/8th) is commemorated by a monument (Sun rules 4th house end-of-the-matter).

Sun-Ascendant Direction #9

| D | Mercury/Cancer | P | conjunction Sun c. → ASC | 8-Jul-1980 |

Black Hills Legal Settlement

On *June 30, 1980*, the Supreme Court ordered payment of $122 million to the Sioux Indians for the taking of the Black Hills by Congress in 1877. To the present day the Sioux have refused acceptance of these funds. Reserved in an interest bearing account, the 1980 settlement has grown to over $1 billion.

Partner: Given the Black Hills Gold Rush was triggered by Sun-Ascendant Direction #6, the Black Hills proposed settlement is an obvious event match. Sun placed in the 8th house of debt ruling the 4th house end-of-the-matter is a delineation match to government funds placed in an interest bearing account (government's debt) for the settlement of legal claims over land appropriated following a gold discovery.

Harvard Medical Center

A newly constructed facility housing four of Harvard University's teaching hospitals opened in early *July 1980*.[19] This event demonstrates the delineation of the Sun ruling the 9th of higher education.

Founding of Cabrini Hospice

The Rev. Vincent Pulicano worked to establish the Cabrini Hospice, which opened in the fall of 1980.[20] Pulicano contacted bone cancer in 1979 and dedicated the last two years of his life to establish the hospice program in New York City. Organization of the hospice was a high profile event supported by celebrity benefits and a grant from the Federal Department of Health and Human Services. Pulicano plays the role of the Sun/Cancer in the 8th ruling the 4th, literally a priest dying of cancer seeking to improve the quality of end-of-life care.

Sun-Ascendant Direction #10

| D | Venus/Virgo | P | sin. sextile Sun d. → ASC | 1-Oct-2007 |

Mortgage Crisis

The nation's largest bank, Citigroup, announced a third quarter loss of $5.9 billion on **October 2, 2007** in the midst of the housing collapse. Sun/Cancer ruling the 8th and 4th matches Citigroup's involvement in the real estate debacle because the Sun placed in the bound of Jupiter/Cancer signifies consumer banking, Sun in the 8th signifies debt, and Sun ruling the 4th signifies real estate. This followed an **October 1, 2007** $3.4 billion write-down of mortgage-backed securities by Union Bank of Switzerland (UBS), the largest loss reported by the largest European bank at that time.[21]

Writing this book a year later with the subprime mortgage crisis having spread to the Credit Default Swap market and the financial markets as a whole, I find it difficult to isolate a single event as candidate for the exact Sun-Ascendant Direction of October 1, 2007. Citigroup and UBS losses are reasonable event matches because they are respectively the largest banks in America and Europe. But it may take some years for a critical evaluation of the early stages of the current financial debacle before a definitive event can be assigned to this participating direction. By contrast, effects of the Distributor are much easier to understand.

<u>Distributor</u>: Venus/Virgo is in the sign of her fall. This placement signifies gambling, drug use, prostitution, pornography, and financial fraud – all perversions of Venus' characteristics. Delineating the fraudulent Venus/Virgo as the national consciousness means that all levels of American society facilitated mortgage fraud – borrowers, lenders, regulators, and Congress. The mortgage bubble was abetted by mortgage lenders who facilitated inflated appraisals, borrowers who falsified incomes, and regulators who looked the other way.

Compare this direction to Sun-Ascendant Direction #8 when Federal agencies were created to facilitate mortgage credit. For that direction, Mercury/Cancer was the Distributor which facilitated credit formation through emotional rhetoric made during a period of financial paralysis.

For this direction, Venus/Virgo set a stage so messy that the Sun could not facilitate mortgage credit. Instead, as an 8th house planet ruling the 4th house end-of-the-matter, the only way the Sun can manifest events is through a forensic financial investigation of fraudulent mortgage finance.

CHAPTER TEN

Partners: Lunar Nodes

North Node	7LE35'42"	**South Node**	7AQ35'42"
Sign	Leo	Sign	Saturn
Bound	Venus/Leo	Bound	Venus/Aquarius
Dwad	Scorpio	Dwad	Taurus
House Position	9th	House Position	3rd
Ruled by:	Sun	Ruled by:	Saturn

Behavior. Other than the ability of the North Node to increase and the South Node to decrease, there are few guidelines in judging the Nodes in the medieval tradition.[1] My experience with the Nodes is to judge them by house position and rulership. In this case, for North Node/Leo/9th, say 'North Node increases affairs of the 9th house because of the Sun.' For South Node/Aquarius/3rd, say 'South Node decreases affairs of the 3rd house because of Saturn.' In addition, because the South Node falls in the same sign as the Moon, say 'South Node diminishes the effects of the Moon.' Viewed this way, events timed by North Node directions should be very similar in effect to Ascendant-Sun directions; events timed by South Node directions, to Ascendant-Saturn directions.

Influence of Sect. From the field of natal astrology, there does appear one additional guideline for judging Nodes which is applicable here. For diurnal nativities with the North Node in the 9th, Bonatti has this to say about judging the native's religious beliefs:

> ...if the Head of the Dragon were in the ninth (in diurnal nativities)...it will signify the native to be of good memory and firm in his own proposals, and he is going to observe his faith and law well; and the more so, and more fervently, if Jupiter and the Sun and Mercury were to aspect that place from the noted aspects: because then his goodness and reputation will be exalted on high, and will fly through many regions or provinces.[2]

In making this delineation, Bonatti acknowledges the role of sect. Since the Sun rejoices in the 9th house, presumably the North Node's ability to increase the affairs of this house is augmented for diurnal figures because the Sun is the sect ruler. For the Regulus USA National Horoscope evaluated by whole sign houses, this condition applies. Moreover, the North Node falls in Leo which is the Sun's sign of rulership. To sum up, because the sect is diurnal and the 9th house is Leo, the North Node's placement in the 9th bodes well for 9th house affairs.

Special Delineation – Military Service. An unexpected finding was the consistent ability of the Nodes to time military service, including drafts for the War of 1812, the Civil War, the Korean War, and the Vietnam War. Placement of the North Node's dwad in Scorpio adds a military flavor to the North Node's delineation; the question is whether the Mars dwad is sufficient to add military service to the North Node's delineation. Mars/Gemini/7th sending its antiscion to the Sun is another possible Martian influence on the North Node; yet a five degree orb for this antiscion relationship is a bit wide. Finally, the antiscion of Mars within two degrees of the fixed star Sirius at 10CA58'18" may be relevant. Robson delineates Sirius with Mars as military preferment.[3] Precession of Sirius to the conjunction of the Sun may also matter.[4] Or the ability of the Nodes to time military conscription may rest on their innate function, regardless of sign, bound, or dwad placement.

Special Delineation – French Peace Treaties. During the rectification process, I discovered the famous WWI armistice on November 11, 1918 was timed within two days by direct solar arc ASC conj. North Node (exact for November 9, 1918). The WWI peace conference was held in Paris the following year. According to mundane choreography rules, Leo is assigned to France.[5] Then it struck me the choice of Paris as location for peace negotiations was a relatively common choice throughout American history:

Table 8. American Peace Negotiations conducted in Paris, France.

Name	Date	Event
Treaty of Paris	1783	Revolutionary War
Paris Peace Conference	1898	Spanish-American War
Paris Peace Conference	1919	WWI
Paris Peace Treaties	1947	WWII – treaty between Germany and European allies
Paris Peace Accords	1973	Vietnam War

I suggest the North Node's placement in Leo is behind the choice of Paris as venue for these Peace Conferences.

CHAPTER 10 - PARTNERS: LUNAR NODES   181

Transits of North Node conjunct Ascendant
Transits of South Node conjunct Descendant

Presentation

This chapter departs from the 'direction-only' format to include transits. For natal astrology, transits of the slow moving Lunar Nodes are one of the most accurate transit measurements for rectification work because Nodal transits connect the native to the world through a public event for which a record is likely to exist.[6] What can be said for natal applications should also be applicable for national horoscopes. This expectation is borne out by the following events timed by the transit of the North Node to the Ascendant and the South Node to the Descendant, which by definition, occur simultaneously. This transit coincides with public events which demonstrate the Sun's rulership of the North Node/9th, Saturn's rulership of the South Node/3rd, and occasionally both planets and Nodes working simultaneously.

December 2, 1787

Special Interests. Of all Federalist Papers published between *October 1787* and *August 1788*, Federalist No. 10 by James Madison published on **November 22, 1787** is ranked as the most famous. In this essay, Madison warned against the rise of *factions*, or special interest groups with goals contrary to the nation as a whole. Part of Madison's solution was formation of a Republic, whose leaders are elected by delegates; in contrast to a Democracy, whose leaders are elected by popular vote. Madison felt special interest groups were capable of manipulating the popular vote in ways which could easily overwhelm the long-term interests of the nation. *Delineation Match*: If Aquarius signifies the common man, then South Node in Aquarius diminishes the will of the people. Transit of North Node to Ascendant by definition moves the South Node to the Descendant, or 7th house of open enemies and legal conflicts. This transit is best delineated as the transit of the South Node to the 7th because it concerns conflict over special interest groups which threaten equal rights for the common man.

July 14, 1806

Pike Expedition. In a 2nd expedition commissioned by General James Wilkinson, Captain Zebulon Pike led the Pike Expedition designed to explore/survey the southwest portion of the Louisiana Purchase. (***July 15, 1806*** – July 1, 1807) Pike was the first to explore the western Great Plains and the Rocky Mountains. Pikes Peak in Colorado was discovered and named for the expedition's leader. *Delineation Match*: North Node in Leo promises an increase in exploration made by Sun/Cancer individuals who risk death. This transit timed an expedition whose goal was exploration of an unknown territory. Sacrifices made by the Sun/Cancer in 8th (men risking death) are evident when one reads some men quit the expedition because of physical exhaustion; others (including Pike) were imprisoned by the Spanish when traveling through New Mexico in early 1807.

February 22, 1825

Expedition. On *March 3, 1825*, Congress authorized a federal survey to mark the Santa Fe Trail in order to link the Missouri River and New Mexico. *Delineation Match*: Usage of the Sante Fe Trail as an international highway between the United States and Mexico confirms the 9th house whole sign placement of the North Node because the 9th signifies foreign travel. During the Mexican-American war of 1846-1848, the trail served as an invasion route for the entry of American troops to Mexico. Sun's placement in the 8th of traded goods matches the importance of the trail as a trade route which facilitated economic development of conquered territory.

October 5, 1843

Humanitarian Service Organization. On *October 13, 1843*, Henry Jones and eleven others founded the B'nai B'rith, a Jewish service organization. The original function of the group was 'to maintain orphanages and homes for the elderly and widows.'[7] Since inception, the organization has expanded its mandate to include supplying disaster relief, funding college scholarships, and the fight against anti-Semitism. *Delineation Match*: The group's original mandate to provide housing assistance for the indigent is similar in objective to Social Security, a New Deal program instituted by FDR and similarly timed by other Sun and Lunar Node directions. Sun rules the 4th of real estate. Supplying disaster relief is consistent with the caring Cancer Sun ruling the 9th of foreign lands. College scholarships match the Node in the 9th of higher education.

May 16, 1862

Military Service. The first of three Confederate Conscription laws was passed on *April 16, 1862*; one month prior to this exact transit date. The next two conscription laws were enacted on September 27, 1862 and during February 1864. While the Union did not make its draft official until July 1863 (which triggered the New York Draft Riot), this transit occurred five weeks after the Battle of Shiloh (*April 6-7, 1862*). After Shiloh, the notion the Union could defeat the Confederates in a single large battle was summarily dismissed. Realization the war would be lengthy and costly demanded additional sacrifices in military service by men on the Union side, with or without a draft. *Delineation Match*: Willingness to die in battle for gains in what was considered a spiritual quest for 'God and Country' for many Civil

CHAPTER 10 - PARTNERS: LUNAR NODES   183

War participants is one delineation of the Sun in 8th of death ruling the 9th of God. Consider also because of controversy over the 'Christians-only' chaplain policy enacted on *August 3, 1861*, qualifications for Civil War chaplains were changed on *July 17, 1862* to include ordained ministers of any religious denomination to accommodate demands for Jewish chaplains.[8] This change occurred two months after the North Node transit, suggesting its relevance.

Homestead Act. On *May 20, 1862*, Lincoln signed the Homestead Act which allowed citizens to acquire up to 160 acres by agreeing to settle public land for five years and pay $1.25 an acre. *Delineation Match*: Lincoln (Sun) provided real estate (Sun-ruled 4th) to facilitate settlement (9th house of journeys). Revenue was used to pay off Federal debts (Sun in 8th).

December 26, 1880

Military Service. On *December 28, 1880*, a statue honoring the memory of General Philip Kearny was unveiled in Newark, NJ.[9] Kearny was a distinguished American military officer who fought in both the Mexican and Civil War, where he was killed in action in the Battle of Chantilly. *Delineation Match*: Sun in the 8th of death ruling the 4th of the end-of-the-matter and the 9th of foreign affairs is a delineation match to a monument honoring an individual who risked death in a foreign land. Kearny also has a connection to France (Leo). In 1839, Kearny traveled to France to study tactics at a famous cavalry school in Saumur. Kearny later participated with the Chasseurs d'Afrique in Algiers.

August 7, 1889

Scientific Expedition. On *August 7, 1889*, the NYT reported a U.S. Government sponsored geodetic survey party was at work determining the boundaries of the newly acquired Alaskan territory.[10] *Delineation Match*: Sun rules the 9th house of exploration.

Death of Missionary. Known as the 'Christian Buddha' by the Chinese, the Rev. J. Crossett died on the steamer El Dorado on June 21, 1889. His life was profiled on *August 14, 1889*.[11] Crossett focused his efforts on the poorest of beggars and those confined in prisons and other institutions. *Delineation Match*: Sun/Cancer/8th ruling the 9th signifies death of a missionary who lived in foreign lands providing care and comfort to the unfortunate.

March 19, 1918

Death of Explorer. Reported *March 19, 1918* was the death of Major William C. Daniels, a Denver Millionaire Merchant and Explorer.[12] *Delineation Match*: Sun/8th ruling the 9th signifies death of an explorer.

October 29, 1936

Death of Missionary. Reported on *October 31, 1936*; death of Mgr. John J. Burke who had secured aid for Mexican Catholics as a member of the Paulist Fathers.[13] *Delineation Match*: Sun/Cancer/8th ruling the 9th signifies death of a missionary who lived in foreign lands providing care and comfort to the unfortunate.

Welfare. Immediately prior to the *November 1936* Presidential elections, Social Security was a hot campaign topic. Arguments over payroll deductions and other features of the program were made daily in the NYT. *Delineation Match*: Sun/Cancer/8th signifies the President's involvement in an investment program (Sun in 8th) designed to provide care and comfort (Sun in Cancer) for retirement (Sun rules 4th). Willingness to provide financial support for the indigent in order to level the playing field among competing ranks of society is traced to John Locke's writings on the welfare state timed by Sun-Ascendant Direction #1. The welfare state is an important construct in the philosophy of America (North Node in 9th of philosophy and religion). In addition, on *October 29, 1936* the NYT reported on a Princeton student who won a debate on Social Security. This event demonstrates the influence of the North Node's placement in the 9th house of higher education.[14]

Statue of Liberty Rededication. For the 50th anniversary of the Statue of Liberty on *October 28, 1936*, President Franklin Roosevelt "re-dedicated the nation yesterday to 'the liberty and the peace' which the Statue of Liberty symbolizes."[15] *Delineation Match*: The Statue of Liberty was a gift from the French which fits the North Node's placement in Leo (France) in the 9th (foreign lands).

June 10, 1955

Death of Explorer. Reported *June 8, 1955* was the death of L. J. Wilth, famous cartographer renown for work in Polar Regions and work during war campaigns.[16] *Delineation Match*: Death of explorer/military personnel is consistent with Sun in the 8th of death ruling the North Node, dwad of Scorpio, in the 9th of foreign lands.

Publicity of Expedition. A notice published *June 9, 1955* promoted an account of the expedition taken by M. Brom to French Equatorial Africa to be published in an American edition on *June 24, 1955*.[17] *Delineation Match*: Sun's rulership of North Node/9th is consistent with publicity for an expedition in a foreign land. Note the Leo-French connection.

Military Service. On *June 16, 1955*, the House of Representatives voted to extend Selective Service until June 30, 1959. *Delineation Match*:

Willingness to die overseas in military service is a match to Sun in 8th of death ruling the North Node, dwad of Scorpio, in the 9th house of foreign lands.

January 19, 1974

Ancestry/Higher Education. On *January 17, 1974*, Clarence E. Lovejoy died. He was the author of *Lovejoy's College Guide* and *The Lovejoy Genealogy*.[18] *Delineation Match*: Sun rules the North Node in the 9th of higher education; Sun also rules the 4th cusp of ancestry.

Higher Education. On *January 18, 1974*, David Crawford died. He was the President of University of Hawaii for 25 years and was born in Hermosillo, Mexico to American missionary parents.[19] *Delineation Match*: Death of a University President is consistent with Sun in 8th ruling the 9th. Crawford's missionary parents demonstrate another 9th house connection.

August 31, 1992

Threat to open communications. In a story reported *August 31, 1992*, The FCC approved 'video dial tone' or the transmission of television and other video services over phone lines. There was concern the FCC would also allow phone companies ownership of program content, creating potential conflict of interests which would ultimately limit free expression.[20] *Delineation Match*: This event matches the transit of the South Node to the 7th cusp of legal conflict. Recall James Madison's warnings on the ability of special interest groups to harm the public interest timed by the December 2, 1787 South Node transit to the Descendant. This event appears a match to Madison's fears espoused more than 200 years earlier.

Expedition – Gold Treasure. On *August 28, 1992*, a Federal Appeals Court ruled insurance companies could share in recovered gold from a September 12, 1857 shipwreck of the steamship Central America.[21] *Delineation Match*: Explorations/expeditions to find gold is one delineation of the Sun ruled North Node in the 9th. Recall Sun-Ascendant Direction #6 which led to the Black Hills Gold Rush. This is one of the few North Node transits which demonstrate placement of the North Node in the bound of Venus/Leo. Gold (Leo) coins (Venus) is an exact match.

End of Transit Section

Node – Ascendant Direction #1

D	Jupiter/Sagittarius	P	sin. trine North Node c. → ASC	4-Apr-1799
D	Jupiter/Sagittarius	P	dex. sextile South Node c. → ASC	4-Apr-1799

Gradual Emancipation of Slaves enacted by New York State

On *March 29, 1799*, the New York State Legislature passed a gradual emancipation law. The law stipulated that children born to slave women after July 4, 1799 were deemed free but the children must serve as their 'mother's master' until the age of 28 (males) or 25 (females). For children who were considered abandoned by the slave master within one year of birth, the slave master was required to register the children with the local overseer of the poor. The overseer would facilitate transfer payments made by the state of New York to slave-owners, up to $3.50 per month per child. The practical effect of this legislation was introduction of compensated emancipation as a palliative in order to secure support from slave masters for the legislation's passage.[22]

Both North and South Node effects are demonstrated by this direction. Sun/Cancer/8th signifies welfare payments. Sun rules the 5th of children by exaltation. North Node times an event which increases the Sun's significations. Moon/Aquarius signifies abolition. South Node diminishes abolition. Slavery was not completely eliminated in New York State until July 4, 1827. Under the 1799 statute, children were not completely free; nor were any adults freed.

Node – Ascendant Direction #2

D	Venus/Aquarius	P	North Node d. → DSC	7-Oct-1814
D	Venus/Aquarius	P	South Node d. → ASC	7-Oct-1814

Hartford Convention

Anger between Federalist-dominated New England and the Republican Party under Jefferson and Madison dates from Jefferson's Embargo Act of 1807. Under this act, New England's trade with Britain effectively ceased which drove the New England economy into a deep recession. Repeal of the Embargo Act a year later helped mend bridges but James Madison's Non-Intercourse Act of 1809 repeated many of the policy errors from Jefferson's 1807 anti-trade measures. Halfway through Madison's second presidential term marked the worst of fighting against the British in the War of 1812. In mid-1814, Madison had become so distrustful of Federalist factions in Massachusetts and Connecticut that Madison refused to delegate control of state militias to the state Governor. With Massachusetts and Connecticut refusing to adhere to Madison's conditions, Madison refused Federal funding for state militia service. At this point there were calls for secession from the Union led by Massachusetts Federalist Harrison Gray Otis.

On *October 10, 1814*, Massachusetts called for a convention at Hartford to discuss constitutional amendments necessary to protect Federalist interests in New England States. What was later known as the 'Hartford Convention' was held on December 15, 1814 with twenty-six delegates representing Massachusetts, Connecticut, Rhode Island, New Hampshire, and Vermont in attendance.

Interpreted as a North Node – Descendant direction, the Hartford Convention is a delineation match to legal conflict over military conscription.

Node – Ascendant Direction #3

D	Venus/Scorpio	P	sin. square North Node c. → ASC	2-Feb-1837
D	Venus/Scorpio	P	dex. square South Node c. → ASC	2-Feb-1837

Supreme Court Decision: *Mayor of New York v. Miln*

Expressing strong anti-immigrant sentiments, New Yorkers demanded and received protection from the New York state legislature. The legislature enacted a statute which required ship masters to report details of each immigrant on board, subject to fines, in order to ascertain whether each immigrant was capable of economic self-sufficiency. This statute was violated by a ship master named Mr. Thompson; ship owner Miln appealed Thompson's conviction on the grounds that the state of New York had overstepped its legal boundary by regulating interstate or foreign commerce over which Congress had authority, not the states.

Arguments in *New York v. Miln* were heard before the Supreme Court on *January 27, 1837*; the case was decided on *February 16, 1837*. The Court upheld the statute enacted by the New York legislature.

Sun/Cancer/8th ruling the 9th signifies a philosophy of providing care and comfort for foreign parties funded through government debt. This is the welfare state delineation of the Sun.

Sun-ruled North Node generates an event consistent with the theme of providing welfare for immigrants; except in this case, welfare is denied because of the interference by Venus/Scorpio as distributor who acts as an accidental malefic. Consider Venus-Scorpio's period as distributor by converse motion: October 3, 1832 – November 3, 1837. This period coincided with public support for Andrew Jackson's attacks against the Second Bank of the United States. Just as Venus in the sign opposite of the money sign of Taurus harbors resentments towards capital and banking, so does Venus/Scorpio turn her stinging side towards immigrants by means of envy and revenge.[23] At this time, Americans were not interested in government support of foreign immigrants because such support was insulting to laboring American workers.

Node – Ascendant Direction #4

D	Venus/Aries	P	dex. trine North Node d. → ASC	9-Jan-1853
D	Venus/Aries	P	sin. sextile South Node d. → ASC	9-Jan-1853

Dispute over Clayton-Bulwar Treaty

The Clayton-Bulwer Treaty was signed on April 19, 1850 by John M. Clayton (USA) and Sir Henry Lytton Bulwer (UK). The treaty established political neutrality in Central America following plans for an interoceanic canal through Nicaragua. (Later the route would be changed to Panama.)

On June 8, 1850, the British Prime Minister Lord Palmerston ordered Bulwer to make a separate declaration that the UK understood the treaty to exclude Honduras and its dependencies. This was apparently a face saving measure in order to make the British look like they were not giving away the store in their treaty negotiations. Clayton was willing to play this diplomatic game and responded with a similarly worded declaration.

At the time of this Ascendant-Node direction, a controversy arose in the Senate over the June 8, 1850 Honduras declaration. Senator Lewis Cass and others complained they thought the purpose of the treaty was to get the British out of Central America; that they were uninformed as to the Honduras declaration; and had they been fully informed they would have not voted to approve the treaty in 1850.

This particular incident is not emphasized by historians. But the controversy was large enough to produce several full page articles in the New York Times; in addition, the Senate met in Executive Session on *January 12, 1853* in order to remove the injunction of secrecy surrounding Treaty documents. Disclosure of Treaty documents and a review of negotiations produced no intent by President Taylor or John Clayton to deceive Congress. The event timed by this direction appears best delineated as a partisan battle.

South Node/Aquarius/3rd diminishes publicity (3rd house) concerning canals (Moon/Aquarius). As ruler, Saturn/Libra/11th is the cause – here an attack by the Senate.

Node – Ascendant Direction #5

D	Venus/Taurus	P	dex. square North Node d. → ASC	14-Sep-1871
D	Venus/Taurus	P	sin. square South Node d. → ASC	14-Sep-1871

Erie Canal Fraud

In late 1871, a scandal broke concerning maintenance contracts for the Erie Canal. Tammany Hall operatives had raised suspicions since accepting contract bids in 1866. On *September 19, 1871*, the New York Times provided a line item financial report for Erie Canal maintenance contracts for the year 1870. The reports shows that Tammany Hall had stolen between one-half and two-thirds of funds appropriated for maintenance contracts.[24]

Similar to the effect of Node-Ascendant Direction #4, news of the Tammany scandal was bad publicity for the nation's canal transportation system.

Node – Ascendant Direction #6

D	Mercury/Libra	P	sin. sextile North Node c. → ASC	6-Dec-1874
D	Mercury/Libra	P	dex. trine South Node c. → ASC	6-Dec-1874

Pacific Mail Company Fraud

On *December 3, 1874*, Russell Sage resigned from his position as President of the Pacific Mail Steamship Company.[25] Sage had decided to distance himself from the company after learning some Directors falsified financial reports to support the stock price. He also learned the financial position of the company was materially worse than what had been reported.

Origins of the Pacific Mail Steamship Company date to the Moon-Ascendant Direction #4 computed for July 27, 1848 – June 9, 1849. This sequence witnessed the formation of Atlantic and Pacific Mail Steamship Companies as well as the Panama Railroad Company designed to facilitate passenger travel to the California gold fields.

This Node-Ascendant direction timed bad publicity for a company organized for mail transportation.

Node – Ascendant Direction #7

D	Jupiter/Gemini	P	dex sextile North Node d. → ASC	2-Jan-1895
D	Jupiter/Gemini	P	sin trine South Node d. → ASC	2-Jan-1895

Deterioration of Gold Supplies

On January 28, 1895, President Grover Cleveland sent a special message to Congress, requesting legislation to halt the run on the nation's gold supply at the Treasury. As explained in Saturn-Ascendant Direction #6, populist political movements forced the introduction of a bimetallic gold-silver standard. Supporters envisioned the inflationary consequences of the Treasury's purchase of silver a remedy for low commodity prices during the deflationary post-Civil War era. Unfortunately it also caused a rise in the supply of silver relative to gold and a corresponding fall in the price of silver relative to gold. A riskless arbitrage was available to those willing to present silver to the Treasury in exchange for Treasury Notes and then turn right around and demand gold for the same Treasury Notes.

Placed eleven signs from Saturn, significator of the United States dollar, North Node conjunct Lot of Fortune both in Leo can be delineated as the gold backing behind the U.S. Dollar. (See Sun-Ascendant Direction #6).

The Partner did indeed time an increase in the nation's currency backing – but by an increase of silver at the expense of gold. The effect of Jupiter/Gemini as Distributor was for the nation to attempt to 'have it both ways' and in doing so saw the nation's gold reserves fall below the statutory level of $100 million on February 8, 1895 which triggered the Panic of 1895.

For further discussion of Distributor Jupiter/Gemini delineated as bimetallism, see Saturn-Ascendant Direction #6.

CHAPTER 10 - PARTNERS: LUNAR NODES

Node – Ascendant Direction #8

D	Venus/Leo	P	conjunction North Node c. → ASC	2-Aug-1950
D	Venus/Leo	P	opposition North Node c. → ASC	2-Aug-1950

Missionaries: Death of Frank Gamewell

On *August 7, 1950*, the Rev. Dr. Frank Dunlap Gamewell died. He was the oldest retired missionary of the Methodist Church and considered a hero of the siege of Peking during the Boxer Rebellion of 1900.[26]

Social Security Legislation

On *August 1, 1950*, Congress approved a compromise bill which added an additional 10 million workers to Social Security and increased benefits for current enrollees.[27] The 1950 legislation was the most significant expansion in the program's mandate since its inception under FDR.

Military Service

On *August 4, 1950*, the U.S. Army called 62,000 reservists for Korean service.

Node – Ascendant Direction #9

D	Venus/Leo	P	conjunction North Node d. → ASC	1-Jun-1962
D	Venus/Leo	P	opposition South Node d. → ASC	1-Jun-1962

Segregation Legislation

It was reported on *May 20, 1962* Congress planned to consider legislation which prohibited segregation in land-grant colleges and universities.[28]

Missionaries: Vietnam Kidnapping

On *May 31, 1962*, three American missionaries were kidnapped in Vietnam's central highlands.[29]

French Satellite Launch

On *May 31, 1962*, France announced its launch date for its first space satellite.[30]

Dollar Stabilization Program

It was reported on *June 1, 1962* the U.S. had accumulated a reserve of almost $18 million in pounds sterling in order to defend the U.S. Dollar against speculative attack from overseas speculators.[31]

Military Draft

On *June 7, 1962*, the U.S. Army announced a 5,000 draft for August 1962.

NEW Out-of-sample event published after 2008 1st edition.

Node – Ascendant Direction #10

D	Jupiter/Gemini	P	sin trine South Node c. → ASC	4-Jan-2018
D	Jupiter/Gemini	P	dex sextile North Node d. → ASC	4-Jan-2018

End of Net Neutrality

Net neutrality is the principle that Internet service providers (ISPs) treat Internet data equally without imposition of any gateways or paywalls which favor specific provider content. Net neutrality was introduced by the Federal Communications Commission (FCC) in 2005 by classifying ISPs as Title II "common carrier services" under the Communications Act of 1934 which gave the FCC permission to regulate internet traffic.

On *December 14, 2017*, the FCC reversed its 2005 decision by reclassifying ISPs as Title I "information services" under the Communications Act of 1934. This action removed ISPs from FCC jurisdiction under the prior 2005 classification. The legal effect of this action was to end net neutrality.[32]

On *January 5, 2018*, the Internet Association whose members include Facebook, Google, and Netflix announced plans to join a lawsuit challenging the FCC's December 14, 2017 decision to end net neutrality.[33]

In *Mozilla v. FCC* decided *October 1, 2019* the US Court of Appeals for the District of Columbia Circuit upheld the FCC's December 14, 2017 decision; however, the court did prevent the FCC from blocking any state or local laws which upheld net neutrality.

South Node/Aquarius/3rd diminishes affairs of the 3rd house of communications. Placement in the bound of Venus/Aquarius adds the theme of social equality. South Node in the bound of Venus/Aquarius diminishes social equality which is a delineation match to the end of net neutrality. One day after the computed primary direction, large tech companies announced legal action against the FCC. The distributor for the direction, Jupiter/Gemini, is an easy delineation match to Jupiter (large business magnates) + Gemini (specializing in communications). The distributor is placed in the 7th house of conflict and legal disputes.

CHAPTER ELEVEN

Partners: Saturn

Longitude	14LI48'24"
Latitude	2n31'01"
Speed	+0deg1'49" (slow)
Sign	Libra
Bound	Jupiter/Libra
Dwad	Pisces
Houses	<u>Occupies</u> 11th
	<u>Rules</u> 2nd, 3rd, 11th (WS), 2nd, 10th (AL)[1]
Rulers	<u>Ruled</u> by Venus/Cancer.
	<u>Rules</u> Moon/Aquarius, South Node/Aquarius.
Additional	Evening star/Occidental
	Most elevated planet, closely conjunct Midheaven
	Ruler of the Chart
	Greatest/Maximum Years = 256

<u>Planet – Saturn</u>: Saturn signifies government, institutions, conservatism, infrastructure, the rule of law, and men.

<u>Sign – Libra</u>: A human sign associated with justice and balance. Saturn/Libra in exaltation means far reaching but unsteady effects.

<u>Bound – Jupiter/Libra</u>: Jupiter/Libra signifies a philosophy of egalitarianism. Jupiter's universal significator as judges and justices adds a judicial delineation to Saturn. For this reason, Saturn should take on a legal dimension; a topic which otherwise might be assigned to the 9th house according to most mundane authors.

<u>Dwad</u>: Saturn in the dwad of Pisces adds a polarizing influence. Though Saturn/Pisces is not technically in detriment or fall, any placement of Saturn in water signs is a difficult because Saturn's dry nature is contrary to Pisces wet nature. Picture a castle surrounded by a moat. Or if Pisces is taken

as the 'collective' in a modern psychological sense, then Saturn/Pisces yields a 'hands off' attitude which can produce a psychology of exclusiveness.

Ruled by Venus/Cancer: Because Venus is corrupted (see Chapter 14 for the complete delineation), she signifies both committal and judgment of financial scandal, consumer bankruptcy, and white racism. These significations of Venus will be the source and outcome of Saturn's actions.

Rules – Moon/Aquarius: The demand for equal treatment of humans in matters of free speech, public education, and local transportation is the primary signification of the Aquarian Moon. As ruler, Saturn is the source and outcome of the Moon's actions.

Synthesis – Saturn

For the Regulus USA National Horoscope, Saturn/Libra is the most important planet to delineate correctly because it is the Ruler of the Chart. Though Saturn is in the sign of his exaltation and powerfully positioned at the Midheaven, upon closer scrutiny Saturn is not as powerful as it first appears. Saturn's first problem is whatever his significations; they cannot be maintained. This is true because whenever Saturn is elevated in the 10th, a sharp rise and fall in reputation is signified, no matter what sign Saturn falls in. Furthermore, planets in the signs of their exaltation produce relatively unsteady effects compared to placements in signs they rule. Both factors of elevation and exaltation predict a fall from grace after initially favorable effects. Saturn's third major problem is the weakness of ruler Venus/Cancer delineated as an accidental malefic mainly for her placement in the bound of Mars and position under the sunbeams. As the source of Saturn's effects, a corrupt Venus gives Saturn ample reasons to create legal institutions designed to clean up Venus-signified problems. Yet as the result of Saturn's actions, Venus ultimately proves too tempting for Saturn to avoid her corrupting influences. This Venus-Saturn ruler pattern of corruption, institutional/legal remedies, and more corruption is the third indication that Saturn will crash badly as time marches on.

Saturn: U.S. Dollar, the New World Order, and Post WWII Institutions

By far the most important signification of Saturn/Libra is its 11th house placement which specifies its actions to America's institutional alliances and the United States Dollar.

Currency. Why does Saturn/Libra signify the U.S. Dollar? Saturn signifies structure and containment. Libra is the air sign ruled by Venus which is the universal significator of money. Structure + money = unit of account. In the 2nd from the 10th by derived houses – literally the 'King's money' –

Saturn is further specified to the nation's treasury. Another clue that Saturn signifies the U.S. Dollar is the expression *The Almighty Dollar* which first entered the popular lexicon in 1836.² The word *Almighty* is indicative of Saturn's exalted status, e.g., almighty = exalted.

New World Order and Post WWII Institutions. The phrase *Novus Ordo Seclorum* means *New Order of the Ages* and appears on the reverse of the Great Seal of the United States. It also appears on the reverse of the One Dollar Bill making a natural linkage between the U.S. Dollar and the New World Order.

Confirming the linkage between Saturn/Libra and the New World Order are events timed by directions of Saturn/Libra to the angles for horoscopes for both the Regulus USA National Horoscope and former President George H. W. Bush. Consider the following directions.

For the Regulus USA National Horoscope:

20-Dec-1946. *d.s.a. ASC trine Saturn.* Timed report stating success of the International Monetary Fund (set up by Bretton Woods) depended on the speed of setting up America's export businesses.³

17-Jul-1947. *c.s.a. Saturn trine ASC.* Timed opening of Paris talks on July 12, 1947 to discuss the structure of the Marshall Plan.

For President George H. W. Bush:

| D | Saturn/Gemini | P | dex. trine Saturn (l=SA) d. → ASC | 8-Jun-1947 |
| D | Saturn/Gemini | P | dex. trine Saturn (l=0) d. → ASC | 12-Jul-1947 |

This primary direction sequence timed the original proposal for the Marshall Plan made on June 5 and the opening of Paris talks on July 12, 1947 to discuss its structure.⁴

The ability of Saturn/Libra directions for both George H. W. Bush and the Regulus USA National Horoscope to time the same 1947 Paris talks for the Marshall Plan is extraordinary. Yet this finding merely confirms the Mundane-Natal Horoscope Connection introduced in Chapter 2. Bush is the only President whose nativity recapitulates the same Saturn/Libra – Venus/Cancer aspect in the Regulus USA National Horoscope. With this connection, there should be no surprise that George H. W. Bush was the first President since Woodrow Wilson to explicitly call for a 'New World Order.'

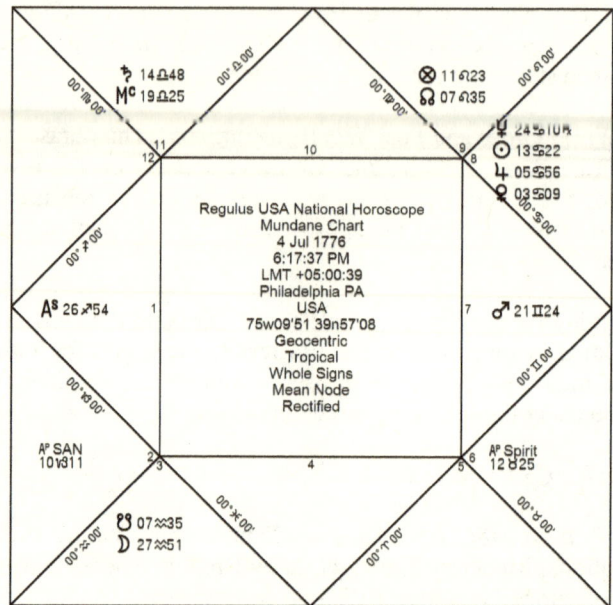

Figure 13. Regulus USA National Horoscope.

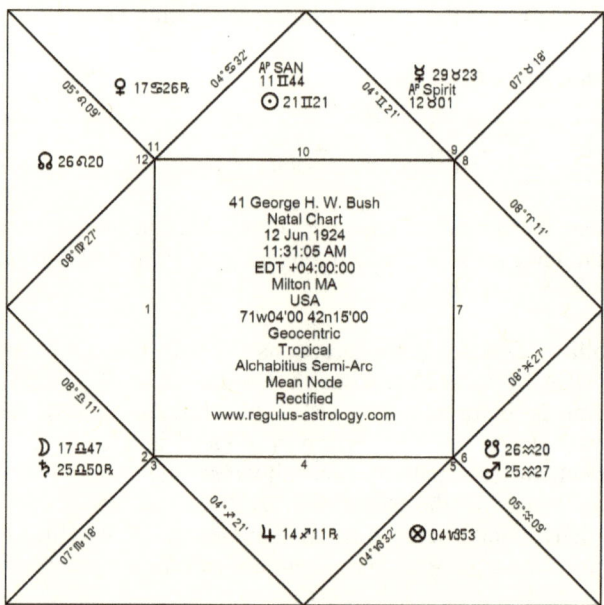

Figure 14. George H. W. Bush.[5]

Wrap-Up: Saturn

The December 1946 Saturn direction timed a report stating the success of the IMF depended on how quickly the U.S. established export businesses. Here we gain an important clue for completing Saturn's delineation.

If Venus signifies both the source and outcome of Saturn's effects *and*

Venus = tainted consumer goods, bankrupt consumers, and traded goods *and*

Saturn = U.S. Dollar, Post WWII institutions, and the New World Order *then*

- Indebted U.S. domestic consumers ('filled to the gills with consumer products') are the trigger for post-WWII institutions designed to expand markets for U.S. multinational corporations by facilitating export of U.S. consumer goods.

- Rescue of failed foreign economies through IMF and World Bank programs of economic stabilization, trade liberalization, and foreign aid designed to promote exports of U.S. traded goods has caused a new cycle of corruption among foreign governments.[6] Corruption and ineffectiveness has caused the IMF and World Bank censure.

- Maturation of developing country economies means these countries are no longer in need of U.S. export goods to meet the demands of their consuming populations. A reduction in exports of U.S. consumer goods reduces net exports, reduces positive capital flows, the strength of the U.S. Dollar, and the ability of the U.S. Dollar to reap seigniorage from its status as a world reserve currency. For these structural reasons the Dollar is guaranteed to decline in the long-term.

Viewed from another perspective, consider conditions which supported strength of the U.S. Dollar in the post-WWII era, arguably timed by the peak measure of U.S. gold reserves on September 21, 1949[7]. America had defeated Germany and Japan in World War II, designed supranational organizations designed to impose the rule of law, and used those same organizations as channels to promote export of U.S. consumer goods. The result was large trade surpluses and a strong dollar. Mars/Gemini/7th signifies warfare fought against Germany and Japan.[8] Saturn/Libra/11th signifies supranational organizations and the U.S. Dollar. Venus/Cancer/8th signifies traded goods. Mars assists Saturn by trine aspect. Venus rules Saturn and allows the export of consumer goods to drive the motivation of supranational organizations.

Saturn-Ascendant Direction #1

D	Venus/Sag.	P	sin. sextile Saturn (l=0) c. → ASC	6-Jul-1790
D	Venus/Sag.	P	sin. sextile Saturn (l=SA) c. → ASC	6-Oct-1792

Weights and Measures

On *July 13, 1790*, Secretary of State Thomas Jefferson submitted his report *Plan for Establishing Uniformity in the Coinage, Weights, and Measures of the United States* to the U.S. House of Representatives. Jefferson submitted two proposals, the first a slight modification of the avoirdupois system[9] commonly in use; the second a more radical extension of the decimal-based currency units to all other weights and measures. Congress took action on neither plan and has historically taken a disinterested approach to the definition of weights and measures.[10]

Jefferson-Hamilton Feud

The origins of America's first two party political system date to the Hamilton-Jefferson feud over federal control of the economy. Between 1790 and 1792, Hamilton's plans for assumption of state and federal debt, a national bank, and protective tariffs to support a domestic manufacturing industry were introduced. At the heart of the debate was Jefferson's opposition to Hamilton's favoritism of commercial interests. Jefferson feared Hamilton's plans would lead to a British-like political-economic system which was the opposite path Jefferson saw for America. Jefferson favored a decentralized economy primarily based on agriculture. This sequence timed Washington's *July 16, 1790* approval of the bill making the District of Columbia the nation's capital. This was a sop to Southern states, primarily debtors, in order to garner approval for the assumption of state Revolutionary War debts. As Hamilton introduced each successive plank to his program of centralized finance, Jefferson became more antagonistic. As the sequence closed, on *October 2, 1792*, Washington met with Jefferson and Hamilton but failed to mediate the feud. Jefferson resigned as Secretary of State in 1793.

Distributor: Venus (money) + Sagittarius (expansion) = inflation. The nation suffered from inflation during 1790-1795, an added impetus for the need to stabilize the nation's financial infrastructure.

Saturn-Ascendant Direction #2

D	Jupiter/Cap.	P	sin. square Saturn (l=SA) d. → ASC	5-Apr-1792
D	Changeover		bound Venus/Capricorn d. → ASC	4-May-1794
D	Venus/Cap.	P	sin. square Saturn (l=0) d. → ASC	12-Feb-1795

Coinage Act of 1792 and creation of the United States Dollar.

Establishment of the United States Dollar as the necessary lubricant for Alexander Hamilton's financial system is the dominant theme of this sequence. Events which lock down this sequence are the Coinage Act of 1792 signed by George Washington on *April 2, 1792* and the presentation of the first deposit of gold bullion for coinage on *February 12, 1795*.[11]

In addition to witnessing Saturn's actions, this direction plainly shows evidence of Saturn's ruler – Venus – as the source of Saturn's effects. As is outlined in Chapter 14, Venus signifies financial scandal. So it is not surprising to learn that the Coinage Act of 1792 was preceded by the first financial crisis in American history. Hamilton's Bank of the United States (BUS) was a key tenet of his centralized national financial plan. Extreme speculation in BUS stock led to America's first stock market crash during March 1792.[12] This panic was a mobilizing factor behind the Coinage Act of 1792 which established the U.S. Mint, regulated coins, established the dollar as the unit of account, declared it lawful tender, and created a decimal system for currency. Venus helped create the U.S. dollar because a financial scandal created sufficient instability in the nation's financial system that currency reform was required.

In natal astrology, Venus in this configuration usually signifies a sex scandal. Hamilton's resignation as Treasury Secretary on *January 31, 1795* was in part due to the growing awareness of his 1791-1792 affair with Maria Reynolds among political operatives (the affair was made public in 1797).

Distributor: Jupiter/Capricorn combines the principles of growth and status through a strong central government, a philosophy known as Federalism in American political history. The creation of the U.S. Dollar as a unit of account was successful because Jupiter/Capricorn favored centralization of control during this Saturn sequence.

Saturn-Ascendant Direction #3

D	Venus/Aquarius	P	sin. trine Saturn (l=SA) d. → ASC	1-Mar-1817
D	Changeover		bound Jupiter/Aquarius d. → ASC	1-Nov-1818
D	Jupiter/Aquarius	P	sin. trine Saturn (l=0) d. → ASC	24-Feb-1820

The Second Bank of the United States and the Panic of 1819

In 1811, the charter of the First Bank of the United States expired, leaving Congress poorly prepared to handle financing of the War of 1812. Following the burning of the White House by the British on August 27, 1814, specie convertibility was suspended. This financial meltdown led to proposals to what would become the Second Bank of the United States. As the sequence opened, the Second BUS was required to resume specie payments on **February 20, 1817**. By this time, the War of 1812 had been over for two years and the country had binged on liberal credit issued by state banks. Far from curbing the post-war speculative frenzy, the BUS merely added fuel to the fire through poor oversight of branch activities and rampant speculation and fraud committed by bank officers and employees.

It was a bad omen that despite a guarantee of specie convertibility when the Bank opened in early 1817 gold remained at a premium to bank notes. As stress in the financial system grew, Spanish dollars started to trade at a premium during March 1818.[13] The peak premium was achieved near *October 1818* during the deepest part of the financial panic. On *February 24, 1820*, Treasury Secretary Crawford proposed paper money with no gold backing, a move rejected by President James Monroe. As the ultimate statement of a collapse in confidence of the dollar uttered by its cabinet level guardian, Crawford's remarks confirm the ability of an exalted and elevated Saturn/Libra-signified U.S. Dollar to fall from grace. By *April 1820* the premium on Spanish dollars was erased signaling the crisis was over.

<u>Distributor</u>: The changeover from Venus to Jupiter as Distributor on November 1, 1818 timed the worst problems for the banking system. Specie demands for settlement of the Louisiana Purchase (October 21) and the last of three BUS policies designed to shrink outstanding loans (October 30) exacerbated the unavailability of bank capital and deepened the financial turmoil. It appears the predisposition of Jupiter/Aquarius towards financing canals and other waterworks worked against stability of capital markets. Consider the Louisiana Purchase allowed Americans control of the Mississippi waterway and the port of New Orleans.

Saturn-Ascendant Direction #4

D	Venus/Aries	P	opposition Saturn (l=SA) d. → ASC	1-May-1854
D	Changeover		bound Mercury/Aries d. → ASC	18-Aug-1855
D	Mercury/Aries	P	opposition Saturn (l=0) d. → ASC	19-Apr-1857

The California Gold Rush, Economic Boom, and the Panic of 1857

Following the 1848 California gold discovery, freshly mined gold expanded the nation's money supply as gold was converted to coin by the U.S. Mint. Peak California placer gold production occurred in 1853.[14] Events of *1854* include the discovery of the largest known mass of gold (195 pounds at Carson Hill), the creation of the San Francisco Mint, and the first minting of a three dollar gold coin. These events suggest the strength of the gold-backed United States dollar as the sequence began.

Unlike other Saturn sequences where an almost instantaneous decline in the value of dollar started as the sequences began; in this case the entire sequence appears to track a relatively high plateau of economic activity. Though California gold production peaked in 1853, the lagged effect of increased money supply on economic activity meant a few years were required for the economy to fully reflect a pickup from earlier gold discoveries. European demand for American railroad securities, industrial products (because of economic dislocations from the Crimean War) and agricultural products (from poor grain harvests) also supported the dollar by capital flows.

In 1857 all of these factors appeared to reverse simultaneously. Gold production declined, the Crimean War ended, and European grain production recovered. In addition, the 1850-1856 expansion was large enough to create a bubble mentality among investors for railroad stocks, the primary beneficiary of western expansion triggered by the California Gold Rush. By 1857, schemes began to unwind as the extent of the rot was realized. The first high profile debacle was the *July 1857* discovery that Robert Schuyler, President of the New Haven and Harlem railroads and grandson of Revolutionary War General Philip Schuyler, had fled to Canada with $2 million from the sale of watered stock. Soon after, the Ohio Life Insurance and Trust Company failed on *August 24, 1857*. Most banks suspended specie payment by October; after the dust settled specie payments were resumed in December 1857.

Distributor: Venus/Aries signifies lust and greed as an underlying social force behind the desire for rapacious profits and speculation; Mercury/Aries, lies to cover up unsound business practices in order to maintain bubble prices.

Saturn-Ascendant Direction #5

D	Jupiter/Libra	P	conjunction Saturn (l=0) c. → ASC	18-Nov-1865
D	Jupiter/Libra	P	conjunction Saturn (l=SA) c. → ASC	13-Nov-1866

Post-Civil War Contraction of Greenbacks

The cost of the Union's expense to fight the Civil War was financed by greenbacks as set forth in the Legal Tender Acts first issued on February 28, 1862. During the Civil War, the price of Greenbacks relative to gold was a proxy for battle success between Union and Confederate military forces. The low price of Greenbacks was made on July 11, 1864 when Confederates made their closest approach to Washington D.C. By this time, greenbacks had lost roughly half their original value relative to gold.

United States public debt reached its maximum of ~$2846 million on *August 31, 1865* following the war's end[15]. Despite Union victory, gold remained at roughly a 40% premium to greenbacks. The low purchasing power of the dollar made many people wish for a return to antebellum pricing power of the dollar. A *November 17, 1865* NYT editorial lamented this situation, but seemed resigned to high prices after rationalizing their causes from an increase in currency circulation, diminished production capacity, and an increase in gold supplies following the 1848 California Gold Rush.[16]

The desire for the country to eliminate the gold premium led to the Contraction Act of April 1866 which removed greenbacks from circulation. As the sequence finished, the NYT reported on *November 9, 1886* the Treasury Department had liquidated $206 million of Greenbacks in the prior fifteen months. The tone of the article was complementary to Treasury Secretary McCulloch citing increased public confidence in the nation's finances.

Distributor: The ability of greenbacks, a purely fiat currency, to regain their parity with the gold-backed United States dollar is one of the rare cases in world history when a fiat currency actually recovered its value. Increased import duties helped Treasury balances. More important was President Johnson's refusal to honor Confederate debt.[17] With less debt for the Union to assume, the Treasury's job was much easier. Jupiter/Libra signifies Johnson's actions as a Judge (Jupiter) weighing the validity of Confederate claims on the scales of justice (Libra) and finding them wanting. Jupiter is also the greater benefic and aided restoration of confidence in the currency.

Saturn-Ascendant Direction #6

D	Jupiter/Gemini	P	dex. trine Saturn (l=SA) d. → ASC	3-Sep-1898
D	Changeover		bound Venus/Gemini d. → ASC	12-Jan-1899
D	Venus/Gemini	P	dex. trine Saturn (l=0) d. → ASC	8-Sep-1901

Bimetallism Discredited as a Populist Policy; Gold Standard introduced

Both the Greenback Party and its successor the Populist Party came to power during the period of post-Civil War deflation which lowered prices for agricultural products and farm income. A dominant plank was free and unlimited coinage of silver as an inflationary remedy. The movement achieved its climax with William Jennings Bryan's famous *Cross of Gold* speech made on July 9, 1896 at the Democratic National Convention. Immediately following Bryan's speech, the August 16, 1896 discovery of placer gold deposits in the Yukon region of Northwest Canada triggered the Klondike Gold Rush. The flow of gold to the American treasury, like the California Gold Rush of the 1850s, increased the nation's money supply, economic prosperity, and confidence in the U.S. Dollar. These events rendered motivations behind third party political movements obsolete.

At the start of the sequence, there were a few remaining holdouts in favor of both silver and gold as a dual monetary standard. Known as bimetallism, this concept was difficult to implement because there was no practical way to manage constant adjustments in relative value between both metals. Secretary of Agriculture J. Sterling Morton convened a three day National Currency Convention in Omaha, Nebraska; during **September 14-16, 1898** as the sequence opened for both sides to hash out these issues. Given McKinley's November 1896 electoral victory against William Jennings Bryan, there was never any doubt that pro-gold forces had taken control. McKinley signed the Gold Standard Act on March 15, 1900 during the sequence which consigned bimetallism to the dust bin.

Corporations, Merger Mania, and the McKinley Assassination

In contrast to other Ascendant-Saturn sequences, the 1898-1901 sequence produced no major financial dislocation. True there was the one day Panic of May 9, 1901; essentially a grudge match over shares of the Northern Pacific Railroad fought by industrialists E. H. Harriman and James J. Hill. The 1901 Panic was symptomatic of the dominance of corporate trusts, whose formation is the key to unlocking the delineation of this sequence.

Between 1898 and 1902, 2,653 companies disappeared in America's biggest wave of corporate mergers.[18] The era included formation of the largest private business organizations, perhaps in all of world history up to that time, with the incorporation of U.S. Steel on February 25, 1901 the quintessence of the era. In an attempt to tie the corporate merger wave to this sequence, I delineate corporate trusts as Saturn/Libra, yet another role played by Saturn/Libra in addition to the U.S. Dollar and the Supreme Court. This is not unreasonable considering the 1898-1901 sequence is the first Ascendant-Saturn set of directions to follow the 1886 Supreme Court decision, *Santa Clara County v. Southern Pacific Railroad*[19], which has been interpreted as the ruling that granted corporations the same rights as natural persons. This was a key legal precept which spurred formation of American corporations and a corresponding increase of their power.

Studying the pattern of other Ascendant-Saturn sequences, the expected pattern is high business activity and confidence in the U.S. Dollar as the sequence starts. A collapse in confidence ensues, typically culminating with the suspension of specie payments. For this sequence the pattern is similar. But instead of dealing with confidence in business and the dollar per se, the focus is on confidence in corporations as a viable form of business organization.

The sequence begins with high business activity and confidence, aided by the Klondike Gold Rush which effectively shuttered the lengthy era of post-Civil War deflation. The formation of behemoths the like of U.S. Steel and the battle fought over Northern Pacific stock, both in 1901, raised the profile of corporations in American discourse but also started a backlash against their excesses. The sequence culminated with McKinley's assassination on **September 6, 1901** and death on **September 14, 1901**. With good reason the business community feared the accession of Teddy Roosevelt to the Presidency. Nicknamed the 'Trust-Buster,' TR enforced the 1890 Sherman Anti-Trust Act in a successful effort to end the most egregious monopolistic practices of the trusts. The power corporations exercised at the beginning of the sequence was symbolically squashed as the sequence closed with TR's accession to the Presidency.

As another event match to the sequence's end marking problems for corporations, consider that during September 1901 Ida Tarbell first proposed to *McClure's* Magazine that she write a series of exposes on Standard Oil (Chapter 6, p. 125). Tarbell's later fame as a muckraker helped trigger increased government regulation which led to the Supreme Court's May 15, 1911 decision to breakup Standard Oil's monopoly.

Distributor: Jupiter/Gemini. The changeover from Mercury/Gemini to Jupiter/Gemini timed the Special Session of Congress convened by Grover Cleveland on ***August 7, 1893*** to deal with the Panic of 1893 which officially started on May 4, 1893. This was an unusual Panic whose origins lie with the Bland-Allison Act of 1878 and the Sherman Silver Purchase Act of 1890. The

Bland-Allison Act required coinage at the ratio of 16 ounces of silver to one ounce of gold, regardless of the metals' relative market values. The Sherman Silver Purchase Act required that the government buy an additional 4.5 million ounces of silver each month over and above the $2-4 million bought according to the terms of Bland-Allison Act. This flood of silver into government coffers caused the ratio to rise well beyond 16:1 and offered an arbitrage opportunity where low value silver could be risklessly exchanged for high value gold. This caused a run on the nation's gold supplies, triggered the Panic of 1893, and resulted in a serious deflation which ironically is what proponents of both Bland-Allison and Sherman Silver Purchase Acts had tried to avoid.

Even more bizarre is the new-found sense of emergency given to the silverites who called for *free and unlimited coinage of silver* to dig the country out of an even deeper hole. The morphing of the Populist Party to accommodate the Free Silver movement can be explained by Jupiter/Gemini as Distributor. Jupiter functions poorly in Gemini, the sign of his detriment, because Jupiter incorrectly assigns too much importance to relatively trivial details. Jupiter/Gemini also signifies a style of rhetoric found commonly in stump speeches of populist political candidates and appeals to a low level of intellectual sophistication. Gemini is also a double-bodied sign; a match to the philosophy of bimetallism espoused by the Populist Party.

Though there was little left of the Populist Party after William Jennings Bryan's defeat in the 1896 Presidential Election, the fact this Distributor was still active for the opening of this sequence on September 3, 1898 explains why bimetallism as a policy consideration still held sway at the National Currency Convention of September 1898.

Distributor: Venus/Gemini. As a method of conducting business, Venus/Gemini signifies rapid transaction turnover. This is in fact the exact situation described by the NYT on *January 16, 1899*, published just days after the changeover to Venus/Gemini.[20] The article described challenges facing banks by the easy availability of credit, low interest rates, and low profits on making loans. Banks had admitted the time had come for an enlargement of the scope of their activities in order to increase profits through higher loan turnover. This matches Venus/Gemini as 'rapid transaction turnover.' This same interest in high turnover was felt not only by banks but by corporations who undertook an enlargement in the scale of operations as a way to profit from an increased number of smaller-sized transactions. To the extent that Venus/Gemini facilitated the concentration of corporate power by inducing an increase in merger activity, Venus/Gemini increased the odds corporations would grow so large that they risked a fall from grace.

Saturn-Ascendant Direction #7

D	Venus/Cancer	P	dex. square Saturn (l=SA) d. → ASC	24-Oct-1931
D	Changeover		bound Mercury/Cancer d. → ASC	23-Jan-1932
D	Mercury/Can.	P	dex. square Saturn (l=0) d. → ASC	17-Mar-1934

Devaluation of Sterling and the U.S. Dollar

While not as well-known as the famous Stock Market Crash of 1929; credit defaults and currency volatility in 1931 ushered in the second and more serious phase of the Great Depression. The May 1931 default of Credit Anstalt in Germany was the figurative straw which broke the camel's back for world capital flows. The crisis quickly spread to England when on *September 21, 1931*, the Bank of England left the gold standard. Initial capital flows were favorable to the United States dollar as the only major currency left with any gold backing. The initial devaluation of the pound from 4.86 dollars to 3.90 corresponded to a 25% rise for the dollar. However the markets greeted the dollar's rise as suspect, figuring it was only a matter of time before the United States joined other nations in taking the dollar off the gold standard. This was a dismal time for domestic finance. In the fall of 1931, hundreds of U.S. banks closed as U.S. citizens hoarded gold.

As the sequence opened, Canada prohibited the export of gold on *October 19, 1931* and on *October 23*, Hoover had talks with French Premier Pierre Laval on topics which included gold reserves and currency stabilization. In currency markets, the gold drain was severe at this time, with the U.S. losing $649 million in gold in the month following the Sterling devaluation, the largest monthly drain on record.[21]

Following his election on November 8, 1932, Franklin Roosevelt took dramatic steps to stave off the deflationary spiral and loss of confidence in the financial system. The most important decisions were his abandonment of the gold standard on April 19, 1933 and passage of the Gold Reserve Act on *January 30, 1934* which fixed the price of gold at $35 per ounce. As the sequence closed, the House passed legislation for the purchase of farm surpluses for silver above the world price on *March 19, 1934*. This was a bit excessive even for FDR and reflects a similar state of panic by Treasury Secretary Crawford in 1820 at the close of Saturn-Ascendant Direction #3.

Between 1931 and 1934, the U.S. dollar was devalued by 41%.

Saturn-Ascendant Direction #8

D	Saturn/Leo	P	dex. sextile Saturn (l=0) c. → ASC	8-Jun-1941
D	Saturn/Leo	P	dex. sextile Saturn (l=SA) c. → ASC	17-Dec-1942

Supreme Court Appointment: Robert Jackson

President Franklin Roosevelt appointed Robert Jackson to the Supreme Court on *June 12, 1941*; the Senate confirmed Jackson on July 7, 1941. During his Supreme Court tenure, Jackson was appointed Chief United States Prosecutor at the International War Crimes Tribunal in Nuremberg, Germany.

Distributor: Saturn/Leo is consistent with totalitarian regimes whose agents were judged at the Nuremberg trials.

Anti-Japanese WWII Legal Measures

Among the ugliest episodes of state actions taken against Americans is the WWII internment of Japanese-Americans. *On July 25, 1941*, FDR issued a Presidential Order freezing Japanese financial assets in the US. This caused a run on Japanese banks. Following Pearl Harbor, President Roosevelt signed Executive Order 9066 on February 19, 1942 which resulted in the forced relocation of over 120,000 Japanese Americans. Manzanar was one of ten camps where Japanese Americans were interned. On *December 6, 1942*, a riot erupted at Manzanar with two deaths and nine injuries. One of the triggers for the riot was the discovery that camp administrators had sold food allowances on the black market for personal profits to the detriment of the camp's food supply. At one point in the day, Joseph Kurihara, the Committee of Five leader negotiating with camp officials burst into 'a fanatical tirade, disclaimed loyalty to the United States, expressed the hope that Japan would win the war, and threatened death to all informers.'[22]

Distributor: Saturn/Leo inhibits the ability of Saturn/Libra to reach balance in matters of law and justice. At the sequence's end, protests erupted against the totalitarian nature of Saturn/Leo policies.

Saturn-Ascendant Direction #9

D	Saturn/Leo	P	dex. sextile Saturn (l=SA) d. → ASC	20-Jan-1970
D	Saturn/Leo	P	dex. sextile Saturn (l=0) d. → ASC,	31-Jul-1971

Rise of Inflation and Collapse of U.S. Dollar under the Nixon Presidency

Perhaps no sequence better demonstrates the U.S. dollar's fall from grace. In January 1970, President Richard Nixon chose to replace the retiring Fed Chairman William Martin with Arthur Burns who took office on *February 1, 1970*. Martin had been appointed Fed Chairman by President Harry Truman on March 21, 1951, after a major change in Fed operating procedures with the Accord of 1951 which Martin helped negotiate. To the present day, Martin has been the longest serving Fed Chairman. He pursued policies designed to maintain the Federal Reserve's independence. As a sign of Martin's success in combating inflation, the price of gold fell to its lowest price in 16 years on *January 16, 1970* as his term culminated.[23] January 1970 marked a major low in gold prices and a high in the value of the dollar; record levels which have never been challenged since.

Nixon and his advisors looked to Arthur Burns as a tool to reverse the Fed's anti-inflation campaign in order to stimulate the economy and aid Nixon's 1972 re-election campaign. Secretary of Labor George Schultz was the first Nixon cabinet member to openly call for the Fed to ease policy on *January 7, 1970*.[24] Burns eventually succumbed to Nixon's desires and is widely considered one of the poorest guardians of inflation since the Fed's inception in 1913. As the sequence closed, Nixon imposed price controls and suspended the convertibility of dollars to gold on *August 15, 1971*. Suspension of gold convertibility all but terminated the Bretton Woods currency management system in place since July 1944.

Distributor: Saturn/Leo signifies a rise in the price of gold because Saturn signifies scarcity and Leo is the sign assigned to gold.

Failed Supreme Court Nomination of G. Harrold Carswell

Delineating Saturn/Libra as the Supreme Court merits attention with Nixon's nomination of G. Harrold Carswell to the Supreme Court on **January 19, 1970** as the sequence began. The Senate rejected the nomination on April 8, 1970.

Saturn-Ascendant Direction #10

D	Mercury/Can.	P	dex. square Saturn (l=0) c. → ASC	22-Oct-1978
D	Changeover		bound Venus/Cancer c. → ASC	13-Dec-1980
D	Venus/Cancer	P	dex. square Saturn (l=SA) c. → ASC	14-Mar-1981

The Carter-Reagan Divide: Recovered Confidence in the U.S. Dollar

The collapse in the U.S. Dollar, initiated by Arthur Burns under the Nixon administration and timed by the Saturn-Ascendant Direction #9 culminated with a major U.S. Dollar low at the end of the 1970s timed by Direction #10. Similar to Direction #5, also computed by converse motion, is the ability of Direction #10 to time *dollar weakness at the outset* and *dollar strength as the sequence culminated*. This is exactly the opposite effect seen in sequences computed by direction motion which open with dollar strength and conclude with dollar weakness.

To see correspondences between world affairs and key turning points in the U.S. Dollar, refer to Figure 15 on the following page.

As the sequence started on *October 22, 1978*, the dollar paused (See #1); a brief resting place before its final eight-day collapse to *October 30, 1978* (See #2). On this date, President Carter initiated a U.S. Dollar support program. The dollar low would hold for nearly ten years until was exceeded in 1987. The dollar retested its October 1978 low on January 7, 1980 (See #3). The intervening period was difficult, marked by Carter's 'malaise' speech on July 15, 1979, seizure of American embassy employees in Tehran on November 4, 1979, and the Soviet invasion of Afghanistan on December 25, 1979. The Distributor changeover from Mercury to Venus on December 12, 1980 marked a short-term high (See #4). By the end of sequence on March 14, 1981 (See #5), confidence in the U.S. Dollar was restored with Reagan's *January 20, 1981* Inauguration.

214 *AMERICA IS BORN: Introducing the Regulus USA National Horoscope*

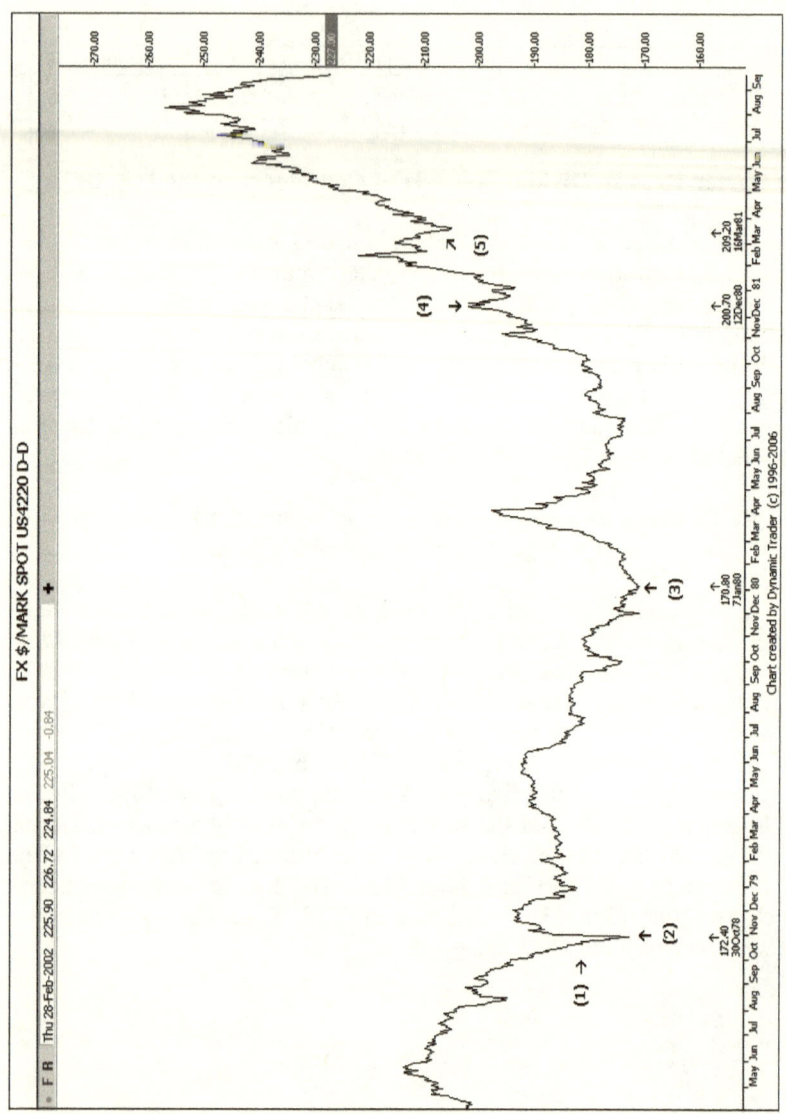

Figure 15. $/Mark Daily Spot Prices, May 1978 to September 1980

NEW Out-of-sample event published after 2008 1st edition.

Saturn-Ascendant Direction #11

D	Venus/Gemini	P	dex trine Saturn (l=BI) c. → ASC	19-Nov-2009
D	Venus/Gemini		dex trine Saturn (l=0) c. → ASC	1-May-2011
D	Jupiter/Gemini	P	dex trine Saturn (l=SA) c. → ASC	5-May-2014

Recovery of the US Dollar following the Great Financial Crisis

This primary direction sequence timed key lows for the U.S. Dollar following the Great Financial Crisis of 2007-2009. Similar to Direction #10 computed by converse motion, once the series of directions completed the U.S. dollar staged a substantial rally. This is consistent with all other Saturn-Ascendant directions documented by this study: Saturn directions computed by direct motion trigger a U.S. Dollar decline after the directions are complete; Saturn directions computed by converse motion trigger a US dollar revival once directions are complete.

During the 2007-2009 Great Financial Crisis. the US Dollar made an all-time record low on 22-Apr-2008. This event was not identified by any Saturn-Ascendant directions listed in the 1st edition. However two of the three most important subsequent U.S. Dollar lows made 4-May-2011 and 8-May-2014 were timed within 3 days of the Saturn-Ascendant directions published in the 2008 1st edition. This implies an accuracy of less than 1 second of time for the proposed rectification.

I list a third direction in the above table, recomputing the Saturn-Ascendant direction based on the latitude adjustment of Bianchini.[25] The recomputed Saturn-Ascendant direction for 19-Nov-2009 using Bianchini's latitude adjustment timed the third most important U.S. Dollar low after the Financial Crisis on 26-Nov-2009 just seven days after the computed direction.

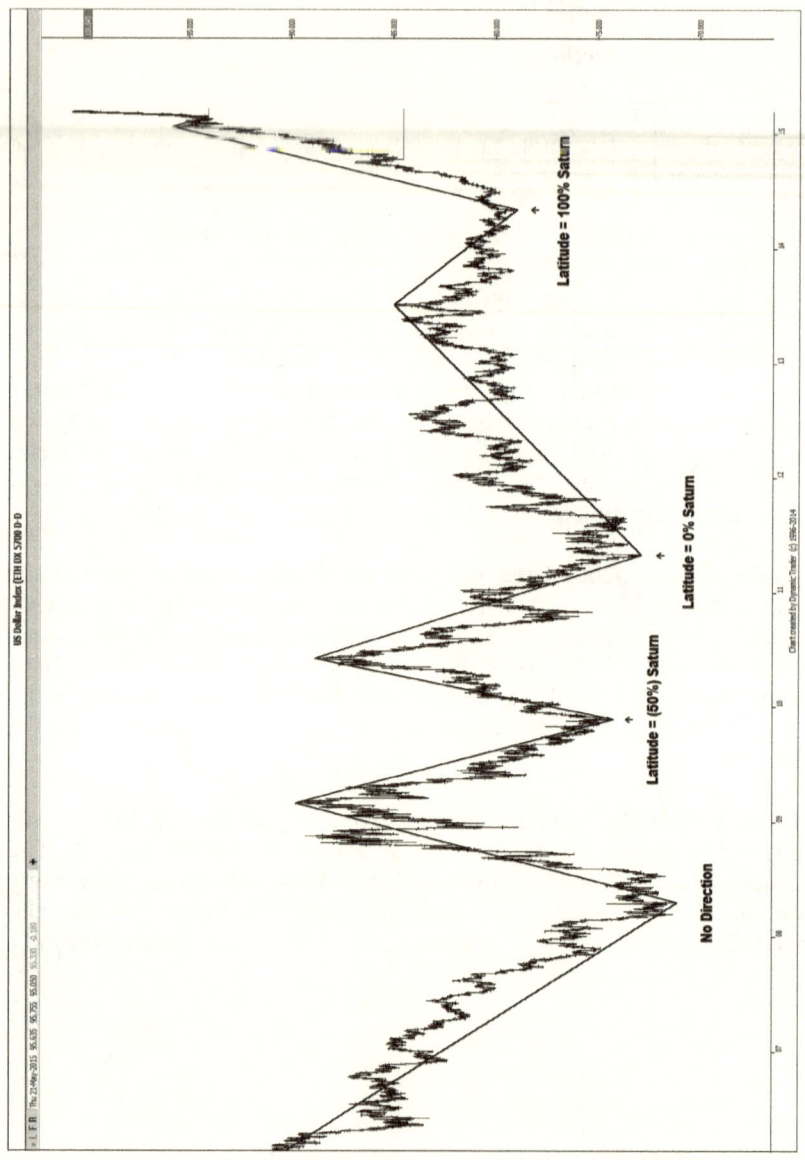

Figure 16. US Dollar Index, January 2007 to December 2014.

CHAPTER TWELVE

Partners: Mars

Longitude	21GE24'28"
Latitude	0N22'56"
Speed	+0deg40'56" (fast)
Sign	Gemini
Bound	Mars/Gemini
Dwad	Aquarius
Houses	<u>Occupies</u> 7th
	<u>Rules</u> 2nd, 5th, 12th (WS); 4th, 11th (AL)
Rulers	<u>Ruled</u> by Mercury/Cancer
Other	Morning star/Oriental
	Recently out the sunbeams
	Sends antiscion to Cancer stellium
	Separates from trine of Saturn

<u>Planet – Mars</u>: Mars signifies physical acts of aggression (e.g., violent crime, warfare), disputes, contentions, and men.

<u>Sign – Gemini</u>: Placed in Gemini means information and business are fought and disputed because sign ruler Mercury is the universal significator of written documents common to business practices. Reckless business investments, speculation, and identity theft are common Mars/Gemini traits. Gemini, the sign of the twins, is also associated with short-term term travel. For these reasons, Mars in Gemini produces railroads because trains move fast over a pair of tracks. The speediness of Mars in Gemini is also conducive to auto racing. As a style of military armament, Mars/Gemini is consistent with incendiary bombs which thrive on oxygen. As a mutable air sign, Mars/Gemini signifies cluster bombs which separate in the air. Or simply consider the line from America's national anthem *The Star Spangled Banner*:

'And the Rockets' red glare, the Bombs bursting in air...'

Bound – Mars/Gemini. Mars placed in its own bound accentuates the effects of Gemini as sign ruler.

Dwad: Mars in the dwad of Aquarius signifies disputes over any type of humanitarian principle which attempts to level the playing field for all social classes. For America, this has played out through segregation and more recently as a backlash against affirmative action. A second topic Mars/Aquarius likes to dispute is land boundaries. The relationship between Aquarius and land boundaries arises because Aquarius is a fixed air sign and land boundaries are effectively created as fixed lines drawn through the air which fall on a given property (or boundary between two countries).

Ruled by Mercury/Cancer: Mercury signifies incoherent emotional reasoning spewed by demagogues and sensational journalism. Mercury will be the source and result of Mars' actions.

Synthesis – Mars

Disputes. Unfortunately for America, incoherent thinking as the cause of disputes is the best delineation of the incendiary Mars ruled by the afflicted Mercury. Was this a natal and not a mundane horoscope, one would predict an individual would become involved in barroom brawls because of sensitivity to imagined slights which are taken out of context. For a national horoscope, the implications are far more severe. They include false flags as a pretext for military activity and high divorce rates resulting from poor communication.

Civil War. Conflict can be internal because Mars rules the 4th of homeland. Perhaps no event better demonstrates the incendiary quality of Mars than the American Civil War. Central to the outbreak of the Civil War were calls for emancipation of slaves made by abolitionists. The threat of emancipation triggered sensationalist news reports in the Southern press which preyed upon the fears of slave owners. The result was Civil War. In this chain of events see the Moon (abolition) rules Mercury (sensationalism) which in turn rules Mars (conflict).

Entertainment. Consider the release of PlayStation's Grand Theft Auto video was timed by Mars-Ascendant Direction #10. The word *play* in *Playstation* reminds us of the relevance of Mars' rulership of the 5th house of entertainment by whole sign houses. Television programs like the Jerry Springer show[1], Divorce Court, and COPS all feature domestic disputes and violence as forms of entertainment.

A less divisive delineation of Mars/Gemini as a source of entertainment is the popularity of NASCAR racing in America as a spectator sport. Mars/Gemini signifies speedy short-term travel and is a match to fast cars.

Consider Mars-Ascendant Directions #7 which timed the Great Auto Race of 1908 and Mars-Ascendant Direction #10 which timed Michael Schumacher's final Formula One victory.

Though not confirmed by directions in this study, another benign example of Mars/Gemini ruling the 5th is competitive marathon races and cycling – including the popularity of spin classes offered at most health clubs presently. More generally, Mars/Gemini ruling the 5th explains America's preference for track and field events relative to water sports like swimming which are associated with water signs on the 5th cusp. America is more a nation of runners and cyclists than swimmers.

Railroads. Completion of the Transcontinental Railroad (May 10, 1869) was an instrumental step made in America's western expansion. As stated earlier, Mars/Gemini signifies railroads because trains move fast (Mars) over a pair of tracks (Gemini=double bodied sign). Consider also Mars' placement in the 7th house which is the angle of the West. Railroads aided *Western* expansion. They also facilitated the wholesale destruction of Native Americans, one of the larger genocides on record.[2] The destruction of buffalo herds was abetted by railroad passengers encouraged to shoot buffalo from moving trains. Recalling the intentional spread of smallpox through contaminated blankets given to Indian tribes, delineation of Mars/Gemini as germ warfare appears appropriate as another Mars/Gemini delineation. Mars (virus/bacteria/fever) infects the lungs (Gemini) which causes illness (Mercury rules 6th) and death (Mercury is placed in the 8th).

England. Because Aries falls on the 4th cusp and Aries is assigned to England by mundane choreography rules, some of Mars' affairs concern land disputes with England. Boundary disputes in the Treaty of Paris at the conclusion of the Revolutionary war and the Venezuela-British Guiana border dispute of 1895 demonstrates a connection between Mars and England. Arguably, so is the 2005 bankruptcy of MG-Rover because Mars/Gemini signifies reckless business investments generally and high performance cars specifically. MG-Rover was England's largest car manufacturer.

Financial loss. The Panics of 1857 and 1907 demonstrate Mars' delineation as reckless business speculation. Reckless speculations are tied to the 7th house because business partnerships are assigned to the 7th; they result in financial loss because Mars rules the 2nd of wealth.

Mars-Ascendant Direction #1

D	Saturn/Sagittarius	P	opposition Mars (l=0) c. → ASC	3-Oct-1782
D	Saturn/Sagittarius	P	opposition Mars (l=MA) c. → ASC	16-Feb-1783

Death of Charles Lee

The British citizen Charles Lee traveled to America in 1773 and took up the colonies' cause against Britain. Because of military experience in the British Army, Lee was assigned the rank of second Major General, the number three spot after Commander George Washington and First Major General Artemas Ward. Charles Lee was captured by the British on December 13, 1776 where he was held for desertion from the British Army. During his confinement, he submitted a plan to his British captors on March 29, 1777 for defeating Washington and his Army. This was not known at the time, even after his release on May 20, 1778. Lee stumbled badly at the Battle of Monmouth, disobeyed Washington's orders, and was court-marshaled on August 12, 1778. Charles Lee died on **October 2, 1782**, as this sequence opened. The direction of Ascendant opposed Mars is identical to the Descendant conjunct Mars. Mars rules the 12th of enemies; direction of Mars to the 7th cusp, 8th from the 12th, times Charles Lee's death.

End of Revolutionary War with England

Benjamin Franklin and John Adams renewed peace negotiations in Paris on **September 27, 1782**, after the British started referring to the '13 United States' and not the 'colonies.' A preliminary treaty was signed on November 30, 1782. A *Declaration for Suspension of Arms and Cessation of Hostilities* was signed by Franklin and John Adams on **January 20, 1783** as the sequence closed. Congress announced the end of hostilities on April 11, 1783, and ratified the preliminary peace treaty on April 15, 1783. The final Treaty of Paris was officially signed on September 3, 1783.

Wars generally start with Mars directions, not end with them. Do these events match the delineation of Mars? Mars in the 7th ruling the 4th signifies legal disputes over property. The dispute is with Britain because Aries signifies Britain in mundane choreography. With the weakness of Mercury, faulty reasoning should cause disputes over legal land settlements. As a delineation match, there were two major problems with land boundaries in the Treaty of Paris. At the same time that Britain signed her treaty with America, she also signed a treaty which ceded Florida to Spain. However the northern border of Florida was not specified. Spain later used control of Florida to block access to the Mississippi River. A second problem was the unspecified Canadian border, not settled until the Jay Treaty of 1794.

Mars-Ascendant Direction #2

D	Mars/Aquarius	P	dex. trine Mars (l=MA) d. → ASC	30-Apr-1824
D	Mars/Aquarius	P	dex. trine Mars (l=0) d. → ASC	13-Oct-1824

End of the 'Era of Good Feelings'

The Distributor changeover from Jupiter to Mars on October 26, 1823 signaled the end of the 'Era of Good Feelings' under President Monroe's administration with a backlash against the implementation of Henry Clay's American System. Monroe's call for new tariffs and tolls to fund internal improvements like the Cumberland Road[3] stirred the ire of Martin van Buren and others in Congress opposed to an increased role for the Federal Government in internal affairs. Clay's American System was essentially an Aquarian approach to economic development based on infrastructure, tariffs, and a national bank. As Distributor, Mars/Aquarius discriminates against infrastructure because it opens up economic opportunities to the masses.

Congressional Nomination of William Crawford for the Presidency

Treasury Secretary William Crawford, with Mars/Aquarius in his own natal figure (b. February 24, 1772), was an important symbol of the Mars/Aquarius theme for Martin van Buren and his Congressional alliances known as the 'radicals.' Congress nominated William Crawford for President on ***February 14, 1824***.[4] This was an unusual choice because Crawford suffered a massive stroke during September 1823 and only resumed his duties on a limited basis during ***September 1824*** as the sequence closed. The fact that Congress saw fit to nominate a stroke victim for President is one of the more bizarre incidents in American history. Why did this happen? Crawford's stroke can be read from the weakness of Mercury as Mars' ruler. Mars in the 7th ruling the 5th of elections signals legal disputes over an election. With natal Mars/Aquarius matching the Distributor, Crawford played the role. In another delineation match, the November election was disputed and thrown into the House of Representatives on ***December 1, 1824*** who selected John Quincy Adams against Andrew Jackson.

Mars-Ascendant Direction #3

D	Mars/Pisces	P	dex. square Mars (l=MA) d. → ASC	10-Feb-1843
D	Mars/Pisces	P	dex. square Mars (l=0) d. → ASC	23-Jul-1843

Oregon Territory

U.S. interest in the Oregon Territory dates from October 20, 1818 when an agreement for joint occupation was signed with Britain. The Oregon Territory was originally defined as the region west of the Rocky Mountains between 42° and 54° 40' N. lat. The northern border was agreed to in a treaty with the Russians on *April 14, 1824*. The Hudson's Bay Company's appointment of John McLoughlin as its chief representative to the Oregon Territory in 1824 was another key milestone for the region's history. McLoughlin built and opened Fort Vancouver on *March 19, 1825*. Both 1824 and 1825 events match projections of Mars-Ascendant Direction #2.

The pace of Oregon settlers picked up in the early 1840s with the Senate's passage of Linn's Oregon Bill on *February 3, 1843* a sign of increased national interest in the Oregon question. Though this legislation did not pass the House, it did give the public increased confidence to migrate. On *May 22, 1843*, the first mass migration of just under 1000 individuals departed from Independence, Missouri. This started what was later known as the 'Great Emigration,' a movement which greatly accelerated following the California Gold Rush of 1848.

Within the Oregon Territory itself, increased uncertainty over competing land claims from both United States and Britain was a motivating factor behind the creation of a provisional government. These meetings were held at Champeog on *May 2* and *July 5, 1843* as the sequence concluded. The provisional government provided a political structure for United States claims to the Oregon Territory.

On December 2, 1845, President James Polk recommended the United States provide Britain a one-year notice for termination of the existing joint occupation agreement for the Oregon Territory. Not content to let Polk peacefully negotiate for northern territory following Polk's willingness to shed blood over Texas, Democratic Party operatives coined the political slogan "Fifty-four Forty or Fight!" in early 1846 as an appeal to warring expansionists.[5][6] Despite this attempt at agitation, Polk settled the matter peacefully and signed the Oregon Treaty on June 15, 1846. The treaty established the northern U.S. border at 49 degrees north latitude.

Mars-Ascendant Direction #4

D	Venus/Libra	P	sin. trine Mars (l=0) c. → ASC	30-Jul-1857
D	Venus/Libra	P	sin. trine Mars (l=MA) c. → ASC	27-Sep-1857

Five Points Riot

On *July 4, 1857*, a riot erupted between rival gangs in New York City's Five Points neighborhood. The dispute concerned implementation of restrictive liquor laws enforced by the newly-organized New York Metropolitan Police. Both the police department reorganization and changes in liquor laws were attempts to reduce power of the Irish-dominated Tammany Hall political machine which had deep roots in the Five Points district. The July 4 riot was a gang fight between the Dead Rabbit Club gang (favoring the local Irish residents) and the Bowery Boys (favoring the police). Though this riot lasted a single day, another riot on *July 13, 1857* and disturbances continuing through *August 1857* are consistent with the sequence.[7]

Panic of 1857

As detailed in Saturn-Ascendant Direction #4, the Panic of 1857 was caused by a simultaneous reversal in factors which supported an economic boom after the 1848 California Gold Rush. The flight of Robert Schuyler to Canada with $2 million from the sale of watered stock in July 1857 was an important trigger for the Panic of 1857. It is a delineation match to this Mars sequence because reckless speculations in railroad stocks and sale of forged stock certificates match the delineation of Mars/Gemini as railroads, reckless speculation, and identity theft.

Death of John McLoughlin

John McLoughlin died on *September 3, 1857*. He functioned as an important facilitator for the settlement of the Oregon Territory from the time he established Fort Vancouver at the end of the Mars-Ascendant Direction #2. His encouragement of American settlers who were ostensibly squatters on Hudson's Bay territory led directly to the Oregon Bill and first mass migration of settlers in 1843 timed by Mars-Ascendant Direction #3.

Mars-Ascendant Direction #5

D	Mars/Aries	P	dex. sextile Mars (l=MA) d. → ASC	4-Nov-1860
D	Mars/Aries	P	dex. sextile Mars (l=0) d. → ASC	18-Apr-1861

Outbreak of Civil War

Lincoln's election to the Presidency on *November 4, 1860*, the outbreak of the Civil War on *April 12, 1861*, and the first report of casualties on *April 19, 1861* lock down this sequence.

Together with the changeover of the Distributor Mars/Aries to Saturn/Aries on July 19, 1863, this primary direction sequence was one of the principal keys used to unlock the rectification of the Regulus USA National Horoscope. See Chapter 2 for details.

Mars/Gemini in the 7th of conflict ruling the 4th of homeland signifies Civil War. As Mars' ruler, Mercury is the cause of Civil War. Mercury rules the 6th of slaves and demonstrates the role of sensationalism and demagoguery regarding slavery as the cause of the Civil War.

Distributor: Mars in the sign of his rulership produces forthright actions in warfare. Mars loves to fight in Aries; he facilitates the direction by imbuing America's social mood with the desire to shed blood.

Note: this is only one of three dexter Ascendant-Mars aspects to occur in United States history. Dexter aspects are considered relatively stronger in effect than sinister aspects. The other two are Mars-Ascendant Directions #2 and #3. Direction #2 timed rise of partisan politics under Andrew Jackson. Direction #3 timed agitation over the Oregon Territory (and likely similar agitation which prevailed prior to the Mexican War).

Mars-Ascendant Direction #6

D	Mars/Virgo	P	sin. square Mars (l=0) c. → ASC	7-Mar-1895
D	Mars/Virgo	P	sin. square Mars (l=MA) c. → ASC	29-Apr-1895

Venezuela-British Guiana Border Dispute

The dispute over Venezuela's eastern border with British Guiana dates from 1830 when Venezuela gained independence from Spain. At the heart of the dispute is a region with high value mineral deposits. the matter was unresolved until 1895 when President Grover Cleveland urged the two parties to submit the matter to arbitration which they did so in 1899. The resulting border was recognized by both parties until 1962 when Venezuela abrogated the arbitration's ruling. The border remains unsolved as of 2008.

This sequence times the origins of American involvement in urging arbitration for the border dispute. As the sequence began, on *February 20, 1895* President Cleveland signed a Congressional resolution urging England and Venezuela to settle their boundary dispute by arbitration. A key player in the dispute, Richard Olney, was elevated to the position of Secretary of State on *June 10, 1895* on the death of Secretary of State Walter Gresham. Under the guidance of President Cleveland, Olney prepared a statement arguing the pro-Venezuelan side of the border dispute. It was presented to Britain by American Minister Thomas Bayard on *July 20, 1895*.

A legal dispute with Britain over property matches Mars in the 7th of disputes ruling the 4th of property. Mercury's sensationalism is evident in Olney's July 20, 1895 statement. Paraphrasing historian Ralph Volney Harlow, Guyana Minister Odeen Ishmael indicates the statement was an emotional appeal designed to gain curry for the Venezuelan border dispute as a topic worthy of American interest.[8]

<u>Distributor</u>: Mars (cutting) in Virgo (earth) signifies natural resource development (e.g., mining) and matches mineral resources of the disputed territory. In addition, Virgo tests well as a mundane choreography significator for many Latin American (including Venezuela). Finally, Mars/Virgo appears in natal charts of those involved in the border dispute. President Benjamin Harrison's Mars/Virgo/7th timed his 1898-1899 role in arguing the Venezuelan side of the border dispute.[9]

Mars-Ascendant Direction #7

D	Mars/Gemini	P	conjunction Mars (l=MA) d. → ASC	9-Oct-1907
D	Mars/Gemini	P	conjunction Mars (l=0) d. → ASC	15-Mar-1908

Panic of 1907

The failure of the Knickerbocker Trust Bank of New York was technically the aftermath of a grudge match fought by Standard Oil against Frederick Heinze over prior business dealings in the Montana copper fields.[10] In late 1907 Heinze set up a trust operation with Charles W. Morse to speculate in copper shares. The share operation was run under the auspices of the Knickerbocker Trust Bank. Motivated by revenge from earlier business deals in Montana, Standard Oil sought the destruction of Heinze and achieved it through strong-arm tactics deployed against other stock operators in order to foil Heinze's stock corner. Leaked information obtained by waiters and busboys during an evening meeting of key Knickerbocker officials was another factor which aided the collapse. As the sequence began, the stock market started to decline on **October 10, 1907** led by copper shares. From this date to the failure of Knickerbocker on **October 22, 1907** stocks essentially collapsed. There were several suicides of Trust Bank customers as well as Knickerbocker President Charles Barney. This panic led to a business contraction because it coincided with a tired economic expansion whose pillar of money supply growth from the Klondike Gold Rush had eroded.

The Great Auto Race of 1908

Still very early in the history of the automobile, car races offered consumers the opportunity to examine engineering in action. Cay buyers wanted to see cars function at high speeds for long durations before committing to buy[11]. News of an auto race from New York to Paris sponsored by the *New York Times* and Paris newspaper *La Matin* was announced on **November 28, 1907**[12]. What would later be dubbed 'The Great Auto Race of 1908' left New York City on **February 12, 1908** and finished on **July 30, 1908** in Paris when the American car named the Thomas Flyer driven by George Schuster Sr. finished after a trek of 22,000 miles. Dwad. On **March 17, 1908**, the New York Times reported that public schools were using the auto race as a pedagogical tool for learning geography.[13] Mars + Aquarius = tracking a *race* by marking road *boundaries* on a map.

Transits of Mars match the progress of the race with Mars 22AR56 near the 4th cusp of homeland at the race's beginning. At the end of the race, Mars moved to 14LE32 in the 9th house of foreign lands, further specified to France because Leo is the sign of France.

Mars-Ascendant Direction #8

D	Mercury/Leo	P	sin. sextile Mars (l=0) c. → ASC	15-Jan-1933
D	Mercury/Leo	P	sin. sextile Mars (l=MA) c. → ASC	30-Mar-1933

Proposed Railroad Reorganization – FDR's 100 Days

There is a great similarity between events of Directions #8 and #9. Both are computed for the same sinister sextile aspect of Mars. Direction #8 is computed by converse motion; #9, by direct motion. Both concern bankruptcies/bailouts for the railroad industry (#8) and the automobile industry (#9). Railroads and cars are signified by Mars/Gemini.

The first quarter of 1933 contained one of the most volatile periods in American financial history including the transfer of presidential power from Hoover to FDR and FDR's nationwide bank holiday from *March 5 – 15, 1933*. As the sequence opened, the House Judiciary Committee held hearings on the revision of bankruptcy laws to aid the railroads on *January 15, 1933*.[14] This was in response to a message from outgoing President Hoover delivered on *January 12*.[15] Railroads issued complaints on the financial costs of newly proposed employee pension requirements.[16] This is a delineation match to an afflicted Mercury in the 8th of investments ruling the 6th of employees. Note the 6th also signifies illness, tarnishing employee health care programs with the same weak Mercury. To this day pension and health care costs remain a major dispute between corporations and employees.

As the sequence closed, the railroad Missouri Pacific filed for bankruptcy on *April 1, 1933*. This was one of the nation's largest railroads which eventually merged with Union Pacific in 1982.[17] Also on *April 1, 1933*, F.H. Prince, the former President of the Pere Marquette Railway, presented a nationwide railroad reorganization plan to Roosevelt which involved consolidating the railroads into seven systems.[18] Industrialists, like Averill Harriman, were generally opposed to direct federal control of railroads. Roosevelt acceded to Harriman's wishes and did not approve Prince's plan.

Distributor: Mercury/Leo signifies an optimistic spirit which describes the mood of the nation following Roosevelt's November 1932 election. The stock market made its low on July 8, 1932 and rallied strongly following the bank holiday. Mercury/Leo mitigates the psychological gloom from reckless business investments which result in bankruptcy. I suggest without the workings of Mercury/Leo as Distributor, the stock market may well have gone to new lows in 1933 under Roosevelt's tenure.

Mars-Ascendant Direction #9

D	Mercury/Leo	P	sin. sextile Mars (l=MA) d. → ASC	8-Oct-1979
D	Mercury/Leo	P	sin. sextile Mars (l=0) d. → ASC	22-Dec-1979

Chrysler Bailout

Congress approved the *Chrysler Corporation Loan Guarantee Act of 1979* on **December 20, 1979** following a petition on **September 7, 1979** by Chrysler to avoid bankruptcy.

Partner: The Chrysler bailout is a delineation match to Mars/Gemini because Mars/Gemini signifies reckless business investments. It is tied to Chrysler because Mars/Gemini signifies auto racing and Chrysler manufactures cars. Placed in the 7th house means these problems are played out as legal disputes. Mercury/Cancer approaching combustion signifies faulty business judgment of consumer trends leading to bankruptcy because Mercury is placed in the 8th of debt. As ruler of the 6th of labor, Mercury/Cancer signifies emotional pleas made by employees fearing job losses made to Congress in order to secure passage of the legislation.

Distributor: Mercury/Leo signifies an optimistic spirit, embodied by Chrysler President and CEO Lee Iacocca (b. October 15, 1924) with natal North Node 19LE43 in the bound of Mercury/Leo ruled by Mercury/Libra. Iacocca's optimism helped Chrysler achieve a successful recovery.

Federal Reserve Targets Money Supply

On **October 6, 1979**, newly installed Federal Reserve Chairman Paul Volcker announced the Federal Reserve would tackle inflation by targeting the money supply. This event was among the singular most important changes in Fed operating policy since its inception in 1913. Large interest rate moves were the norm following the changeover to money supply targeting. Policy decisions were marred by mistakes in money supply data interpretation, whose very definition was rapidly changing in the wake of financial deregulation. Taming inflation led to business bankruptcies and the 1981/1982 recession.

Delineating Mars/Gemini as excessive risk taking matches the style of the early Volcker Fed in combating inflation with increased financial market volatility. Weakness of Mercury is consistent with policy errors. Mars' placement in the 7th of open enemies is a match to Volcker's declaration of inflation as 'public enemy number one.'

Mars-Ascendant direction #10

D	Mars/Gemini	P	conjunction Mars (l=0) c. → ASC	24-Oct-2004
D	Mars/Gemini	P	conjunction Mars (l=MA) c. → ASC	30-Mar-2005

Formula One Auto Racing

Michael Schumacher won his 7th and final Formula One World Drivers Championship on *October 24, 2004* as the sequence opened. Schumacher is considered the greatest driver in auto racing history. How a German driver winning a race in Belgium is relevant to the history of the United States is not obvious until one sees that Schumacher also won the 2005 United States Grand Prix on *June 19, 2005* just after the sequence closed. This race was marred by Michelin tire failures, leaving only cars equipped with Bridgestone tires left to race. The tire problem was a catastrophic publicity event for Formula One racing in the U.S. with many calling the race a farce. The tire problem shows the weakness of the Mercury as Mars' ruler. Note the same sequence by direct motion timed the Great Auto Race of 1908.

Grand Theft Auto: San Andreas

Following its North American PlayStation 2 release on *October 26, 2004*, the video game San Andreas became the best-selling video game in North America. Windows and Xbox ports were released on *June 7, 2005* just after the end of the sequence. Plot features include gang violence, an urban riot, drug dealing, dishonest policemen, and covert intelligence operations. Plot features match Mars in the 7th of disputes ruling the 5th of entertainment.

Bankruptcy of MG-Rover

MG-Rover was the last locally-owned large-scale car manufacturer in the UK car market. Demand had slowly waned over time as popularity diminished. A possible rescue of MG-Rover announced during *June 2004* by the Shanghai Automotive Industry Corporation (SAIC) and SAIC joint venture announcement during *November 2004* corresponded to the start of the sequence.[19] This was a high profile corporate rescue attempt which attracted the attention of Prime Minister Tony Blair. Due to various problems, including a false statement of Tata of India to cease marketing agreements with MG-Rover should the SAIC deal go through, the SAIC deal collapsed. On *April 7, 2005*, MG-Rover announced it was suspending production and sought bankruptcy protection. This event concerns a legal dispute over cars (Mars) threatening bankruptcy (Mercury) occurring in England (Aries/4th).

NEW Out-of-sample event published after 2008 1st edition.

Mars-Ascendant direction #11

D	Mars/Virgo	P	sin square Mars (l=MA) d. → ASC	9-Sep-2017
D	Mars/Virgo	P	sin square Mars (l=0) d. → ASC	1-Nov-2017

End to DACA Program (Deferred Action for Childhood Arrivals)

On *September 5, 2017*, President Donald Trump ordered an end to the DACA program in one of the most contentious measures taken against illegal immigrants during his administration. As distributor for this primary direction sequence, Mars/Virgo signifies conflict with Mexico based on the prosecution of the Mexican-American War of 1846-1848 timed by Mars/Virgo directions in the horoscope of President James Polk. Mexican territorial claims relinquished after the Mexican-American War include Texas, Utah, Nevada, California, most of Arizona/New Mexico and portions of Wyoming/Colorado/Kansas/Oklahoma. These are the current states where illegal immigration remains a political lightning rod.

Nationwide Antifa rally

On *November 4, 2017*, the group Refuse Facism sponsored nationwide multi-city Antifa rallies. Actual attendance was sparse.[20] Mars/Gemini ruling the 4th is consistent with civil unrest. See however the Partner for this direction was a sinister aspect which is less powerful than a dexter aspect. Attendance was low, there were no deaths, and there were no mass arrests.

The rise of Antifa as a USA political force appears tied to the Ascendant Distributor changeover from Jupiter/Virgo to Mars/Virgo on *April 28, 2017*. The first USA Antifa event tagged by Googletrends was *February 1, 2017* when Antifa protestors at Berkeley protested the appearance of Breitbart editor Milo Yiannopoulos.[21] However cancellation of Portland's annual Avenue of Roses Parade and Carnival on *April 29, 2017* – because of multiple groups planned to protest - was the first recorded USA incident where Antifa planned to confront right-wing demonstrators in public.[22] This falls 1 day after the Ascendant Distributor changeover to Mars/Virgo.

On *August 14, 2017*, Mark Bray published *Antifa: The Anti-Fascist Handbook*.[23] This occurred two days after the *August 11/12, 2017* Unite the Right rally in Charlottesville, Virginia. August 2017 is the peak Googletrends Antifa score for 2017, though a secondary peak occurs in November 2017 the same month as the *November 4, 2017* nationwide Antifa rally cited above.

CHAPTER THIRTEEN

Partners: Mercury

Longitude	24CA10'32"
Latitude	3s52'47"
Speed	-0deg27'08" (slow)
Sign	Cancer
Bound	Jupiter/Cancer
Dwad	Aries
Houses	<u>Occupies</u> 8th
	<u>Rules</u> 7th, 10th (WS); 6th, 7th, 9th, (AL)
Rulers	<u>Ruled by</u> Moon/Aquarius
Additional	Evening star/Occidental
	Retrograde
	Under the Beams approaching the Sun
	Member of Venus-Jupiter-Sun-Mercury stellium

<u>Planet – Mercury</u>: Media, communications, education, literature, boys.

<u>Sign – Cancer:</u> Mercury/Cancer is noted for sensitivity to the immediate environment because the Moon rules Cancer and the Moon governs instinct and sensory perception. Though Mercury/Cancer is not technically in detriment, his manifestation as 'fleeting sensitivity' underlies problems faced by Mercury in all water signs. Here the facts Mercury tries to communicate can be clouded or dissolved by the water element. With Moon-ruled Cancer assigned to the public in mundane astrology, Mercury/Cancer's better application is found in deciphering and manipulating crowd behavior. Stump speaking and demagoguery are common Mercury/Cancer communication styles.

<u>Bound – Jupiter/Cancer</u>: In the sign opposed to Capricorn, Jupiter/Cancer opposes Capricorn traits of accumulated wealth and status through a philosophy favorable to the consuming public. With consumer banking and consumer legal protection two consistent themes timed by

Jupiter-Ascendant directions (see Chapter 15), these themes are added to Mercury's signification.

Dwad – Aries: Adds aggressiveness to communication. Headstrong logic, military strategy, forceful debate, and rashness are common manifestations.

Ruler – Moon/Aquarius/3rd: The demand for equal treatment of humans in matters of free speech, public education, and local transportation is the primary signification of the Aquarian Moon. All of these effects will prove the source and result of Mercury's effects.

Rules – Mars/Gemini/7th: Signifies an incendiary style of firepower, lying/deceit, and identity theft which harm marriage, legal disputes, and open enemies. As ruler, Mercury is the source and outcome of Mars' actions.

Additional Considerations: Mercury's position, retrograde and under the beams moving quickly towards the Sun, is a significant debility. So is Mercury's position five signs from his ruler the Moon (in aversion). Schoener cites Moon and Mercury in aversion as one indication of mental illness.[1]

Synthesis – Mercury

Mercury peregrine in Cancer, placed in the dwad of Aries, in aversion to its ruler, retrograde, and under the sunbeams are sufficient conditions to classify Mercury as an accidental malefic. The most succinct delineation of this combination is irresistibility to sensationalism and demagoguery. Placement in the bound of the benefic Jupiter/Cancer appears *not* to improve the quality of Mercury's actions, but to confer consumer banking and consumer protection as topics Mercury chooses to debate. This delineation is consistent with banking and consumer protection as reoccurring themes in populist political movements.

Insanity is another delineation of Mercury and is a plausible reason behind the relatively high number of serial killers in the United States compared to their ranks in other industrialized nations. (See actions of Richard Speck timed by Mercury-Ascendant Direction #9.)

Because Mercury is the universal significator of slaves and rules the 6th and 9th, immigrant labor is another common Mercury theme.

Mercury as the cause of Mars-signified disputes is so commonly found it is sometimes difficult to separate the effects of Mercury and Mars for a given Mercury or Mars direction.

Mercury-Ascendant Direction #1

D	Saturn/Capricorn	P	opposition Mercury (l=0) d. → ASC	23-Sep-1803
D	Changeover		bound Mars/Capricorn d. → ASC	26-Apr-1805
D	Mars/Capricorn	P	opposition Mercury (l=ME) d. → ASC	16-Jul-1808

Impeachment of John Pickering

Accused of insanity, John Pickering was the first federal official to be removed from office after conviction on impeachment charges. Because the Constitution specified impeachment could only occur for high crimes or misdemeanors – with insanity not meeting either classification – Federalists accused Jefferson's party of violating the Constitution.

Key dates: On *February 4, 1803*, Jefferson sent evidence against Pickering to the House of Representatives. On *March 2, 1803*, Pickering was impeached on charges of drunkenness and unlawful rulings; on *March 12, 1804*, Pickering was convicted of impeachment charges.

Partner: Mercury (insanity) is directed to the 7th cusp (lawsuits).

Distributor: The Distributor changeover to Saturn/Capricorn on October 19, 1801 timed the ascendancy of John Marshall on the Supreme Court who helped cement Federalist control of the Constitution. Saturn/Capricorn tied the effects of this direction to legal questions of Constitutionality.

New England – Canadian Smuggling

Passage of the Embargo Law on December 22, 1807 had a destructive impact on the New England economy because it restricted trade with Britain. In response, a vast smuggling network was established between New England and Canada, primarily by Federalists opposed to Jefferson and Madison. In *late summer 1808*, James Madison took note of Canadian smuggling operations and complicity between New England shippers and the British.[2]

Partner: Mercury in the 8th house of traded goods is consistent with smuggled goods because a smuggler is a thief (Mercury) who operates in hiding (under the sunbeams). Direction to the 7th cusp shows a legal dispute.

Distributor: Mars/Capricorn can be read as James Madison. See Chapter 6, Mars/Capricorn Distribution, for this delineation.

Mercury-Ascendant Direction #2

D	Saturn/Scorpio	P	sin. trine Mercury (l=ME) c. → ASC	5-Apr-1813
D	Saturn/Scorpio	P	sin. trine Mercury (l=0) c. → ASC	9-Jan-1816

West Florida Occupation

The capture of Mobile, Alabama on *April 13, 1813* and occupation of West Florida on *April 15, 1813* during the War of 1812 are the logical event matches for this sequence based on the ability of the same Mercury trine ASC solar arc direction to time Madison's initial annexation of West Florida. See Appendix E, p. 376 for the solar arc section for description of the West Florida episode as a 'false-flag' operation for land-grabbing through military means.

The Negro Fort at Prospect Bluff

The entire 1813-1816 sequence can be tied to propaganda surrounding American military battles against the Creek and Seminole Indian tribes with Andrew Jackson at the helm. Jackson's March 27, 1814 victory at the Battle of Horseshoe Bend ended what was effectively a civil war within the Creek Indian tribe. Some remaining Creek Indians traveled to Florida which would become the next battleground. At the conclusion of the War of 1812, the British evacuated a fort built at Prospect Bluff on the Apalachicola River. Major Edward Nicholls of the British Royal Marines remained briefly in order to instruct the Seminoles how to defend their land guaranteed by the Treaty of Ghent. The fort was supplied with cannon, muskets, and ammunition. The Seminoles didn't care much for the fort and Nicholls gave the fort over to fugitive slaves before leaving in 1815. Quickly the fort gained a reputation as the 'Negro Fort,' much feared by Southerners as a potential rallying point for slave revolts. It is likely that wildly exaggerated statements fearing slave revolts were uttered near the sequence's end date of *January 9, 1816* because Nicholls left the fort in the *summer of 1815* and by *April 1816* Andrew Jackson threatened to eliminate the fort should the Spanish refuse. In a military confrontation with Gen. Edmund Gaines on July 27, 1816, the Fort exploded when a cannon ball made a direct hit in the fort's gunpowder magazine. The explosion killed more than 250 of the 320 people in the fort and was heard more than 100 miles away in Pensacola.[3]

Partner: Statements made by Southerners fearing a slave revolt are a delineation match to Mercury/Cancer as sensationalist rhetoric designed to spur military action by a false flag operation.

Distributor: Saturn/Scorpio signifies the need for security fueled by paranoia. Matches fears of the Negro Fort espoused by white settlers.

Mercury-Ascendant Direction #3

D	Mars/Pisces	P	dex. trine Mercury (l=0) d. → ASC	7-Mar-1845
D	Changeover		bound Saturn/Pisces d. → ASC	2-Jun-1847
D	Changeover		bound Jupiter/Aries d. → ASC	2-Aug-1848
D	Jupiter/Aries	P	dex. trine Mercury (l=ME) d. → ASC	24-Sep-1849

Texas and the Mexican War
(May 13, 1846 – February 2, 1848)

Faced with Senate refusal to pass a formal treaty to annex Texas during 1844, John Tyler signed a Joint Congressional Resolution for annexation on *March 1, 1845* which required simple majority support. Mexico's Santa Anna had long stated that American annexation of Texas would constitute a declaration of war. Mexico still considered Texas a renegade province following the 1836 Texas Declaration of Independence. Circumstances surrounding Texas annexation, the Mexican War, and the California Constitutional Convention were imbued with Mercury-Cancer's sensationalism because annexation would add to the balance of slave states in the Union. Debate between abolitionists and slave states was so emotional that the Mexican War would be cited later as one of the primary causes of the Civil War.

California Constitutional Convention
(*September 1 – October 12, 1849*)

Mercury's debilities extend to immigrant labor because Mercury rules the 6th (labor) and the 9th (foreign affairs). During the debate, labor leaders and organizations turned against the annexation of Texas because of their experience that free white workers could not compete against slave labor, effectively shutting out employment prospects in Texas were annexation to proceed.[4]

California's Constitutional Convention limited suffrage to white males. Despite Congressional extension of suffrage to aliens in many other Western territories in the middle 1800s, aliens in California, Texas, and those living in other territories gained by the Mexican War were denied suffrage.[5] Debate notes from both Texas (1846) and California (1849) conventions are indicative of the tendency of debate to descend to demagoguery.[6] Failure of aliens to achieve suffrage made these individuals second class citizens.

Mercury-Ascendant Direction #4

D	Venus/Libra	P	sin. square Mercury (l=ME) c. → ASC	15-May-1852
D	Venus/Libra	P	sin. square Mercury (l=0) c. → ASC	1-Feb-1854

Uncle Tom's Cabin

Hatred of slavery widened beyond abolitionist circles following publication of *Uncle Tom's Cabin* by Harriet Beecher Stowe on **March 20, 1852** which described sadistic practices borne by slaves. *Uncle Tom's Cabin* had a sensational impact on popular opinion and was the second best-selling book of the 19th century after the Bible.[7] As the sequence opened, a NYT notice **May 14, 1852** indicated Stowe received $4,000 based on 10 cents per copy sold and was offered $10,000 for copyright of the book. Outrage over treatment of fugitive slaves, fueled by *Uncle Tom's Cabin*, was one of many factors which led to the Civil War. When first introduced to Stowe in 1862, Lincoln allegedly said "So this is the little lady who caused the Great War."[8]

Partner: The book's sensationalism matches the delineation of Mercury/Cancer generally; its effects are specified to slaves because Mercury rules the 6th house. As ruler of Mars, Mercury is the cause of Martian events; in this case, the Civil War.

Kansas-Nebraska Act

Stephen Douglas introduced the Kansas-Nebraska Act on **January 23, 1854**. The Act essentially repealed the Missouri Compromise of 1820 by letting each state choose whether or not to allow slavery in a concept known as 'popular sovereignty.' Douglas' original motivation for introducing this legislation was greed: he stood to profit from railroad expansion which would increase the value of his personal Chicago real estate holdings.

Partner: Like *Uncle Tom's Cabin*, the Kansas-Nebraska Act had a sensational impact on Americans. It caused an influx of pro-slavery immigrants to Kansas who planned to act as swing votes in favor of slavery. The resulting violence known as *Bloody Kansas* was a direct result of the Kansas-Nebraska Act. This is consistent with Mercury as the source of Mars/Gemini-signified civil strife.

Distributor: Venus/Libra as peacemaker signifies Douglas' attempts at mediating differences between slave and free states.

Mercury-Ascendant Direction #5

D	Mars/Aries	P	dex. square Mercury (l=0) d. → ASC	3-Jan-1863
D	Changeover		bound Saturn/Aries d. → ASC	9-Jul-1863
D	Changeover		bound Venus/Taurus d. → ASC	9-Sep-1866
D	Venus/Taurus	P	dex. square Mercury (l=ME) d. → ASC	16-Jul-1867

Emancipation Proclamation

Following the Emancipation Proclamation which went into force on *January 1, 1863*, emancipated slaves, now referred to as 'Freedmen,' were allowed to serve as Union military forces. Their service was generally confined to support roles as cooks and teamsters. When captured by Confederate soldiers, Freedmen were executed on site.[9]

Partner & Distributor: Properly delineated, the direction of the Ascendant to an afflicted Mercury in the bounds of a malefic (Mars/Aries) promises the annihilation of slaves through military action. Why? Because Mercury rules the 6th of slaves, Mercury is afflicted, and Mars/Aries as Distributor promises harm through warfare. This delineation matches the fate of captured freedman serving in the Union military.

Reconstruction

On *July 17, 1867*, the NYT reported Freedmen were leaving cotton fields unattended in order to attend educational programs with the goal of learning voting procedures.[10] Concern was expressed on the negative impact on the cotton crop as weeds were left to grow intermingled with cotton.

Partner: The incident describes a labor problem. Mercury under the sunbeams ruling the 6th of slaves is a delineation match to freedman disappearing from agricultural fields. The NYT also confirms the role of the Moon as the cause of Mercury's effects. Educational programs were paid for by philanthropists who sought suffrage for freedman. Moon in the 3rd of education rules the 5th of elections, the 8th of bequests, and Mercury in the 8th.

Distributor: As Distributor, Venus/Taurus contributes agricultural cotton fields as backdrop to this event because cotton is a land-grown crop (Taurus) which is fashioned into clothing (Venus).

Mercury-Ascendant Direction #6

D	Saturn/Taurus	P	dex. sextile Mercury (l=0) d. → ASC	11-Oct-1883
D	Changeover		bound Mars/Taurus d. → ASC	8-Jan-1886
D	Mars/Taurus	P	dex. sextile Mercury (l=ME) d. → ASC	1-May-1888

Pittsburgh Manifesto

Held during **October 1883** as the sequence opened, the Pittsburgh Convention of the Revolutionary Socialist Party featured a pro-trade union platform.[11] Trade unionism was favored by western attendees. The Eastern faction favored more radical action espoused by the German anarchist Johann Most. Most was an advocate of 'propaganda by deed,' a seemingly harmless slogan which in truth advocated the murder of capitalists and theft of property.

<u>Distributor</u>: The NYT editorial described the speakers as demagogues, matching the type of rhetoric spewed by an afflicted Mercury/Cancer.

<u>Partner</u>: Calls for the destruction (Saturn) of capitalism (Taurus) are consistent with Saturn/Taurus as distributor.

Disarray of Labor Movements

Formed after the Civil War, the Knights of Labor was the first nationwide labor organization whose basis was equality among workers. Knights' membership peaked in 1886 but declined following an unsuccessful strike against the Missouri-Pacific railroad on March 6, 1886. Following the Haymarket Riot of May 14, 1886, labor unions suffered a death blow. With police and civilian fatalities, Haymarket was labeled an anarchist attack. In response the national mood recoiled against organized labor as a social movement. With calls for 'Knights of Labor, the Farmers' Alliance ... Grangers, Greenbacks, [and] Anti-Monopolists'[12], the Union and United Labor Parties both held political conventions during **May 1888** in order to jump start trade union activism. The conventions were unsuccessful. Typical of the disarray of Labor Unions in 1888 were squabbles among the New York Brewer's Union. In an NYT article dated **May 4, 1888**, a threat signed by 'A Working Bull who is on a Rampage'[13] captures Mars/Taurus as the distributor for this direction.[14]

Mercury-Ascendant Direction #7

D	Mars/Virgo	P	sin. sextile Mercury (l=ME) c. → ASC	7-Apr-1890
D	Mars/Virgo	P	sin. sextile Mercury (l=0) c. → ASC	18-Sep-1891

Immigration Reform: Creation of Ellis Island

Originally constructed as Castle Clinton for defense of New York's harbor (1808-1811), the renamed Castle Garden served as the Immigrant Landing Depot between 1855 and 1890. By 1890, high numbers of immigrants had given rise to unscrupulous hucksters who swindled naive immigrants, many non-English speaking. As the sequence opened, on *April 8, 1890*, the Sub-Committee of the Joint Congressional Committee started hearings on the operations of Castle Garden.[15] The chair of the Committee indicated the purpose of the hearings was fact-finding. Following the hearings, Congress decided to close Castle Garden and construct a new facility on Ellis Island which opened *January 1, 1892* just after the end of the sequence. The money changing concession was soon given to American Express in order to eliminate immigrant swindles.

Partner: The vulnerability of immigrants at the hands of swindlers is shown by the weakness of Mercury/Cancer as the ruler of the 9th of foreign affairs and the 6th of the working class.

Birth of Princess Stephanie Juliann von Hohenlohe

Hohenlohe was born on *September 16, 1891* as the sequence closed. She was one of the most famous and influential Nazi spies in the period prior to WWII. After war broke out, she moved to San Francisco and later supplied the American Office of Strategic Services (predecessor to the CIA) with information helpful in completing a psychological profile of Adolph Hitler.

Mercury-Ascendant Direction #8

D	Jupiter/Cancer	P	conjunction Mercury (l=0) d. → ASC	6-Aug-1945
D	Changeover		bound Saturn/Cancer d. → ASC	9-Nov-1947
D	Saturn/Cancer	P	conjunction Mercury (l=ME) d. → ASC	7-Aug-1948

Detonation of nuclear weapons over Hiroshima and Nagasaki

Hiroshima (*August 6*) and Nagasaki (*August 9*) were bombed with nuclear weapons. The ability of Mercury in the Regulus USA National Horoscope to time the offensive use of nuclear weapons is not generally recognized by American astrologers who assign nuclear activity to Pluto. A review of significant nuclear events of the 20th Century reveals 24th-25th cardinal degrees a common placement. They include Trinity, Joe-1, and 596. Mercury is retrograde which signifies a repeated event; there were two bombs.

The sinking of USS Indianapolis on *July 30, 1945* is relevant to this direction because this ship delivered the nuclear components of 'Little Boy' (for Hiroshima) to Tinian Island on *July 26, 1945*. The ship's Captain Charles Butler McVay III was later court-marshaled for placing his ship in harm's way. These claims were hotly disputed with McVay's reputation exonerated in October 2000 by a Congressional resolution, but not before McVay committed suicide on November 6, 1968 after mounting guilt from families of deceased servicemen who blamed him for casualties suffered in 1945.

White – Hiss Congressional Testimony

Congressional testimony of Whittaker Chambers against Alger Hiss on *August 25, 1948* was the first televised Congressional hearing in American history. This followed the death of Harry Dexter White on *August 16, 1948*; three days after he denied Chambers' accusations of Soviet complicity. Subsequent evidence from the Venona project confirmed the guilt of both Hiss and White as Soviet spies, a conclusion made by the bipartisan Moynihan Commission on Government Secrecy.

Partner: The sensationalism of the hearings matches the delineation of an afflicted Mercury/Cancer. Richard Nixon was instrumental in persuading Chambers to testify against Hiss; Nixon leveraged the Chambers-Hiss controversy for his own political purposes.

Distributor: Saturn/Cancer is a polarizing influence; literally denying (Saturn) the people (Cancer). It is a delineation match to the witch-hunts of the McCarthy era.

Mercury-Ascendant Direction #9

D	Saturn/Cancer	P	conjunction Mercury (l=ME) c. → ASC	11-May-1964
D	Changeover		bound Saturn/Cancer c. → ASC	27-Feb-1965
D	Jupiter/Cancer	P	conjunction Mercury (l=0) c. → ASC	3-Jun-1967

Bugged American Intelligence Embassy in Moscow

On *May 19, 1964*, the U.S. State Department reported more than 40 hidden microphones were found in the walls of the American Embassy in Moscow. They dated from the 1950s under Stalin. This episode appears linked to the January 20, 1964 defection of KGB Colonel Yuri Nosenko who supplied details of the hidden microphones and other intelligence matters.[16]

Death Sentence of Mass Murderer Richard Speck

The mass murderer Richard Speck, who killed eight student nurses on July 14, 1966, was sentenced to death on *June 8, 1967*. The conviction was appealed to the Illinois Supreme Court the same day and had a lengthy post-trial history. The U.S. Supreme Court upheld the murder conviction but overturned Speck's death penalty on June 28, 1971. Potential jurors opposed to the death penalty had been systematically excluded during the jury selection process. According to the Supreme Court, the resulting bias unfairly tilted the jury towards the death penalty.

As the source of Mercury's actions, Moon/Aquarius signifies student nurses as the cause of Speck's murderous rampage. As the result of Mercury's actions, Moon/Aquarius exhibits its concern for human rights and causes Speck's death penalty to be overturned.

Attack on USS Liberty

The American surveillance vessel USS Liberty was mistakenly attacked by the Israelis on *June 8, 1967* during the Six-Day War. It was the single deadliest attack against a U.S. Naval vessel since the end of World War II and the single greatest loss of life by the U.S. Intelligence community. Multiple communications failures occurred on both Israeli and American sides. The event remains hotly debated among military and intelligence circles.

Compare this incident to the sinking of the USS Indianapolis, timed by the Mercury-Ascendant Direction #8 (same Distributor).

CHAPTER FOURTEEN

Partners: Venus

Longitude	3CA09'45"
Latitude	0n06'04"
Speed	+1deg 13'29" (fast)
Sign	Cancer
Bound	Mars/Cancer
Dwad	Leo
Houses	<u>Occupies</u> 8th
	<u>Rules</u> 4th, 6th, 11th (WS); 3rd, 5th, 10th (AL)
Rulers	<u>Ruled</u> by Moon/Aquarius
	<u>Rules</u> Saturn/Libra
Other	Morning star/Oriental
	Under the sunbeams approaching combustion
	Applying to conjunction of Jupiter
	Member of Venus-Jupiter-Sun-Mercury stellium

<u>Planet – Venus</u>: Peace, diplomacy, food, art, romance, and women.

<u>Sign – Cancer</u>: Venus in Cancer combines her significations with consumers because Cancer is ruled by the Moon, significator of the public. Cancer's signification of care and comfort also translate to the home; accordingly, Venus/Cancer signifies consumer and home products. Other significations include the love of the color white, dairy products, and female breasts as a preferred sexual erogenous zone.[1]

<u>Bound – Mars/Cancer</u>: Mars in Cancer is placed in the sign of his fall. At its simplest delineation, this malefic bound taints consumer product quality by the introduction of foreign substances (e.g. Martian type of liquid). As a significator of martial acts generally, Mars in Cancer functions with timidity unless home turf is threatened. Back a Mars/Cancer individual into a corner and watch Mars replace his timidity with acts of unspeakable cruelty as he lashes out to defend home turf. Given the ability of many Ascendant-Venus directions to time race riots in American history, it appears Venus/Cancer as

'love of white' and Mars/Cancer as 'defense of home turf by cruelty when threatened' is best delineated as white racism.

Dwad – Leo: Venus in the dwad of Leo adds flair and publicity. The consumer advertising industry is a delineation match. Another is publicity of lynchings and race riots in the popular media.

Ruled by Moon/Aquarius: The demand for equal treatment of humans in matters of free speech, public education, and local transportation is the primary signification of the Aquarian Moon. All of these effects will prove the source and result of Venus' effects.

Rules Saturn/Libra: The United States Dollar and affiliations with supranational organizations who wish for imposition of the New World Order through trade and financial policies are the primary significations of Saturn/Libra. These actions will be the result of Venus' effects.

Approaching Superior Conjunction: Venus under the sunbeams is quickly approaching her superior conjunction. Medieval texts state planets under the sunbeams are one of the worst debilities because the Sun burns up planets under its rays. In my opinion, Mayan astrology does a much better job at explaining Venus' actual behavior relative to the Sun. A thumbnail sketch of Bruce Scofield's pioneering work in this area[2] finds the Mayans feared the first appearance of Venus as a morning star for its ability to reveal sex scandals. In the Mayan model, information about scandalous behavior becomes fully known at Venus' maximum elongation as a morning star and is judged when Venus makes her superior conjunction. In watching this cycle closely the past few years, I have observed that Venus' superior conjunction marks both the end cycle (judgment of scandal) and the start of a new cycle (committal of new scandalous behavior). In my opinion, as Venus approaches her superior conjunction, Venusian temptations are titillating and unstoppable. The expressions 'like a moth to a flame' and 'blinded by the light' are apropos. Though the Mayans emphasized sexual sins, any perversion of Venus is possible: misuse of food, alcohol, drugs, money laundering, and all types of financial fraud. For the USA, Venus/Cancer approaching her superior conjunction can be delineated as 'unstoppable desires' for participation in all Venus/Cancer delineated activities. These 'unstoppable desires' will both occur (as the cycle starts) and be judged (as the cycle ends).

Synthesis – Venus

White racism. Judgment of white racism is the most frequent event timed by Ascendant-Venus directions. To recap, Venus/Cancer loves home and family but because Cancer's color is white, the love of Venus/Cancer is restricted to white homes and white families. As a bound, Mars/Cancer adds the theme of defense of home/family when threatened. This Venus-Mars combination signifies white racism. Venus approaching the Sun signifies its judgment.

As ruler of Venus, Moon/Aquarius/3rd shows both the source and cause of white racism. As significator of fair and equal treatment of all humans, the Moon's placement in the 3rd ties its significations to public education and transportation. Integration of schools (Little Rock) and buses (Rosa Parks) were two of the most prominent Civil Rights battlegrounds in the 1950s and 1960s. By exaltation, Moon also rules the 5th of recreation and elections and the 6th of slaves. Integration of professional sports (Jackie Robinson), obtaining suffrage for minorities, and abolition of slavery were other seminal events in American Civil Rights history. All of these events – ranging from abolition to school integration – triggered America's worst episodes of white racism. In this way the Moon/Aquarius caused white racism as white citizens rebelled against the Moon's need for fair and equal treatment of all humans.

The inability of the void of course Moon to perfect matters means recourse to Saturn as the Moon's ruler is required to judge white racism. Saturn/Libra signifies Congress and the Supreme Court; both institutions have mandated Civil Rights legislation since the 1950s. The Moon, with help from Saturn, brings about judgment of white racism and implementation of Civil Rights legislation to meet the need of fair and equal treatment of all humans.

<u>Tainted Consumer Products</u>. Though most of the following Venus-Ascendant directions time events concerning white racism, the ability of a pair of Venus-Ascendant solar arc directions in 1905/1906 to time revelation of unsanitary practices in the meatpacking industry speaks to the delineation of Venus/Cancer as tainted consumer food products. (See Appendix E, p. 382).

Besides tainted food products, placement of Venus/Cancer in the bound of Mars/Cancer is consistent with tainted pharmaceutical products. Arguably, Venus/Cancer/8th also signifies the relatively high incidence of breast cancer among American women. It is also consistent with medical problems from silicone gel breast implants which emerged in the early 1990s.

Venus-Ascendant Direction #1

D	Mercury/Capricorn	P	opp. Venus (l=VE) d. → ASC	18-Mar-1783
D	Mercury/Capricorn	P	opp. Venus (l=0) d. → ASC	27-Apr-1783

Newburgh Conspiracy

Washington's *March 15, 1783* famous Newburgh Address was a surprise speech made to a group of his soldiers prepared for mutiny. At the Revolutionary War's end, the American colonies were bankrupt. Promises made by states to levy taxes to back Continental Currency were repudiated and replaced by the issuance of an even greater pool of fiat money by the states. Hyperinflation resulted. The phrase 'not worth a Continental' dates from this period. Soldiers were disgusted with Congress for failure to honor promised wages, pensions, and other financial assistance. Petitions to Congress were presented during December 1782 and January 1783. Some progress was made but continued inaction led to the planned mutiny in *March 1783*.[3] After the Newburgh Address, Congress did make a settlement with the soldiers.

Partner: Venus at her superior conjunction denotes judgment of failed Congressional financial pledges because of worthless currency. Venus falls in the 8th of pensions/taxes and rules the 11th of currency.

Distributor: Mercury/Capricorn signifies the strategy (Mercury) of Federalists (Capricorn) to manipulate soldiers' demands as a publicity tool in order to demonstrate the Federal Government's need to levy taxes.

British Abolitionist Movement

Olaudah Equiano, a former American slave living in London, convinced the abolitionist Granville Sharpe to prosecute a slave trader for drowning 133 slaves at sea in order to claim insurance benefits. The Equiano-Sharpe incident was triggered by the publication of a letter to the editor on *March 18, 1783*, as the sequence began. Author Adam Hochschild traces the repercussions of this event to the eventual abolition of slavery in the British Empire on August 1, 1838.[4] The boycott of sugar by abolitionists was a key element in the success of the campaign to eliminate slavery.

Partner: Judgment of white racism is one delineation match to this direction. In addition, sugar is a Venus-ruled commodity.

Venus-Ascendant Direction #2

D	Venus/Pisces	P	dex. trine Venus (l=VE) d. → ASC	17-May-1832
D	Venus/Pisces	P	dex. trine Venus (l=0) d. → ASC	30-Jun-1832

Jump Jim Crow

Thomas Dartmouth (T.D.) "Daddy" Rice originated blackface comedy, a later staple of minstrel shows, with his song and dance routine *Jump Jim Crow*. While I was unable to find an exact sequence match to Rice's move to New York in 1832, variants of the lyrics endorsing Andrew Jackson's Presidential Campaign suggest the connection between *Jump Jim Crow* and the Democratic Party Convention held during **May 21-22, 1832** as the sequence opened.[5]

Partner: The first performance of the song and dance routine which gave rise to the *Jim Crow* segregation moniker is a delineation match to Venus/Cancer as white racism.

Distributor: Because the feet are assigned to Pisces, Venus/Pisces is a match to *Jump Jim Crow* because it was performed as a part of a dance. Venus/Pisces also signifies a melodramatic and sentimental musical style common to Minstrel Show performances.

Veto of the Second Bank of the United States

On **July 10, 1832**, Andrew Jackson vetoed the recharter of the Second Bank of the United States. As just cause, Jackson cited business practices which favored the wealthy at the expense of the common man. In addition, because the capital structure of the bank, many profits would accrue to bank owners and foreign investors were the Bank to be rechartered. Unwittingly, Jackson helped set into motion the next scandal with his bank veto. Without the anchor of gold, state banks engaged in rampant issuance of private banknotes. Excessive money creation fueled a speculative boom and the Panic of 1837 as leverage was unwound.

Partner: Jackson's actions match the delineation of Venus at her superior conjunction as judgment of a financial scandal.

Distributor: Venus/Pisces signifies sacrifice. Public willingness to part with a bulwark of the financial system is consistent.

Venus-Ascendant Direction #3

D	Mars/Scorpio	P	sin. trine Venus (l=0) c. → ASC	18-Sep-1842
D	Mars/Scorpio	P	sin. trine Venus (l=VE) c. → ASC	6-Oct-1842

Muncy Abolition Riot

In April 1842, Enos Hawley, a Quaker abolitionist, invited an outside speaker to Muncy, Pennsylvania, to speak on behalf of the abolitionist movement at a local schoolhouse. A riot ensued with eighteen men breaking school windows with thrown rocks and other debris. Hawley and the guest speaker were injured. Local law enforcement eventually quelled the violence. This primary direction sequence matches the indictment of rioters during *September 1842* and their trial during *October 1842*. The jury was eventually swayed by jury member Abraham Updegraff and convicted thirteen of the eighteen men. Shortly after the trial, Governor David Porter effectively nullified the jury decision with his pardon of all convicted rioters.[6]

Partner: Judgment of a race riot is a delineation match to Venus/Cancer. Note also that Moon/Aquarius/3rd – significator of abolitionist speeches – was the cause of the riot.

Distributor: Mars/Scorpio adds violence motivated by revenge which was a likely motivator behind the riot. The Governor's pardon may have also been motivated by revenge against abolitionists but this observation is speculative.

Venus-Ascendant Direction #4

D	Jupiter/Aries	P	dex. square Venus (l=VE) d. → ASC	25-Apr-1850
D	Jupiter/Aries	P	dex. square Venus (l=0) d. → ASC	7-Jun-1850

Missouri Compromise Debate and the Nashville Convention

This sequence times several events during the Missouri Compromise debate. On *April 17, 1850*, pro-slavery Senator Henry Foote (Mississippi) brandished his pistol at Senator Thomas Hart Benton (Missouri) following Benton's heated arguments with Vice-President Millard Fillmore. Benton had recently opposed slavery in 1849.

The Nashville Convention of *June 3 – 11, 1850*, was set into motion by the October 1, 1849 Mississippi Convention's resolution to fight the abolitionist movement's goal to eliminate slavery. Moderate Whig and Democrat attendees were able to hold in check those Southerners who favored immediate secession should slavery be restricted in new territories. The mood of compromise at the Nashville Convention carried to the Senate which approved the Missouri Compromise in *September 1850*.

Partner: On first glance, *judgment of a race riot* does not match the Foote-Benton violence. Yet Venus rules the 11th of Congress and threats of physical violence within the Senate chambers over white racism surely mirrored agitated constituencies living in Foote and Benton's Senate districts. Important is Foote's failure to actually shoot Benton. Further research is required to see how Foote was *judged* to demonstrate the ability of the Sun to essentially burn up Foote's white racism. *Judgment of white racism* is an easier match to the Nashville Convention. Secessionist sentiments espoused by radical Southerners were essentially burned up by moderate forces.

Distributor: Jupiter/Aries signifies the public's 'Westward Ho!' migration following the 1848 California gold discovery. Western migration brought the issue of slavery in western territories to a head.

Venus-Ascendant Direction #5

D	Venus/Taurus	P	dex. sextile Venus (l=VE) d. → ASC	16-Aug-1868
D	Venus/Taurus	P	sex. sextile Venus (l=0) d. → ASC	29-Sep-1868

Race Riots: Pulaski, New Orleans and Camilla, Georgia

The effective lame duck period following President Andrew Johnson's acquittal on impeachment charges on May 26, 1868 was taken over by the newly-formed Ku Klux Klan which instituted a reign of terror in order to influence national elections to be held during the fall. Over 1,300 lynchings were attributed to the KKK prior to the November 1868 Presidential election.[7]

Notable disturbances include the Pulaski Riot (town in which the KKK was founded), St. Augustine, Florida (August 15, 1868)[8], Camilla, Georgia (September 19, 1868)[9], and New Orleans (September 22, 1868)[10]. The Camilla riots were so violent that Congress reinstated military rule of Georgia; consistent with the delineation of Venus/Cancer approaching her superior conjunction as judgment of white racism.

Distributor: With Venus/Taurus as distributor, riots timed by this direction should be muted compared to other Venus directions with malefic distributors. Given the violence of riots timed by this sequence, this appears hard to swallow; yet consider the events of the New Orleans riot. The conflict in New Orleans started as a shouting match between a group of marching African Americans who supported the Grant Presidential ticket (favorable to Freedmen) and a supporter of the Seymour and Blair ticket (favorable to white Southerners). The initial brawl started in a confectionary and restaurant with male restaurant patrons jumping up to defend female patrons who were eating ice cream. Restaurants serving high quality food are consistent with Venus in Taurus, the sign of her rulership, as Distributor. Ice cream is signified by Venus/Cancer because Venus is food and Cancer signifies milk from which ice cream is made. With less than a dozen African Americans killed and a few injured in the New Orleans riot, the benefic distributor Venus/Taurus appears to have limited total casualties by providing a restaurant setting as the backdrop for the confrontation.

Venus-Ascendant Direction #6

D	Saturn/Libra	P	sin. square Venus (l=0) c. → ASC	21-Jun-1880
D	Saturn/Libra	P	sin. square Venus (l=VE) c. → ASC	5-Jul-1880

Reconstruction

On *June 15, 1880*, President Rutherford Hayes vetoed an attempt by Democrats to weaken election laws by replacing Deputy Marshals with unseasoned officers.[11] At the time, Deputy Marshals helped enforce election laws which enfranchised the Freedmen. Judgment of an attempt to disenfranchise African Americans is a delineation match to Venus/Cancer ruling the 5th of elections. Hayes' citation of the constitutionality of his veto shows the influence of Saturn/Libra as distributor.

Mining Swindles

On *June 21, 1880*, the NYT published an exposé on fraudulent advertising practices used to promote investments in mining properties adjacent to the famous Nevada Comstock Lode silver deposit. Salting barren ores neighboring Comstock in order to increase their assay value was a typical tactic.[12]

According to astrological sign–metal correspondences, silver is assigned to the Moon which rules Cancer. Because Venus signifies money/investments and Cancer signifies silver, Venus/Cancer signifies a silver mine investment. 'Salting the ore' is a process which matches the adulteration of the bound Mars/Cancer. Dwad of Leo is technically gold; for this example the Leo dwad most likely adds a flamboyant promoter to the mix. Venus at her superior conjunction signifies judgment of scandals, reinforced by Saturn/Libra as distributor.

On *July 8, 1880*, the NYT published another laundry list of commonly perpetuated mining frauds.[13] The article also mentioned cases of overeager French investors who overpaid for Utah mines which were profitable, but not at the level necessary to make a sufficient return on their investment. Willingness to overpay confirms the delineation of Venus as the 'unstoppable desire' to own a silver mine investment which caused investors to overpay.

Venus-Ascendant Direction #7

D	Mercury/Virgo	P	sin. sextile Venus (l=0) c. → ASC	18-Feb-1918
D	Mercury/Virgo	P	sin. sextile Venus (l=VE) c. → ASC	6-Mar-1918

Food Scarcity – World War I

On *February 21, 1918*, Food Administrator Herbert Hoover stated the next two months

> would be the most critical period in the food history of the nation and the countries allied with it in the war.[14]

By this time, the devastation of World War I caused food production in Europe to collapse. Massive U.S. food exports, primarily cereals, were required to keep citizens of Allied countries from starvation. Relevant to this direction, the NYT aired dirty laundry between Hoover and William Gibbs McAdoo over the unwillingness of railroads to make further schedule adjustments in order to facilitate shipments to Eastern ports for European delivery. Besides his post as Treasury Secretary, McAdoo was Director General of Railroads at this time. Another of Hoover's concerns was the risk of rotting crops should reduce rail capacity delay their transport to drying terminals.

Distributor: Mercury/Virgo establishes the business affairs (Mercury) of sown crops (Virgo) as this direction's theme.

Partner: Export (8th house) of consumer goods (Venus/Cancer) matches the event timed by this direction. Note Cancer is a water sign and Hoover complains of the high moisture content of agricultural products. Hoover's call for wet grains to be promptly shipped to drying terminals matches the configuration of the Sun attempting to burn up Venus under his beams. Finally, problems with rail transportation as cause of the shipping problem are consistent with the inability of the void of course Moon/Aquarius in the 3rd of local transportation to function properly. Even the Moon's separation from Mars/Gemini delineated as a legal dispute about homeland affairs can be read as the Hoover-McAdoo dispute because Mars/Gemini signifies railroads.

Venus-Ascendant Direction #8

D	Mars/Cancer	P	conjunction Venus (l=VE) d. → ASC	22-Aug-1920
D	Mars/Cancer	P	conjunction Venus (l=0) d. → ASC	30-Sep-1920

Passage of the 19th Amendment – Women's Suffrage

Passed by Congress on June 4, 1919 and ratified on *August 19, 1920*, the 19th Amendment granted women the right to vote. Venus signifies women and rules the 5th of elections. At first glance, there seems little relationship between women's suffrage and race riots, yet truth is stranger than fiction. Is it a coincidence that immediately following Congressional passage of the 19th Amendment on June 4, 1919 that America saw its worst summer of race riots in the nation's history? No, say historians who have struggled to explain the paradox of the passage of both racist and social welfare legislation during the Progressive Era. Barbara Holden-Smith[15] advances the thesis that the fear of interracial sex between black men and white women was a powerful motivator of white racism in general and lynching in particular. According to Holden-Smith, voters considered the 19th Amendment as a way to enfranchise white women as a protective measure against blacks. Viewed this way, the contribution to racism by Mars/Cancer as both Distributor and bound of the Partner was a powerful motivator for granting female suffrage.

Warren Harding's Anti-Lynching Campaign

Consistent with the delineation of Venus/Cancer as the judgment of white racism is Warren Harding's willingness to redress the ills of lynching and segregation during his fall 1920 front porch Presidential Campaign. On *September 10, 1920* Harding spoke before several Negro delegations and met privately with Negro leaders promising progress on these issues.[16] Harding was instrumental in promoting an anti-lynching bill in Congress. The bill passed the House but was killed by a Senate filibuster on January 26, 1922. The failure of Harding to pass anti-lynching legislation can be traced to the racism of Mars/Cancer which interferes with the judgment of white racism.

Venus-Ascendant Direction #9

D	Mars/Cancer	P	conjunction Venus (l=0) c. → ASC	7-Apr-1992
D	Mars/Cancer	P	conjunction Venus (l=VE) c. → ASC	16-May-1992

The Rodney King Verdict

The Los Angeles riots of 1992 following the acquittal of four police officers accused in the beating of Rodney King were among the most violent in American history. Casualties included 53 dead, thousands injured, and destruction of several hundred million dollars' worth of property from looting, arson, and general destruction. Rioting began *April 29* following the acquittal verdict, peaked during *April 30/May 1*, and ran its course by *May 4*.

Partner: The riots matched Venus' *judgment of white racism* because a retrial of the four officers acquitted was ordered on federal charges of civil rights violations. Announced a year later on April 17, 1993, two officers were found guilty and two were acquitted. Note also that Venus in the dwad of Leo signifies luxury goods; a match to the type of item commonly stolen during the riots.

For the event chart of the riot's outbreak, cast for **6:45 PM, April 29, 1992**, Los Angeles, California; the South Node at 3CA26 was partile conjunct the USA Venus/Cancer at 3CA09. As a destroyer, the South Node contributed to the judgment of white racism timed by this direction.

Distributor: Though not as violently racist as the April 5, 1917 – January 29, 1925 Distribution defined by Mars/Cancer in *direct motion*, the December 8, 1987 – October 3, 1995 time period defined by Mars/Cancer by converse motion was nevertheless imbued with white racism. Memorable is the reverse discrimination backlash against affirmative action programs during the tenure of George H. W. Bush as President. The period culminated with the O.J. Simpson verdict on October 3, 1995. (For computation, see Chapter 5, Example 4, pp. 77-81).

Venus-Ascendant Direction #10

D	Mercury/Virgo	P	sin. sextile Venus (l=VE) d. → ASC	2-Nov-1994
D	Mercury/Virgo	P	sin. sextile Venus (l=0) d. → ASC	18-Nov-1994

California Proposition 187

The *November 8, 1994* passage of and the *November 11, 1994* restraining order against California's Proposition 187 matches delineation of Venus/Cancer as judgment of white racism because the measure failed to be honored in the courts. The Proposition was designed to eliminate government benefits to illegal immigrants. Services to be denied included public education, health care, and social services. In opposing the bill, State Senator Art Torres stated Proposition 187 was 'the last gasp of white America in California.' The measure passed with 58.5% of the vote but was eventually set aside following lengthy legal proceedings.

Distributor: Mercury/Virgo links this direction to California through choreography. My own research assigns Virgo to most Central and South American Latino nations as well as lands acquired by America in the 19th century beginning with the Louisiana Purchase.[17] As for Mercury, the direction concerned a ballot initiative which is the domain of Mercury.

Denny's Restaurant Settlement

Just prior to *November 6, 1994*, Denny's sold 17 of its restaurants to a black-owned company in order to honor a deal it made with the NAACP.[18]

Coke vs. Pepsi Ad Campaign addresses Sugar Content

Venus/Cancer also signifies comfort food. Bound of Mars/Cancer adds adulteration. In the case of soft drinks, the ingredient high fructose corn syrup has been linked to diabetes. How was this tainted consumer product judged by this direction? Coke began an advertising campaign to highlight its 20% lower sugar content compared to its rival Pepsi.[19]

Distributor: Coke's ad campaign started airing on Spanish-television, matching the Virgo-Latino choreography link described above.

CHAPTER FIFTEEN

Partners: Jupiter

Longitude	5CA56'38"
Latitude	00s04'12"
Speed	0deg13'34" (fast)
Sign	Cancer
Bound	Mars/Cancer
Dwad	Virgo
Houses	<u>Occupies</u>: 8th
	<u>Rules</u>: 1st, 4th, 8th (WS); 1st, 3rd, 12th (AL)
Rulers	<u>Ruled by</u>: Moon/Aquarius
Additional	Member of Venus-Jupiter-Sun-Mercury stellium
	Applies to Saturn by square aspect
	Conjunct Mars by antiscion
	Morning star, oriental, leaving combustion

<u>Planet – Jupiter</u>: Signifies religion, judges, legal systems, wisdom, higher education, banking, magnates, and philanthropy.

<u>Sign – Cancer</u>: Jupiter placed in the cardinal water sign of Cancer means the public is exalted in Jupiter's realm of religion, justice, wisdom, higher education and financial affairs.

<u>Bound – Mars/Cancer</u>: Mars placed in the sign of his fall produces timidity unless home turf is threatened. If challenged, Mars/Cancer responds with cruelty. The defensiveness of Mars/Cancer appears a match to the historical reluctance of states to allow expansion of national branch banking networks to their regions. It also appears consistent with redlining.

<u>Dwad – Virgo</u>: Jupiter in the dwad of Virgo, sign of detriment, interferes with Jupiter's activity through legalese, excessive paperwork, and bureaucracy.

Ruled by Moon/Aquarius: The demand for equal treatment of humans in matters of free speech, public education, and local transportation is the primary signification of the Aquarian Moon. All of these matters will prove the source and result of Jupiter's effects.

Synthesis – Jupiter

Placement in the 8th house ties these Jupiterian concepts to death, taxes, pensions, inheritance, and traded goods. Legal protection for the consumer against risk of death and unfair business practices are themes which exemplify Jupiter's ties to the legal establishment. With the horoscope's Part of Spirit in the capitalistic earth sign of Taurus (12TA25), banking and financial themes emphasize Jupiter's function as a financial magnate. Indebted family farmers are another Jupiter/Cancer/8th house theme.

Consumer Protection. Legal protection afforded the consumer against the risk of death is the most straightforward delineation of Jupiter/Cancer in the 8th house. Ralph Nader and his role in establishing the Consumer Product Safety Commission is one of the better examples of this theme. Substitute the words 'traded goods' for 'death' and create the Federal Trade Commission designed to protect consumers from monopolistic practices of businesses. The FTC was created in 1914 (Jupiter-Ascendant Direction #7) and launched its suit against Microsoft in 1998 (Jupiter-Ascendant Direction #10).

Consumer Banking. By far, banking is most consistent type of Jupiterian activity timed by Jupiter-Ascendant Directions. How does Jupiter's placement in the sign of Cancer, the bound of Mars, and the dwad of Sagittarius modify its effects? First consider the planet **Jupiter** as a universal significator for magnates. In a society where each planet assigned to a social class[1], Jupiter as the greater benefic occupies a position within the upper class because of its abundant wealth and wisdom. A 'pure' Jupiterian banking system provides banking access to the upper class because that is Jupiter's domain. **Jupiter in the sign of Cancer** extends banking access beyond the upper class to all levels of society because Cancer is ruled by the Moon who signifies the public at large. The defensiveness of the **bound Mars/Cancer** takes Jupiter a step back by reacting against the potential for non-whites to garner upward social mobility through access to bank capital. In banking parlance, this practice is named *redlining*, a term created in the late 1960s by Chicago community organizers. Residents living within districts outlined by red lines drawn on maps were denied banking services with discrimination against mortgage lending the most common occurrence. Jupiter in the **dwad of Virgo** is best delineated as not being able to see the forest through the trees. In financial affairs, it adds a level of bureaucratic red tape bristling with legalese and excessive paperwork.

The combined influence of sign, bound, and dwad means Jupiter provides banking services reaching beyond the upper class to middle and lower class consumers. Non-white minorities are restricted from access. Bureaucracy impedes the delivery of banking services.

National Branch Banking. Among the unusual features of the American banking system is the lack of universal national branch banking. Though money center banks have gradually expanded their domains through mergers, these changes have been very gradual. Today there remains no single bank with brick and mortar operations in all 50 states. The United States is a rarity among the developed world for its lack of a universal national branch banking network. I suggest the defensiveness of local and state banking authorities when faced by the encroachment of national branch banks can be attributed to the bound of Mars/Cancer. Mars/Cancer defends home turf, an apt descriptor for actions taken by local and state banking authorities against national branch banking.

Family Farmers. Besides consumer banking, Jupiter/Cancer also signifies agricultural food production because Jupiter signifies growth and Cancer signifies nourishment. Cancer also signifies the family with many American farms family-owned. The theme of family farms is also repeated through Jupiter's rulership of the 4th house of family and real estate. Placement in the 8th means family farmers are in debt. For this reason, the struggling family farmer has been a reoccurring theme in American history. Though relatively small, Shays' Rebellion (Jupiter-Ascendant Direction #1) was the first major incident of civil unrest faced by America following the Revolutionary War. It so unnerved members of the upper class that the Constitutional Convention was called in order to strengthen Federal authority. Indebted farmers were the trigger for the revolt.

Debtor-Creditor class division. More generally, Jupiter/Cancer's signification as consumer banking activates the Cancer/Capricorn axis as a polarizing division between debtors and creditors. Capricorn signifies accumulated wealth; its ruler Saturn the means used to hoard and contain money. Moon rules the people; its sign of Cancer on the 8th house of debt shows a flow of wealth to the people through debt instruments. Moon's placement in Aquarius means the demand for Lockean equality among all humans is the motivating force behind the rise of the debtor class. Jupiter in the sign of Cancer aids flow of money from established interests to the public through consumer banking. Because Jupiter rules the 4th of real estate, mortgage lending is a mainstay of consumer banking products.

Jupiter-Ascendant Direction #1

D	Mercury/Capricorn	P	opposition Jupiter (l=0) d. → ASC	31-Mar-1786
D	Mercury/Capricorn	P	opposition Jupiter (l=JU) d. → ASC	29-Apr-1786

Shays' Rebellion

Though Shays' Rebellion didn't draw blood until **September 26, 1786**, events surrounding the rebellion match the delineation of this primary direction sequence.

Played out against a backdrop of postwar inflation, Shays' Rebellion was a classic battle between creditors and debtors fought over settlement of outstanding debts. Normally in an inflationary environment, debtors repay outstanding loans with cheaper currency. As long as creditors continue to accept payment in inflated currency, debtors benefit under inflation. In 1786 the terms were different. Because paper currency had suffered a material decline (e.g., 'not worth a Continental'), creditors required hard assets for loan repayment and co-opted the courts to enforce their demands. As a result, farmers were either forced to pay with goods-in-kind (such as oxen essential to farm production) or went to debtors' prison. As a result, the farm economy suffered. Shay led a group of indebted farmers who wished to rebel against what they considered were unreasonable demands imposed by merchant creditors.

Partner: Jupiter/Cancer is a delineation match to farming whose objective is food production for human consumption. Shays' Rebellion is a delineation match because Jupiter in the 8th matches farmers' indebtedness and Jupiter rules the 4th of real property. Bound of Mars/Cancer adds cruelty when threatened and matches the farmers' anger following the harsh terms imposed by creditors. Jupiter in dwad of Virgo, sign of sown crops, reiterates the ties between Jupiter/Cancer and farming.

Distributor: The combination of Mercury (merchants) and Capricorn (established social class) signifies established merchants who were creditors.

Jupiter-Ascendant Direction #2

D	Venus/Pisces	P	dex. trine Jupiter (l=0) d. → ASC	29-Mar-1834
D	Venus/Pisces	P	dex. trine Jupiter (l=JU) d. → ASC	28-Apr-1834

Andrew Jackson's Bank War

Jackson's Bank War dates from July 10, 1832 when he vetoed the recharter for the Second Bank of the United States. (See Venus-Ascendant Direction #2). On September 25, 1833, Jackson ordered federal deposits be shifted to state banks. The order was effective October 1, 1833 and was largely completed by December 1833. Congress believed Jackson usurped his Presidential powers in making this decision and censured Jackson on *March 27, 1834*. Shortly thereafter Jackson made a new proposal on currency and banking reforms on *April 21, 1834*.

Partner: If Jupiter/Cancer signifies consumer banking, then Jackson's deposit removal to what historians refer to as his 'Pet Banks' is arguably the first primitive attempt made to create consumer banking in American history. As significator of Jackson, the Cancer Sun ruled by the Moon (sign) and Jupiter (exaltation) shows Jackson motivated by the need for universal access to consumer credit (Moon ruling 8th) and for consumer banking as the vehicle (Jupiter in 8th). Sun applying to square of Saturn, significator of Congress and ruler of Capricorn, shows the conflict between Jackson and Congress which led to his censure.

Distributor: Venus/Pisces signifies sacrificial love. Replacing 'love' with 'money' is consistent with the American people willing to side with Jackson in his decision to 'sacrifice' the Second Bank of the United States.

Jupiter-Ascendant Direction #3

D	Mars/Scorpio	P	sin. trine Jupiter (l=JU) c. → ASC	23-Feb-1839
D	Mars/Scorpio	P	sin. trine Jupiter (l=0) c. → ASC	8-Mar-1839

Aroostook War

Controversy over settlement of the Maine/New Brunswick border between America and Canada culminated with the Aroostook War of 1838-1839. On *February 19, 1839*, the Maine legislature called for a general draft of militia in order to fight incursions by New Brunswick on disputed territory. On *March 2, 1839*, based on testimony from Maine Representative Smith, Congress authorized a force of 50,000 men and appropriated $10 million for the intervention.[2] These dates appear to represent the peak measurements for the Aroostook War; threatened but never fought.

Precursor Events. The Maine/New Brunswick border was left disputed after the War of 1812 and might have remained that way unless a struggle over timber resources developed. In late 1825, a devastating New Brunswick forest fire left lumberjacks looking south for fresh stands of timber. A key player in the Aroostook War was the American lumberjack John Baker (b. January 17, 1796). Baker's natal figure with North Node in the bound of Jupiter/Cancer and Mars/Scorpio in the 7th of disputes[3] replicates both distributor and Partner for this sequence. Baker was essentially a squatter in disputed territory whose efforts were supported by Maine officials but not by New Brunswick. Baker raised a flag on July 4, 1827 in disputed territory he renamed the 'Republic of Madawaska' and was later arrested by the British. Twelve years later the border remained disputed.

Distributor and Partner: It turns out the dissolution of the Second Bank of the United States (Jupiter-Ascendant Direction #2) is relevant here. After the Bank's dissolution, Maine residents who paid taxes were issued tax refunds. British authorities accused Maine officials of using the tax refunds as a cover for offering bribes to residents in the disputed territory to curry favor for American annexation. This led to the 1839 dispute. It appears tax refunds played a similar role astrologically as the movement of funds to pet banks did in Jupiter-Ascendant Direction #2. Both episodes timed shifts in funds from established moneyed interests (Bank of the United States) to consumers. With Mars/Scorpio as Distributor in Direction #3, there was risk of war.

Jupiter-Ascendant Direction #4

D	Jupiter/Aries	P	dex. square Jupiter (l=0) d. → ASC	22-Jan-1852
D	Changeover		bound Venus/Aries d. → ASC	3-Feb-1852
D	Venus/Aries	P	dex. square Jupiter (l=JU) d. → ASC	21-Feb-1852

Retail Banking

This sequence timed the launch of several consumer banks. A notice dated *January 26, 1852* reported the organization of *The Merchants' and Mechanics' Bank of Chicago*.[4] Just after the sequence closed, *Wells Fargo & Company* was founded on *March 18, 1852*.

Partner: The Chicago Bank epitomizes consumer banking because its implied customers – merchants and mechanics – were typical middle class borrowers who had difficulty in accessing cheap capital. In the mid-1800s, states had not yet completely abandoned usury laws which disproportionately affected middle class borrowers.

Venus/Aries as Distributor: As the sequence closed, a front page NYT letter to the editor was published on *February 28, 1852* asking the New York legislature to follow twenty two other states who had already abandoned their usury laws. The letter specifically addressed the plight of merchants and mechanics.[5] As distributor, Venus/Aries matches the apparent greediness of lenders who supported usury laws.

Jupiter/Aries as Distributor: As Distributor for the period August 2, 1848 to February 2, 1852, Jupiter/Aries signaled the westward migration of Americans wishing to partake in the California Gold Rush and fulfill America's Manifest Destiny. It was this growing mass of people in pursuit of unbridled riches which attracted Henry Wells and William G. Fargo to the California economy. Without the optimistic spirit of Jupiter/Aries as Ascendant Distributor, there would have been no clients in California for Wells Fargo to serve.

Jupiter-Ascendant Direction #5

D	Venus/Taurus	P	dex. sextile Jupiter (l=0) d. → ASC	5-Aug-1870
D	Venus/Taurus	P	dex. sextile Jupiter (l=JU) d. → ASC	4-Sep-1870

Bank Act of 1870

The Bank Act of 1870 (July 12, 1870) was one in a series of adjustments to the more sweeping National Bank Act of 1863 which created a system of national banking charters. Designed to encourage the formation of additional National Banks in order to add stability to the banking system as a whole, the 1863 Act levied a discriminatory tax of 2 percent on state bank notes. The Bank Act of 1870 reapportioned the circulation of bank notes away from Eastern and Middle states (considered to have excess notes in circulation) to Southern States. The 1870 Act also allowed bank notes backed by gold.[6] Another change in 1870 (no exact date found) was the ability of state banks to issue personal checks in order to avoid the discriminatory tax on state bank notes. As the sequence opened, a notice appeared on *August 3, 1870* that Kidder, Peabody, & Co.'s had filed an application to open the first national bank which planned to issue gold notes under the auspices of the new 1870 Bank Act.[7] A subsequent bulletin dated *August 14, 1870* indicated several other national banks planned to begin operations under the new Banking Law in the following week.[8]

Partner: The reapportionment of bank notes to Southern States is consistent with delineation of Jupiter/Cancer as consumer banking. Like Jackson's Pet Banks of the 1830s, the 1870 Bank Act moved money away from established banking centers (Eastern and Middle states) to citizens in need of credit (Southern states). Introduction of personal checks is another feature which facilitated consumer banking.

Distributor: Venus/Taurus is the classic money placement of Venus in the sign she rules. It suggests the strength of banks formed under its influence and matches the additional surety of its notes provided by gold backing.

Additional: Birth of Amadeo Giannini, founder of Bank of America, on *May 6, 1870.* Pioneered branch banking as a way to deliver banking services to the consumer. North Node falls in the bound of Jupiter/Cancer.

Jupiter-Ascendant Direction #6

D	Saturn/Libra	P	sin. square Jupiter (l=JU) c. → ASC	18-Dec-1876
D	Saturn/Libra	P	sin. square Jupiter (l=0) c. → ASC	27-Dec-1876

Banks, Debt, Taxation, and Insolvency

Following the Panic of 1873, the United States entered an economic depression which lasted until 1877. By the time of this sequence in 1876, lackluster loan demand had caused bank capital to rise. Because of the vagaries of tax laws which subjected bank capital to a high level of taxation, banks with surplus capital paid higher taxes compared to what banks paid prior to the depression. As a result of higher taxation, some banks returned capital to shareholders; others declared bankruptcy.

A NYT editorial dated *December 22, 1876* advised the New York Superior Court to overturn a lower court ruling regarding bank taxation. At issue was the apparent zeal taken by the lower courts which increased bank taxes. The editorial writer accused the court of taking an illogical anti-bank stance.[9]

Partner: In this event the same anti-national and pro-consumer banking attitude which permeated Jackson's Bank War is acted out by Lower Courts which ruled against the banks.

Distributor: Saturn/Libra signifies the Superior Court, called forth to administer justice to a legal banking case.

Jupiter-Ascendant Direction #7

D	Mercury/Virgo	P	sin. sextile Jupiter (l=JU) c. → ASC	3-Aug-1914
D	Mercury/Virgo	P	sin. sextile Jupiter (l=0) c. → ASC	14-Aug-1914

Expansion of Bank Lending on the outbreak of WWI

On *July 31, 1914*, Treasury Secretary McAdoo proposed a loosening of restrictions on bank lending so national banks could issue additional currency based on State, county, and municipal securities held as assets.[10] Both the Senate and House passed the measure on the same day. McAdoo met with bankers the evening of *August 2* and promised an immediate issuance of $100 million in currency.[11] The final form of Congressional legislation approved on *August 3, 1914* provided an effective $1 billion increase in currency.[12] The objective of this currency issuance was made to substitute bank currency backed by government bonds with bank currency backed by other assets including State, county, and municipal securities. Currency backed by government bonds could be redeemed for gold; not so for currency backed by the other instruments. Bankers were worried about an outflow of gold after the outbreak of WWI days earlier. Should an outflow occur, banks would have to shrink their outstanding loans to maintain compliance with reserve requirements. This sequence times an emergency measure taken to head off such a scenario. As the sequence closed, there was a movement among New York banks to allow national bank notes to be used directly as reserves.[13] This proposal was considered too much of a giveaway to the banks and was opposed by the Federal Reserve on *August 15*.[14]

Partner: Expansion of bank reserves = Jupiter/Cancer as banking.

Distributor: The second event mentions *legislative busybodies* involved in unsuccessful lobbying of national bank notes as reserves, a match to the style of Mercury/Virgo as distributor. Mercury in its own sign of rulership also signifies smart businessmen, a match to bankers. Finally, Virgo is the sign of sown crops. The bankers knew that whatever gold they had to send to Europe would be quickly returned in payment for U.S. grain exports after the fall harvest. Bankers were attempting to maintain their capital in the interim.

Jupiter-Ascendant Direction #8

D	Mars/Cancer	P	conjunction Jupiter (l=0) d. → ASC	17-Nov-1923
D	Mars/Cancer	P	conjunction Jupiter (l=JU) d. → ASC	13-Dec-1923

Defeat of Branch Banking

On *November 7, 1923*, the Federal Reserve Board adopted a resolution effective February 1, 1924 that restricted state banks from opening branches outside their home towns.[15] In response as a countermeasure, eighteen states filed a brief before the Supreme Court joining Missouri in its efforts to continue restrictions on National branch banking activities.[16] On *December 15, 1923*, Controller of the Currency Henry M. Dawes appealed for support of Branch Banking which would serve the interests of National Banks in their expansion plans.[17] On January 29, 1924, the Supreme Court sided in favor of Missouri by stating that National Banks are declared subject to State Laws which prohibit Branches.[18]

Events timed by this sequence are similar in character to the Jupiter-Ascendant direction #9 (see next) computed by converse motion.

Partner: Jupiter/Cancer signifies growth of consumer banking and matches the desire of the Federal Reserve Board and the Controller of the Currency to allow National Banks the right to open additional branches in new states to facilitate access to consumer credit.

Distributor: Mars/Cancer signifies cruelty when threatened. Though not reaching the level of cruelty, the reaction of Missouri against the potential intrusion of National bank branches on their home turf matches the defensiveness of Mars/Cancer.

Consider also that Jupiter/Cancer itself falls in the bound of Mars/Cancer. This means Mars/Cancer serves double duty for this direction: As Distributor and the Partner's bound. Given the ability of Mars/Cancer to stop the spread of branch banking in this direction, it appears Jupiter's placement in the bound of Mars/Cancer explains the relative paucity of National branch banking compared to other developed economies as a first order condition. Only when Jupiter/Cancer is accompanied by benefic distributors (as in 1870) is the reluctance to form branch banking overcome.

Jupiter-Ascendant Direction #9

D	Mars/Cancer	P	conjunction Jupiter (l=JU) c. → ASC	24-Jan-1989
D	Mars/Cancer	P	conjunction Jupiter (l=0) c. → ASC	19-Feb-1989

Kidder Peabody Reorganization

A report published *January 19, 1989* announced an expected reorganization of Kidder, Peabody & Company. Its owner G. E. Capital had grown disappointed with its retail and institutional sales operations. A new Chief Executive was expected to be appointed. G. E. eventually sold Kidder to PaineWebber in October 1994; afterwards the Kidder name was dropped.

Savings & Loan Crisis: Loss of Branch Banking and Minority Access

This sequence occurred during the rapid meltdown phase of the Savings & Loan Crisis, whose worst years were between 1986 and 1991. One result was the curtailment of credit available to households from tightened lending standards. The elimination of superfluous bank branches also rolled back the physical proximity of bankers to consumers, a hallmark of consumer banking practice. In one report published *February 20, 1989* on Lewis Ranieri's purchase and workout of the failed United Savings Association of Texas, the number of branches had fallen from 104 in 1983 to 19 with no new loans made in the prior 30 months.[19] In the New York metropolitan region, it was reported on *January 30, 1989* that branch closings disproportionately hurt minority communities. Dorothy Adadi, national executive board member of ACORN, the Association of Community Organizations for Reform Now, cited the inconvenience of having to travel two miles to visit a bank branch and reduced access to loan officers with knowledge of the community and its needs.[20] A *February 19, 1989* article cited difficulties faced by a proposed Hispanic-owned bank to raise capital in New Haven, CT.[21]

Distributor and Partner: Recall the 1870 formation of Kidder Peabody and growth of consumer banking timed by Jupiter-Ascendant Direction #5. For the earlier direction, Venus/Taurus was the Distributor. Compare this result to events timed by this direction with Mars/Cancer as Distributor which timed Kidder's reorganization, reduction of branch banking networks, and reduced availability of consumer credit. These two examples demonstrate the power of the Distributor to materially alter the outcome of Partners.

Jupiter-Ascendant Direction #10

D	Mercury/Virgo	P	sin. sextile Jupiter (l=0) d. → ASC	25-May-1998
D	Mercury/Virgo	P	sin. sextile Jupiter (l=JU) d. → ASC	5-Jun-1998

Federal Trade Commission – Formation

Formation of the Federal Trade Commission is a delineation match to legal protection for the consumer against unfair business practices. It fits the timing of Jupiter-Ascendant Direction #7 computed for *August 3-14, 1914*. The Senate passed the FTC Bill on *August 5, 1914*, and after House and Senate conference negotiations in late August, both houses passed the legislation which went into force on September 26, 1914.[22] I suggest the outbreak of World War I led to a delay in passage of the final legislation. Note both the 1914 and 1998 sequences share Mercury/Virgo as Distributor.

Distributor: Mercury/Virgo signifies the details of business operations and specifies consumer protection to the realm of business dealings.

Federal Trade Commission – Lawsuits against Microsoft and Intel

The NYT reported the FTC was planning to sue Intel on *May 28, 1998* which it did so on *June 9, 1998*. This followed anti-trust actions filed against Microsoft on May 18, 1998. The Microsoft case was one of the most publicized anti-trust cases in the last twenty years.

Distributor: Besides significator of business details, Mercury/Virgo is arguably a delineation match to computer chips because the small size and detailed nature of chips is a Virgo characteristic. As significator of communication, Mercury is the information which passes through the chips. Mercury/Virgo also signifies 'busybodies' and matches the disparaging comments made about FTC lawyers by members of the business community.

Death of Miles Kirkpatrick

Miles Kirkpatrick died on *May 17, 1998*. Kirkpatrick was among the most celebrated FTC attorneys and chairmen. He gained prominence in 1969 by leading the American Bar Association's FTC Commission after a report which highlighted the agency's weaknesses. As a result, Nixon appointed Kirkpatrick Chairman of the FTC.

CHAPTER SIXTEEN

Final Thoughts

Scope. Rectification of a National Horoscope for the United States Declaration of Independence is the objective of this book. To meet that goal and keep the project to a reasonable length, I limited the scope to Ascendant directions. What this means is thousands of events await future research. That I have made no attempt to explain specific events such as World War II may disappoint many but the goal was never to test a list of events.

Further Research. Given the power of directing the Ascendant through the Bounds to identify prominent themes in American social history, I suggest readers experiment with directing other significators through the bounds. Taking this step requires wrestling with interplanetary primary directions. Of the three methods for zodiacal directions used prior to 1700 – Ptolemy's method, Regiomontanus under the Pole, and Placidus under the Pole - preliminary testing suggests Ptolemy's method holds the most promise for directing the Sun, Moon, and Lot of Fortune through the bounds.

Relocation. Many modern mundane astrologers recommend relocating National Horoscopes according to the current position of capital cities. Despite the capital's location in New York, Princeton, and Washington, the Philadelphia chart still works. I suggest relocation is not required.

Transits. Those astrologers preoccupied with transits often say directions and progressions cannot act alone; they require transits to trigger their effects. I have used perhaps a dozen transit examples in this entire book. I suggest astrologers favoring transits in the predictive hierarchy are sloppy rectifiers.

Solar Arcs vs. Primary Directions. Many medieval astrologers eschew solar arc directions because they are symbolic and do not have any bearing on actual planetary movements. Many solar arc practitioners dismiss primary directions because they consider their mathematics archaic and incomprehensible. My findings suggest both methods of directing are valid. Furthermore, the **Solar Arc – Primary Directions Proposition** presents a possible Rosetta stone capable of unifying both systems. It's a proposition worth exploring.

APPENDIX A

Event Catalog for Initial Rectification Phase, July 2002

4-Jul-1776	Declaration of Independence
25-Dec-1776	Washington Victory at Trenton
6-Feb-1778	French-US Alliance
19-Oct-1781	Washington Victory at Yorktown
17-Sep-1787	Constitution Signed
4-Mar-1789	Constitution Into Force
30-Apr-1789	Washington Inauguration
14-Jul-1789	France: Storming of the Bastille
4-Aug-1790	Birth of Bond Market
25-Feb-1791	Bank of United States Charter approved
23-Mar-1792	Duer Stock Market Panic of 1792
2-Apr-1792	Birth of U.S. Dollar
17-May-1792	New York Stock Exchange started
1-Feb-1793	France declared War on UK, Spain, Netherlands
22-Apr-1793	Washington issued Neutrality statement on French-UK War
7-Aug-1794	Washington intervened in Whiskey Rebellion
14-Aug-1795	Washington signed John Jay's treaty with Britain
18-May-1796	Land Act passed regarding NW Territory settlement
18-Oct-1797	"XYZ" Affair in Paris/results in US/French Naval war to 1800
14-Dec-1799	President Washington Died
17-Feb-1801	Jefferson elected President
2-May-1803	Louisiana Purchase
18-May-1804	Napoleon crowned Emperor of France
22-Jun-1807	HMS Leopold Incident – U.S. vs. Britain
22-Dec-1807	Embargo Act crimped international trade
2-Feb-1811	Bank of United States renewal denied
19-Jun-1812	Madison officially declared War with Britain (War of 1812)
24-Aug-1814	British burned White House
24-Dec-1814	Treaty of Ghent ended War of 1812
8-Jan-1815	Battle New Orleans won by Andrew Jackson
14-Mar-1816	Second Bank of the United States passed by Congress
15-Mar-1817	Erie Canal construction authorized
20-Oct-1818	Convention of 1818 established Canadian border
3-Mar-1820	Missouri Compromise
4-Sep-1821	Czar Alexander claimed Pacific Coast North of 51st parallel
2-Dec-1823	Monroe Doctrine
9-Feb-1825	John Quincy Adams won disputed Presidential Election
26-Oct-1825	Erie Canal completed
19-May-1828	"Tariff of Abominations" is passed
7-Apr-1831	Most of Jackson's cabinet resigned on Eaton Affair
10-Jul-1832	Jackson vetoed renewal of Second Bank of the United States
10-Sep-1833	Jackson announced "Pet Bank" policy

31-Jul-1834	Coinage Act of 1834
30-Jan-1835	Assassination attempt against Jackson
11-Jul-1836	Jackson issued Specie Circular
10-May-1837	Panic of 1837
4-Jul-1840	Martin Van Buren signed Independent Treasury Act into law
16-Aug-1841	Tyler vetoed Third Bank of the United States bill, riots ensued
11-Sep-1841	Tyler's cabinet resigned over Bank of the United States veto
30-Mar-1842	Tariff Act of 1832
9-Aug-1842	Webster-Ashburton Treaty signed with Britain
13-May-1846	Congress approved Polk's request for war against Mexico
24-Jul-1847	Brigham Young arrived at the Great Salt Lake
4-Jan-1848	Sutter's Mill Gold discovery started California Gold Rush
2-Feb-1848	Treaty of Guadalupe Hidalgo ended War with Mexico
19-Jul-1848	Women's Suffrage Movement began
24-Feb-1853	Coinage Act of 1853
18-Dec-1860	Crittenden Compromise
4-Mar-1861	Lincoln Inauguration
11-Mar-1861	Confederate States formed Constitution
12-Apr-1861	Attack on Fort Sumter launched Civil War
5-Aug-1861	Revenue Act – First income tax levied
27-Jan-1862	Lincoln issued War Order against Confederacy
11-Mar-1862	Lincoln removed General McClellan
17-Mar-1862	First Greenback Issue
6-Apr-1862	Battle of Shiloh (6-7 April)
20-May-1862	Homestead Act
1-Jan-1863	Emancipation Proclamation Act
10-May-1863	General Stonewall Jackson died
3-Jul-1863	Last day of Battle of Gettysburg – Pickett's Charge
19-Nov-1863	Lincoln delivered Gettysburg Address
30-Jun-1864	Congress passed Internal Revenue Act to finance war
11-Jul-1864	Low price of Greenbacks – traded down to 9 grams of gold
13-Jul-1864	Confederate troops within 5 miles of Washington D. C.
2-Sep-1864	Sherman burned Atlanta
1-Feb-1865	Congress proposed 13th Amendment
8-Apr-1865	General Lee surrendered at Appomattox
14-Apr-1865	Lincoln Assassination
18-Dec-1865	13th Amendment to abolish slavery is ratified
9-Apr-1866	Congress overruled Johnson on Reconstruction Law
16-Jun-1866	Congress Proposed 14th Amendment
2-Mar-1867	First Reconstruction Act passed by Congress
23-Mar-1867	Second Reconstruction Act passed by Congress
30-Mar-1867	US acquired Alaska
19-Jul-1867	Third Reconstruction Act passed by Congress
25-Nov-1867	Impeachment of President Johnson proposed
13-Mar-1868	Impeachment trial of Johnson began
16-Mar-1868	Johnson acquitted
28-Jul-1868	14th Amendment Ratified
10-May-1869	First Continental Rail line completed
24-Sep-1869	Black Friday Gold Panic
10-Jan-1870	Standard Oil Incorporated
8-Oct-1871	Chicago Fire
4-Sep-1872	Credit Mobilier Scandal Erupted
12-Feb-1873	Coinage Act of 1873 "Crime of '73"
18-Sep-1873	Panic of 1873/Failure of Jay Cooke & Co.
14-Jan-1875	Specie Resumption Act passed
25-Jun-1876	Battle of the Little Bighorn
3-Mar-1877	Desert Land Act

APPENDIX A - EVENT CATALOG FOR INITIAL RECTIFICATION PHASE   275

28-Feb-1878	Bland-Allison Act
15-Oct-1878	Edison Electric Light Company established
9-Dec-1878	Greenbacks reach face value in advance of 1-Jan-1879
2-Jul-1881	Garfield Assassination
2-Jan-1882	Standard Oil Trust created
24-May-1883	Brooklyn Bridge opened
4-May-1886	Haymarket Riot
28-Oct-1886	Statue of Liberty dedicated
31-May-1889	Johnstown PA flood
14-Jul-1890	Sherman Silver Purchase Act signed
1-Oct-1890	McKinley Tariff Bill
1-Jan-1892	Ellis Island opened
21-Apr-1893	Gold reserves fell below $100 MM
27-Jun-1893	Panic of 1893/Stock Market Crash
11-May-1894	Pullman Worker Strike
9-Jul-1896	Bryan: Cross of Gold Speech
12-Aug-1896	Klondike Gold Rush began
15-Feb-1898	Explosion of Battleship Maine in Cuba
24-Apr-1898	Spain declared war on America
1-Jul-1898	Battle of San Juan Hill, Cuba
10-Dec-1898	Treaty of Paris ended Spanish American War
14-Mar-1900	Gold Standard Act
8-Sep-1900	Galveston Hurricane
10-Jan-1901	Spindletop Oil Discovery Texas
9-May-1901	Northern Pacific Stock Corner
6-Sep-1901	McKinley Assassination
3-Dec-1901	Roosevelt speech – Trust Regulation
18-Nov-1903	Panama Canal treaty
17-Dec-1903	Wright Brothers achieved flight at Kitty Hawk
8-Jun-1905	Roosevelt helped negotiate Russo-Japanese War Treaty
1-Oct-1907	Stock Market Panic – Knickerbocker Trust Co
1-Oct-1908	Model T Introduced
15-May-1911	Supreme Court Decision against Standard Oil
15-Apr-1912	Titanic Disaster
23-Dec-1913	US Federal Reserve Act
9-Apr-1914	Diplomatic crisis in Mexico
28-Jun-1914	Archduke Ferdinand assassination
28-Jul-1914	WWI Declaration
15-Aug-1914	Panama Canal opened
7-May-1915	Sinking of Lusitania
2-Apr-1917	Wilson Declaration of War against Germany
8-Jan-1918	Wilson Fourteen Points speech
17-Jul-1918	Second Battle of the Marne
26-Sep-1918	Battle of Verdun
11-Nov-1918	Armistice WWI
29-Jan-1919	19th Amendment passed (prohibition)
28-Jun-1919	Treaty of Versailles
26-Aug-1920	19th Amendment passed (women's suffrage)
27-May-1921	Emergency Tariff Act
2-Aug-1923	Death of President Harding in office
25-Oct-1923	Senator Walsh presented evidence of Teapot Dome Scandal
5-May-1925	Scopes arrested for teaching Evolution
26-Feb-1926	Revenue Act passed by Coolidge, reduced tax rates
18-Sep-1926	Florida tornado killed/injured many seekers of "land-boom"
27-Aug-1928	Kellogg-Briand Pact signed
14-Feb-1929	St. Valentine's Day Massacre
29-Oct-1929	Black Tuesday Stock Market Crash

17-Jun-1930	Smoot Hawley Tariff Act
1-May-1931	Empire State Building Completed
18-Sep-1931	Japan invaded Manchuria
8-Nov-1932	FDR elected President in landside election
30-Jan-1933	Hitler assumed office as Chancellor in Germany
4-Mar-1933	FDR Inauguration, Bank Holiday
5-Dec-1933	21 Amendment passed (repealed Prohibition)
30-Jan-1934	Gold Reserve Act, U. S. Dollar Devaluation
3-Oct-1935	Italy invaded Ethiopia
6-May-1937	Hindenburg Disaster
30-Oct-1938	Welles broadcast: Invasion from Mars
10-May-1940	Germany invaded Low Countries
14-Jun-1940	Paris fell to the Germany Army
7-Dec-1941	Pearl Harbor
18-Apr-1942	Air Raid on Tokyo
2-Feb-1943	Germans surrendered at Stalingrad
6-Mar-1944	First air raid on Berlin
6-Jun-1944	Operation D-Day
22-Jul-1944	Bretton Woods Agreement
16-Dec-1944	Battle of the Bulge
12-Apr-1945	Death of President Roosevelt in office
7-May-1945	Germans surrendered to Allies
16-Jul-1945	First Atomic Bomb detonated in New Mexico
6-Aug-1945	US dropped atomic bomb on Hiroshima
2-Sep-1945	Japanese surrendered aboard USS Missouri
5-Mar-1946	Churchill coined "Iron Curtain" terminology
5-Jun-1947	Marshall Plan proposed
14-May-1948	Israeli declared independence, recognized by USA
26-Jun-1948	Berlin Blockade
2-Nov-1948	Truman surprise defeat of Dewey
21-May-1949	Federal Republic of Germany established
23-Sep-1949	Truman announced Russian nuclear capability
25-Jun-1950	North Korean troops crossed 38th parallel, Korean War
1-Nov-1950	Truman Assassination Attempt
8-Sep-1951	Japanese Peace Treaty – recognized Japan's sovereignty
16-Nov-1952	Successful Hydrogen Bomb testing Marshall Islands
19-Jun-1953	Execution of Julius and Ethel Rosenberg
27-Jul-1953	Korean War – Armistice – US/North Korea/China
1-Mar-1954	Shooting in House of Representatives
17-May-1954	*Brown v. Board of Education* ended school segregation
2-Dec-1954	McCarthy condemned by Senate
24-Sep-1955	Eisenhower heart attack
26-Jul-1956	Nasser nationalized Suez Canal
5-Nov-1956	Suez Canal cease fire
4-Sep-1957	Little Rock: African American students blocked by militia
25-Sep-1957	US Army troops escorted African American students to school
4-Oct-1957	USSR launched Sputnik
19-Jan-1960	US signed mutual defense treaty with Japan. Protests in Japan.
1-Feb-1960	Greensboro NC African Americans staged lunch counter sit-in
5-May-1960	U-2 Plane shot down – announced by Khrushchev
16-May-1960	Paris Peace Conference disaster – Khrushchev stormed out
26-Sep-1960	First televised Presidential debates
8-Nov-1960	Kennedy elected President
17-Apr-1961	Bay of Pigs Invasion
25-May-1961	Kennedy committed U.S. to landing Man on Moon
20-Feb-1962	John Glenn orbited the earth in Project Mercury
10-Apr-1962	Kennedy denounced hike in steel prices

APPENDIX A - EVENT CATALOG FOR INITIAL RECTIFICATION PHASE

22-Oct-1962	Cuban Missile Crisis announced by Kennedy
28-Oct-1962	Russia withdrew missiles
12-Apr-1963	Martin Luther King arrested in Birmingham jail
18-Jul-1963	Kennedy – Interest Equalization Tax
28-Aug-1963	Martin Luther King "I Have a Dream speech"
22-Nov-1963	Kennedy Assassinated
7-Aug-1964	Gulf of Tonkin Resolution
4-Jan-1965	Johnson proposed "Great Society Program" in State of Union
11-Aug-1965	Watts race riots Los Angeles
12-Jul-1966	Race riots Chicago's West Side
8-Mar-1968	Gold buying Panic on U.S. Balance of Payments Deficit
4-Apr-1968	Martin Luther King Assassinated
20-Jul-1969	Neil Armstrong landed on the Moon
18-Aug-1969	Woodstock Concert
15-Nov-1969	Largest antiwar rally in history of USA
4-May-1970	Kent State shootings
15-Aug-1971	Nixon closed gold window, U.S. Dollar floats
18-Dec-1971	Smithsonian accords
21-Feb-1972	Nixon to China
17-Jun-1972	Watergate Arrest
12-Aug-1972	Last of U.S. ground troops withdrew from Vietnam
27-Jan-1973	Kissinger signed Paris Peace Treaty ending Vietnam
12-Feb-1973	U. S. Dollar Devaluation
6-Oct-1973	Yom Kippur War
17-Oct-1973	OPEC Oil Embargo
24-Jul-1974	Supreme Court ruled that Nixon must turn over tapes
8-Aug-1974	Nixon resigned
22-Sep-1975	Assassination Attempt President Ford
17-Sep-1978	Camp David Accords – Sadat & Begin
1-Nov-1978	U. S. Dollar Bailout
28-Mar-1979	Three Mile Island Nuclear Accident
1-Oct-1979	US formally gave up Panama Canal
6-Oct-1979	US Federal Reserve adopted money supply targets
4-Nov-1979	Iranian Hostage Crisis began in Tehran
21-Jan-1980	Gold peaked at $873
27-Mar-1980	Silver Panic
18-May-1980	Mt. St. Helens volcano erupted
4-Nov-1980	Landslide win for Reagan
20-Jan-1981	Reagan took office, Iranians released hostages
30-Mar-1981	Reagan is shot
13-Aug-1981	ECRA signed
2-Oct-1981	Reagan announced military expansion
28-Dec-1981	Reagan imposed sanctions on Soviet Union
8-Jan-1982	AT&T Breakup announced
23-Oct-1983	US Marines killed in Lebanon bombing
11-Mar-1985	Gorbachev took office
13-Aug-1982	Mexican Debt Crisis
22-Sep-1985	Plaza Accord
28-Jan-1986	Space Shuttle Challenger exploded
5-Apr-1986	Bombing in West Germany by Libya against U.S. servicemen
14-Apr-1986	Retaliation bombing in Libya
22-Oct-1986	Tax Reform Act of 1986
14-Nov-1986	Boesky pleaded guilty on insider trading charges
17-May-1987	USS Stark attacked by Iraq in Persian Gulf
19-Oct-1987	Stock Market Crash
8-Dec-1987	Reagan and Gorbachev signed INF Treaty
24-Mar-1989	Exxon Valdez accident

17-Oct-1989	San Francisco Bay earthquake
9-Nov-1989	Fall of Berlin Wall
2-Aug-1990	Iraq invaded Kuwait
16-Jan-1991	US attacked Iraq
27-Feb-1991	US declaring victory in Gulf War
25-Dec-1991	Gorbachev resigned
30-Apr-1992	Peak in LA violence following Rodney King verdict
31-Aug-1997	Princess Diana Died
11-Sep-2001	WTC Attack

APPENDIX B

Catalog of Ascendant Directions

The following Table summarizes all Ascendant Directions computed by primary motion presented in Chapters 6-15. Included are the following:

- Distributor: Name and date of changeover.

- Partner: Name and date of computation.

- Motion: Distributors and Partners computed for both direct and converse motion.

- Aspects: Partners labeled sinister ("sin.") or dexter ("dex.") as appropriate.

- Latitude of Promissor: Zero latitude is designated by '0.' If full latitude of promissor is used, the two character abbreviation for the planet is listed, e.g., 'MA' means full latitude of Mars is used to calculate the direction.

The table is designed to be read starting from the middle column and moving right for direct directions or left for converse directions. Distributors appear next to the middle date column. The advantage of this presentation is the easy identification of the assignment of Partners to Distributors. This is especially helpful when a primary direction sequence for a single Partner straddles two Distributions. For example, the primary direction sequence for directing the Moon to the Ascendant is the date range February 2, 1829 to May 10, 1831. The 1829 direction falls in the bound of Saturn/Aquarius; the 1831 direction, bound of Venus/Pisces. (See p. 278).

APPENDIX B - CATALOG OF ASCENDANT DIRECTIONS

CONVERSE					DATE	DIRECT				
asp	PARTNER	lat	DISTRIBUTOR			DISTRIBUTOR	asp	PARTNER	lat	
			26SA-Mars		4-Jul-1776	26SA-Mars				
					11-Jul-1777		dex	sextile Moon	0	
					20-Jul-1777		dex	sextile Moon	MO	
	opposed Mars	0			8-Aug-1779					
	opposed Mars	MA			30-Nov-1779	0CP-Mercury				
					3-Oct-1782					
					17-Feb-1783			opposed Venus	VE	
			21SA-Saturn		18-Mar-1783					
					24-Mar-1783					
					27-Apr-1783			opposed Venus	0	
					31-Mar-1786			opposed Jupiter	0	
					29-Apr-1786			opposed Jupiter	JU	
					5-May-1787	7CP-Jupiter				
			17SA-Mercury		27-Nov-1787					
sin	sextile Saturn	0			6-Jul-1790					
sin	sextile Saturn	SA			5-Apr-1792		sin	square Saturn	SA	
			12SA-Venus		6-Oct-1792					
					21-Sep-1793			opposed Sun		
					19-Nov-1793					
					4-May-1794	14CP-Venus				
sin	trine N Node	0			12-Feb-1795		sin	square Saturn	0	
					4-Apr-1799					

280

APPENDIX B - CATALOG OF ASCENDANT DIRECTIONS

CONVERSE					DIRECT			
asp	PARTNER	lat	DISTRIBUTOR	DATE	DISTRIBUTOR	asp	PARTNER	lat
dex	sextile S Node			4-Apr-1799				
				19-Oct-1801	22CP-Saturn		opp Mercury	0
				24-Sep-1803				
				26-Apr-1805	26CP-Mars		opp Mercury	ME
				16-Jul-1808				
			0SA-Jupiter	8-Sep-1808				
dex	square Moon	MO		12-Sep-1808	0AQ-Mercury			
dex	square Moon	0		23-Dec-1809				
sin	trine Mercury	ME		22-May-1811				
				5-Apr-1813	7AQ-Venus			
				24-Apr-1814				
sin	trine Mercury	0		7-Oct-1814			conjunct S Node	
				9-Jan-1816				
			24SC-Saturn	30-Mar-1816				
				1-Mar-1817		sin	trine Saturn	SA
				1-Nov-1818	13AQ-Jupiter			
				24-Feb-1820		sin	trine Saturn	0
			19SC-Jupiter	1-Aug-1822				
				26-Oct-1823	20AQ-Mars			
				30-Apr-1824		dex	trine Mars	MA
				13-Oct-1824		dex	trine Mars	0
				18-Mar-1827	25AQ-Saturn			

APPENDIX B - CATALOG OF ASCENDANT DIRECTIONS

CONVERSE					DIRECT				
asp	PARTNER	lat	DISTRIBUTOR	DATE	DISTRIBUTOR	asp	PARTNER	lat
sin	trine Sun			1-Feb-1829			conjunct Moon	0
				29-Sep-1829				
				25-Jun-1830	0Pl-Venus			
				18-May-1831			conjunct Moon	MO
				17-May-1832		dex	trine Venus	VE
			11SC-Mercury	30-Jun-1832		dex	trine Venus	0
				2-Oct-1832				
sin	square N Node			29-Mar-1834		dex	trine Jupiter	0
dex	square S Node		7SC-Venus	28-Apr-1834		dex	trine Jupiter	JU
				2-Feb-1837				
				2-Feb-1837				
				3-Nov-1837				
sin	trine Jupiter	JU		14-Dec-1837	12Pl-Jupiter			
sin	trine Jupiter	0		11-Oct-1838		dex	trine Sun	
				23-Feb-1839				
				8-Mar-1839				
				9-May-1840	16Pl-Mercury			
sin	trine Venus	0		19-Feb-1842	19Pl-Mars			
sin	trine Venus	VE		18-Sep-1842				
				6-Oct-1842				
				10-Feb-1843		dex	square Mars	MA
				23-Jul-1843		dex	square Mars	0

APPENDIX B - CATALOG OF ASCENDANT DIRECTIONS

CONVERSE					DATE	DIRECT			
asp	PARTNER	lat	DISTRIBUTOR			DISTRIBUTOR	asp	PARTNER	lat
					7-Mar-1845		dex	trine Mercury	0
			0SC-Mars		21-Sep-1846				
dex	trine Moon	MO			2-Jun-1847	28PI-Saturn			
					25-Jul-1848				
dex	trine Moon	0	28LI-Mars		2-Aug-1848	0AR-Jupiter			
					3-Apr-1849				
					11-Jun-1849				
					24-Sep-1849		dex	trine Mercury	ME
					25-Apr-1850		dex	square Venus	VE
					7-Jun-1850		dex	square Venus	0
					22-Jan-1852		dex	square Jupiter	0
					3-Feb-1852	6AR-Venus			
					21-Feb-1852		dex	square Jupiter	JU
sin	square Mercury	ME			15-May-1852				
					9-Jan-1853		dex	trine N Node	
					9-Jan-1853		sin	sextile S Node	
sin	square Mercury	0			1-Feb-1854				
					1-May-1854			opposed Saturn	SA
					18-Aug-1855	12AR-Merc			
					9-Jun-1856		dex	square Sun	0
					19-Apr-1857			opposed Saturn	0
sin	trine Mars	0			30-Jul-1857				

APPENDIX B - CATALOG OF ASCENDANT DIRECTIONS

CONVERSE						DIRECT				
asp	PARTNER	lat	DISTRIBUTOR		DATE	DISTRIBUTOR	asp	PARTNER	lat
sin	trine Mars				27-Sep-1857				
			21LI-Venus		3-Feb-1858				
					7-Jun-1860	20AR-Mars			
					4-Nov-1860		dex	sextile Mars	MA
					18-Apr-1861		dex	sextile Mars	0
					3-Jan-1863		dex	square Mercury	0
					9-Jul-1863	25AR-Saturn			
	conjunct Saturn	0			25-Apr-1865		sin	sextile Moon	0
	conjunct Saturn	SA			18-Nov-1865				
					9-Sep-1866	0TA-Venus			
					13-Nov-1866				
			14LI-Jupiter		23-Nov-1866				
					16-Jul-1867		dex	square Mercury	ME
					25-Jul-1867		sin	sextile Moon	MO
	square Sun				9-Sep-1867				
sin					16-Aug-1868		dex	sextile Venus	VE
					29-Sep-1868		dex	sextile Venus	0
					5-Aug-1870		dex	sextile Jupiter	0
					4-Sep-1870		dex	sextile Jupiter	JU
					14-Sep-1871		dex	square N Node	
					14-Sep-1871		sin	square S Node	
					25-Dec-1871	8TA-Mercury			

APPENDIX B - CATALOG OF ASCENDANT DIRECTIONS   285

| CONVERSE ||||| DATE | DIRECT ||||
asp	PARTNER	lat	DISTRIBUTOR			DISTRIBUTOR	asp	PARTNER	lat
sin	sextile N Node			6-Dec-1874					
dex	trine S Node			6-Dec-1874					
				18-Sep-1875			dex	sextile Sun	
			6LI-Mercury	1-Mar-1876	14TA-Jupiter				
				2-Dec-1876					
sin	square Jupiter	JU		18-Dec-1876					
sin	square Jupiter	0		27-Dec-1876					
sin	square Venus	0		21-Jun-1880					
sin	square Venus	VE		5-Jul-1880					
				2-Feb-1882	22TA-Saturn				
				11-Oct-1883			dex	sextile Mercury	0
			0LI-Saturn	5-Jun-1884					
				8-Jan-1886	27TA-Mars				
				16-Sep-1886			sin	square Moon	0
			28VI-Saturn	5-Dec-1886					
				1-May-1888	0GE-Mercury		dex	sextile Mercury	ME
				21-Jun-1888					
sin	sextile Mercury	ME		21-Dec-1888			sin	square Moon	MO
sin	sextile Mercury	0		7-Apr-1890					
				18-Sep-1891	6GE-Jupiter				
				6-Aug-1893					
				2-Jan-1895			dex	sextile N Node	

APPENDIX B - CATALOG OF ASCENDANT DIRECTIONS

CONVERSE				DATE	DIRECT			
asp	PARTNER	lat	DISTRIBUTOR		DISTRIBUTOR	asp	PARTNER	lat
sin	square Mars	0		2-Jan-1895		sin	trine S Node	
sin	square Mars	MA		7-Mar-1895				
			12VI-Mars	29-Apr-1895				
				10-Sep-1895		dex	trine Saturn	SA
				3-Sep-1898	12GE-Venus			
			17VI-Jupiter	12-Jan-1899				
				15-Sep-1900		dex	trine Saturn	0
				8-Sep-1901	17GE-Mars			
				23-Oct-1903				
				8-Apr-1905			conjunct Mars	MA
				9-Oct-1907			conjunct Mars	0
				15-Mar-1908				
sin	sextile Sun			14-Nov-1910	24GE-Saturn			
			7VI-Venus	14-Apr-1913				
sin	sextile Jupiter	JU		3-Aug-1914				
sin	sextile Jupiter	0		14-Aug-1914				
				8-Dec-1914		sin	trine Moon	0
				18-Dec-1916		sin	trine Moon	MO
				5-Apr-1917	0CA-Mars			
sin	sextile Venus	0		18-Feb-1918				
sin	sextile Venus	VE		6-Mar-1918				
				22-Aug-1920			conjunct Venus	VE

APPENDIX B - CATALOG OF ASCENDANT DIRECTIONS 287

CONVERSE					DATE	DIRECT			
asp	PARTNER		lat	DISTRIBUTOR		DISTRIBUTOR	asp	PARTNER	lat
				0VI-Mercury	30-Sep-1920			conjunct Venus	0
					18-Feb-1922			conjunct Jupiter	0
	opposed Moon		MO		17-Nov-1923			conjunct Jupiter	JU
	opposed Moon		0		11-Dec-1923				
					13-Dec-1923				
					9-Nov-1924				
				24LE-Mars	30-Jan-1925	**7CA-Venus**			
					29-Sep-1929				
					25-Oct-1931		dex	square Saturn	SA
sin	sextile amrs		0		23-Jan-1932	**13CA-Merc**		conjunct Sun	
sin	sextile Mars		MA		30-Jun-1932				
					15-Jan-1933				
					30-Mar-1933		dex	square Saturn	0
				18LE-Mercury	17-Mar-1934				
					16-May-1937				
dex	sextile Saturn		0		4-Apr-1939	**19CA-Jupiter**			
dex	sextile Saturn		SA		8-Jun-1941			coni Mercury	0
				11LE-Saturn	17-Dec-1942				
					6-Aug-1945				
					10-Apr-1946				
					9-Nov-1947	**26CA-Saturn**			
					26-Aug-1948			coni Mercury	ME

APPENDIX B - CATALOG OF ASCENDANT DIRECTIONS

CONVERSE					DATE	DIRECT			
asp	PARTNER	lat	DISTRIBUTOR			DISTRIBUTOR	asp	PARTNER	lat
	conjunct N Node				7-Aug-1950				
			6LE-Venus		11-Aug-1952				
					5-Nov-1952	0LE-Jupiter			
			0LE-Jupiter		2-Mar-1960				
					27-May-1960	6LE-Venus			
	conj Mercury	ME			1-Jun-1962				
			26CA-Saturn		11-May-1964				
					27-Feb-1965				
					28-Sep-1966	11LE-Saturn			
	conj Mercury	0			2-Jun-1967				
					20-Jan-1970		dex	sextile Saturn	SA
					31-Jul-1971		dex	sextile Saturn	0
			19CA-Jupiter		4-Oct-1973				
					22-Aug-1975	18LE-Merc			
dex	square Saturn	0			22-Oct-1978				
					8-Oct-1979		sin	sextile Mars	MA
	conjunct Sun				22-Dec-1979		sin	sextile Mars	0
			13CA-Mercury		8-Jul-1980				
					13-Dec-1980				
dex	square Saturn	SA			14-Mar-1981				
			7CA-Venus		9-Apr-1983	24LE-Mars			
					7-Dec-1987				

288

APPENDIX B - CATALOG OF ASCENDANT DIRECTIONS

CONVERSE					DATE	DIRECT			
asp	PARTNER	lat	DISTRIBUTOR			DISTRIBUTOR	asp	PARTNER	lat
	conjunct Jupiter	JU			26-Feb-1988			opposed Moon	0
	conjunct Jupiter	0			24-Jan-1989			opposed Moon	MO
					25-Jan-1989				
	conjunct Venus	0			19-Feb-1989				
	conjunct Venus	VE			18-Nov-1990	0VI-Mercury			
					7-Apr-1992				
					16-May-1992		sin	sextile Venus	VE
					2-Nov-1994		sin	sextile Venus	0
			0CA-Mars		18-Nov-1994				
sin	trine Moon	MO			3-Oct-1995				
sin	trine Moon	0			19-Jan-1996		sin	sextile Jupiter	0
					29-Jan-1998		sin	sextile Jupiter	JU
					25-May-1998				
					5-Jun-1998	7VI-Venus			
			24GE-Saturn		24-Sep-1999				
	conjunct Mars	0			23-Feb-2002		sin	sextile Sun	
	conjunct Mars	MA			24-Oct-2004				
					31-Mar-2005				
			17GE-Mars		1-Oct-2007				
					17-Mar-2009				
dex	trine Saturn	0			1-May-2011				
					23-Apr-2012	17VI-Jupiter			

APPENDIX B - CATALOG OF ASCENDANT DIRECTIONS

CONVERSE					DATE	DIRECT				
asp	PARTNER	lat	DISTRIBUTOR			DISTRIBUTOR	asp	PARTNER	lat	
			12GE-Venus		25-Dec-2013					
dex	trine Saturn	SA			5-May-2014					
					28-Apr-2017	21VI-Mars				
					9-Sep-2017		sin	square Mars	MA	
					1-Nov-2017		sin	square Mars	0	
sin	trine S Node		6GE-Jupiter		4-Jan-2018					
dex	sextile N Node				4-Jan-2018					
					2-Jun-2019					
					20-Apr-2021		sin	sextile Mercury	0	
					1-Oct-2022		sin	sextile Mercury	ME	
sin	square Moon	MO	0GE-Mercury		16-Jan-2024					
					17-Jul-2024					
dex	sextile Mercury	ME			6-Sep-2024					
					31-Jan-2026	28VI-Saturn				
sin	square Moon	0	27TA-Mars		22-Apr-2026					
					29-Dec-2026					
					2-Aug-2028	0LI-Saturn				
dex	sextile Mercury	0	22TA-Saturn		28-Mar-2029					
					4-Dec-2030					
					3-Jul-2032		sin	square Venus	VE	
					17-Jul-2002		sin	square Venus	0	
					9-Jan-2036		sin	square Jupiter	0	

APPENDIX B - CATALOG OF ASCENDANT DIRECTIONS

CONVERSE					DIRECT			
asp	PARTNER	lat	DISTRIBUTOR	DATE	DISTRIBUTOR	asp	PARTNER	lat
				19-Jan-2036	6LI-Mercury	sin	square Jupiter	JU
				4-Feb-2036				
			14TA-Jupiter	6-Nov-2036				
dex	sextile Sun		8TA-Mercury	19-Apr-2037				

APPENDIX C

Supplement: Directing through the Bounds

Thesis: The Mundane-Natal Horoscope Connection

Mundane astrology works because planetary configurations in mundane charts sympathetically trigger actions by individuals with similar natal configurations. These individuals are 'lifted up' from the masses to play out events promised by mundane horoscopes.

Appendix C presents natal figures for prominent individuals who influenced the national consciousness as defined in Chapter 6. If the thesis is correct, then natal horoscopes of prominent individuals should mirror the National Horoscope in some way. Results of this sample identified several types of mundane-natal connections which support the thesis:

1. *Recapitulation of the same Distributor planet/sign combination in the natal chart.* <u>Example</u>: Saturn/Gemini is a planet/sign combination found in the natal figure for Frederick Winslow Taylor. Taylor's concept of *Scientific Management* rose to national attention when the USA Ascendant Distributor changed to Saturn/Gemini.

2. *Placement of another planet, aspect, or point in the relevant bound.*
<u>Example</u>: Charles Coughlin's natal Ascendant (15CA20) falls in the bound of Mercury/Cancer. This was a sufficient connection to make Coughlin the leading radio demagogue during the Mercury/Cancer Distribution even though Coughlin's own Mercury falls in Scorpio not Cancer.

3. Dynamic activation of the Distributor's sign by Firdaria or ZRS. <u>Example</u>: Minnie Hauk's L1 Taurus period using Zodiacal Releasing from Spirit encapsulates the Venus/Taurus distribution even though her natal Venus is placed in Sagittarius, not Taurus.

4. In some cases, a connection could not be found. <u>Example</u>: James Folger.

    For rectification details, see www.regulus-astrology.com.

Mars/Sagittarius ~ July 4, 1776 – November 29, 1779

Benjamin Franklin ~ Beaumarchais and Gun Smuggling

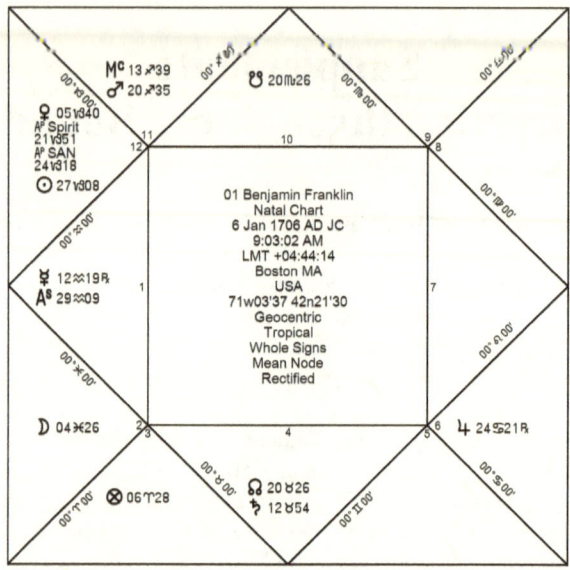

On January 29, 1774, Benjamin Franklin faced the British Privy Council in the 'Cockpit' as he stood accused of stealing the Hutchinson letters which detailed repressive measures favored by Massachusetts Governor Thomas Hutchinson. Prior to this time, Franklin's politics were anti-British but within the context of reforming the politics of British rule. After this date, no more; Franklin was radicalized to the course of the American revolution.

<u>dsa ASC conj Mars</u>. *2-Jul-1773*
<u>csa Mars conj ASC</u>. *20-Apr-1774*
>Forms bookends to the Hutchinson affair.
>Hutchinson letters read to Massachusetts assembly, June 1773.
>Franklin admits responsibility of transmission of letters, 25-Dec-1773.
>Franklin faces the Privy Council, 29-Jan-1774.
>Effigies of Hutchinson hanged and burned in Philadelphia, 3-May-1774.

D	Saturn/Aquarius	P	ASC d. => Mars (MA)	24-Mar-1776
D	Saturn/Aquarius	P	ASC d. => Mars (0)	30-Mar-1776

>The same measurement computed by primary directions follows Franklin's 2-Mar-1776 decision while serving on the Committee of Secret Correspondence to send Silas Deane to France. This led to French loans and weapons smuggling arranged by Silas Deane and Beaumarchais for the benefit of the American Revolution.

Mercury/Capricorn ~ November 30, 1779 – May 4, 1787

Isaiah Thomas ~ The Massachusetts Spy

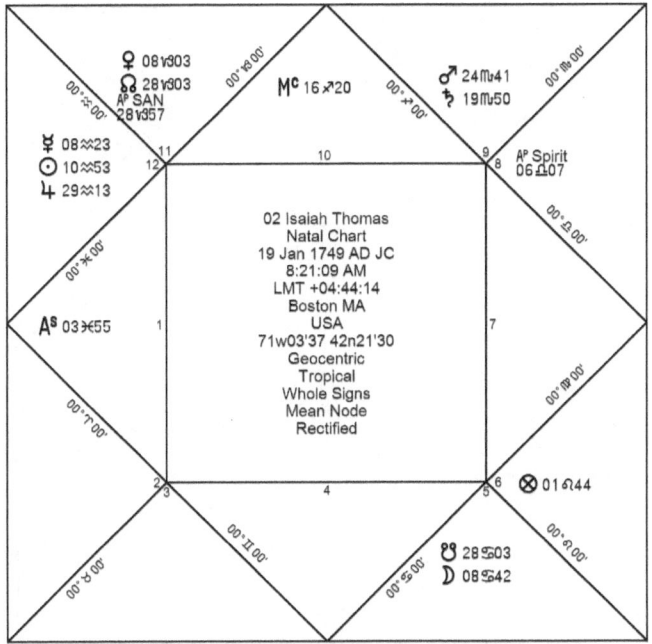

Isaiah Thomas was America's leading printer during the Federalist Era. He began publishing the *Massachusetts Spy* in 1770 and supported the cause of colonial patriots. Besides publishing the *Massachusetts Spy*, he also published books, including spellers and dictionaries of Edinburgh professor William Perry in order to compete with the popularity of Noah Webster's speller published during Mercury/Capricorn's Distribution. Besides printing, Thomas also founded the American Antiquarian Society. After retirement in 1802, Thomas spent years researching the history of printing in America from the mid-17th century to 1800. His two volume work *The History of Printing in America with a Biography of Printers, and an Account of Newspapers (1810)* remains the primary reference on history of early American printing to the present day.

The printing career of Isaiah Thomas is contained within his major Mercury Firdaria period: January 8, 1767 to January 7, 1780 and continues through Mercury/Capricorn's Distribution for the National Horoscope.

Linkage to Mercury/Capricorn is indirect. At the time of the prenatal syzygy, a solar eclipse, Mercury's position was 19CP00.

Jupiter/Capricorn ~ May 5, 1787 – May 3, 1794

Alexander Hamilton ~ The Federalist Papers

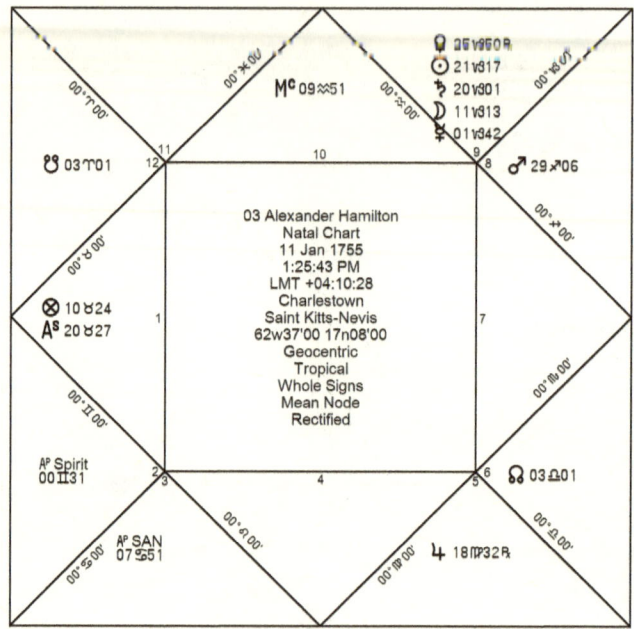

For Hamilton, Moon/Capricorn/9th signifies the need for a strong centralized government. The Moon falls in the bound of Jupiter/Capricorn.

D	Venus/Aquarius	P	MC d. → Moon (l=MO)	5-Aug-1785
D	Venus/Aquarius	P	MC d. → Moon (l=0)	17-Oct-1785

The path to the 1787 Constitutional Convention was not a straight line. Hamilton worked behind the scenes to agitate for the convention in 1785 and during January 1786 proposed the first Constitutional Convention in Annapolis; held September 1786 with only 5 states in attendance. The full Convention was held in Philadelphia from *May 2 to September 28, 1787.*

Arguably Firdaria is the simpler predictive technique which links Hamilton's Moon to his Federalist agenda. The Moon's major Firdaria period begins January 11, 1786 as Hamilton calls for the Annapolis Convention. The subsequent Moon-Saturn minor Firdaria period from 25-Apr-1787 to 6-Aug-1788 includes the Constitutional Convention and Hamilton's contribution to the Federalist Papers.

APPENDIX C - SUPPLEMENT: DIRECTING THROUGH THE BOUNDS 297

Venus/Capricorn ~ May 4, 1794 – October 18, 1801

John Jay ~ The Jay Treaty

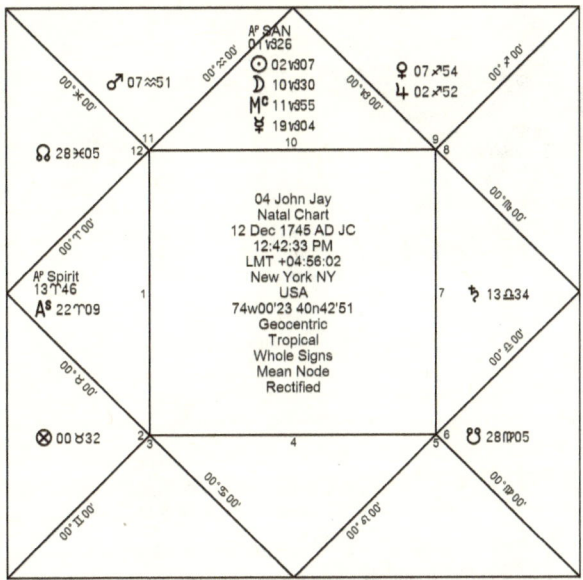

The Capricorn stellium in the 10th house ties Jay to the Federalist Era. Mercury is placed in the bound of Venus/Capricorn which is the active Ascendant distributor for the length of time between treaty signature and implementation. During the balance of the Venus/Capricorn distribution, John Jay served as Governor of New York.

REG	D	Venus/Pisces	P	sin sextile MC d. → Mercury (l=ME)	5-Oct-1794
REG	D	Venus/Pisces	P	sin sextile MC d. → Mercury (l=0)	27-Oct-1795
PT	D	Venus/Pisces	P	sin sextile MC d. → Mercury (l=ME)	19-May-1796
PT	D	Venus/Pisces	P	sin sextile MC d. → Mercury (l=0)	28-Jan-1797

19-Nov-1794 Jay Treaty signed by John Jay in England.
14-Aug-1795 Jay Treaty signed by President Washington.
30-Apr-1796 House of Representatives funded Jay's Treaty.
1797 John Jay elected Governor of New York (to 1-Jul-1801).

Saturn/Capricorn ~ October 19, 1801 – April 25, 1805

John Marshall ~ The Nationalist Supreme Court

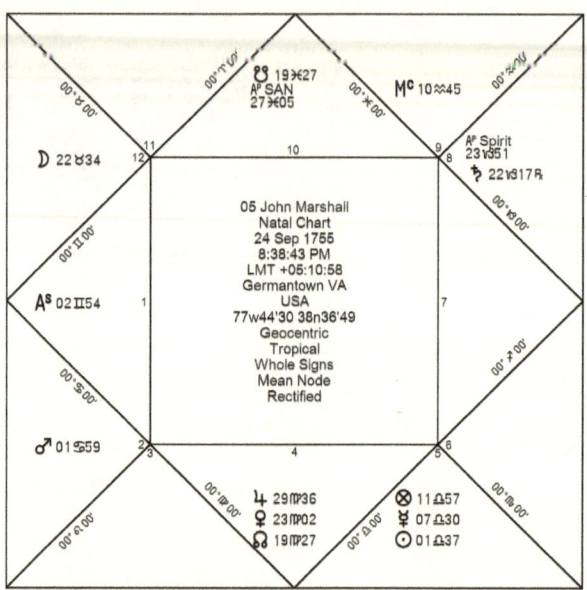

Lot of Spirit 23CP51 and Saturn 22CP17-rx both in the bound of Saturn/Capricorn tie John Marshall to the Saturn/Capricorn distribution. By quadrant houses (not shown), Saturn/Capricorn-rx is placed within 5 degrees of the 9th house cusp 17CP37. The 9th house signifies law and the Judicial system. Marshall was sworn in as Chief Justice of the Supreme Court on January 31, 1801, nine months before the start of the Saturn/Capricorn distribution.

How Saturn/Capricorn retrograde is capable of connecting Marshall to the Saturn/Capricorn distribution on first glance initially raises questions. Especially since Marshall started work on the Supreme Court just after the Federalist Party had lost to Thomas Jefferson's Democratic-Republican Party. Facts of *Marbury v. Madison*, Marshall's first major case, explain how Saturn's retrograde position assisted, and did not detract from, the corralling of power within the Judiciary Branch under Marshall's tenure.

Marbury v. Madison established the principle of judicial review which grants the Supreme Court the power to rule laws unconstitutional. In this case, the Supreme Court nullified a Congressional law regarding its own conduct (nullification of a law shows the effect of retrogradation). This ruling increased the power of the Supreme Court.

APPENDIX C - SUPPLEMENT: DIRECTING THROUGH THE BOUNDS

Mars/Capricorn ~ April 26, 1805 – September 11, 1808

James Madison ~ Opposition to British Trade

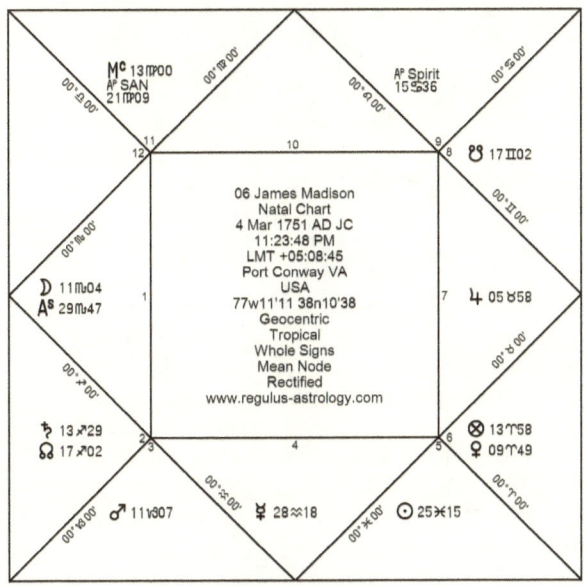

With natal Mars/Capricorn, James Madison was a staunch opponent of banking and manufacturing promoted by Alexander Hamilton. Madison was also a Federalist hater and an English hater. As President, Madison launched the War of 1812 against the British, nicknamed 'Mr. Madison's War.' Events during this Mars/Capricorn Distribution can be viewed as precursor events which led to the War of 1812.

| D | Mercury/Scorpio | P | dex. sextile Mars (l=MA) d. → MC | 26-May-1805 |
| D | Mercury/Scorpio | P | dex. sextile Mars (l=0) d. → MC | 21-Jul-1805 |

Occurring just days before the official start of the Mars/Capricorn Distribution on April 26 was James Madison's letter to James Monroe on ***April 12, 1805*** with complaints on Britain's Rule of 1756 used as legal justification for seizure and impressment of neutral vessels. During the ***summer and fall of 1805***, coincident with the Mars-MC primary direction sequence above, Madison reviewed legal precedents and maritime laws and concluded that Britain's Rule of 1756 was without merit. He wrote, published, and distributed to Congress *An Examination of the British Doctrine which Subjects to Capture a Neutral Trade not Open in Time of Peace.* It laid the intellectual framework for Jefferson's trade embargos which followed in ***1807/1808***.

Mercury/Aquarius ~ September 12, 1808 – April 23, 1814

John Elihu Hall ~ *American Law Journal*

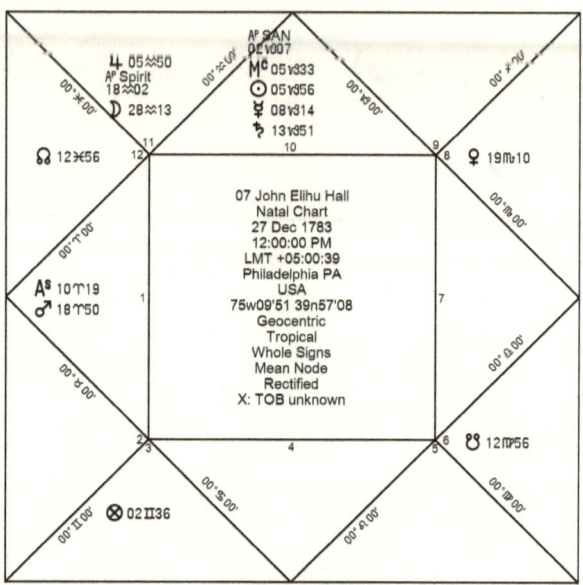

Note: this is an untimed horoscope, set for a default time of 12 Noon.

Lawyer and editor John Elihu Hall published the *American Law Journal*, America's first legal periodical, in six volumes from January 1808 to 1817. Compared to modern legal periodicals largely comprised of peer-reviewed scholarly articles, the *American Law Journal* was more of a digest of ongoing legal decisions, laws, and statutes. Hall's intent in producing the *American Law Journal* was to promote a uniform and systematic legal system for America in the post-Revolutionary War era.[1]

Jupiter's placement in the bound of Mercury/Aquarius links Hall with the Mercury/Aquarius distribution. Jupiter + Aquarius combines philosophy (Jupiter) with the fixed air sign (Aquarius) and is consistent with Hall's attempt to create a uniform American legal system.

Venus/Aquarius ~ April 24, 1814 – October 31, 1818

John C. Calhoun ~ Bonus Bill of 1817

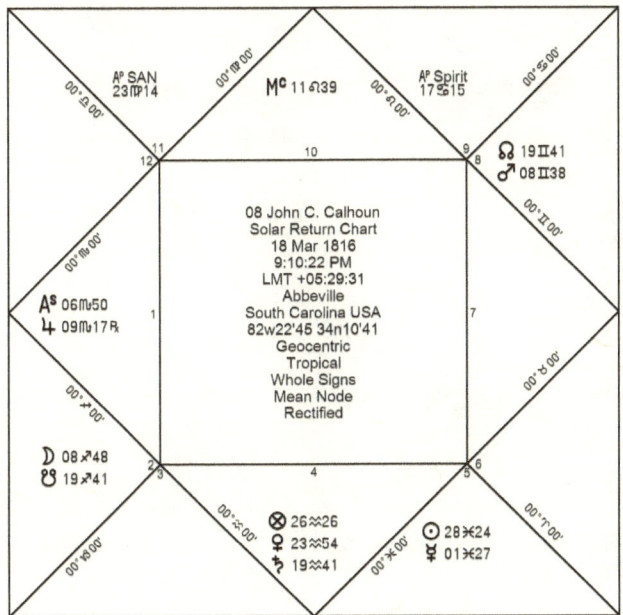

John C. Calhoun's current out-of-favor reputation is based on his states' rights philosophy and advocacy of slavery. However during his lifetime he was one of America's leading politicians serving in Congress, as Secretary of War (Monroe administration), Secretary of State (Tyler administration) and as Vice President (Jackson administration).

The 1816 solar return[2] takes Calhoun back to his last days in Congress under Madison and his first days under Monroe as Secretary of War. This was a time when Calhoun was sympathetic to the needs of national improvements (e.g., infrastructure) following the nation's poor military preparedness and near defeat by the British during the War of 1812. On *February 4, 1817*, Calhoun made a speech in favor of the Bonus Bill which called for the diversion of profits from the Central Bank for internal improvements. In one of the last measures taken before he left office, President Madison vetoed the measure on *March 3, 1817*.

The linkage between Calhoun and support for the ill-fated Bonus Bill is shown by the 1816 solar return with Venus, Saturn, and LOF all in Aquarius with the Lot closely conjunct the USA's Moon 27AQ51 which signifies internal improvements in the Regulus USA National Horoscope.

Jupiter/Aquarius ~ November 1, 1818 – October 25, 1823

DeWitt Clinton ~ Erie Canal

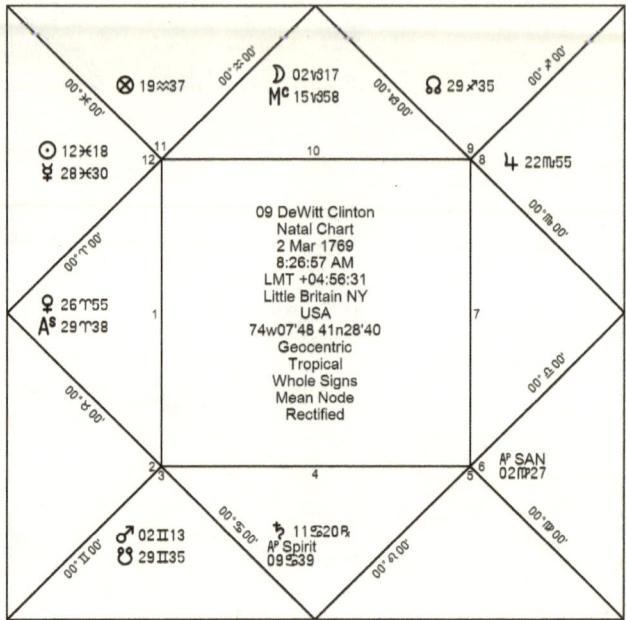

DeWitt Clinton was the dominant force in New York politics in the first quarter of the 19th century. He served nonconsecutive terms as New York Mayor, Governor of New York, and was the unsuccessful Federalist Party candidate for the 1812 Presidential race. He is best remembered for his role in constructing the Erie Canal.[3]

<u>30-Dec-1815</u>. *csa LOF conj Moon*
<u>3-Feb-1817</u>. *dsa Moon conj LOF*

Clinton is tied to the Jupiter/Aquarius Distribution through placement of his natal Lot of Fortune in the bound of Jupiter/Aquarius.

The first measurement timed his ***December 30, 1815*** meeting called to solicit support for construction of a canal in New York State. The second measurement preceded passage of the New York Canal bill on ***April 15, 1817*** by 10 weeks but coincided with the founding of the Lyceum of Natural History with which Clinton was involved. Besides his interest in canal construction, Clinton was intensely involved as President of the Literary Philosophical Society, the American Academy of Arts, and the Free School Society; also Second Vice President of the Historical Society.

Mars/Aquarius ~ October 26, 1823 – March 17, 1827

William Crawford ~ Election of 1824

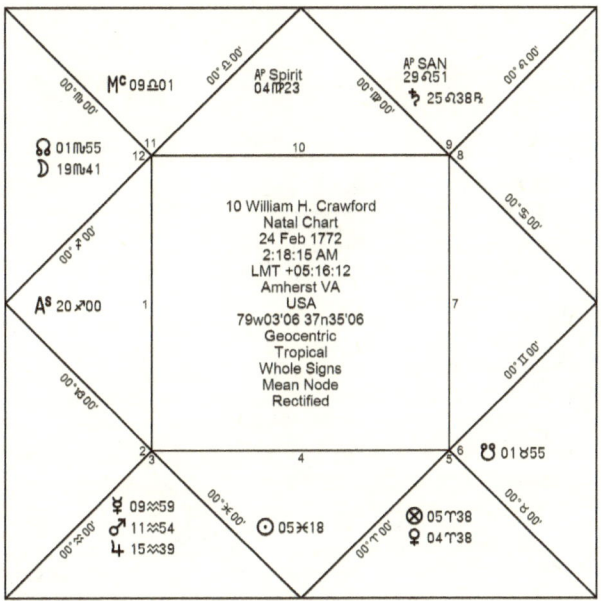

With Mars/Aquarius the 12th house spoiler in William Crawford's horoscope, William Crawford plays an accidental role in the rise of partisan politics with the fractious Presidential Election of 1824.[4] The year 1824 was the last year that Presidential candidates were nominated through the Congressional caucus. By 1824, Crawford was the lone supporter of the caucus procedure among Presidential contenders. Crawford was supported in his successful caucus election held *February 14, 1824* by the up-and-coming political operative Martin Van Buren who made his first attempt at kingmaker with his selection of William Crawford. Martin Van Buren would later prove successful with Andrew Jackson in 1828. Unfortunately for Van Buren, in 1824 he backed the wrong man. What made the 1824 election so unusual was Crawford's unwillingness to exit the Presidential race following a debilitating stroke in late September 1823.[5] Had Crawford exited the race after this illness and released his votes, the probability of the election falling to the House of Representatives as it did on *December 1, 1824* would have been much less likely. The divisive election results with Andrew Jackson winning an insufficient majority vote, Congressional choice of John Quincy Adams as President, and partisan attacks made by pro-Jackson forces against Adams can ultimately be traced back to Mars/Aquarius resonating through Crawford's horoscope.

Saturn/Aquarius ~ March 18, 1827 – June 24, 1830

Benjamin Silliman ~ Scientific Education in America

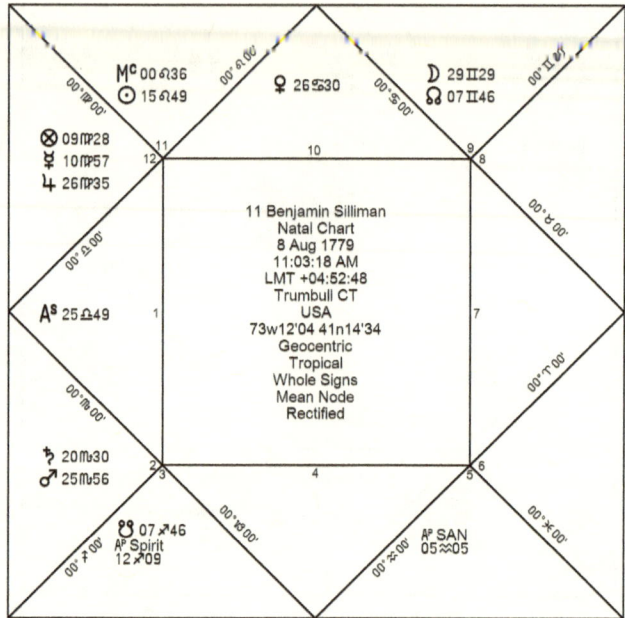

Lacking accurate birth data for Josiah Holbrook, I have chosen to present the figure for his teacher, Benjamin Silliman. Silliman is one of the most important figures in the development of science in the United States. At Yale University, he is remembered for teaching natural history, which covered geology, mineralogy, botany, and zoology. His acquisitions of rocks, minerals, and fossils made Yale's collection the largest in the United States.[6]

At the end of his Yale teaching career, Silliman was the first individual to successfully distill petroleum into component products. His research efforts were publicized by his son Benjamin Silliman Jr. on April 16, 1855. What was later referred to as the *Silliman Report* presented the economics of petroleum and was instrumental in attracting the first major oil industry investment capital.

The connection between Silliman, scientific education, and Aquarius is not obvious until one applies Zodiacal Releasing from Spirit. The start of Silliman's L1 Aquarius period on 16-Jan-1818 coincides with Silliman's role in founding the *American Journal of Science*, the first such publication in the US.

APPENDIX C - SUPPLEMENT: DIRECTING THROUGH THE BOUNDS

Venus/Pisces ~ June 25, 1830 – December 13, 1837

Thomas Cole ~ Hudson River School

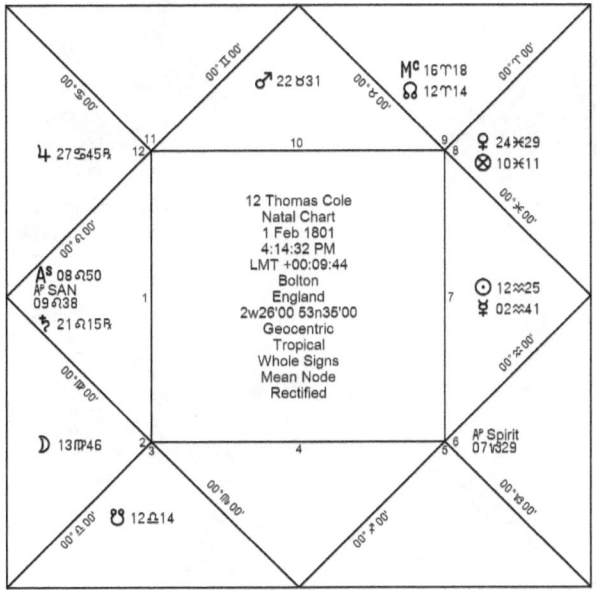

D	Mercury/Aries	P	MC d. => Venus (0)	22-May-1825
D	Mercury/Aries	P	MC d. => Venus (0)	5-Jun-1825

Thomas Cole moved to New York City during April 1825 and shortly thereafter traveled up the Hudson River for sketching trips. By October 1825 he completed three paintings of Hudson River landscapes which came to public attention with a favorable review in the New York Evening Post on *November 22, 1825*.[7] The Hudson River School was born. The romantic and idealistic style of Hudson River painting is signified by Venus in Pisces, a sign where Venus is exalted. It is recapitulated in Cole's horoscope.

Cole's best known paintings are five gigantic mural-sized paintings titled *The Course of Empire*, commissioned by patron Luman Reed and now on display at the New York Historical Society. Started in *1834*, the series was completed in *1836*. Planets in their exaltation produce effects which represent the purest form of the planet in question, though their effects are ephemeral. *The Course of Empire* portrays the rise and fall of a Romanesque civilization with the Hudson River Valley used as a backdrop. Depiction of a rise and fall is consistent with the ability of an exalted planet to rise yet unable to sustain its gains.

Jupiter/Pisces ~ December 14, 1837 – May 8, 1840

Charles Wilkes ~ The United States Exploring Expedition

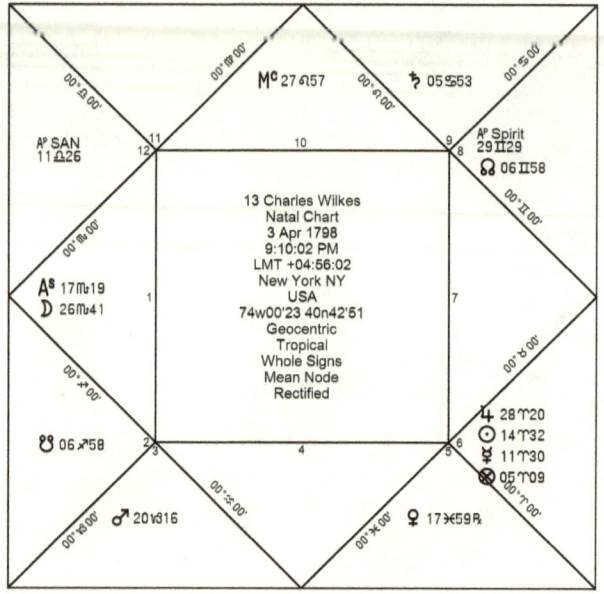

Historian Nathanial Philbrick attributes the relative anonymity of Charles Wilkes and the U.S. Exploring Expedition to Wilkes' harsh treatment of his crew which resulted in his court-marshal in July 1842.[8] Philbrick traces this behavior to Wilke's physical exhaustion (and possible nervous breakdown) while in Rio de Janeiro between *November 23, 1838* and *January 6, 1839*.[9]

Be that as it may, the United States Exploring Expedition, sometimes referred to as the "U.S. Ex. Ex." for short, was a significant milestone in the development of oceanography as a discipline. Ships under command of Charles Wilkes set sail on *August 18, 1837* and returned to New York on *June 10, 1842*, a date range which captures the Jupiter/Pisces distribution. Two months after the distribution changed from Jupiter/Pisces to Mars/Pisces, a dispute arose on Fiji leaving two sailors killed and about 80 islanders killed in retaliation.

The victor of Wilkes' horoscope is Jupiter/Aries which transited the MC of the horoscope when he set sail in 1837. Linkage to Jupiter/Pisces as Ascendant Distributor is weak, but Pisces is the rising Ascendant decan ruled by Jupiter/Aries.

Mercury/Pisces ~ May 9, 1940 – February 18, 1842 **(OMIT)**

APPENDIX C - SUPPLEMENT: DIRECTING THROUGH THE BOUNDS 307

Mars/Pisces ~ February 19, 1842 – June 1, 1847

The Folgers of Nantucket ~ A Whaling Family Dynasty

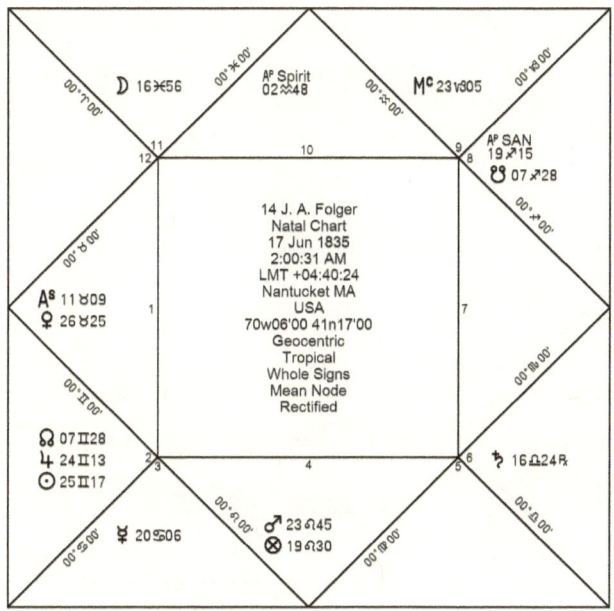

The Folger family dates from one of the first Pilgrim Mayflower migrations, has an extensive genealogy, and includes Benjamin Franklin among its clan. See also the nativity of Mayhew Folger (b. 9-Mar-1774) with a strong Mars/Pisces placement for a delineation match to whaling.

James 'J. A.' Folger's horoscope shows little connection to the Mars/Pisces whaling signature. He does not inherit the mantle of his family's whaling heritage. Towards the end of the Mars/Pisces distribution, Nantucket was struck by a fire on *July 13, 1846* which burned the business district to the ground. After The Great Fire of 1846, the 11 year old boy J. A. helped his father reconstruct his family's burned try works and ships. But he did not stay. Representative of the many restless workers of the New England whaling industry which peaked in *1846*, J. A. and his two older brothers went west to seek their fortunes in the California Gold Rush in the fall of 1849 and arrived in San Francisco on May 5, 1850. J. A. would go on to found Folger's Coffee. Venus/Taurus signifies green coffee beans; Mars/Leo signifies fire; their square aspect denotes the roasting process; Venus separates from Mars ("roasted beans ready for brewing"); Moon applies to Mercury, both of which are collected by Venus. The Moon-Mercury configuration signifies Folger's marketing skills which are applied to coffee.

Saturn/Pisces ~ June 2, 1847 – August 1, 1848

Nicholas Trist ~ Treaty of Guadalupe Hidalgo

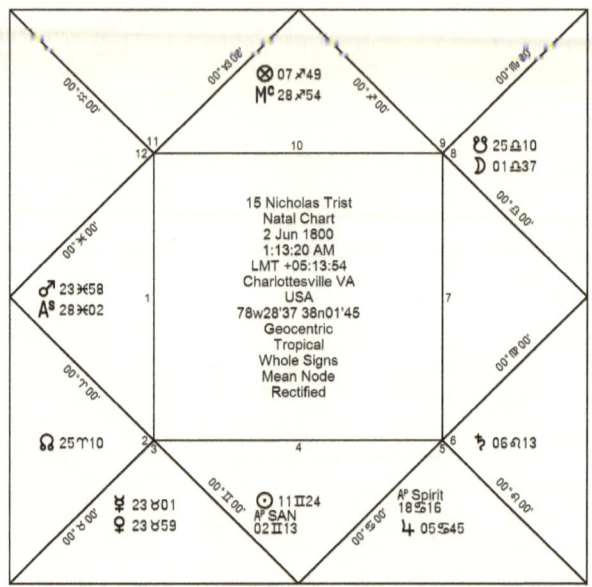

Polk found an unlikely executor of his grand strategy for territorial acquisition in State Department clerk Nicholas Trist. Polk, eager to avoid political grandstanding by politicians attempting to parlay diplomatic success into a future Presidential Bid, chose the unknown Trist as his Mexican envoy.

D	Jupiter/Gemini	P	dex. sextile Saturn (l=SA) d. → ASC	29-Mar-1847
D	Jupiter/Gemini	P	dex. sextile Saturn (l=BI) d. → ASC	7-Sep-1847
D	Jupiter/Gemini	P	dex. sextile Saturn (l=0) d. → ASC	15-Feb-1848

Though Trist's natal Saturn is placed in Leo, not Pisces, his Ascendant does fall in the bound of Saturn/Pisces. The primary direction sequence of Ascendant bound ruler Saturn/Leo is a close match to specific incidents during Trist's diplomatic tenure in Mexico and the overall Saturn/Pisces Distribution. After General Winfield Scott's victory at Veracruz on *27-Mar-1857*, President Polk considered this an auspicious time for peace talks and sent Nicholas Trist. The second direction computed with the Bianchini latitude variation occurs a week after Scott captured Mexico City and two weeks before Trist wrote to Polk stating his Mexican negotiations exceeded his instructions. Two events sandwich the final direction: the Treaty of Guadalupe Hidalgo (February 2, 1848) and Buchanan's treaty presentation to President Polk February 19, 1848).

Jupiter/Aries ~ August 2, 1848 – February 2, 1852

Phrenology ~ Lorenzo Fowler

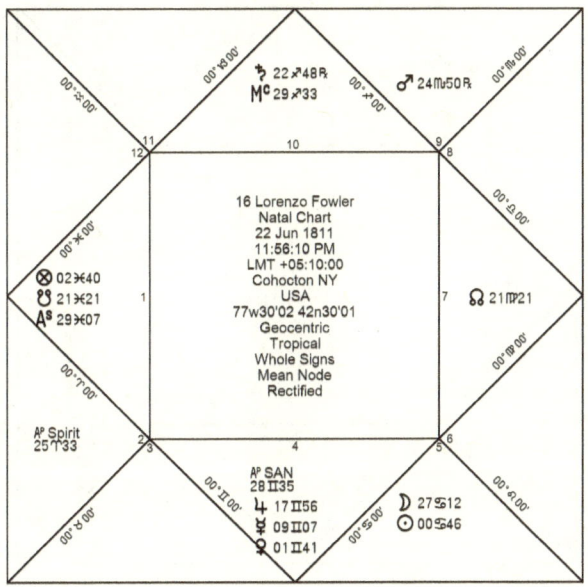

Jupiter/Aries is the logical significator for phrenology as it combines Jupiter's teaching and advising with the head assigned to Aries according to medical astrology. As a discipline, phrenology was introduced to America by Johann Gaspar Spurzheim in the fall of 1832 with a lecture series at Boston's Athenaeum. Siblings Orson, Lorenzo, and Charlotte quickly formed a phrenology business and opened shop in 1836 on Park Row in one of Manhattan's prime business districts. By the time of the Jupiter/Aries distribution, phrenology was a well-established business. The Fowler's publishing department claimed to have the largest mail-order list in the city. During the time of the Jupiter/Aries distribution, the American Phrenological Society was inaugurated in *May 1849*, Lorenzo Fowler conducted his famous phrenology reading of Walt Whitman's head on *July 16, 1849* [Note Whitman's Mars is closely conjunct Fowler's Lot of Spirit], and on *October 29, 1851*, a Boston office opened. Shortly after the end of the distribution, Orson Fowler left the firm to launch an independent career as itinerant lecturer on sex, the apostle of nature, and octagon houses.

As presented, the horoscope shows few ties to Jupiter/Aries with only the Lot of Spirit placed in Aries as a sign linkage. Brother Orson (b. 11-Oct-1809), the best known of the siblings, has Jupiter/Aries-rx in his horoscope.

Venus/Aries ~ February 3, 1852 - August 17, 1855

Harriet Beecher Stowe ~ Uncle Tom's Cabin

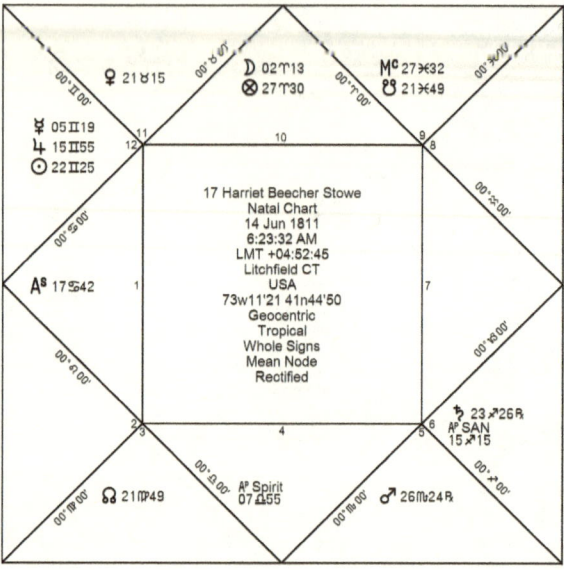

It was passage of the Fugitive Slave Act on September 18, 1850 which motivated Harriet Beecher Stowe to write *Uncle Tom's Cabin*. First published as a serial in the *National Era* starting June 5, 1851, *Uncle Tom's Cabin* was published in book form on **March 20, 1852** just after the changeover. Stowe is tied to the Distribution through her natal Venus entering the bound of Venus/Aries on **May 8, 1852** by converse solar arc just after the changeover.

D	Mercury/Cancer	P	ASC (l=0) d. → Mercury	29-Dec-1851
D	Mercury/Cancer	P	ASC (l=ME) d. → Mercury	2-Jan-1855

Stowe's writing career took off with this Mercury primary direction sequence. Mercury is another link between Stowe's natal figure and the Venus/Aries Distribution because Mercury rules the North Node in the third of writing whose antiscion (as well as the Lot of Faith's) falls in the bound of Venus/Aries. That her writing would engender a rebellion over slavery can be read through Mercury's rulership of both Sun and Jupiter in the 12th. The classical delineation for slave revolts is the ruler of the 6th placed in the 12th. Here Jupiter/Gemini - significator of intellectual curiosity - is the cause of slave revolts[10], in turn triggered by ruler Mercury which signifies Stowe's authorship of *Uncle Tom's Cabin*.

Mercury/Aries ~ August 18, 1855 - June 6, 1880

Walt Whitman ~ Leaves of Grass

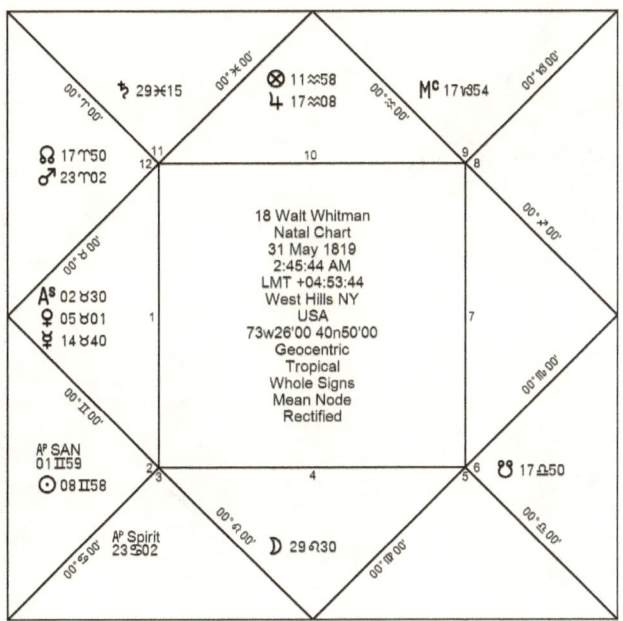

At its simplest Mercury/Aries signifies writing about war; a theme fully embodied by the poet Walt Whitman. From *Poem of Joys* (1860):

To go to battle - to hear the bugles play and drums beat!
To hear the crash of artillery - to see the glittering of the bayonets
    and musket-barrels in the sun!
To see men fall and die and not complain!
To taste the savage taste of blood - to be so devilish!
To gloat so over the wounds and deaths of the enemy.[11]

North Node in the bound of Mercury/Aries ties Whitman to the Mercury/Aries Distribution. The first edition of *Leaves of Grass* was published on **July 4, 1855** and on **June 14, 1860** just after the Distribution ended, Whitman's publishers informed him the first printing of his third edition had sold out and a second printing was ready for binding.[12]

| D | Mars/Gemini | P | sin. sextile North Node (l=MA) d. → Mars | 10-Aug-1860 |

This direction occurred prior to the Civil War outbreak on April 12, 1861. In Whitman's own words, 'My book and war are one...'[13]

Mars/Aries ~ June 7, 1860 - July 8, 1863

Alexander Stephens ~ Launch of Civil War

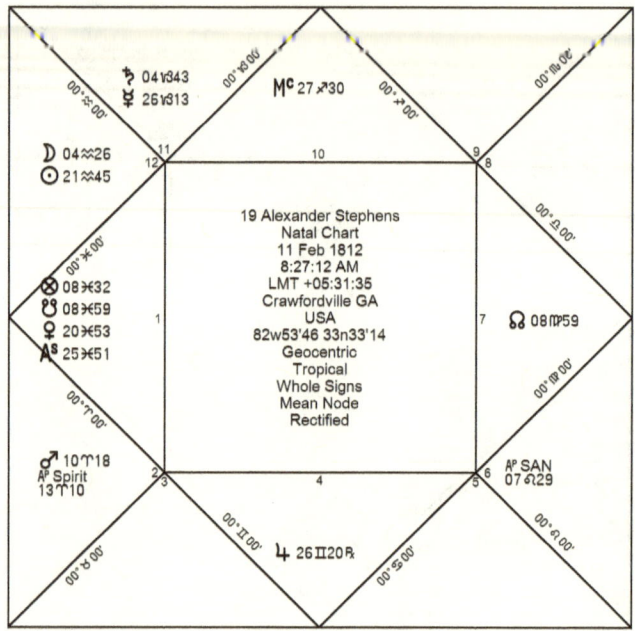

A life-long supporter of States Rights, Alexander Stephens punctuated his affiliation with various States Rights political parties in the late 1830s and early 1850s with an uneasy alliance with the Whigs in the 1840s. Stephens was an instrumental figure behind passage of both the Missouri Compromise and the Kansas-Nebraska Act through complex parliamentarian tactics.

Stephens argued against secession but eventually fell in line with the South and served as Jefferson Davis' Vice President for the duration of the Civil War. Mars/Aries directly links Alexander Stephens to the Distribution.

As one dynamic timer of the conflict, Stephens' draft of the Confederate Constitution held at the Montgomery Convention during **February 1861** coincided with L1 Cancer – L2 Scorpio (29-May-1850 – 21-Aug-1861) using Zodiacal Releasing from Spirit. The L2 Scorpio subperiod is ruled by Mars/Aries.

Saturn/Aries ~ July 9, 1863 - September 8, 1866

Clement Vallandigham ~ General Order Number 38

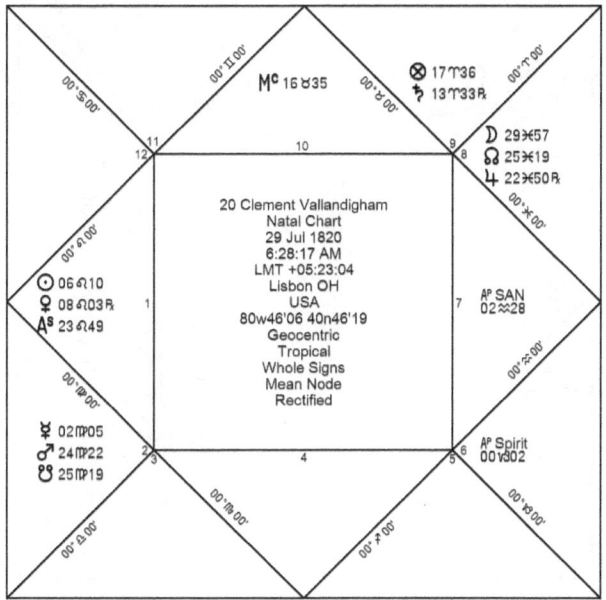

During *April 1863*, Union General Ambrose Burnside issued General Order Number 38 which outlawed antiwar sentiment. An excerpt:

> *The habit of declaring sympathies for the enemy will no longer be tolerated in the department. Persons committing such offences will be at once arrested, with a view to being tried as above stated, or sent beyond our lines into the lines of their friends.*[14]

Ohio Congressmen Clement Vallandigham, operating in the state where Burnside made his order effective, denounced Lincoln on *May 1, 1863* and called for his removal from office. For his comments, Vallandigham was arrested on *May 5* for violation of Order Number 38. After a series of legal maneuvers, President Lincoln ordered Vallandigham banished to the Confederacy. After released in Tennessee, Vallandigham traveled to Canada where he won the Democratic Nomination for Governor of Ohio in absentia on *June 11, 1863* using an anti-war platform. He was defeated by pro-Union Democrat John Brough on *October 13, 1863*.

Vallandigham's anti-war statements are consistent with delineation of Saturn/Aries as the frustration of war.

Venus/Taurus ~ September 9, 1866 - December 24, 1871

Minnie Hauk ~ America's First Opera Diva

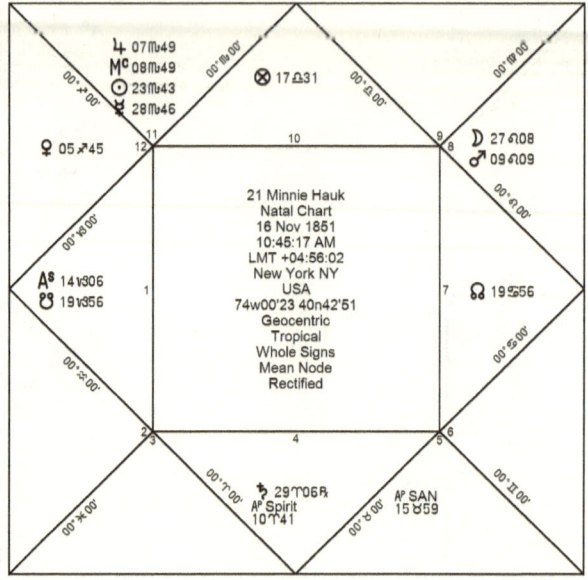

Though singer Jenny Lind's 1850-1852 famous tour preceded Minnie Hauk by two decades, Lind was a Swedish national and her P. T. Barnum-sponsored tour preceded construction of the Academy of Music by several years. In my opinion, Lind's popularity was indicative of a personality cult rather than a sign that opera had entered the national consciousness.

Minnie Hauk's vocal career began in 1862 when Academy of Music's impresario Max Maretzek arranged vocal training for Hauk with Achille Errani. Her public debut in *La Sonnambula* at the Brooklyn Academy of Music on **October 13, 1866** was favorably received. The following year she took the role of Juliette in the American premiere of Gounod's *Romeo et Juliette* on **November 15, 1867**. The next three years saw premieres in London, Paris, and in Vienna. Using Zodiacal Releasing from Spirit, Hauk's L1 Taurus period from August 29, 1866 to July 18, 1874 sandwiches the Venus/Taurus distribution. Her *La Sonnambula* debut occurred 6 weeks after the start of L1. After the distribution was complete, Hauk premiered the New York production of *Carmen* in the title role on October 23, 1878. This occurred during the Jupiter/Taurus Distribution which triggered such increased interest in opera the rival Metropolitan Opera House was formed so the nouveau riche could secure seats.

Mercury/Taurus ~ December 25, 1871 - February 28, 1876

J. P. Morgan ~ Patron of Metropolitan Museum of Art

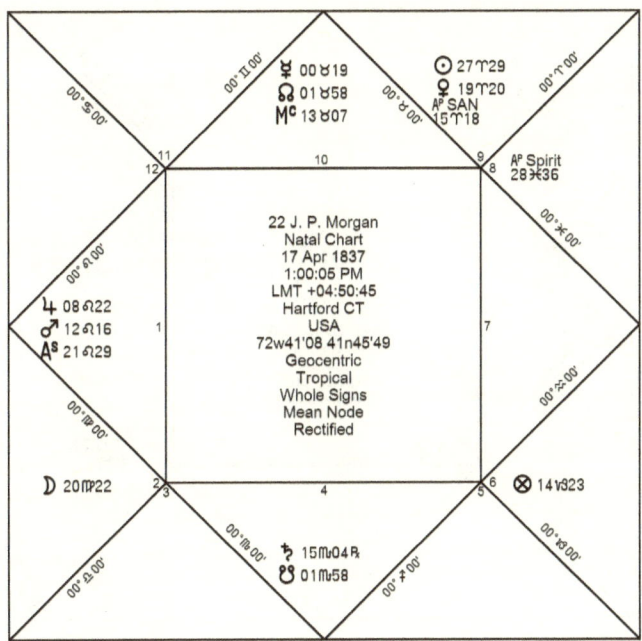

Though J. P. Morgan did not exercise his maximum influence on the Metropolitan Museum of Art until he took the reins of President in 1904, J. P. Morgan did start accumulating drawings, books, manuscripts, and an art reference collection in the 1870s.[15] J. P. Morgan's natal figure, with Mercury/Taurus conjunct North North/Taurus, both in the bound of Venus/Taurus, exemplifies his reputation as an art collector and museum patron. Like the Metropolitan Museum, to which he first made a donation in *1871*, his surviving Morgan Library and Museum has a strong focus on education. It also features a large collection of manuscripts, a nod to Mercury's literary signification. For his 1871 solar return (not shown), Mercury/Venus conjunct in the 8th house of bequests timed his first donation to the Metropolitan Museum during the first year of the Mercury/Taurus Distribution.

Jupiter/Taurus ~ March 1, 1876 - February 1, 1882

Jay Gould ~ Union Pacific Railroad

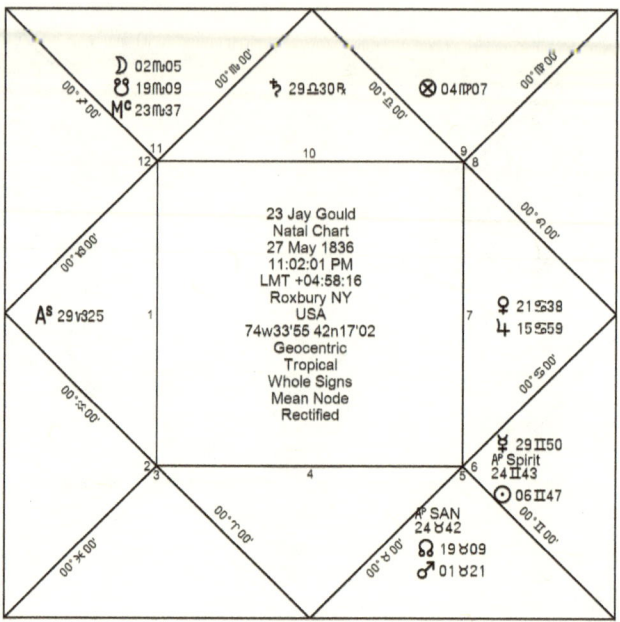

Jay Gould is tied to the Jupiter/Taurus Distribution through placement of North Node/Taurus in the bound of Jupiter/Taurus. Sign and bound rulers, Venus and Jupiter respectively, fall in the 7th of business partnerships. Gould was known for his investments in the railroad and telegraph industries. Railroads are signified by Mars/Gemini which is the bound placement of the Lot of Spirit. Jupiter rules the 3rd house of short-term travel and communication which is a delineation match to railroads and communications.

During the Jupiter/Taurus distribution, Gould's business milestones included Western Union's purchase of rival Atlantic and Pacific on *August 21, 1877*, approval of Union Pacific's consolidation (and Gould's resignation) on *January 24, 1880*, creation of the Missouri Pacific Railway during *Summer 1880*, and an agreement with rival railroad magnate Collis P Huntington on *November 25, 1881* to resolve competing claims on railroad routes in order to avoid duplication of efforts. Towards the end of the distribution, Gould had garnered notoriety for his business dealings. The New York Times printed a 5000-word, page 1 article on *February 22, 1881* reporting on a meeting of the National Anti-Monopoly League where resolutions against monopolists were offered.[16] The Times followed with the excoriating editorial 'His Majesty Jay Gould' published *February 23, 1881*.[17]

Saturn/Taurus ~ February 2, 1882 - January 7, 1886

Philip Armour ~ Chicago Meatpacking Industry

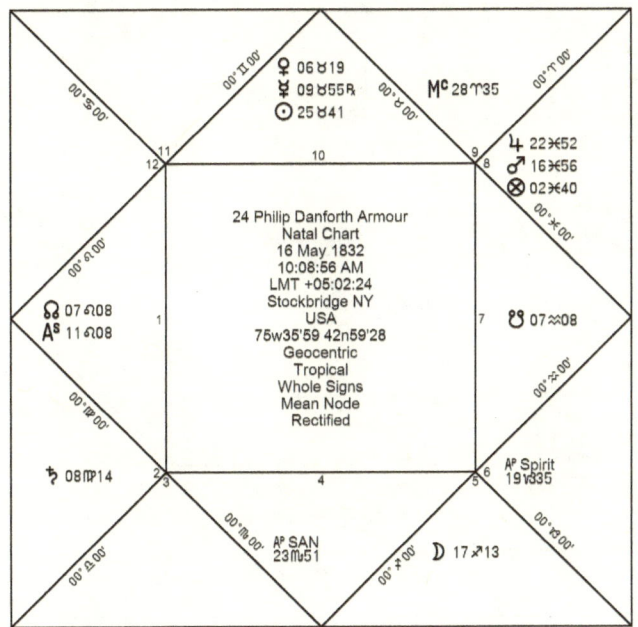

With his brother Herman, Philip Armour created Armour & Company in 1867, soon to become the world's largest food processor. Together with business rival Gustavus Swift (Swift & Company), the Armour brothers helped establish Chicago as a major industrial center in post-Civil War America. Armour & Company is remembered for the following:

- first company to produce canned meat

- first company to use assembly-line methods of production

- followed lead of Swift in establishing refrigerated rail cars

- reduced waste by using 'everything but the squeal.'

- charged for selling tainted beef in 1898-1899 which provided the impetus for Upton Sinclair to write his meatpacking expose *The Jungle* in 1906.

Armour is tied to the Distribution through Venus/Taurus (cattle) ruling Sun/Taurus in the bound of Saturn/Taurus (meatpacking).

Mars/Taurus ~ January 8, 1886 - June 20, 1888

Louis Lingg ~ Haymarket Riot and Suicide

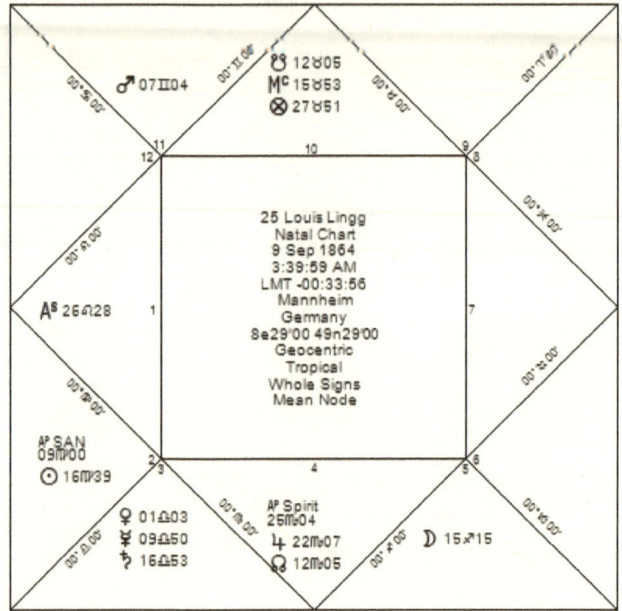

As one of the seven men sentenced to death for the death of police officer Mathias J. Degan during the Haymarket Riot of *May 4, 1886*, Louis Lingg is linked to labor protests by his Lot of Fortune placed in the bound of Mars/Taurus. For the Haymarket Riot event chart cast for 10:30 PM Chicago, IL, trSun 14TA34 and trMoon 27TA29 were closely conjunct Lingg's MC and LOF degree respectively.

Lingg's suicide death on *November 10, 1887* is also notable for its method and connection to Mars/Taurus as Distributor. Mars signifies fire, fighting, and the like. Placed in the fixed sign of Taurus, sign of his detriment, Mars often stores its anger for long periods of time before releasing in an explosive manner.[18]

Taurus is also assigned to the lower jaw and throat. Mars/Taurus signifies injuries to this area of the body. Accordingly, on November 10, 1887 at 9:00 a.m. Louis Lingg detonated a dynamite cap in his mouth which blew off his lower jaw and destroyed much of his face. After suffering in agony for six hours, he died near 3:00 p.m.

Mercury/Gemini ~ June 21, 1888 - August 5, 1893

William S. Burroughs I ~ Patent for a 'Calculating-machine'

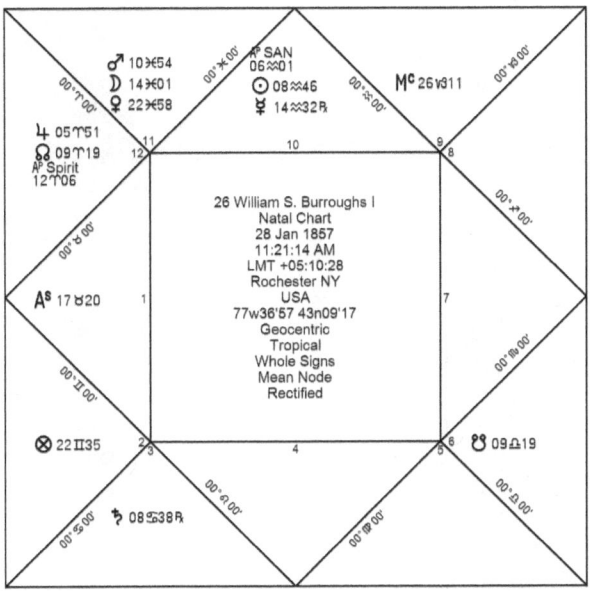

Working as a bank clerk, William Burroughs first considered the idea of a machine to guard against common math errors made while performing simple accounting functions. After developing this idea in 1882, Burroughs borrowed $300 from friends, constructed a rudimentary adding machine, and applied for basic patents in 1885 which were granted on *August 21, 1888*. His American Arithmometer Company was formed on January 20, 1886 and paid its first dividend to stockholder in 1895 after selling several hundred machines. Renamed the Burroughs Adding Machine Company in 1905 after his death, Burroughs specialized in mainframe computer applications for the banking industry. In 1986, Burroughs merged with Sperry Corporation to form Unisys Corporation, still extant in 2008.

Burroughs received his initial patent on **August 21, 1888** during the Mercury/Gemini Distribution and received another patent on *September 12, 1893* just after the Jupiter/Gemini Distribution began. Following his death on September 14, 1898, sales took off during the Venus/Gemini Distribution as the high volume of business transactions increased demand for adding machines (see Saturn-Ascendant Direction #6). Lot of Fortune/Gemini connects Burroughs to the Mercury/Gemini distribution. ZRS L1 Gemini (30-Sep-1879 – 17-Jun-1899) times his career success with L2 subperiods in mutable signs, all angular from the Lot of Fortune, timing career milestones.

Jupiter/Gemini ~ August 6, 1893 - January 11, 1899

Alexander Graham Bell ~ Growth of Telephone Industry

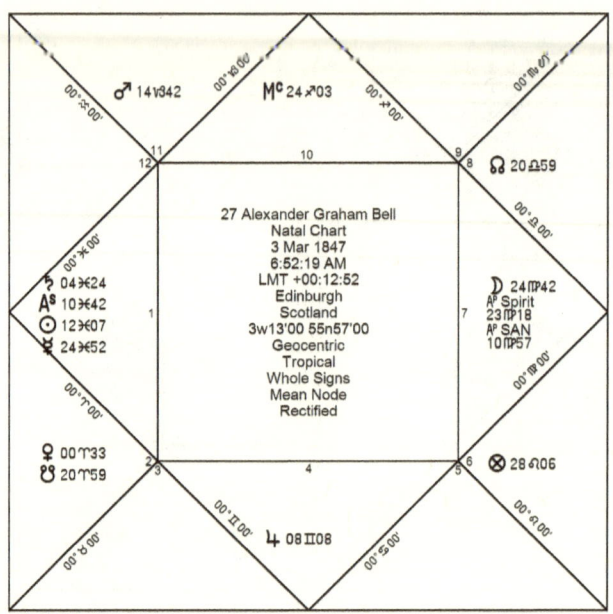

Of thirteen patents issued to Alexander Graham Bell for the telephone, the two most important were for the telephone and the receiver.[19]

No. 174,465	March 7, 1876	Telegraphy (telephone)
No. 186,787	January 30, 1877	Electric Telegraphy (receiver)

With a life of seventeen years, the patents expired on **March 7, 1893** and **January 30, 1894**, straddling the start of the Jupiter/Gemini Ascendant Distribution. For inventor Alexander Graham Bell, Jupiter/Gemini is the Ascendant ruler and is in mutual reception with Mercury/Pisces ruler of the 7th. With this configuration, Bell's partners attracted many patent challenges.

In 1894 Bell Telephone Company lawyers were caught overstepping the patent process. In a case heard by the U.S. Circuit Court on **June 14-20, 1894** during his Jupiter return, Bell Telephone Company was charged with fraudulently attempting to extend monopoly control through abuse of patent laws. The case was decided against Bell on **December 19, 1894** after Jupiter left Gemini for Cancer. In the six years following the decision, more than 6,000 new telephone companies commenced operations.[20]

Venus/Gemini ~ January 12, 1899 - October 22, 1903

Frank Woolworth ~ the Five and Dime Store

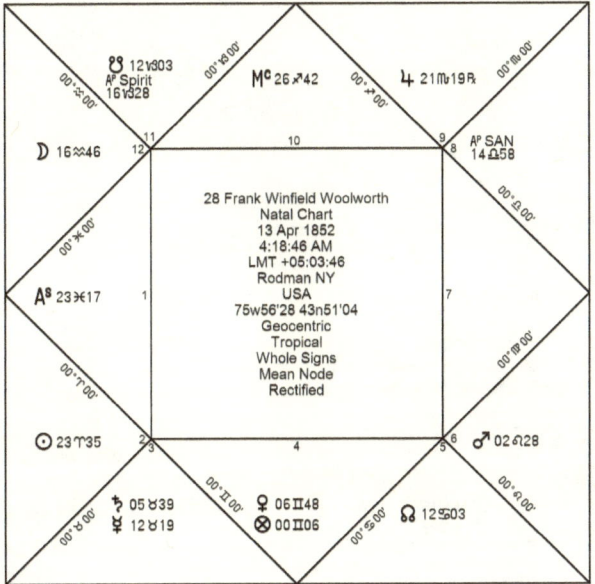

From his first successful store opening in Lancaster, Pennsylvania on June 21, 1879, Frank Woolworth built his chain of 5 and 10 cent stores to one of America's most successful merchandising corporations.

Though Woolworth & Co was not incorporated until February 1905 after the completion of the Venus/Gemini distribution, the prior years were ones of rapid growth in the Woolworth franchise. To celebrate Woolworth's 25th anniversary, in *early 1904* Woolworth's began to display colorful arrangements of mittens, scarves, and muffs in their window displays. These items are a delineation match to Venus/Gemini in generosity with Mercury/Taurus. In medical astrology, Gemini is assigned to the hands; Taurus to the throat. Gemini is also one of two signs ruled by Mercury which signifies speech and hearing. Accordingly, mittens cover the hands, scarves the neck, and muffs the ears. Venus/Gemini adds beauty; the duality of Gemini is exemplified in mittens which are sold in pairs and Woolworth's window display which exhibited multiple pairs of mittens.[21] Venus/Gemini rules the 3rd house of publicity.

Woolworth's career capstone was the April 24, 1913 opening of the Woolworth Building in lower Manhattan, at the time on the world's tallest buildings. This occurred during the Venus-Sun Firdaria subperiod.

Mars/Gemini ~ October 23, 1903 - November 13, 1910

John D. Rockefeller ~ Standard Oil

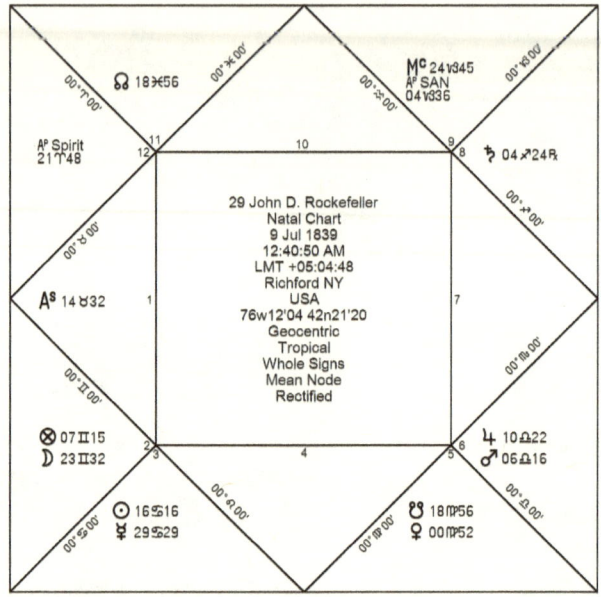

As the protagonist of Ida Tarbell's Standard Oil investigation[22], John D. Rockefeller received intense scrutiny for his business dealings. Of all corporate operations, Standard Oil was the poster child for corporate lawlessness which proved fodder for Ida Tarbell and other muckrakers. Tarbell's expose was serialized in *McClure's Magazine* from **November 1902** to **August 1905**. In response to Tarbell's reports of illicit activity, the US government filed an antitrust suit against Standard Oil on **November 18, 1906**.

D	Jupiter/Aries	P	sin trine Saturn (0) d. => MC	14-Nov-1906

Natal Saturn/Sagittarius-rx functions like Saturn placed in the opposite sign of Gemini. Functionally, Saturn/Gemini signifies regulation and is relevant to the antitrust case since Saturn rules the 9th house of the law and is placed in the 8th house of investments. As Saturn and Mars are enemies, Saturn/Gemini is the malefic capable of hemming in the lawlessness of Mars/Gemini. The breakup of Standard Oil is ordered on **May 15, 1911** after the Ascendant Distribution changes to Saturn/Gemini.

Placement of natal Moon in the bound of Mars/Gemini links Rockefeller to this distribution. Moon serves double duty as variable railroad pricing contracts as well as a female journalist who uncovers the illicit deals.

Saturn/Gemini ~ November 14, 1910 - April 4, 1917

Frederick Taylor ~ *Principles of Scientific Management*

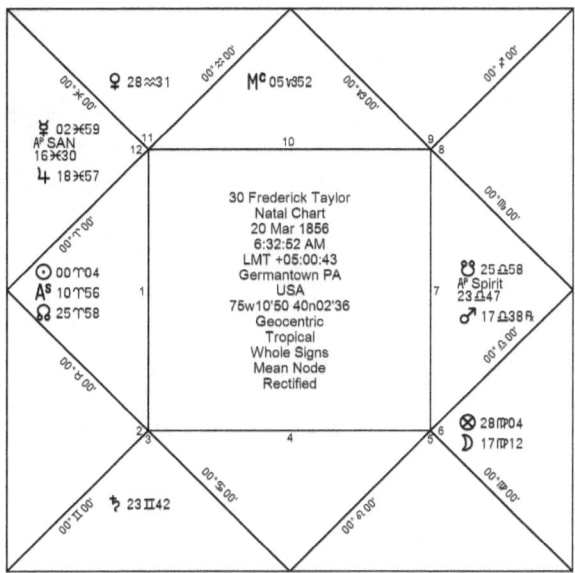

Frederick Winslow Taylor was the first American to apply the rigors of scientific analysis to business operations. Taylor has been alternately described as the first management consultant, an efficiency expert, and the father of *Scientific Management*. Taylor's professional career captured the industrial wave following the Civil War largely in machine shops of steel companies. The witness of inefficient production processes and employee practices grated on Taylor who devised various methods of improving manufacturing productivity which included stop watches on the shop floor.

D	Mars/Gemini	P	Saturn (0) d. => ASC	24-Sep-1911
D	Mars/Gemini	P	Saturn (SA) d. => ASC	11-Oct-1912

Workers decried Taylor as the man who reduced them to mechanical cogs on a wheel by his insistence that management make all manufacturing and production decisions. With this attitude towards workers, a backlash against Taylorism set in. On *August 21, 1911*, the House passed a resolution authorizing investigation of shop management and released its report on *March 9, 1912*. Taylor's reputation remained unscathed. On *October 6, 1912*, the NYT published a full-page story quoting the statistician Roger Babson who predicted that application of scientific management to the US Dollar will be the next great step in the efficiency movement.[23]

Mars/Cancer ~ April 5, 1917 - January 29, 1925

D. C. Stephenson ~ Grand Dragon of the Indiana Ku Klux Klan

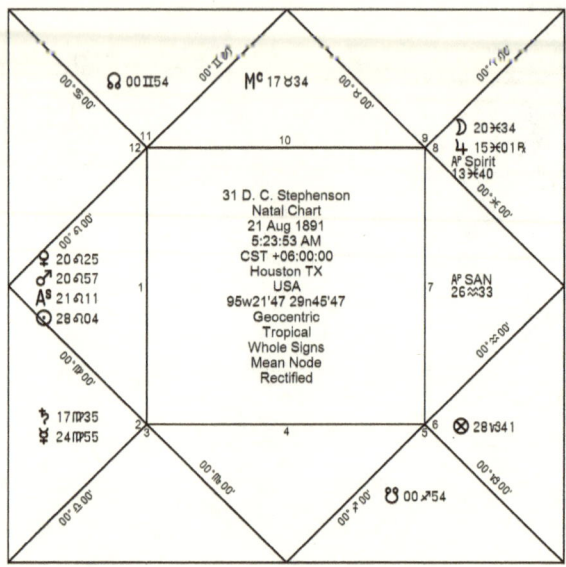

Twelve days after the start of the Mars/Cancer distribution, D. C. Stephenson volunteered for WWI army service. His military service was cut short in 1919 after discipline problems, sex adventurism, drinking, and theft. His fortunes improved during the Red Scare launched by Attorney General Palmer in 1920; the same year Stephenson was recruited by the Indiana Klan.

22-Jul-1922	Published first issue of *The Fiery Cross*.
4-Jul-1923	Declared the Grand Dragon of Indiana Klansmen.
Sep-1923	Severed ties with national group and formed rival KKK.
13-May-1924	Elected Grand Dragon of rival KKK faction.
1924	National KKK membership peaked at 6 million.
15-Mar-1925	Raped and mutilated Madge Oberholtzer.
16-Nov-1925	Sentenced to life in prison.
1925	National KKK membership collapsed.

Mars/Cancer signifies defense of the white race through measures of cruelty when threatened. Linkage between Stephenson's horoscope and the Mars/Cancer planet/sign combination occurs dynamically with his KKK recruitment during **September 1920** two months after the start of the L2 Cancer period [20-Jul-1920 to 8-Aug-1922] using Zodiacal Releasing from Spirit. His **July 4, 1923** promotion to Grand Dragon of the Indiana Klan is marked by both Sun and Mars in Cancer transiting is 12th house.

Venus/Cancer ~ January 30, 1925 - January 22, 1932

Mae West ~ Diamond Lil as Female Sex Icon

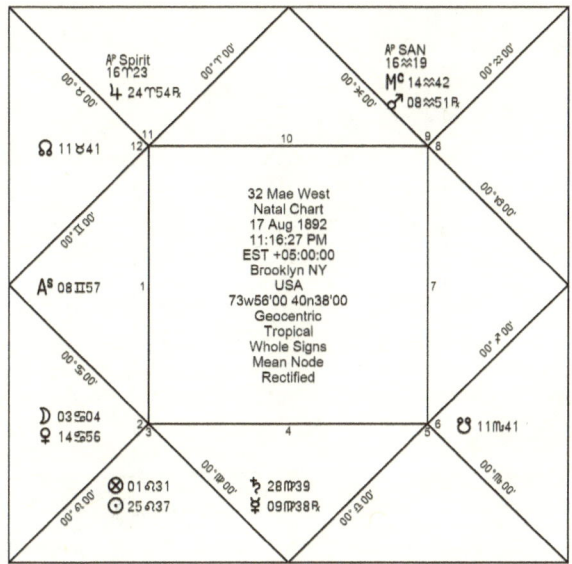

On *April 26, 1926*, Mae West transitioned from Vaudeville to Broadway with the opening of her show *Sex*, a title chosen for its shock value. The show raised enough eyebrows that West was arrested for indecency and served a 10 day sentence beginning *April 19, 1927* for 'corrupting the morals of youth.' She used notoriety to her advantage in advancing her career with another controversial production *The Wicked Age* in *November 1927* before landing her signature role as *Diamond Lil* on *April 9, 1928*. With many Broadway rivals and a later film version, Diamond Lil's persona as a 'bad girl with a heart of gold' impressed her humorous persona on an American public during the Roaring Twenties and the early days of the Great Depression.

By mainstream Hollywood standards, Mae West's full-bodied, hourglass physique was not considered attractive. But the addition of humor through carefully executed one-liners filled with double entendre proved a successful combination. She made sex funny. Mae West also tapped into the American male's desire for the curves and fleshiness of Venus/Cancer long before breast implants became a common cosmetic procedure in America. As Ascendant distributor, Venus/Cancer timed her initial rise to national prominence. Apart from Directing through the Bounds, Venus/Cancer is also present in the Regulus USA National Horoscope.

Mercury/Cancer ~ January 23, 1932 - April 3, 1939

Charles Coughlin ~ Radio Demagogue

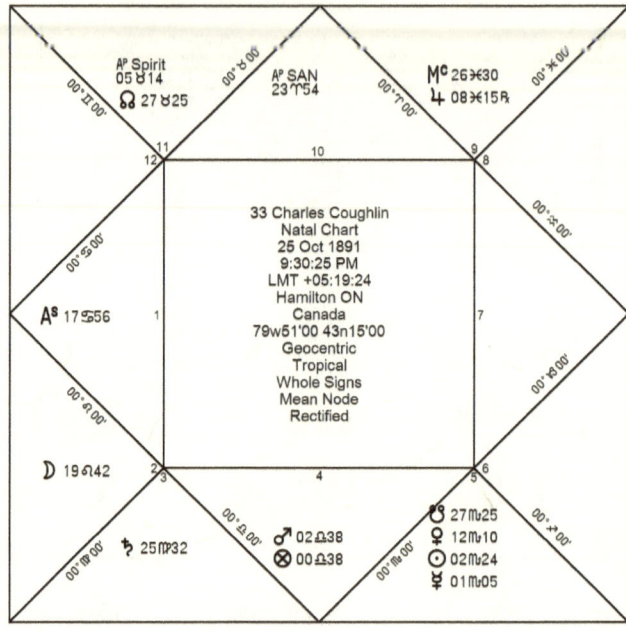

| D | Mercury/Leo | P | Moon (l=0) d. → ASC | 19-Aug-1932 |

Coughlin's Ascendant in the bound of Mercury/Cancer ties his activities as a populist demagogue to the Mercury/Cancer Distribution. Coughlin launched his radio broadcast career on October 17, 1926 from the Church of the Little Flower in Detroit, Michigan. By the time of the Moon-ASC primary direction listed above in the summer of 1932 he was an active campaigner for FDR's presidential campaign; in fact, FDR co-opted some of Coughlin's themes in an *October 2, 1932* address. By *February 1934*, Coughlin was named as most useful citizen politically after the President in an audience poll taken by WOR Radio listeners (New York). However by the 1934 midterm elections Coughlin had soured on FDR after FDR's devaluation of the dollar, an action Coughlin considered unconstitutional. On *November 11, 1934*, Coughlin founded a competing political organization, the *National Union for Social Justice*. Coughlin's popularity peaked in *1935* with a Madison Square Garden gathering with 23,000 in attendance on *May 22*. On *September 10, 1935*, the same day Huey Long was assassinated, Coughlin met with FDR which resulted in their final split. After this meeting, Coughlin's rhetoric became increasingly anti-Semitic.[24] The Catholic Church eventually forced him off the air.

Jupiter/Cancer ~ April 4, 1939 - November 8, 1947

Henry A. Wallace ~ Secretary of Agriculture

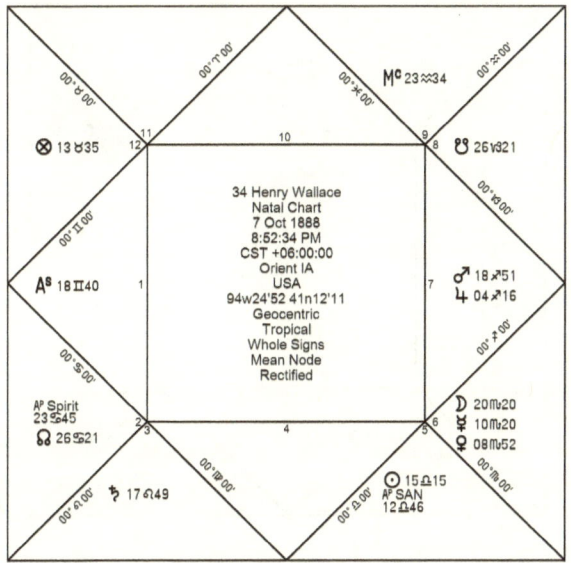

Hailing from a prominent Iowa farm family, Henry A. Wallace served as Secretary of Agriculture (1933-1940) following in the footsteps of his father. In 1926 Wallace founded Hi-Bred Corn, later Pioneer Hi-Bred Corporation; today the second largest hybrid seed producer after Monsanto.

After service as Secretary of Agriculture, Wallace was elevated to the VP slot in 1940. On the eve of Pearl Harbor, Wallace chaired the Supply Priorities and Allocations Board and was a key player in war planning. After US entry to WWII, Wallace opposed the imperialist view of American foreign policy espoused by TIME Magazine editor Henry Luce (see "American Century" essay in *February 17, 1941* issue of TIME) with his "The Century of the Common Man" speech given on *May 8, 1942*. Wallace later fell out with the administration and was dumped as Vice-President from the 1944 ticket. Wallace continued to garner high popularity as a political figure by positioning himself as the hero of the average American in the same way that William Jennings Bryan did 50 years earlier. He announced an unsuccessful third-party Presidential bid on *December 29, 1947* just after the conclusion of the Jupiter/Cancer distribution. Most historians cite *February 1948* as the high-water mark of the Progressive Party under Wallace.

Placement of the Lot of Spirit in the bound of Jupiter/Cancer ties Wallace to this distribution. Jupiter/Sagittarius is the victor of the horoscope.

Saturn/Cancer ~ November 9, 1947 - November 4, 1952

Joseph McCarthy ~ Communist Witch Hunt

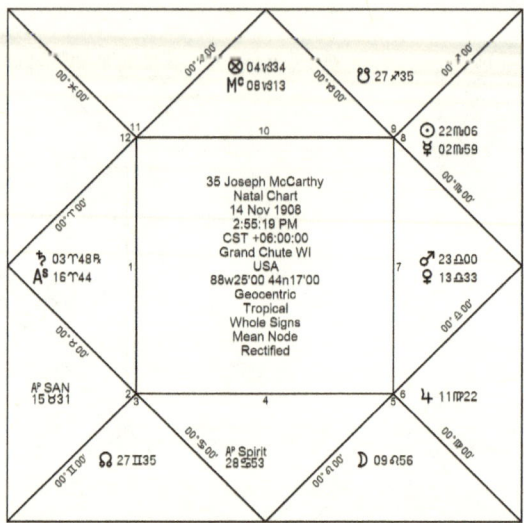

The transition from Progressive politics during early WWII years to the anti-Communist reactionary phase of America's social mood can be traced by the loss of Wisconsin's Progressive Senator Robert La Follette Jr. to Joseph McCarthy on *November 5, 1946* a year before the official start of the Saturn/Cancer distribution. La Follette's father was the titan of the Wisconsin progressive movement three decades earlier during Woodrow Wilson's era. Tragically, Robert la Follette Jr. never forgave himself for his loss to McCarthy and committed suicide on February 24, 1953.

McCarthy arrived in Washington at the perfect time to ride the wave of Saturn/Cancer paranoia. The House Un-American Activities Committee was made a permanent House committee charted to investigate Communist subversion the same year of McCarthy's election. On *February 9, 1950*, McCarthy delivered his infamous speech in Wheeling, West Virginia stating "I have here in my hand a list of 205 – a list of names that were made known to the Secretary of State as being members of the Communist Party and who nevertheless are still working and shaping policy in the State Department." But McCarthy overstayed his welcome as an anti-Communist crusader with his chairmanship of the Senate Permanent Subcommittee on Investigations on *January 20, 1953* after the end of the Saturn/Cancer distribution. Senate condemnation on *December 2, 1954* ended his political career.

McCarthy's Lot of Spirit is placed in the bound of Saturn/Cancer.

Jupiter/Leo ~ November 5, 1952 - May 26, 1960

Fulton Sheen ~ *Life is Worth Living*

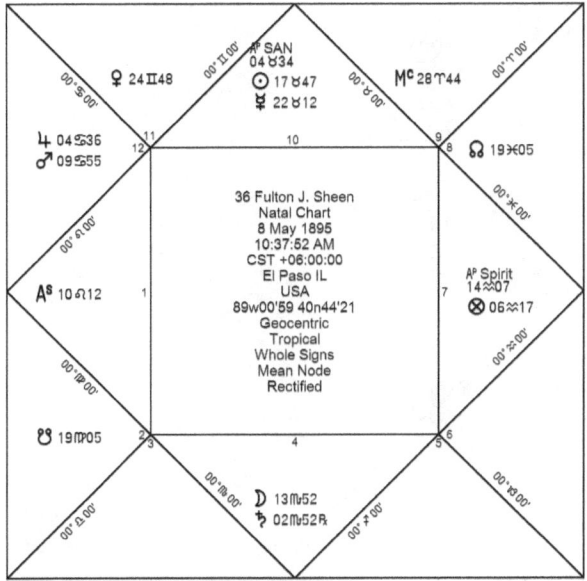

On the air from 1952 to 1957, Fulton Sheen's weekly television program *Life is Worth Living* reached American audiences as large as 30 million. Sheen spoke in front of live television audiences on religious topics with anti-Communism a frequent message. On *February 24, 1953*, Sheen made the prophetic statement that 'Stalin must one day meet his judgment' in a dramatic reading of the burial scene from Shakespeare's Julius Caesar which replaced the names of Caesar, Cassius, Mark Antony, and Brutus with Stalin, Beria, Malenkov, and Vishinsky. Stalin died shortly thereafter on *March 5, 1953*.

Life is Worth Living made its debut on *February 12, 1952* and Sheen quickly became a celebrity with his *Time* Magazine cover of *April 14, 1952*. Sheen's television career continued until Cardinal Spellman forced Sheen off the air in *October 1957* after a dispute over charitable financial matters.

Jupiter/Leo is a planet/sign combination which signifies moral authority. Sheen's Ascendant is placed in Leo, but in the bound of Venus not in the bound of Jupiter for this speculative rectification. There is no doubt that Jupiter is the victor of Sheen's horoscope with trJupiter 10LE12 conjunct the ASC degree on the date of his September 20, 1919 ordination and conjunct the MC degree on April 23, 1952 nine days after his TIME magazine cover. The direct connection between Jupiter/Leo and Sheen's horoscope is not obvious.

Venus/Leo ~ May 27, 1960 - September 27, 1966

Frank Sinatra ~ The Rat Pack

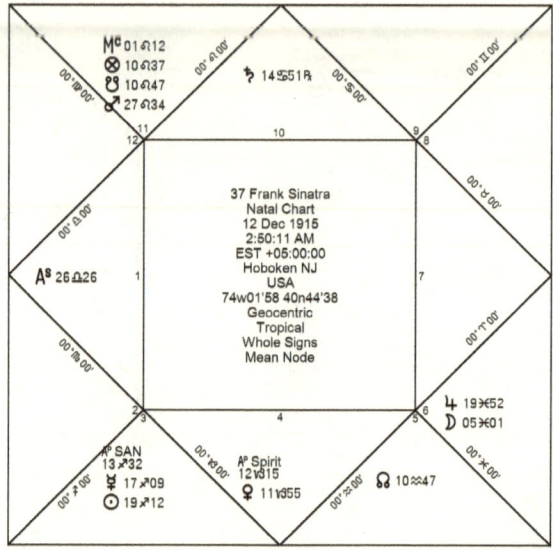

The term 'Rat Pack' was coined by Lauren Bacall as a descriptive term for the 'debauched appearance' of Frank Sinatra, Humphrey Bogart, and others at the Las Vegas Desert Inn in June 1955.[25] But it was not until 1960 the Rat Pack truly jelled as a social phenomenon. Frank Sinatra's legendary *Summit at the Sands* held from **January 26 to February 16, 1960** established the Rat Pack's iconic status and provided the backdrop for filming *Ocean's Eleven*. Though their influence as popular icons waned after the Kennedy assassination, film production until 1966 suggests the Rat Pack's continued influence, albeit at a lower level of popular appeal.

10-Aug-1960   *Ocean's Eleven* (Sinatra, Martin, Davis, Lawford, Bishop)
10-Feb-1962   *Sergeants 3* (Sinatra, Martin, Davis, Lawford, Bishop)
25-Feb-1963   *4 for Texas* (Sinatra, Martin)
24-Jun-1964   *Robin and the 7 Hoods* (Sinatra, Martin, Davis)
24-Sep-1965   *Marriage on the Rocks* (Sinatra, Martin)
26-Oct-1966   *Texas Across the River* (Martin, Bishop)

Sinatra is tied to the Distribution by both Lot of Fortune and South Node in the bound of Venus/Leo. South Node placed in 10th house (quadrant houses) of the King explains why Sinatra's status fell after JFK's assassination.

Saturn/Leo ~ September 28, 1966 - August 21, 1975

Robert F. Williams ~ Negroes with Guns

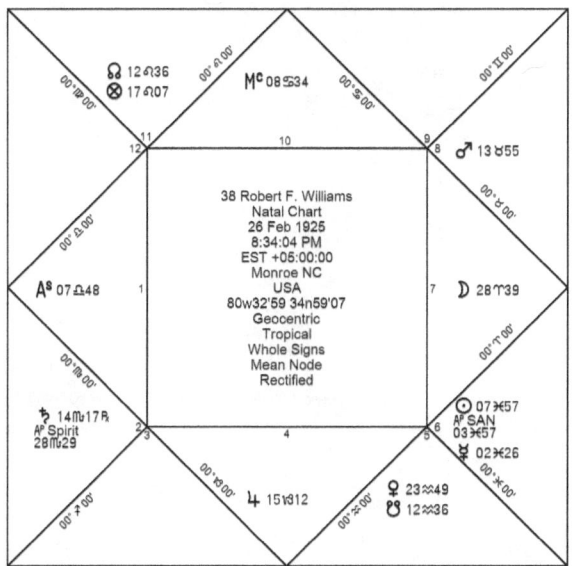

Predating the political activities of Stokely Carmichael, Huey P. Newton, and Bobby Seale by roughly a decade, Robert F. Williams was the first prominent African American of the mid-20th Century to advocate gun use as an alternative to Martin Luther King's peaceful civil disobedience. Williams is relevant to Saturn/Leo as Distributor because his 1962 book *Negroes with Guns* was one of several formative influences on Black Panther co-founders Huey P. Newton and Bobby Seale. In 1965, the year before the Panthers were founded in *1966*, Both Newton and Seale joined the Revolutionary Action Movement; a group who had earlier elected Robert Williams president-in-exile during Williams' years in Cuba and China.

Williams is linked to the Saturn/Leo distribution by placement of both the North Node and the Lot of Fortune in the bound of Saturn/Leo. Dynamic activation of the North Node and its bound lord Saturn timed key milestones in William's development as an advocate for arming African Americans with weapons in order to defend themselves.

Most relevant as supporting evidence for Saturn/Leo as Ascendant Distributor is Williams' North Node Firdaria period spanning *February 26, 1964* to *February 26, 1967*. During this time Newton and Seale studied Williams' book **Negroes with Guns** and founded the Black Panther Party.

Mercury/Leo ~ August 22, 1975 - April 8, 1983

Sylvester Stallone ~ Rocky Balboa

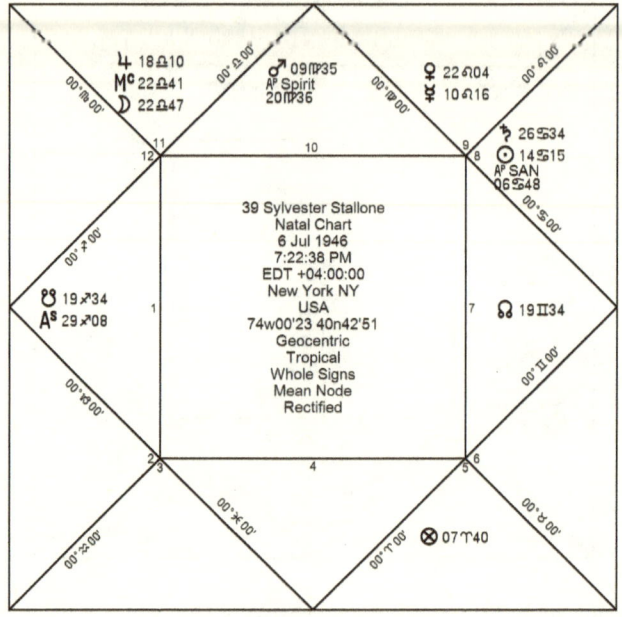

'I've never considered myself intelligent; I've considered myself clever. I have the gift of taking the negative and making it into a positive.'[26]

…Sylvester Stallone

On March 24, 1975, Chuck Wepner challenged Heavyweight Boxing Champion Muhammad Ali to a boxing match. The mere ability of Wepner to survive Ali for all rounds of the fight was a symbolic victory for the underdog.

It was also the inspiration for Sylvester Stallone's movie script *Rocky*. Written in the **summer of 1975**, *Rocky* established Stallone as a leading Hollywood film actor following the film's **November 21, 1976** release.

| D | Mercury/Taurus | P | dex. square Mercury (l=0) c. → ASC | 17-Aug-1975 |
| D | Mercury/Taurus | P | dex. square Mercury (l=ME) c. → ASC | 12-Oct-1975 |

As Distributor, Mercury/Leo appears in Stallone's figure as ruler of the Part of Spirit and signifies the 'feel good' positive philosophy of the *Rocky* franchise.

Mars/Leo ~ April 9, 1983 - November 18, 1990

Mr. T. ~ the *A-Team*

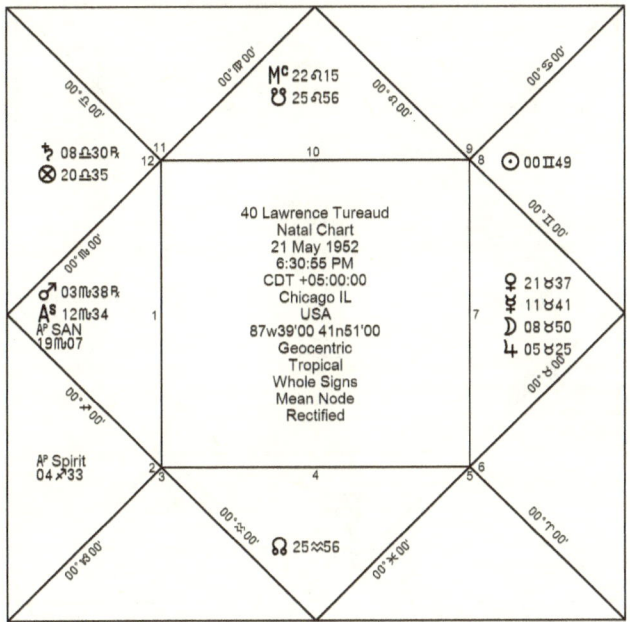

Former bouncer and bodyguard Laurence Tureaud, a.k.a. 'Mr. T,' rose to prominence when Sylvester Stallone hired Tureaud to play the role of James 'Clubber' Lang as Rocky Balboa's opponent in the film Rocky III which opened May 28, 1982. After Rocky III, Mr. T. was chosen as one of four actors in the television series 'The A-Team;' a series he would quickly dominate by public popularity. The A-Team's run from ***January 23, 1983*** to ***March 8, 1987*** is a close match to the Distribution of Mars/Leo.

The structure of the series is based on a successful bank theft in Vietnam ordered by the team's commanding officer which is not recognized by the team's remaining superiors after the commanding officer is murdered. The A-Team is arrested for a 'crime they didn't commit' but avoids military prison by escape. Returning to America, the A-Team operates as mercenaries for 'the little guy' in plots based largely on fights surrounding property rights. In the final series the A-Team reconciles with the government and executes espionage operations for the military. South Node in the 10th of career in the bound of Mars/Leo means Mr. T's career as a rescue/action hero is diminished by banking activities because the Sun ruled 10th falls in the 8th of debt and banking. Jupiter/Taurus conjunct the antiscion of the South Node placed in the 7th of conflict matches the A-Team's interest in property rights battles.

Mercury/Virgo ~ November 19, 1990 - September 23, 1999

Bill Gates ~ Microsoft, Windows, and the World Wide Web

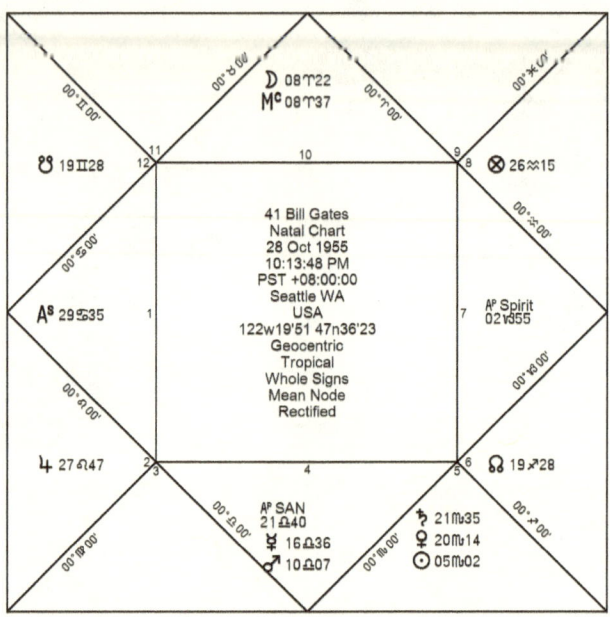

Under the leadership of Bill Gates, Microsoft was a significant driver of increased business productivity through computer software.

22-May-1990. Windows 3.0 launch. First Windows product to achieve broad commercial success.

19-Nov-1990. Microsoft Office launch. For the first time Microsoft Word, Excel, and PowerPoint were bundled together. Taking advance of Windows 3.0, multiple software programs could be open at a single time. This was a milestone for improved productivity for the business community.

5-Nov-1999. Judge Thomas Penfield Jackson issued initial findings of fact that Microsoft held monopoly power and used it to harm consumers, rivals, and other companies. This decision was later overturned.

13-Jan-2000. Bill Gates turned over CEO position to Steve Ballmer.

While there is no linkage between Gates' horoscope and a Mercury/Virgo signature, the launch of Microsoft Office on the exact date of the start of the Mercury/Virgo distribution is an event too obvious to ignore.

APPENDIX C - SUPPLEMENT: DIRECTING THROUGH THE BOUNDS 335

Venus/Virgo ~ September 24, 1999 - April 22, 2012

Martha Stewart ~ Makeovers and Fraud

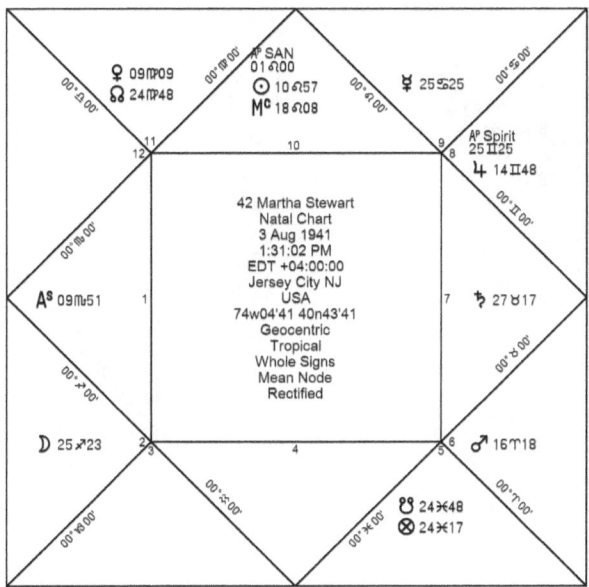

If Venus/Virgo signifies homely women in need of a makeover, look no further to *Martha Stewart Living* as a total solution to the Venusian realm of clothing, adornment, food, and decoration. Stewart's media empire dates to the December 13, 1982 publication of her first book but it is the ***October 19, 1999*** initial public offering of her company Martha Stewart Living Omnimedia which appears relevant to the start of the Venus/Virgo Distribution.

For Stewart, Venus/Virgo in the 11th ruled by Mercury/Cancer in the 9th signifies alliances with women who are need of Stewart's publications. Her flagship magazine *Martha Stewart Living* is a delineation match to writing (Mercury) about the home (Cancer) in a published product (9th house).

D	Venus/Scorpio	P	ASC d. → Venus (l=VE)	17-May-2004
D	Venus/Scorpio	P	ASC d. → Venus (l=0)	1-Jul-2004

Venus/Virgo in the 11th ruling the 12th also signifies mistakes and imprisonment from the fraudulent activities of friends. In 2004, Stewart was found guilty of conspiracy, obstruction of an agency proceeding, and making false statements to federal investigators. The Ascendant-Venus sequence matches the announced hiatus of *Martha Stewart Living* on ***May 18, 2004*** and the denial of motion for a new trial on ***July 8, 2004***.

Jupiter/Virgo ~ April 23, 2012 – April 27, 2017

Google IPO ~ Rise of Big Data

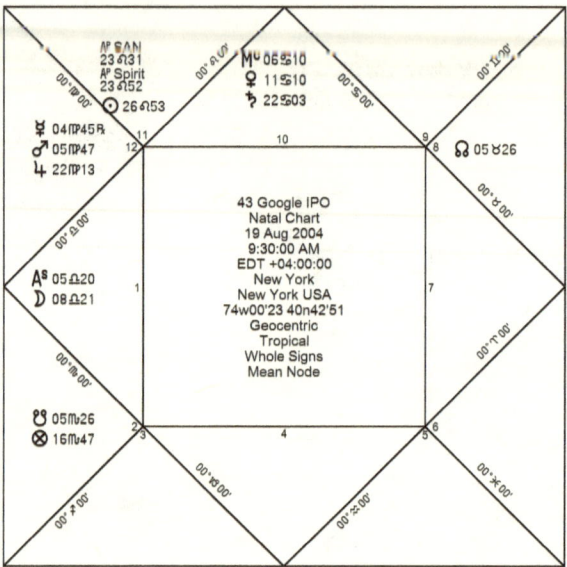

Wikipedia defines big data as 'a field that treats ways to analyze, systematically extract information from, or otherwise deal with data sets that are too large or complex to be dealt with by traditional data-processing application software.'[27] If Jupiter + Virgo = "Big Data" and Mars + Virgo = "Mining Data" then Google is connected to both Jupiter/Virgo and Mars/Virgo distributions with both planet/sign combinations recapitulated in its 2004 IPO horoscope (shown above) as well as its reorganization under the Alphabet umbrella on *October 2, 2015* (untimed, not shown).

Two months before the official Ascendant distributor changeover, the NYT declared the arrival of big data with a feature story "The Age of Big Data" on *February 11, 2012*.[28] Googletrends, itself a big data analysis tool, scores the search term 'big data' the highest for the month of *October 2014* two years into the distribution. In the final month of the distribution, Googletrends 'big data' ranking dropped by 30% from its peak.

Mars/Virgo also has a military theme. On *April 26, 2017* just one day before the close of the distribution, the Pentagon established Project Maven, a battlefield artificial intelligence application. Google briefly partnered with the Defense department on Project Maven before Google withdrew its participation in June 2018 after employee protests and resignations.

APPENDIX C - SUPPLEMENT: DIRECTING THROUGH THE BOUNDS

Mars/Virgo ~ April 28, 2017 – January 30, 2026

Peloton IPO ~ Metrics of Fitness Training

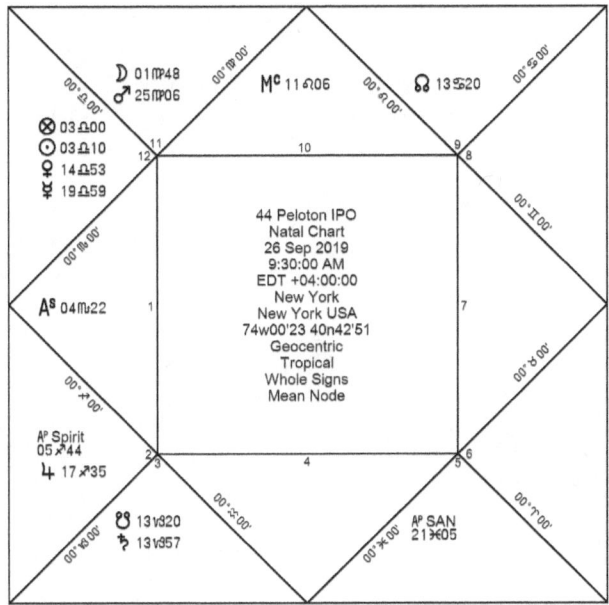

Other than a select number of nationwide equipment manufacturers which supply the fitness industry with machines which power workouts, the American fitness industry is widely decentralized with most gyms locally owned. Peloton is an example of one such nationwide equipment manufacturer which successfully targets at-home fitness users with high-end spin cycles complete with audiovisual linkups to group workouts and biometric data for tracking fitness performance. Its IPO was launched a few months before the 2020 COVID pandemic outbreak with Peloton stock a Wall Street favorite during the *2020* lockdowns. From its IPO price of $27, the stock soared to a high of $166.10 on *January 14, 2021*. The Peloton IPO horoscope recapitulates the Mars/Virgo plant/sign combination of the Ascendant distributor. Note that Mars is also placed in his own bound (between 17VI00 and 20VI59) which accentuates the Mars/Virgo theme.

With Mars/Virgo a universal significator for physical exercise, it has been interesting to witness the exercise theme manifest through in-home workouts even as the gym industry faced substantial financial losses and bankruptcies during the pandemic. Still exercise, just not at the local gym.

APPENDIX D

Tests of Egyptian versus Ptolemaic Bounds

Historically there has been a debate over competing sets of bounds with Egyptian and Ptolemaic bounds the most often cited. The majority of medieval astrologers used the Egyptian system, but William Lilly's (1602-1681) usage of Ptolemaic bounds has spawned a strong following among modern day horary practitioners who use Lilly's *Christian Astrology* as a primary sourcebook.

Directing through the Bounds. In *ARM*, I suggested two methods for evaluating competing sets of bounds.[1] In the first recommended test, Directing through the Bounds is applied to natal significators for both sets of bounds. Next, both Distributor chronologies are compared to natal events. The set of bounds which yields the best fit chronology to life events is selected the winner. In ARM, I computed the directed Midheaven for Theodore Roosevelt under both systems and concluded that the Egyptian system for the bounds of Mars/Aries and Saturn/Aries was a better fit to Roosevelt's renewed career as a politico (Mars/Aries) and difficulties he faced from Woodrow Wilson who denied his request to form and lead a military contingent in France during World War I (Saturn/Aries).

Placement of Luminaries. The second recommended test is based on the assumption the bound imparts its own characteristics to any planet, cusp, or part placed in its degree range. With surviving aphorisms which support this style of analysis applied to the luminaries, I suggested studying the effects of both sets of bounds on the Sun and Moon. Because the Sun and Moon often signify the native's father and mother, a qualitative assessment of which bound placement most closely matches affairs of the father or mother is one method of testing the impact of bound placement for the relevant luminary. Another is assessment of the nature of events timed dynamically by directions of luminaries to the angles. The bound which best matches the specifics of the event wins. In ARM, I compared six placements of the Moon in Capricorn and concluded that Egyptian bounds were correct.

Both tests presented in *ARM* confirmed the validity of Egyptian bounds, a choice consistent with my teacher Robert Zoller. With the obvious limitations of a small sample, I cited the need for further testing on a much wider sample.

Regulus USA National Horoscope - Directing through the Bounds

What follows are results of applying the first recommended test to the Ascendant of the Regulus USA National Horoscope. As stated in Chapter 6, what follows is the largest known empirical test of bounds using this procedure ever attempted or presented.

Analysis presented in this Appendix culls data from both Chapter 6 and Appendix C in order to take a closer look at changeovers between individual bounds within a single sign. For the forty-two bounds tested ranging from Mercury/Capricorn to Venus/Virgo, I was able to identify events for the majority of changeovers which are consistent with Egyptian bounds.

Pisces is an exception. While both systems position planets in the same order within Pisces, changeovers are different. In some cases, I identified changeovers more consistent with Ptolemy's system. These exceptions must be treated cautiously because they may not be repeated in other samples. Keeping in mind that Egyptian bounds are designed so the sum of each planet's degrees across all signs equal the planet's major years, should these exceptions in Pisces be borne out, adjustments in other signs will be required to balance out any discrepancies within Pisces.

Given their consistency across Capricorn, Aquarius, Aries, Taurus, Gemini, Cancer, Leo, and early Virgo, I loathe tinkering with Egyptian bounds. Yet I must be faithful to research findings of this project. More research will be required to definitively settle this debate, though it appears likely that Egyptian bounds, or a slightly modified version of them, are the correct system of bounds to use.

APPENDIX D - TESTS OF EGYPTIAN VS PTOLEMAIC BOUNDS

Table 9. Comparison of Egyptian vs. Ptolemaic Bounds

♈-Egyptian	0–Jupiter	6–Venus	12–Mercury	20–Mars	25-Saturn
♈-Ptolemy	0–Jupiter	6–Venus	14–Mercury	21–Mars	26-Saturn
♉-Egyptian	0-Venus	8-Mercury	14-Jupiter	22-Saturn	27-Mars
♉-Ptolemy	0-Venus	8-Mercury	15-Jupiter	22-Saturn	26-Mars
♊-Egyptian	0-Mercury	6-Jupiter	12-Venus	17-Mars	24-Saturn
♊-Ptolemy	0-Mercury	7-Jupiter	13-Venus	21-Mars	25-Saturn
♋-Egyptian	0-Mars	7-Venus	13-Mercury	19-Jupiter	26-Saturn
♋-Ptolemy	0-Mars	6-Jupiter	13-Mercury	20-Venus	27-Saturn
♌-Egyptian	0-Jupiter	6-Venus	11-Saturn	18-Mercury	24-Mars
♌-Ptolemy	0-Saturn	6-Mercury	13-Venus	19-Jupiter	25-Mars
♍-Egyptian	0-Mercury	7-Venus	17-Jupiter	21-Mars	28-Saturn
♍-Ptolemy	0-Mercury	7-Venus	13-Jupiter	18-Saturn	24-Mars
♎-Egyptian	0-Saturn	6-Mercury	14-Jupiter	21-Venus	28-Mars
♎-Ptolemy	0-Saturn	6-Venus	11-Jupiter	19-Mercury	24-Mars
♏-Egyptian	0-Mars	7-Venus	11-Mercury	19-Jupiter	24-Saturn
♏-Ptolemy	0-Mars	6-Jupiter	14-Venus	21-Mercury	27-Saturn
♐-Egyptian	0-Jupiter	12-Venus	17-Mercury	21-Saturn	26-Mars
♐-Ptolemy	0-Jupiter	8-Venus	14-Mercury	19-Saturn	25-Mars
♑-Egyptian	0-Mercury	7-Jupiter	14-Venus	22-Saturn	26-Mars
♑-Ptolemy	0-Venus	6-Mercury	12-Jupiter	19-Mars	25-Saturn
♒-Egyptian	0-Mercury	7-Venus	13-Jupiter	20-Mars	25-Saturn
♒-Ptolemy	0-Saturn	6-Mercury	12-Venus	20-Jupiter	25-Mars
♓-Egyptian	0-Venus	12-Jupiter	16-Mercury	19-Mars	28-Saturn
♓-Ptolemy	0-Venus	8-Jupiter	14-Mercury	20-Mars	26-Saturn

How to read:

Each zodiacal sign of 30 degrees is subdivided into five unequal divisions. Each division is known as a 'bound.' Examining Egyptian bounds for the sign of Aries, see the first 6 degrees assigned to Jupiter; next 6, Venus; next 8, Mercury; next 5, Mars; last 5, Saturn.

In speaking about bounds, say that the first six degrees are Aries are the 'bound of Jupiter in Aries' and that any planet, point, or aspect falling in the first six degrees of Aries 'falls in' or 'lies in' the bound of Jupiter in Aries.

CAPRICORN

	Egyptian		Ptolemaic
4-Jul-1776	ASCENDANT	4-Jul-1776	ASCENDANT
30-Nov-1779	0CP-Mercury	30-Nov-1779	0CP-Venus
5-May-1787	7CP-Jupiter	21 Apr 1786	6CP-Mercury
4-May-1794	14CP-Venus	20-May-1792	12CP-Jupiter
19-Oct-1801	22CP-Saturn	25-Jan-1799	19CP-Mars
26-Apr-1805	26CP-Mars	13-Jun-1804	25CP-Saturn

For Capricorn, there are substantial differences between Egyptian and Ptolemaic bounds. The key delineation step required to unlock the true character of these bounds is to assign Capricorn to pro-Federalist factions because Capricorn's trait of accumulated wealth matches Federalist objectives espoused during the Federalist Era (1789-1801).

Mercury/Capricorn

- Egyptian bounds assign Mercury to the first degrees of Capricorn; Ptolemy assigns Venus. Noah Webster's grammar books, published 1783-1785, favor Egyptian bounds for their delineation match to Mercury/Capricorn as a methodical system of learning.

- <u>Changeover Event</u>. Jefferson's reorganization of William & Mary in 1779 (no exact date found) included formation of America's first Law School. Installed as the first law chair, Wythe appears to be a textbook Mercury/Capricorn personality.

Jupiter/Capricorn

- For the late 1780s and early 1790s, the Egyptian system assigns Jupiter/Capricorn as Distributor; the Ptolemaic system, Mercury/Capricorn. This time period features establishment of the United States Constitution, the tripartite system of government, and Alexander Hamilton's financial system. Though delineation of Mercury/Capricorn as a written document designed to establish central control is a possible match to the Constitution, I suggest the Constitution's philosophy embodies something on a larger scale (Jupiter) than a Federalist edict (Mercury).

- <u>Changeover Event</u>. James Madison's arrival in Philadelphia on *May 3, 1787* (-2 days) for the Constitutional Convention which opened *May 25, 1787* (+20 days) is a match to the start of Jupiter/Capricorn Distribution.

APPENDIX D - TESTS OF EGYPTIAN VS PTOLEMAIC BOUNDS

Venus/Capricorn

- Since Venus and Mars are enemies, the key to confirming Venus as the active bound in the late 1780s is to contrast events which occur during Distributions of Venus and Mars. Delineating Venus/Capricorn as a trade treaty with England which allowed Federalists to gain from war profiteering is a match to the Venus Distribution under the Egyptian system. This contrasts with Jefferson's 1807 Embargo Act which effectively shuttered trade with Britain. Under the Venus Distribution, Federalists gained financially; under Mars, they suffered.

- <u>Changeover Event</u>: President George Washington's appointment of John Jay to England on *April 16, 1794* (-18 days), James Monroe to France on *May 27, 1794* (+23 days), and John Quincy Adams to the Netherlands on *May 27, 1794* (+23 days) flank the May 4, 1794 changeover.

Saturn/Capricorn

- The Egyptian system places Saturn before Mars; Ptolemy reverses the order. Placed in the sign he rules, Saturn/Capricorn likes to build walls in order to maintain social status. These may be legal measures or strategies designed to maintain accumulated wealth through conservative investments (usually bonds). Known for its legal measures taken to secure the Court's independence through judicial review, the rise of the Marshall Court in 1801 favors Saturn's placement in the Egyptian system.

- <u>Changeover Event</u>. Convening of John Marshall's Supreme Court on *August 4, 1801* (-76 days) is a delineation match to Saturn/Capricorn, a planet/sign combination recapitulated in Marshall's own natal figure.

Mars/Capricorn

- As stated above, because Mars and Venus are enemies, the Mars/Capricorn Distribution yields events opposed to the objectives of Venus/Capricorn. Jefferson's Embargo Acts drove Federalist New England into a recession as Federalist gains from war profiteering under Venus/Capricorn were reversed.

- <u>Changeover Event</u>. Commencement of the Battle of Derne on *April 27, 1805* (+1 day) is a precise match. Victory of American Marines in this battle is a delineation match to the warrior Mars in the sign of Capricorn where he is exalted.

AQUARIUS

	Egyptian		Ptolemaic
12-Sep-1808	0AQ-Mercury	12-Sep-1808	0AQ-Saturn
24-Apr-1814	7AQ-Venus	13-Jul-1813	6AQ-Mercury
1-Nov-1818	13AQ-Jupiter	5 Feb 1818	12AQ-Venus
26-Oct-1823	20AQ-Mars	26-Oct-1823	20AQ-Jupiter
18-Mar-1827	25AQ-Saturn	18-Mar-1827	25AQ-Mars

Substantial differences exist between bound systems for the sign of Aquarius. Just as understanding the enmity between Venus and Mars was helpful in deciphering the correct bound system for Capricorn, the same principle applies to Aquarius. Delineation of Venus/Aquarius as pleasant social intercourse and Mars/Aquarius as partisan politics is born out through actions of the directed Ascendant in the Egyptian bound system.

Mercury/Aquarius

- For Egyptian bounds, Mercury is assigned to the first seven degrees of Aquarius; for Ptolemy's bounds, Saturn to the first six degrees. Delineation of Mercury/Aquarius as maritime law matches the nation's concern over impressments and cargo seizures during the first phase of the War of 1812. It is also consistent with codification of laws which matches production of the *American Law Journal*.

- Changeover Event: John Elihu Hall produced the first issue of his *American Law Journal* during ***January 1808*** (-8 months).

- Culminating Event: Repeal of all embargo and non-importation laws on ***April 14, 1814*** (-10 days) signaled the end of fair maritime law as an American priority during the War of 1812.

Venus/Aquarius

- Venus/Aquarius is consistent with pleasant social intercourse embodied in the moniker 'The Era of Good Feelings' coined on July 12, 1817. Venus/Aquarius is also consistent with John Calhoun's February 4, 1817 speech in favor of the Bonus Bill for funding internal improvements, timed by Venus/Aquarius in Calhoun's active solar return.

- No specific changeover events were identified for Venus/Aquarius. As plugs, see the culminating event for the prior Mercury/Aquarius Distribution and the changeover event which kicks off the subsequent Jupiter/Aquarius Distribution as indirect support for the bound of Venus.

Jupiter/Aquarius

- Constructed over the period from July 4, 1817 to October 26, 1825, the bulk of the Erie Canal was completed during the Jupiter/Aquarius Distribution. Judicial and magnate support for internal improvements confirm Jupiter, not Venus, as the correct bound from 1818 to the early 1820s.

- Changeover Event. Canvass White's limestone discovery and demonstration of hydraulic cement in *1818* (+/- ??) was a pivotal event which sped the construction of the Erie Canal. I was unable to document the exact date of White's demonstration at Elisha Carey's barroom.

Mars/Aquarius

- With the rise of partisan politics and anti-intellectualism, the 'Era of Good Feelings' during James Monroe's early administration came to an end under the Mars/Aquarius Distribution. Partisan politics which gave rise to Andrew Jackson during the mid-1820s confirms Mars, not Jupiter, as the correct bound.

- Changeover Events. William Crawford's *September 1823* stroke (-1 month) is a match. His unwillingness to drop out of the race after his stroke was a contributing factor to the resurgence of partisan politics leading up to the disputed 1824 Presidential election. Publication of John Henry Eaton's *The Letters of Wyoming* in *1823* is another probable changeover match (exact publication date not found).[2]

Saturn/Aquarius

- Saturn is assigned to the final degrees of Aquarius using Egyptian bounds; Ptolemy assigns Saturn to the first degrees. Combined with the sign of fixed knowledge, Saturn in Aquarius is the pre-eminent placement for science and engineering. Rise of the Lyceum and Abolition movements during the late 1820s is another delineation match to Saturn/Aquarius as Distributor, not the partisan Mars/Aquarius.

- Changeover Events. President John Quincy Adams' order to close ports to British goods on *March 17, 1827* (-1 day) is a delineation match to closure (Saturn) of ports (a type of 'waterworks' signified by Aquarius). Launch of *Freedom's Journal*, the first African American newspaper, on *March 16, 1827* (-2 days) is a delineation match to black (Saturn) equality (Aquarius). Finally, the Lyceum Movement launched their first cooperative in *early 1827*.

PISCES

	Egyptian		Ptolemaic
25-Jun-1830	0PI-Venus	25-Jun-1830	0PI-Venus
14-Dec-1837	12PI-Jupiter	6-Jul-1835	8PI-Jupiter
9-May-1840	16PI-Mercury	27-Feb-1839	14PI-Mercury
19-Feb-1842	19PI-Mars	23-Sep-1842	20PI-Mars
2-Jun-1847	28PI-Saturn	1-Apr-1846	26PI-Saturn

For the sign of Pisces, there is no difference between the order of planets for both Egyptian and Ptolemaic systems. However the changeovers vary and findings suggest discrepancies for bounds as defined by the Egyptian system. As stated in the opening pages of this Appendix, given the consistency of Egyptian bounds in other signs, these results must be treated cautiously. Further research is required to assess these differences.

Venus/Pisces

- Both systems begin with Venus/Pisces which is consistent with the import of European romanticism to America through landscape painters of the Hudson River School founded by Thomas Cole.

- Culminating Event. Romanticism of the Hudson River School culminated with Thomas Cole's series *The Course of Empire* in the spring of 1836 which were shown to the public during October 1836. This corresponds to the start of Jupiter/Pisces on September 26, 1836 calculated as 10 Pisces. This raises the question whether the bound of Venus/Pisces extends beyond 8 degrees of Pisces in the Egyptian system.

Jupiter/Pisces

- Delineated as maritime expeditions, Jupiter/Pisces is a match to the United States Exploring Expedition. Given the association between the symbol of Pisces and Christianity[3], studying the impact of Christianity on the temperance movement of the early 19th century may be helpful in gaining additional insight for the Jupiter/Pisces Distribution.

- Changeover Event. Congressional approval of the U.S. Exploring Expedition on May 18, 1836 and Charles Wilkes' trip to Europe for the purpose of acquiring equipment in the fall of 1836 suggest the bound of Jupiter/Pisces begins slightly earlier than 12 Pisces as specified by the Egyptian system whose changeover is December 14, 1837.

- Culminating Event. Between December 1838 and January 1839, Charles Wilkes likely suffered a nervous breakdown.[4] If true, Wilkes' problems are consistent with the changeover to Mercury/Pisces on February 27, 1839 calculated under Ptolemy's system. His expedition started to have problems with the loss of the USS Sea Gull in May 1839. As another tragedy, two members of his crew were killed by natives in July 1840.

Mercury/Pisces

- Debut of the comedic talents of Master Juba in the spring of 1841 is consistent with both Egyptian and Ptolemaic systems. Not surprising, Mercury placed in the sign of his fall means that written records for the Mercury/Pisces Distribution have proven difficult to locate.

Mars/Pisces

- Delineation of Mars/Pisces as whaling is key step required to unlock the final two changeovers in Pisces. Because Mars and Saturn are inimical, Mars assists and Saturn inhibits whaling operations.

- Changeover Event. Here the debate is whether the changeover to Mars/Pisces occurs on February 19, 1842 (Egyptian) or September 23, 1842 (Ptolemy). Peter Ewer's September 21, 1842 successful test of pontoon camels designed to facilitate the offloading of returning whale ships to Nantucket's harbor matches Ptolemy's bounds. The significance of this event in the annals of the whaling industry needs further vetting.

Saturn/Pisces

- Besides a planet/sign combination which is inimical to whaling, Saturn/Pisces can also be delineated as control (Saturn) of a river (Pisces).

- Changeover Event. Does the Saturn/Pisces changeover occur on June 2, 1847 (Egyptian) or April 1, 1846 (Ptolemy)? Arrival of General Taylor's troops to the Rio Grande on March 24, 1846 suggests the accuracy of Ptolemy's system. Given President Polk's desire to protect American interests by sealing off the northern Mexico border (see Chapter 6), Taylor's arrival to the Rio Grande is an excellent fit to Saturn/Pisces delineated as 'control of a river'. In addition, two events inimical to whaling occur shortly after the April 1, 1846 changeover computed using Ptolemy's bounds. First is the capture and interrogation of survivors of the whale ship *Lawrence* in May 1846 by the Japanese. This was an international incident which was a precursor event for Commodore Perry's later 1853 Japanese Expedition.[5] Second is Nantucket's July 13, 1846 fire which destroyed their land-based whaling infrastructure.

ARIES

	Egyptian		Ptolemaic
2-Aug-1848	0AR-Jupiter	2-Aug-1848	0AR-Jupiter
3-Feb-1852	6AR-Venus	3-Feb-1852	6AR-Venus
18-Aug-1855	12AR-Mercury	25-Oct-1856	14AR-Mercury
7-Jun-1860	20AR-Mars	17-Jan-1861	21AR-Mars
9-Jul-1863	25AR-Saturn	23-Feb-1864	26AR-Saturn

For the sign of Aries, planets follow the same order. Only changeovers for Mercury, Mars, and Saturn vary.

Jupiter/Aries

- Changeover Event. There is no difference between both systems for the bound of Jupiter. The *New York Herald's* publication of the gold discovery at Sutter's Mill on **August 19, 1848** (+17 days) was the first major East Coast news media to publicize what would become the California Gold Rush. Delineated as a warlike (Mars) philosophy (Jupiter), the westward migration of Americans triggered conflict with Indians from whom Americans no longer shirked engagement. In the same year as the 1848 European revolutions, the changeover also gave an increased voice to the Young America Movement; whose leader John L. O'Sullivan penned an *August 1848* editorial calling for Americans to send arms and troops to Europe in support of America's Manifest Destiny.[6]

Venus/Aries

- Changeover Event. Publication of Uncle Tom's Cabin on **March 20, 1852** (+47 days) followed the Venus/Aries changeover by seven weeks. The book's depiction of sadistic treatment of slaves further inflamed the nation on the topic of slavery. Sadism, or the love (Venus) of fighting (Aries) is a delineation match.

- Culminating Event. At issue is whether the bound of Venus/Aries extends to 12 degrees (Egyptian) or 14 degrees (Ptolemy). Publication of *Leaves of Grass* on July 4, 1844 is the logical changeover event to Mercury/Aries (see next section) and supports the Egyptian bound default.

Mercury/Aries

- At its simplest, Mercury/Aries signifies writing about war which is epitomized in the poetry of Walt Whitman. Mercury/Aries also signifies legal disputes and is consistent with the Kansas Constitutional Crisis.

- Changeover Events. Walt Whitman published the first edition of *Leaves of Grass* on ***July 4, 1855*** (-45 days). The Topeka Constitutional Convention held ***October 1855*** (+ 2 months) was the first attempt to establish a Kansas State Constitution. Approved by Free-State voters on December 15, 1855, the Topeka Constitution triggered a Constitutional crisis as pro- and anti-slavery forces held a series of competing Conventions in order to impose their slavery views on Kansas as a whole.

- Culminating Event. Walt Whitman's publisher informed him that the first printing of his third edition of *Leaves of Grass* had sold out on ***June 14, 1860*** (+7 days) and that a second printing was ready for binding.

Mars/Aries

- Mars is assigned five degrees in both systems. The period corresponding to Mars/Aries using Egyptian bounds covers 1860-1863; Ptolemy's system covers the slightly later period 1861-1864. Mars in the sign of his rulership signifies offensive warfare.

- Changeover Event. As detailed in Chapter 2, Lincoln's ***May 18, 1860*** (-20 days) Presidential Nomination is the proposed changeover event because his nomination crystallized the South's growing antagonism towards the North. Many in the South indicated Lincoln's election would force them to secede from the Union, an action first taken by South Carolina on December 20, 1860. (See Chapter 2 for further discussion).

Saturn/Aries

- Both systems assign Saturn to the final degrees of Aries; the last five degrees using Egyptian bounds; the last four using Ptolemy's system.

- Changeover Event. The changeover from Mars to Saturn is best delineated as protests against the Union Draft which broke out in New York City on ***July 13, 1863*** (+4 days). The New York Draft Riots are a delineation match to Saturn/Aries as the frustration against fighting. Saturn/Aries also matches the conduct of the Civil War following Gettysburg. Increased use of siege tactics matches the delineation of Saturn/Aries as guerilla warfare. (See Chapter 2 for further discussion).

TAURUS

	Egyptian		Ptolemaic
9-Sep-1866	0TA-Venus	9-Sep-1866	0TA-Venus
25-Dec-1871	8TA-Mercury	25-Dec-1871	8TA-Mercury
1-Mar-1876	14TA-Jupiter	18-Nov-1876	15TA-Jupiter
2-Feb-1882	22TA-Saturn	2-Feb-1882	22TA-Saturn
8-Jan-1886	27TA-Mars	21-Mar-1885	26TA-Mars

Planets occupy the same order for the sign of Taurus. Only changeovers for Jupiter, Saturn, and Mars vary.

Venus/Taurus

- There is no difference on the definition of the bound of Venus/Taurus.

- <u>Changeover Event</u>: Operatic debut of Minnie Hauk, America's first international opera superstar, on *October 13, 1866* (+34 days) is a match to delineation of Venus/Taurus as vocal (Taurus) music (Venus).

Mercury/Taurus

- Both systems assign the start of Mercury's bound to 8 Taurus. They differ on the whether the bound extends to 14 Taurus (Egyptian) or 15 Taurus (Ptolemy).

- <u>Changeover event</u>: Formation of Drexel, Morgan & Co. on *July 1, 1871* (-177 days) established J. P. Morgan's own business organization distinct from operations of his father Junius.[7] A reasonable argument can be made to date the modern Morgan banking dynasty from this event. As further evidence of the Mundane-Natal Horoscope Connection, J. P. Morgan recapitulates the Distributor with Mercury/Taurus in his own natal figure. Mercury/Taurus signifies the business (Mercury) of money (Taurus).

Jupiter/Taurus

- The bound of Jupiter/Taurus begins as early as March 1, 1876 (Egyptian) or as late as November 18, 1876 (Ptolemaic).

- <u>Changeover Event</u>. Continuing to follow changes in the Morgan banking family, in the fall of 1875 partner Joseph Drexel retired. Drexel was replaced with Egisto P. Fabbri on January 1, 1876. Biographer Strouse suggests Fabbri and other Morgan associates revealed a growing strength of J. P. Morgan's inner circle.[8] This is the kind of improvement we should expect to see for the banking industry as the Distributor changes from Mercury to Jupiter the greater benefic.

Saturn/Taurus

- Both systems assign the beginning of Saturn's bound to 22 Taurus and differ only on the extent of Saturn's rulership to 26 Taurus (Ptolemy) or to 27 Taurus (Egyptian).

- <u>Changeover Event</u>. The invention of refrigerated rail cars by Gustavus Swift and his 1880 formation of the Swift Refrigerator Line was a critical step in the evolution of the Chicago Meatpacking District. From 2,622 in *1882*, the number of Refrigerator Cars rose to 69,769 by 1886.[9] The combination of Saturn (cold/dry) and Taurus (beef) is a delineation match to the use of refrigerated rail cars as a method to preserve meat. Preservation and storage are saturnine methods.

Mars/Taurus

- Protests (Mars) against Capitalists (Taurus) match the zeitgeist of the era labor historians now refer to as 'The Great Upheaval' defined as the period from September 1885 to September 1888.[10] It included the famous Haymarket Riot of May 4, 1886.

- <u>Changeover Event</u>. Does Mars/Taurus take over from Saturn/Taurus on January 8, 1886 (Egyptian) or as early as March 21, 1885 (Ptolemy)? A membership surge in the Knights of Labor beginning in November 1885 which required the Knights to establish a new headquarters in *late December 1885* (-1 month) favors the January 8, 1886 changeover computed using Egyptian bounds.[11]

GEMINI

	Egyptian		Ptolemaic
21-Jun-1888	0GE-Mercury	21-Jun-1888	0GE-Mercury
6-Aug-1893	6GE-Jupiter	24-Jun-1894	7GE-Jupiter
12-Jan-1899	12GE-Venus	20-Dec-1899	13GE-Venus
23-Oct-1903	17GE-Mars	16-Oct-1907	21GE-Saturn
14-Nov-1910	24GE-Saturn	30-Nov-1911	25GE-Mars

In addition to the reversal of the order for Mars and Saturn, slightly different changeovers for Jupiter and Venus distinguish Egyptian and Ptolemaic bound systems.

Mercury/Gemini

- Company development of calculators and punch card systems whose fortunes would eventually lead to the Burroughs and IBM Corporations are consistent with Mercury/Gemini delineated as office automation.

- <u>Changeover Events</u>. Patents granted for the Burroughs Calculating Machine on **August 21, 1888** (+61 days) and the Hollerith Tabulating Machine on **January 8, 1889** (+201 days) matches the delineation of Mercury/Gemini as organizing bits of information through office automation.

Jupiter/Gemini

- <u>Changeover Events</u>. Alexander Graham Bell's patent expirations on **March 7, 1893** (-152 days) and **January 30, 1894** (+177 days) straddle the August 6, 1893 changeover from Mercury to Jupiter for Egyptian bounds. Bell's patent expirations created an explosion of telephone service as thousands of new telephone companies entered the market. Both of these patent expirations preceded the suggested changeover from Mercury to Jupiter on June 24, 1894 under Ptolemy's system.

Venus/Gemini

- Founding of the 5 and 10 cent store S. S. Kresge (later renamed K-Mart), rapid growth of Woolworth's, and formation of the Victor Talking Machine Company (1901) are all consistent with Venus/Gemini delineated as the 'love of talk' and rapid transaction turnover.

- Changeover Events. S. S. Kresge's formation of his retailing company during 1899 (no exact date found) is consistent with the start of Venus/Gemini under both systems.

Mars/Gemini and Saturn/Gemini

- In the last degrees of Gemini, Mars precedes Saturn in the Egyptian system; Ptolemy reverses the order. The rise of the muckraker movement, reckless risk taking culminating with the Panic of 1907, and *The Great Auto Race of 1908* are consistent with the speed and lawlessness of Mars/Gemini. Increased business regulation, including the famous order to break up the Standard Oil monopoly on May 15, 1911 matches the investigative and regulatory nature of Saturn/Gemini. This event sequence which identifies lawlessness prior to regulation is a delineation match to Mars preceding Saturn in the Egyptian bound system.

- Changeover Event for Mars/Gemini. The *January 1903* (-9 months) issue of *McClure's Magazine* inaugurated the Muckraker Era. A review of Standard Oil's operations may yield another event which more closely times the changeover.

- Changeover Event for Saturn/Gemini. The *November 10, 1910* (-4 days) decision of Louis Brandeis to invoke *Scientific Management* in support of his veto of railroad price increases launched Frederick Winslow Taylor to national fame. Taylor invented the concept of *Scientific Management* and as the father of this field is still studied and revered in academic business circles to the present day. Assigning Taylor to the Saturn/Gemini Distribution using Egyptian bounds is supported by the recapitulation of Saturn/Gemini in Taylor's own natal figure.

CANCER

	Egyptian		Ptolemaic
5-Apr-1917	0CA-Mars	5-Apr-1917	0CA-Mars
30-Jan-1925	7CA-Venus	11-Dec-1923	6CA-Jupiter
23-Jan-1932	13CA-Mercury	23-Jan-1932	13CA-Mercury
4-Apr-1939	19CA-Jupiter	21-Jun-1940	20CA-Venus
9-Nov-1947	26CA-Saturn	5-Feb-1949	27CA-Saturn

Mars/Cancer

- Both systems assign Mars to the first degrees of Cancer. Influence of KKK on the 1924 Democratic National Convention, nicknamed the 'Klanbake Convention' for the KKK's ability to jettison Catholic candidate Al Smith from the Democratic ticket suggest continued influence of the bound of Mars/Cancer well past the December 11, 1923 ending date computed under Ptolemy's system.

- Changeover Events. American isolationism of the 1920s can be traced to Woodrow Wilson's *April 2, 1917* war message (-3 days) as the nation quietly rebelled against a President who had won re-election six months previously on an anti-war platform. Most precise is the *April 5, 1917* (exact date) meeting of the Anti-Saloon League of America[12] when General Superintendent Purley Albert Baker recommended closing a perceived loophole in the proposed constitutional amendment for prohibition.[13]

- Culminating Event. Indiana Grand Dragon D. C. Stephenson's rape and mutilation of Madge Oberholtzer on *March 15, 1925* (+44 days) precipitated a nationwide collapse in KKK membership.

Venus/Cancer

- The 'Roaring 1920s' was known for the rise of consumerism and is a better delineation match to Venus/Cancer, signifier of consumer goods, than Jupiter/Cancer which is associated with farming and real estate.

- Changeover Events. Though no specific events were uncovered, a report that America led the globe in annual consumption of cotton at thirty pounds per capita on *January 21, 1925* (-9 days) is indicative of high demand consistent with Venus/Cancer delineated as consumer products.[14]

Mercury/Cancer

- The debate is whether Mercury's bound extends to April 4, 1939 (Egyptian) or June 21, 1940 (Ptolemy). Given the importance of demagogues Huey Long and Charles Coughlin to the Mercury/Cancer era, the coincidence of Huey Long's September 8, 1935 assassination and Charles Coughlin's break with FDR on September 10, 1935 (the same day Huey Long died) offers an important clue. A chart cast for Long's assassination on September 8, 1935, Baton Rouge, LA, 9:20 PM CST features the South Node positioned at 18CA56. September 8 was the very day the transiting South Node made its ingress to the bound of Mercury/Cancer using Egyptian bounds.[15] I suggest this event confirms the extension of the bound of Mercury/Cancer to 18CA59'59" because not until the South Node crossed the 19CA00'00" barrier did Long die.

- Changeover Events. Franklin Roosevelt's attempt to appease William Randolph Hearst on *February 2, 1932* (+10 days) is a reasonable changeover event because Hearst's association with sensationalism journalism matches the propensity of Mercury/Cancer for propaganda.[16]

Jupiter/Cancer

- For the early 1940s, Jupiter/Cancer (Egyptian) competes with Venus/Cancer (Ptolemy). The exaltation of farming epitomized by the popularity of Agriculture Secretary Henry Wallace favors Jupiter/Cancer.

- Changeover Events. Congressional support for farm programs and Wallace on *April 1, 1939* (-3 days), Wallace's public relations campaign on farm programs publicized by the NYT on *April 2, 1939* (-2 days), and the launch of Food Stamps on *May 16, 1939* (+42 days) confirm the changeover.

- Culminating Event. Wallace's *December 2, 1947* (+24 days) Presidential nomination by the Progressive Citizens of America Party marked Wallace's high water mark of political influence.

Saturn/Cancer

- Saturn is assigned to the final degrees of Cancer under both systems but begins sooner in the Egyptian system.

- Changeover Event. The Hollywood blacklist issued on *November 25, 1947* (+17 days) is a delineation match to Saturn/Cancer as a witch-hunts taken against the populace.

LEO

	Egyptian		Ptolemaic
5-Nov-1952	0LE-Jupiter	5-Nov-1952	0LE-Saturn
27-May-1960	6LE-Venus	27-May-1960	6LE-Mercury
28-Sep-1966	11LE-Saturn	13-Apr-1969	13LE-Venus
22-Aug-1975	18LE-Mercury	29-Nov-1976	19LE-Jupiter
9-Apr-1983	24LE-Mars	15-Jul-1984	25LE-Mars

Jupiter/Leo

- Under Ptolemy's bounds, Saturn/Leo is assigned to 1952-1960 which coincides with Eisenhower's two Presidential terms. Delineation of Saturn/Leo as a totalitarian leadership style which stifles dissent is a mismatch to the 1950s which is remembered as an era of social conformity. It is true that totalitarianism can produce conformity. But as I argue in Chapter 6, the 1950s era of social conformity appears the result of a 'carrot' approach led by Jupiter/Leo delineated as state-supported religion. The addition of 'Under God' to the Pledge of Allegiance, the addition of 'In God We Trust' to paper currency, growth in Catholic School enrollment, growth of God and Country awards in the Boy Scouts, and the popularity of Catholic priest Fulton Sheen suggest the overriding importance of Christianity to the national consciousness.

- <u>Changeover Events</u>. Resolutions by the Catholic service organization The Knights of Columbus made on *August 21, 1952* (-76 days) and *September 24, 1952* (-37 days) in favor of adding the phrase 'under God' to the Pledge of Allegiance are precursor events which triggered the national movement for modification of the Pledge of Allegiance.

Venus/Leo

- Venus (Egyptian) and Mercury (Ptolemy) compete as Ascendant Distributors in the early 1960s. Delineation of Venus/Leo as cocktail culture, love of gold, love of French culture, and the love of Kings is more accurate match to the era's penchant for James Bond's film success in *Goldfinger* ("shaken not stirred"), Jackie Kennedy's adoption of French fashion and cuisine, launch of Julia Child's French cooking television series, and the Kennedy Camelot Era.

- <u>Changeover Events</u>. Filming of the Rat Pack film Ocean's 11 during the Sands Summit (*January 26 to February 16, 1960*) (-101 days) and the film's *August 10, 1960* (+75 days) premiere straddle the start of the Venus/Leo Distribution. John F. Kennedy's *July 13, 1960* (+47 days)

Presidential nomination as a significator of the Camelot Era is more precise in marking the changeover.

- Culminating Events. The Rat Pack's final movie *Texas Across the River* premiered on ***October 26, 1966*** (+28 days).

Saturn/Leo

- The difference between Saturn/Leo (Egyptian) and Venus/Leo (Ptolemy) bounds is stark. Delineation of Saturn/Leo as the Black (Saturn) Panther (Leo/lion family) Party is one of the most straightforward matches for the keyword method of delineation.

- Changeover Events. The LSD crackdown, made illegal on ***October 6, 1966*** (+8 days), and the founding of the Black Panther Party on ***October 15, 1966*** (+17 days) mark the onset of an authoritarian government and a rebellious citizenry.

Mercury/Leo

- Mercury/Leo (Egyptian) is favored over Jupiter/Leo (Ptolemaic) for its delineation match to blockbuster entertainment and the 'feel-good' *Rocky* film franchise created by Sylvester Stallone.

- Changeover Events. Debut of the film *Jaws* on ***June 20, 1975*** (-63 days) and Sylvester Stallone's completion of the film script for *Rocky* (***summer 1975***) confirm the changeover.

Mars/Leo

- Both systems assign Mars to the last degrees of Leo with six degrees assigned using Egyptian bounds and five degrees assigned under Ptolemy.

- Changeover Events. The television series *The A-Team* featuring Laurence Tureaud, a.k.a. 'Mr. T', made its debut on ***January 23, 1983*** (-76 days). The military invasion of Grenada known as Operation Urgent Fury was launched ***October 25, 1983*** (+199 days). Both events match the delineation of Mars/Leo as action heroes and the defense of honor. Preceding the changeover to Mars/Leo on July 15, 1984 using Ptolemy's bounds; both of these events favor the Egyptian system.

VIRGO

	Egyptian		Ptolemaic
18-Nov-1990	0VI-Mercury	18-Nov-1990	0VI-Mercury
24-Sep-1999	7VI-Venus	24-Sep-1999	7VI-Venus
23-Apr-2012	17VI-Jupiter	15 Apr 2007	13VI-Jupiter
28-Apr-2017	21VI-Mars	25-Jul-2013	18VI-Saturn
31-Jan-2026	28VI-Saturn	29-Jan-2021	24VI-Mars

Mercury/Virgo

- Identical for both systems.

- <u>Changeover Events</u>. Bill Gates' concept of 'instantly accessible data' presented at Comdex on *November 12, 1990* (-6 days) followed launch of Microsoft Windows 3.0 on *May 22, 1990* (-180 days).

- <u>Culminating Events</u>. Bill Gates published *Business @ the Speed of Thought* on March 24, 1999. Note the Federal Trade Commission's preliminary decision in their antitrust case against Microsoft did not occur until November 5, 1999, forty-two days after the end of the Distribution.

Venus/Virgo

- Fills out ten degrees in Egyptian bounds; six degrees in Ptolemy's system.

- <u>Changeover Events</u>. HBO television series The Sopranos debuted on January 10, 1999 and was nominated for 16 Emmy Awards including best drama on *July 23, 1999* (-63 days). The initial public offering for Martha Stewart Living Omnimedia took place on *October 19, 1999* (+25 days).

On first glance, the end of *The Sopranos* (June 10, 2007), *Extreme Makeover* (May 15, 2007), *Pimp My Ride* (May 24, 2007), and *Queer Eye for the Straight Guy* (October 30, 2007) fall so near to the end of the Venus/Virgo Distribution on April 15, 2007 computed under Ptolemy's system that Ptolemy's system appears to win out. But these cancellations can be explained by transits of the South Node and Saturn. The South Node transited through the bound of Venus/Virgo (Egyptian) from February 21, 2007 to August 28, 2007 when most of these series ended. *Queer Eye for the Straight Guy* was able to hold out a little longer, with transiting Saturn entering the bound of Venus/Virgo on November 8, 2007, just nine days after the show's final episode.

APPENDIX E

Solar Arc Directions

Public Nature of Solar Arc Directions. Because solar arc directions often time events with a public character, they are likely to receive media publicity. For this reason, recent online availability of the *New York Times* archives since 1850 has been a significant research aid for this project. The relative ease in finding events which match the delineation of each planet using the paper's online archives suggests the *New York Times* is valid as a representative indicator for the nation as a whole.

Solar Arc - Primary Directions Proposition. An unusual finding from the researching the Presidential database for *ARM* was the ability to link events of a public nature timed by solar arc directions to events of an individual nature timed by primary directions. I update this proposition with selected directions for the Regulus USA National Horoscope.

Database and Conventions. What follows are the complete set of solar arc directions between planets and the Ascendant, computed by direct and converse motion. Ptolemaic aspects are used. These conventions differ from Reinhold Ebertin's Cosmobiology School which restricts solar arc measurements to hard aspects and computation to direct motion. My empirical work suggests soft aspects (e.g., sextile and trine) and converse motion work just as well. For the 172 solar arc measurements presented, event matches were identified for approximately 85% of the sample.

The Solar Arc - Primary Directions Proposition

In researching the Presidential database, I discovered a curious phenomenon. While computing Dwight Eisenhower's rectification, it struck me quite odd the direction of ASC opposed Mars timed the Pearl Harbor attack *by solar arc* yet the same ASC opposed Mars timed Eisenhower's own response to the attack through his own travel and military operations during WWII *by primary direction*. Woodrow Wilson's figure showed a similar configuration for the outbreak of WWI. For Wilson, an ASC opposed Mars direction timed Archduke Ferdinand's assassination *by solar arc* and the same ASC opposed Mars timed Wilson's failed negotiations at the Paris Peace talks of 1919 *by primary direction*. Observations from Eisenhower, Wilson, and other Presidential nativities led me to the following proposition:

> **Proposition:**
> **The Relationship between Solar Arcs and Primary Directions**
>
> Primary directions time the direct effects of planetary behavior for the native. While the effects are similar, solar arc directions time more public manifestations of the same planetary behavior for which the native may be only an indirect participant.
>
> Public events timed by solar arc directions may directly draw the native into similar events timed later by primary directions. The reverse order, events first timed by primary directions; later by solar arcs, is also possible.
>
> It also may be true that solar arcs, unlike primary directions, have a more public manifestation generally, whether or not the same type of event is mirrored in primary directions at some other time.

The initial finding is enough solar arc-primary direction relationships exist to maintain the proposition. Consider the following event pairs:

September 8, 1901.
Assassination of President William McKinley (September 5).
Primary Direction: dex. trine Saturn d. → ASC, lat=0.

July 5, 1826.
Deaths of Presidents John Adams and Thomas Jefferson (July 4).
Solar Arc Direction: dsa ASC trine Saturn.

Both events time Presidential deaths and both events were timed by Saturn trine Ascendant directions.
December 17, 1942.

Riot at Manzanar Japanese internment camp (December 6).
Primary Direction: dex sextile Saturn c. → ASC, lat=Saturn.

July 14, 2006.
Supreme Court rules military tribunals created by George W. Bush a violation of American law and the Geneva Conventions (July 14).
Solar Arc Direction: csa Saturn sextile ASC.

Both events concern the legal status of enemies confined during wartime.

May 20, 1872.
Present Grant sent message to Congress on remedies to correct abuses faced by immigrants on arrival to American soil (May 15).
Solar Arc Direction: dsa Mercury sextile ASC.

September 18, 1891.
Construction of Ellis Island (1981/1892).
Primary Direction: sin. sextile Mercury c. → ASC, lat=zero.

Both events concern remedies taken to mitigate immigrant fraud.

January 29, 1932
Biography of Clarence Darrow published (February 5). Gained notoriety for defending murder cases. Was opposed to capital punishment and was able to spare the vast majority of his clients from the death penalty.
Solar Arc Direction: dsa Mercury conj. ASC.

June 3, 1967
Mass murderer Richard Speck was sentenced to death (June 8, 1967). Following a lengthy appeals process, Speck's death penalty was later overturned.
Primary Direction: conj. Mercury c. → ASC, lat=zero.

Both events are related to capital punishment for convicted murderers.

Though I have deliberately cherry picked these examples, I believe connections between these event pairs provide sufficient support to maintain the proposition. To reach a definitive conclusion on the proposition, what is required is fine tuning of what direction pair constitutes a match. Consider the following permutations for Saturn trine Ascendant directions:

Solar Arc Directions

direct Ascendant trine Saturn
direct Saturn trine Ascendant
converse Ascendant trine Saturn
converse Saturn trine Ascendant

Primary Directions

dexter trine Saturn c. → ASC, lat=Saturn
dexter trine Saturn c. → ASC, lat=zero
dexter trine Saturn d. → ASC, lat=Saturn
dexter trine Saturn d. → ASC, lat=zero
sinister trine Saturn c. → ASC, lat=Saturn
sinister trine Saturn c. → ASC, lat=zero
sinister trine Saturn d. → ASC, lat=Saturn
sinister trine Saturn d. → ASC, lat=zero
dexter trine Ascendant c. → Saturn, Pole of Saturn, lat=Saturn
dexter trine Ascendant c. → Saturn, Pole of Saturn, lat=zero
dexter trine Ascendant d. → Saturn, Pole of Saturn, lat=Saturn
dexter trine Ascendant d. → Saturn, Pole of Saturn, lat=zero
sinister trine Ascendant c. → Saturn, Pole of Saturn, lat=Saturn
sinister trine Ascendant c. → Saturn, Pole of Saturn, lat=zero
sinister trine Ascendant d. → Saturn, Pole of Saturn, lat=Saturn
sinister trine Ascendant d. → Saturn, Pole of Saturn, lat=zero

Which solar arc should be mapped to which primary direction?

Good question.

Right now I cannot say. In addition, by choosing to limit this study to Ascendant directions calculated with the Ascendant as significator, I did not compute the last eight types of Saturn-Ascendant directions listed with Saturn as the significator. Computation and research of these additional directions would be required to fully populate the sample of Saturn-Ascendant primary directions. Once this additional step is taken, the proposition can be fully investigated using the Regulus USA National Horoscope as a data sample.

Now on to the directions.

Moon - Ascendant Solar Arc Directions

1-Jul-1777. *dsa ASC sextile Moon.*
2-Jul-1777. *csa Moon sextile ASC.*

Both directions fall near the battlefield service of Sybil Ludington (April 26, 1777) and Molly Pitcher (June 28, 1778) which timed the sequence #1. No additional events were found to match this pair of directions.

4-Dec-1806. *dsa Moon square ASC.*
18-Dec-1806. *csa ASC square Moon.*

Considering the connection between the Aquarian Moon and the abolition movement, Jefferson's **December 2, 1806** request for Congress to ban all slave importation to the United Stated effective January 1, 1808 is a delineation match.

12-Jan-1838. *dsa Moon trine ASC.*
7-Mar-1838. *csa ASC trine Moon.*

To protest the gag rule, on **February 14, 1838** John Quincy Adams submitted to the House 350 petitions against slavery and the annexation of Texas. This is a match to the Moon as significator of the abolition movement.

24-Dec-1839. *dsa ASC conj. Moon.*
18-Feb-1840. *csa Moon conj ASC.*

This pair of directions times the first phase of legal proceedings of the Amistad affair and its favorable impact on the Abolition movement. Following the discovery of slaves on the Spanish vessel La Amistad on August 26, 1839, John Quincy Adams published an influential letter in support of the captured slaves on **December 25, 1839**.[1] Arguments were presented before the U.S. District Court, Connecticut; on January 7, 1840 who ordered the slaves returned to their homeland later that month. Given the prominence of John Quincy Adams in the abolitionist movement, his letter published on Christmas Day 1839, one day from an exact hit to the first solar arc direction, is arguably the best delineation match because it captures the 'publicity' potential found in many solar arc directions.

10-Oct-1898. *dsa Moon opposed ASC.*
18-Mar-1899. *csa ASC opposed Moon.*

This sequence corresponds to agitation against annexation of the Philippines at the conclusion of the Spanish-American War fought between the American Anti Imperialist League founded on June 15, 1898 and Congressional pro-imperialist forces. After the Treaty of Paris was signed on **December 10, 1898**, it was ratified on **February 6, 1899** following heated arguments between anti-imperialist and imperialists in the Senate. Anti-imperialism is consistent with the Aquarius Moon because Aquarius opposes the sign of Leo which is associated with royalty and imperialism.

28-Aug-1900. *dsa ASC sextile Moon.*
6-Feb-1901. *csa Moon sextile ASC.*

On **August 28, 1900**, a New York Central passenger train collided with a freight train. Train accidents like this demonstrate the power of the Moon to carry with it the properties of Mars from which the Moon separates. Mars/Gemini signifies reckless speeding.[2]

27-Apr-1930. *dsa ASC square Moon.*
12-Nov-1930. *csa Moon square ASC.*

Following a series of prison riots in 1929, discussions on remedies to prevent prison riots were published **April 27, 1930**[3]; followed by President Hoover's message to Congress on prison reform the following day. On May 11, 1930, Ohio debated prisoner rehabilitation.[4]

On **May 6, 1930**, the Senate debated whether the Federal government should acquire the Erie and Oswego Canals in New York.[5]

On **November 18, 1930**, President Hoover extended the Civil Service's merit system by executive order.

1-Dec-1957. *dsa Moon trine ASC.*
1-Jul-1958. *csa ASC trine Moon.*

On **December 9, 1957**, Attorney General William Rogers established the Civil Rights Division to provide better enforcement of the Civil Rights Act of 1957. On **July 2, 1958**, President Eisenhower pledged the Federal Government would enforce the law on civil rights issues 'as laid down by the Supreme Court procedures.'[6] This pair of directions also marked the second half of the 1957-1958 school year when nine African American students attended Little Rock High School under military protection.

APPENDIX E - SOLAR ARC DIRECTIONS

9-Oct-1959. *dsa ASC trine Moon.*
8-May-1960. *csa Moon trine ASC.*

On **October 15, 1959**, the Civil Rights Commission disclosed an expansion in the scope of its investigations to include discrimination in employment and justice administration.[7] On February 29, 1960, the Senate began debate on the Civil Rights Act of 1960 which passed and received President Eisenhower's signature on **May 6, 1960**.

27-May-1987. *dsa Moon square ASC.*
13-Dec-1987. *csa ASC square Moon.*

Three Civil Rights legal actions corresponded to the first direction:

1. On **May 21, 1987**, the Senate Labor and Human Resources committee approved the Civil Rights Restoration Act by 12 to 4 margin.

2. On **May 24, 1987**, the Supreme Court expanded the Civil Rights Act of 1866 to afford protection beyond African Americans to any people subject to discrimination because of 'ancestry or ethnic characteristics.'[8]

3. On **May 27, 1987**, New Jersey director of the State Division of Civil Rights Panela S. Poff ordered the remaining all-male eating clubs at Princeton University to begin admitting women.[9]

Reagan's nomination of Robert Bork to the Supreme Court on **July 1, 1987**, the Senate's rejection of Bork on October 2, 1987, and confirmation hearings for Reagan's third appointee, Anthony M. Kennedy, on **December 14, 1987** occupied much of the nation's attention for the time period between both directions.

Sun - Ascendant Solar Arc Directions

3-Oct-1793. *dsa ASC opposed Sun.*
9-Oct-1793. *csa Sun opposed ASC.*

Born *October 10, 1793,* Harriet Newell was part of the first wave of American-born Christian missionaries to travel overseas. She preached in India, Burma, and Mauritius where she died on November 30, 1812 during her first year abroadsa 19th century Christians considered her a hero and named many children for her following her death.

29-Dec-1821. *dsa Sun trine ASC.*
30-Jan-1822. *csa ASC trine Sun.*

Born *December 25, 1821*, Clara Barton later established the American Red Cross on May 21, 1881. See Sun-Ascendant Direction #5.

Born *February 4, 1822*, Edward Fitzgerald 'Ned' Beale was a famous 19th Century American who embodied the adventurism and compassion signified by the Sun/Cancer ruling the 9th. He was a naval officer, military general, explorer, frontiersman, Indian affairs superintendent, California rancher, diplomat, and friend of Kit Carson and Ulysses S. Grant.[10] He was also the first American to bring gold samples back East from the California Gold Rush of 1848 achieving immediate fame; a match to the Sun's rulership of the POF/Leo in the 9th.

20-Nov-1852. *dsa Sun square ASC.*
7-Feb-1853. *csa ASC square Sun.*

On *November 24, 1852*, President Millard Fillmore authorized Matthew Perry to seek diplomatic & trade relations with Japan.

Michael Owens, born *February 6, 1853*, was a U.S. Marine who was injured during the Korean Expedition of 1871 and awarded the Medal of Honor.[11] The Korean Expedition was designed to support an American diplomatic effort to establish trade relations with Korea, to determine the fate of the *General Sherman* merchant ship, and to establish a treaty for providing assistance to shipwrecked sailors.[12] Sun's placement in the 8th house of traded goods is a delineation match to the primary objective of the Korean Expedition that Owens would participate in later in life.

12-Nov-1855. *dsa ASC trine Sun.*
4-Feb-1856. *csa Sun trine ASC.*

The American philanthropist and eugenicist Ezra Seymour Gosney was born on *November 6, 1855*. Gosney's activities in philanthropy match the Sun in the 8th of bequests; his interest in education matches the Moon/Aquarius/3rd as the Sun's ruler. Gosney's belief in eugenics can be attributed to his natal Jupiter 23AQ17 in the bound of Mars/Aquarius with natal Mars in Virgo. Jupiter/Aquarius is a humanitarian placement and matches the stated goal of his Human Betterment Foundation "to foster and aid constructive and educational forces for the protection and betterment of the human family in body, mind, character, and citizenship."[13] Jupiter's placement in the bound of Mars/Aquarius – significator of discrimination – mars Jupiter's otherwise open ended humanitarian philosophy. Mars/Virgo in the natal figure signifies sterilization as the type of discrimination he favored.[14]

Birth of Frederick William Vanderbilt, *February 2, 1856*. Vanderbilt was the only one of four sons of William Henry Vanderbilt to leave a greater estate than what he inherited. He was a known philanthropist and graduated from Yale's Sheffield Scientific School.

7-Apr-1883. *dsa Sun sextile ASC.*
18-Aug-1883. *csa ASC sextile Sun.*

On *April 10, 1883*, orders were given for the first scientific expedition for the purpose of collecting and preserving marine invertebrates aboard the U.S. Fisheries Steamer Albatross.[15]

Birth of Jonathan Mayhew "Skinny" Wainwright IV, *August 23, 1883*. Wainwright was a four-star general who was forced to surrender Allied forces in the Philippines on May 6, 1945. Wainwright and his men were held in prison camps until freed by the Russians in August 1945. Wainwright was subsequently awarded a Medal of Honor.

March 10, 1886. *dsa ASC square Sun.*
July 27, 1886. *csa Sun square ASC.*

On *March, 10 1886*, Grover Cleveland sent to Congress the 1st of his pension bills.

In *July 1886*, The Dunnottar Castle Freightliner, an iron-hulled cargo ship carrying coal from Sydney, Australia, to Wilmington, California, crashed in the Kure Atoll. It was discovered on July 3, 2006 during an expedition conducted by marine archaeologists funded by the NOAA Maritime Heritage Program.[16] Note the event is tied to the direction not by the vessel's initial mission or crash, but through its subsequent discovery by a government-sponsored foreign expedition designed for scientific research.

13-Jan-1916. *dsa ASC sextile Sun.*
15-Jul-1916. *csa Sun sextile ASC.*

January 1916 marked the return of delegates to America from the Henry Ford Peace Expedition which held peace meetings among nonbelligerent European nations.[17]

On **July 17, 1916**, President Wilson signed into law the Federal Farm Loan Act. This system created a long-term credit system for farmers, similar to structures already in place for industry and commerce.

10-Sep-1942. *dsa Sun conj. ASC.*
7-Apr-1943. *csa ASC conj. Sun.*

On **September 17, 1942**, FDR began a nonpartisan/no publicity re-election campaign with visits to large number of war plants and defense sites.[18]

On **April 13, 1943**, FDR dedicated the Jefferson memorial and began a sixteen day tour of military facilities.[19]

31-Dec-1974. *dsa ASC conj. Sun.*
27-Jul-1975. *csa Sun conj. ASC.*

On **December 31, 1974**, gold was legalized for American ownership for the first time since the Great Depression.

Reported **July 20, 1975** was the find of a Spanish Galleon off the Florida Coast containing gold and silver.[20]

21-Sep-2001. *dsa Sun sextile ASC.*
25-Mar-2002. *csa ASC sextile Sun.*

On **September 21, 2001**, gold traded to a short term high of $296 following the 9-11 attacks. The stock market made a temporary low on the same date.

Lunar Node-Ascendant Solar Arc Directions

28-Sep-1796. *dsa North Node trine ASC.*
28-Sep-1796. *dsa South Node sextile ASC.*

No events found. Consider Washington's Farewell Address of September 17, 1796.

6-Oct-1796. *csa ASC sextile South Node.*
6-Oct-1796. *csa ASC trine North Node.*

Dorr Expedition. In a convoluted fashion, Captain Dorr's decision to include political reformer Thomas Muir as passenger matches the Sun-ruled North Node delineated as increase in exploration/travel because of a diplomat who risks death. Sun's rulership of the 5th house by exaltation is relevant to Muir because ambassadors and legates are 5th house affairs. Muir's ties to France also suggest his relevance to this direction. Now the event:

The sea-otter hunter and sea captain Ebenezer Dorr was the first American explorer to sail along the California coastline. In early 1796, Captain Dorr stopped at Sydney for supplies and allowed the Scottish lawyer and political reformer Thomas Muir to travel on Dorr's ship. Muir originally intended to travel to the United States on a French passport but was captured and sent to Botany Bay as a political prisoner. Muir transferred from Dorr's ship to another vessel and landed in Monterrey during ***June 1796***. Muir was subsequently recaptured, wounded and disfigured in a sea battle. He was finally released and made contact with the French Directory where he shared his ideas to the French on an invasion of England. His health shattered, Muir faded away quickly and died January 26, 1799 at Chantilly.[21]

What is the relevant event timing to the solar arc direction of October 6, 1796? Four weeks later, Captain Door landed in Monterrey on ***October 29, 1796*** for supplies but the Spanish refused to trade for Dorr's otter skins. It was this event which led me to Muir as a possible connection to this Lunar Node-Ascendant solar arc direction.

12-Jan-1819. *dsa ASC conjunct South Node.*
12-Jan-1819. *dsa ASC opposed North Node.*

No events found.

9-Feb-1819. *csa North Node opposed ASC*.
9-Feb-1819. *csa South Node conjunct ASC*.

Trustees of Dartmouth College v. Woodward. By siding with Dartmouth College on **February 2, 1819**, the Supreme Court stated New Hampshire had no right to invalidate Dartmouth's private charter in its attempt to depose the College President. The decision was generally opposed by the public, including the former President Thomas Jefferson, because it strengthened private contract rights at the expense of the public interest. *Delineation Match*: Moon/Aquarius/3rd signifies the need for education by all citizens; South Node/Aquarius/3rd diminishes the public's equal treatment on matters of education. Saturn (Supreme Court) as ruler of the South Node is the cause.

Tallmadge Amendments. Following introduction of the Missouri Compromise legislation on **February 13, 1819**, NY Representative James Tallmadge introduced two anti-slavery amendments. The first banned further introduction of slavery to Missouri. The second allowed children of slaves after admission of Missouri into the Union to be declared free at age 25. Tallmadge delivered a widely circulated speech in support of his amendments on **February 15, 1819**. The Tallmadge amendments were defeated. *Delineation Match*: South Node in same sign as the Moon diminishes any signification of the Moon; here abolition.

10-Oct-1858. *dsa South Node trine ASC*.
10-Oct-1858. *csa North Node sextile ASC*.

Solar Eclipse Scientific Expedition. Updated travelogue of Lieutenant Gillis' expedition to observe the solar eclipse at Payta, Peru dated August 30, 1858 and published ***October 5, 1858***.[22]

7-Jan-1859. *csa ASC trine South Node*.
7-Jan-1859. *csa ASC sextile North Node*.

Nicaragua Canal Project. A detailed history of interest in constructing a canal through the Isthmus of Panama and technical details of a French Proposal were outlined on ***January 8, 1859***.[23]

24-May-1880. *dsa ASC sextile South Node*.
24-May-1880. *dsa ASC trine North Node*.

Nicaraguan Canal Contract. The Panama *Star and Herald* reported on *May 15, 1880* that a contract was signed between an American Company and the Republic of Nicaragua for the construction of a Nicaraguan canal. The story was reported by the NYT on ***May 24, 1880***.[24]

Arctic Exploration Discussion. The American Geographical Society was addressed on *May 25, 1880* on the topic of 'Arctic Exploration – Ancient and Modern.'[25] Given the ability of two subsequent solar arc directions to time later Arctic expeditions, this event appears relevant to the direction.

30-Sep-1880. *csa South Node sextile ASC.*
30-Sep-1880. *csa South Node trine ASC.*

No events found.

28-Apr-1910. *dsa ASC square South Node.*
28-Apr-1910. *dsa ASC square North Node.*

South Pole Expedition Abandoned. A South Pole expedition led by Navy Commander Peary under the auspices of the Peary Arctic Club and the National Geographic Society was abandoned on *April 24, 1910* after failure to secure $50,000 in financing.[26]

23-Oct-1910. *csa South Node square ASC.*
23-Oct-1910. *csa North Node square ASC.*

Unsuccessful Atlantic Airship Crossing. The American explorer Walter Wellman attempted to cross the Atlantic in the airship America, departing Atlantic City, NJ on *October 16, 1910* in a high profile media event.[27] The airship went down on *October 19, 1910*. Wellman and his crew received a favorable reception at Atlantic City for their attempt on *October 23, 1910*.[28]

9-Nov-1918. *dsa North Node conj ASC.*
9-Nov-1918. *dsa South Node opposed ASC.*

WWI Armistice. On *November 11, 1918* at 11:00 AM, the WWI ceasefire entered into force. The ceasefire was signed at Compiègne, France. Success of the American Expeditionary Force during the Meuse-Argonne Offensive, September 26 – November 11, 1918, was responsible for the German surrender. Note the connection between the terminology 'expeditionary force' and 'expeditions' which are assigned to the 9th house, the North Node's location by whole sign houses. (See Chapter 10 for a delineation of North Node/Leo/9th as peace treaties negotiated in France.)

15-May-1919. *csa ASC conjunct North Node.*
15-May-1919. *csa ASC opposed South Node.*

Solar Eclipse Scientific Expedition. Professor David Todd, head of Amherst's Astronomical Observatory, sailed on *May 13, 1919* in order to prepare for taking a picture of the total solar eclipse of *May 29, 1919* from an airplane at an altitude of 10 to 15,000 feet. His trip received widespread support from the scientific community.[29]

War Bond Drive. Completion of the nation's fifth and final war loan drive was celebrated by the entry of the Navy destroyer Calhoun who entered New York's 'Victory Harbor' at 3:00 p.m. on *May 11, 1919*.[30]

21-Nov-1939. *dsa ASC trine South Node.*
21-Nov-1939. *dsa ASC sextile North Node.*

Byrd Ship Accident and Launch of Third Antarctic Expedition. Antarctic explorer Richard Byrd's ship crashed its bow into a dock in Philadelphia's shipyard. Byrd was docking to procure additional supplies for its third government-sponsored Antarctic expedition. The vessel North Star later departed Boston on *November 15, 1939*.[31][32]

Red Cross Pioneer Honored. On *November 17, 1939*, a dinner was given in honor of Mrs. William Kinnicutt Draper. She had been active in the Red Cross since the society's inception during the Spanish-American War.[33]

Death of Presbyterian Minister active in European War Relief. The Rev. Dr. James I. Vance died (obituary printed *November 25, 1939*). Vance was a Minister and Moderator of the Presbyterian Church (1918-1919) who led Protestant Relief in Europe after World War I.[34]

16-Jun-1940. *csa South Node trine ASC.*
16-Jun-1940. *csa North Node sextile ASC.*

Salvation Army War Relief Appeal. On *June 10, 1940*, the Salvation Army announced it would begin soliciting funds for European war relief.[35] The campaign was started on *June 14, 1940*.[36]

21-Oct-1977. *dsa South Node trine ASC.*
21-Oct-1977. *dsa North Node sextile ASC.*

Concorde Flight Approval. On *October 17, 1977*, the U.S. Supreme Court approved trial flights of the Concorde airline to New York's Kennedy airport.[37] Increase (North Node) of foreign travel (North Node in 9th) to France (Leo) is a delineation match. First flight was *October 19, 1977*.

Popular Interest in Food Relief Programs. On **October 19, 1977**, the NYT described America's increasing interest in tackling world hunger as an emerging long-term social movement.[38]

Reinstatement of the Gold-Clause in Contracts. On **October 20, 1977**, the NYT reported that President Carter was expected to approve a ruling which allowed Americans to include the value of gold as a form of payment in business contracts.[39] The so-called 'gold-clause' had been illegal since 1933 (under FDR). Carter approved the legislation (date of passage not found).

Illness of Sir Edmund Hillary. The famous mountaineer Sir Edmund Hillary returned to his camp in the Himalayas after spending a few days in a military hospital from high-altitude sickness.[40]

16-May-1978. *csa ASC trine South Node.*
16-May-1978. *csa ASC sextile North Node.*

Supreme Court Rulings. On **May 15, 1978**, the Supreme Court ruled against Native Americans by prohibiting use of Federal courts to sue their own tribes for Civil Rights violations.[41]

22-Nov-1998. *dsa ASC opposed South Node.*
22-Nov-1998. *dsa ASC conjunct North Node.*

Social Security. On **November 20, 1998**, Republican Bill Archer, chair of the House Ways and Means Committee, held a hearing of Social Security reform.[42] President Bill Clinton held the first-ever White House Conference on Social Security on **December 8 & 9, 1998**.

30-May-1999. *csa South Node opposed ASC.*
30-May-1999. *csa North Node conjunct ASC.*

Social Security Surplus. On **May 27, 1999**, the House passed legislation that would restrict spending any accrued surpluses from the Social Security program.[43]

Mormon Missionaries. A **May 23, 1999** NYT article profiled the success of the Mormon Missionary program, a force of 60,000 missionaries in 163 nations, the largest program of its kind in North America.

Saturn-Ascendant Solar Arc Directions

<u>12-Mar-1789</u>. *dsa Saturn sextile ASC.*
<u>17-Mar-1789</u>. *csa ASC sextile Saturn.*

On *March 4, 1789*, the U.S. Government (under the Constitution) went into effect.

<u>6-Apr-1795</u>. *dsa ASC square Saturn.*
<u>12-Apr-1795</u>. *csa Saturn square ASC.*

(?) This pair of directions may involve debate surrounding Jay's Treaty after its terms were made public during *March 1795*. It was ratified by the Senate on *June 24, 1795*.

<u>5-Jul-1826</u>. *dsa ASC trine Saturn.*
<u>11-Aug-1826</u>. *csa Saturn trine ASC.*

Deaths of former President John Adams and Thomas Jefferson on **July 4, 1826**. Saturn is the killing planet of the Sun. These deaths were high profile media events, fitting the public nature of solar arc directions. Note also the corresponding Saturn-Ascendant Direction #6 timed the McKinley assassination.

No events found for the August 11, 1826 measurement.

<u>2-Jun-1851</u>. *dsa Saturn conj. ASC.*
<u>18-Aug-1851</u>. *csa ASC conj. Saturn.*

No events found for the June 2, 1851 measurement.

On **August 22, 1851**, the racing yacht *America* won the Royal Yacht Squadron's 'One Hundred Guinea Cup,' later renamed as America's Cup. *America* was built for John Cox Stevens who served as the first Commodore of the New York Yacht Club. Stevens' connection appears important in refining the delineation of Saturn/Libra because Stevens was also a founding member of the Union Club, New York's oldest gentlemen's society. In mundane astrology, Saturn signifies old men. Saturn falling in the 11th house of groups/organizations/clubs fits with Steven's ties to the Union Club.

As stated at the opening of Chapter 7 (pp. 140-141), Abū Ma'shar gives high marks to Saturn/Libra for the ability to trigger winds which are useful for sailing races.

APPENDIX E - SOLAR ARC DIRECTIONS   375

<u>19-Aug-1887</u>. *dsa ASC opposed Saturn.*
<u>6-Jan-1888</u>. *csa Saturn opposed ASC.*

In a story reported *August 20, 1887*, President Cleveland and the American Minister to Argentina, The Hon. Bayless W. Hanna, discussed increased advantages of trade with Argentina.[44] At this time, the Cleveland administration was concerned with the impact of high tariffs on trade policy. In his Annual Message to Congress on December 6, 1887, Cleveland made a sweeping indictment of the tariff system.

Cleveland's *January 16, 1888* appointments of Lucius Lamar to the Supreme Court, William Freeman Vilas to the Secretary of the Interior, and Donald McDonald Dickinson to Postmaster General are a delineation match because the President's cabinet is signified by the 11th house where Saturn is positioned.

<u>22-Sep-1911</u>. *dsa Saturn sextile ASC.*
<u>20-Mar-1912</u>. *csa ASC sextile Saturn.*

Canadians vetoed trade reciprocity agreement with United States on *September 21, 1911*; a major disappointment to the Taft administration.

The U.S. Steel Corporation sought voluntary dissolution to prevent prosecution by the Government through the Sherman Anti-Trust Act; reported *September 22, 1911*.[45]

In *March 1912*, Harvey Washington Wiley, known as the 'crusading chemist' and the 'Father of the Pure Food and Drugs Act' resigned from the U.S. Food and Drug Administration over a conflict with Secretary of Agriculture Wilson. Note the role of Venus/Cancer as Saturn's ruler in this direction e.g., Venus/Cancer = tainted food and drugs.

<u>12-Apr-1941</u>. *dsa Saturn square ASC.*
<u>7-Nov-1941</u>. *csa ASC square Saturn.*

On *April 12, 1941*, an American organization named 'The Committee to Defend America by Aiding Allies' proposed clamping down on war profiteers (neutral ship-owners trading with Germany and Italy) by prohibiting the right to purchase 'marine insurance and other facilities.'[46]

On *November 9, 1941*, the U.S. and Canada convened a three-day meeting of economists from both countries to study trade and other issues in post-war scenario planning.[47]

20-Dec-1946. *dsa ASC trine Saturn*.
17-Jul-1947. *csa Saturn trine ASC*.

The White House reinstated receptions and state dinners following cessation of World War II. First reception to honor Supreme Court was held on *December 10, 1946*.

This pair of directions appears relevant to the New World Agenda through post-WWII establishment of institutions designed to facilitate foreign trade. In a story reported *December 20, 1946*, success of the International Monetary Fund under the Bretton Woods agreement was seen to depend on the speed of setting up America's export businesses.[48] The 16-nation conference held in Paris to discuss the Marshall Plan opened on *July 12, 1947*.

Both the state diner in honor of the Supreme Court and the Paris Conference held to discuss the Marshall Plan were high profile public events matching the penchant of solar arc directions for publicity.

19-Sep-1970. *dsa Saturn trine ASC*.
19-Apr-1971. *csa ASC trine Saturn*.

Former Fed Chair William Martin stated "We are in a process of evolution toward a world central Bank" in his first speech *September 14, 1970* following retirement as Fed Chairman.[49]

On *September 17, 1970*, U.S. and IMF announced transactions which reduced U.S. gold stocks by $322 million[50]. (See the same type of event for the May 30, 1976 solar arc.)

In a Johns Hopkins University conference attended by leading authorities on currency issues, Prof. Fritz Machlup of Princeton University warned on *April 18, 1971* the rapid growth of the Eurodollar market could have severe consequences for the U.S. Dollar.[51]

On *April 18, 1971* started National Coin Week with the theme of 'Numismatics – the Hobby of All Ages.'[52] The event was advertised to be the most interesting since 1924.

30-May-1976. *dsa ASC square Saturn.*
23-Dec-1976. *csa Saturn square ASC.*

On *June 2, 1976*, the IMF held its first gold auction. Gold auctions continued periodically until May 7, 1980.

On *December 20, 1976*, President-elect Jimmy Carter nominated Griffin Bell to the position of Attorney General. The nomination was considered controversial because of Bell's membership in segregated social clubs and prior decisions on school integration.[53]

17-Jan-2006. *dsa ASC sextile Saturn.*
14-Jul-2006. *csa Saturn sextile ASC.*

Confirmation hearings for Supreme Court Justice Samuel Alito were held *January 9-13, 2006*. His confirmation was voted out of Senate Judiciary Committee *January 24* and confirmed by Senate on *January 31*.

On *July 14, 2006*, the NYT reported two recent incidents involving the Supreme Court and Congress which effectively reprimanded President Bush for overstepping the legal boundaries of the Presidency.[54] The first was a Supreme Court decision which ruled President Bush's creation of military tribunals to process terror suspects was a violation of American law and the Geneva Conventions. The second was a confrontation between Congress and President Bush over obtaining warrants for domestic wiretapping.

Mars-Ascendant Solar Arc Directions

12-Apr-1782. *dsa Mars opposed ASC.*
13-Apr-1782. *csa ASC opposed Mars.*

These directions timed the start of negotiations between Britain and the American colonies at the end of the Revolutionary War. British representative Richard Oswald met with Benjamin Franklin on *April 12, 1782*. Compare these solar arcs with the corresponding primary direction sequence #1.

2-May-1833. *dsa ASC trine Mars.*
17-Jun-1833. *csa Mars trine ASC.*

(?) Possible event match. On May 6, 1833, Robert Randolph, a disgruntled naval officer, assaulted President Andrew Jackson at the Alexandria, Virginia waterfront. Appearing to shake hands with Jackson, Randolph instead punched him in the face which left Jackson bleeding.

28-Aug-1844. *dsa Mars trine ASC.*
1-Nov-1844. *csa ASC trine Mars.*

(?) No events found.

17-Jan-1864. *dsa ASC square Mars.*
24-Apr-1864. *csa Mars square ASC.*

The Confederate massacre of Union troops at Fort Pillow, primarily African American, made national headlines on *April 15, 1864*. Perhaps the most serious war crimes of the entire Civil War were committed at Fort Pillow when surrendered Union troops were killed, bayoneted, burned alive, and in some cases buried alive after being forced to dig their own graves.

6-Mar-1875. *dsa Mars square ASC.*
3-Jul-1875. *csa ASC square Mars.*

26-Mar-1894. *dsa ASC sextile Mars.*
24-Aug-1894. *csa Mars sextile ASC.*

8-Mar-1905. *dsa Mars sextile ASC.*
25-Aug-1905. *csa ASC sextile Mars.*

Incidents of petty theft surfaced when testing these directions. These may be relevant to the direction given the October 27, 1964 Mars-Ascendant solar arc direction timed the largest jewelry theft in American history. But their insignificance makes them irrelevant for confirming the rectification.

12-Jun-1953. *dsa ASC conj Mars*.
9-Jan-1954. *csa Mars conj ASC*.

On *June 9, 1953*, CIA psychologist Sidney Gottlieb approved the use of LSD in the CIA mind-control research program known as Project MK-ULTRA.

American Motors Corporation was formed after the merger of the Hudson Motor Car Company and the Nash-Kelvinator Corporation on *January 14, 1954*. This was the largest corporate merger in U.S. history up to that time.

28-Mar-1964. *dsa Mars conj ASC*.
27-Oct-1964. *csa ASC conj Mars*.

On *March 26, 1964*, Secretary of Defense Robert McNamara reiterated the importance of America's military and economic aid to South Vietnam in its war against Communists.

The biggest jewel theft in American history occurred on *October 29, 1964*, when Jack Roland Murphy (a.k.a. Murf the Smurf) and two accomplices easily breached lax security measures at the American Museum of Natural History. Stolen were the Star of India, the Eagle Diamond, the DeLong Star Ruby, and other gemstones. The Star of India was recovered in a locker in a Miami bus station. The DeLong Star Ruby was recovered at a phone booth in Florida. The Eagle Diamond was not recovered. The thieves were arrested within two days and received a three-year prison sentence. Murphy later committed a murder in a separate crime; yet after serving a lengthy prison sentence started to preach Christianity as a method of criminal rehabilitation.

Mercury-Ascendant Solar Arc Directions

<u>21-Jan-1805</u>. *dsa ASC opposed Mercury.*
<u>3-Feb-1805</u>. *csa Mercury opposed ASC.*

Both directions time events surrounding the impeachment trial of Supreme Court Justice Samuel Chase. Drawing the ire of Jefferson for his Federalist stance on court decisions, Chase stood trial in the Senate on ***February 4, 1805*** and was acquitted of all charges on March 1, 1805. The trial was organized around weak legal reasoning consistent with an expectation of flawed legal proceedings timed by the direction of an afflicted Mercury to the 7th cusp of legal conflict. Says Henry Adams of the impeachment affair:

> *The impeachment, then, was a criminal prosecution, and the Senate was a criminal court; yet no offence was charged which the law considered a misdemeanor, while error of judgment, with no imputed ill-intent, was alleged as a crime. Staggering under this load of inconsistencies, uncertain what line of argument to pursue, and ignorant whether the Senate would be ruled by existing law or invent a system of law of its own, the managers, February 9, 1805, appeared in the Senate chamber to open their case and produce their witnesses.*[55]

<u>5-Oct-1810</u>. *dsa Mercury trine ASC.*
<u>23-Oct-1810</u>. *csa ASC trine Mercury.*

Both directions time the rise and fall of the Republic of West Florida, proclaimed on ***September 26, 1810*** after a September 23, 1810 raid and capture of the Spanish fort at Baton Rouge. President James Madison announced annexation of parts of West Florida on ***October 27, 1810***. This episode appears one of the earliest false-flag operations used to justify an illegal land acquisition by the U.S. Government. Of this episode, historian Robert Higgs remarks: "…this venture, born of low-level filibuster and high-level intrigue, illustrates the same ingrained American propensity for land-grabbing so evident in other U.S. acquisitions of territory."[56]

<u>25-Oct-1841</u>. *dsa Mercury square ASC.*
<u>23-Dec-1841</u>. *csa ASC square Mercury.*

On September 13, 1841, President John Tyler was repudiated by the Whig congressional caucus and declared expelled from the party. This disaster followed his veto of the Second Bank of the United States on September 9, 1841. Both directions in the fall of 1841 appear tied to Tyler's desire to resuscitate his administration through expansionist policies regarding Texas and Oregon territories. On ***October 11, 1841***, the same day Abel

Upshur was appointed to Secretary of the Navy (who would later be accused of negotiating a secret treaty for Texas annexation with Sam Houston), Tyler wrote Daniel Webster indicating the publicity benefits of Texas annexation for his administration.

Another event which may be relevant, but requires further research to confirm event timing, is Tyler and Webster's secret authorization of a preferential transportation deal with Alfred Benson in order to ship American settlers to Oregon – with expenses paid for by the United States government. If timing of the deal matches dates of either direction, it would be consistent with other Mercury-Ascendant directions which time secret deals made to facilitate land acquisition (e.g., 1810, West Florida; 1896/1897, Cuba & Hawaii).

8-Nov-1866. *dsa ASC trine Mercury.*
19-Feb-1867. *csa Mercury trine ASC.*

Both directions time the rise of the Radical Republicans and the early phases of Reconstruction. Radical Republicans took over the House during mid-term elections held in **November 1866**. On **February 14, 1867**, the House passed the First Reconstruction Act which placed Ten Confederate States under military control of the United States Army. The House overrode President Andrew Johnson's veto making the First Reconstruction Act effective on **March 2, 1867**.

20-May-1872. *dsa Mercury sextile ASC.*
11-Sep-1872. *csa ASC sextile Mercury.*

On or about **May 15, 1872**, Ulysses Grant sent a special message to Congress on remedies to correct abuses faced by immigrants. Grant requested that immigrants receive improved accommodations on ships in order to guarantee minimum standards of health and comfort. He also recommended changes to eliminate frauds heaped on immigrants on arrival to the United States by unscrupulous hucksters.[57]

A NYT editorial dated **September 11, 1872** bemoaned the situation of murderers acquitted from the death penalty on charges of insanity, only to appeal for release after regaining their sanity shortly after beginning their imprisonment.[58] The writer suggested creation of a new style of confinement where an extended period of observation could occur under conditions less harsh than suffered by duly convicted criminals.

28-Dec-1896. *dsa ASC square Mercury*.
2-Jun-1897. *csa Mercury square ASC*.

These two directions correspond to William Randolph Hearst's yellow journalism campaign to whip up American support for action against Spain regarding Cuba. Following purchase of the *New York Journal* in 1896, Hearst followed competitor Joseph Pulitzer's formula at the *New York World* by introducing sensationalism in reporting to increase sales. Circulation of the *New York Journal* rose by 125,000 in late 1896.[59] Following the first direction is the *New York Journal*'s article 'Death of Rodriquez' of **January 19, 1897** providing the details of the execution of the Cuban rebel Adolfo Rodriquez by a Spanish firing squad.[60] This was the type of sensationalist reporting Hearst encouraged in order to turn American opinion against Spain. Just after the second direction, McKinley appointed General Stewart Woodford as the American Minister to Spain. On **July 16, 1897**, Woodford presented a letter from Secretary of State John Sherman demanding Spain end the Cuban Civil War or risk United States entry in the conflict.[61] Spain responded with a letter on August 4, 1897 describing American accusations in sensationalist terms.

Hawaii also fell victim to expansionist rhetoric in the age of yellow journalism. On **June 6, 1897**, McKinley sent the Hawaii annexation treaty to the Senate for approval.

12-Sep-1926. *dsa ASC sextile Mercury*.
27-Mar-1927. *csa Mercury sextile ASC*.

This direction appears related to the one which follows based on publicity surrounding the Sacco-Vanzetti case. The May 26, 1926 confession of Celestino Madeiros gave the Sacco-Vanzetti defense sufficient evident to appeal for a new trial. The Medeiros motion was argued before Judge Thayer during **September 13-17, 1926**. Thayer denied the appeal on October 23, 1926.[62] On **April 8, 1927**, Sacco and Vanzetti were sentenced to death in the electric chair after exhausting the appeals process.

As a measure of anti-immigrant sentiment at the time of the Sacco-Vanzetti case, there was a movement in Congress to completely shut the doors for immigration accompanied by a prediction that all aliens would be barred from entering the United States within the next 25 years.[63]

29-Jan-1932. *dsa Mercury conj. ASC*.
18-Aug-1932. *csa ASC conj. Mercury*.

Railroad companies and unions workers signed an agreement for a 10% wage cut, **January 31, 1932**.

Clarence Darrow's autobiography was published on **February 5, 1932**. Darrow had gained notoriety defending murder cases. He was vehemently opposed to capital punishment and was able to spare the vast majority of his clients from the death penalty.

The second direction timed an **August 18, 1832** report stating that almost three times as many immigrants left the U.S. compared to immigrant arrivals in 1932.[64]

<u>12-Aug-1985</u>. *dsa ASC conj. Mercury.*
<u>10-Mar-1986</u>. *csa Mercury conj. ASC.*

The first direction timed Russia's **August 22, 1985** complaint over U.S. intent to test an anti-satellite weapon in space.[65] The test was later completed on September 13, 1985.

Three events were timed by the second direction.

First was a **March 9, 1986** report of effects of radiation exposure from an August 29, 1949 nuclear experiment at the Hanford Nuclear Reservation which released more than 100 times as much radiation compared to the 1979 Three Mile Island accident.[66] (Note connection to Hiroshima/Nagasaki).

Second was a request by six world leaders, published **March 10, 1986**, requesting Reagan and Gorbachev to halt nuclear testing until the next summit meeting.

Third was former Senator John Tower's resignation as an arms negotiator on **March 11, 1986**.

<u>12-Jan-1991</u>. *dsa Mercury sextile ASC.*
<u>28-Jul-1991</u>. *csa ASC sextile Mercury.*

Congress authorized use of military force to drive Iraq out of Kuwait on **January 12, 1991**. The vote was influenced by a public relations campaign organized by Citizens for a Free Kuwait which manufactured 'a campaign in which a nurse working in the Kuwait City hospital described Iraqi soldiers pulling babies out of incubators and letting them die on the floor.'[67] Though determined to be a fabricated hoax a year later, the story was influential in tipping sufficient swing votes towards support of the war.

The USA and USSR signed the START I treaty on **July 31, 1991**.

Venus-Ascendant Solar Arc Directions

25-Jan-1783. *dsa ASC opposed Venus.*
26-Jan-1783. *csa Venus opposed ASC.*

Following the *January 20, 1783* preliminary peace treaty between France and Spain, Lafayette wrote a letter to George Washington on *February 5, 1783* with a proposal that slaves be emancipated and employed as tenant farmers.[68] This incident matches the delineation of Venus/Cancer as judgment of white racism.

23-Jul-1832. *dsa Venus trine ASC.*
6-Sep-1832. *csa ASC trine Venus.*

Both directions follow Andrew Jackson's *July 10, 1832* veto of the Bank Bill and his *July 14* approval of the Tariff of 1832. Both directions bracket the Congressional recess with Jackson gone from *July 22* to *October 19*.

During the recess period, Jackson continued to pursue anti-corruption measures by deciding to block funds spent on public works projects.[69] Though no actions were taken during Congressional recess, Jackson's consideration of shelving wasteful spending matches the delineation of Venus/Cancer as judgment of scandal.

It's also possible that civil unrest in South Carolina, reported in *early August and September 1832*[70], is a delineation match to Venus/Cancer as the burning of cotton because Venus/Cancer = clothing/cotton and the Tariff of 1832 signed *July 14, 1832* did not lower cotton tariffs sufficiently for South Carolina businessmen. This incident would lead to the Nullification crisis a few months later.

6-Jun-1845. *dsa ASC trine Venus.*
11-Aug-1845. *csa Venus trine ASC.*

James C. Napier was born on *June 9, 1845* in Nashville, Tennessee. Born of free parents he relocated to Ohio temporarily after race riots closed free black schools in Nashville. After his return to Nashville, he rose quickly in political circles and became Nashville's most powerful African American politician between 1872 and 1913.[71]

Frederick Douglas departed for Europe on *August 16, 1845* after publication of his autobiography, *Narrative of the Life of Frederick Douglas*. This book became an immediate best seller and was used extensively by the abolitionist movement.

Both Napier and Douglas were devoted to providing education for African Americans.

13-Apr-1863. *dsa Venus square ASC.*
19-Jul-1863. *csa ASC square Venus.*

On *April 13, 1863*, the Anti-Gold Speculation bill was introduced in the Senate. This measure was made to counteract excessive speculation in gold, whose price was tightly correlated to battlefield success of Union soldiers on Civil War battlefields. The measure was later passed but rescinded fairly quickly. *Judgment of scandal* is similar in spirit to *squashing speculation* which better describes the actions of the Senate for this direction.[72]

Following the New York City Council's *April 22, 1863* approval of the Harlem Company to run a new rail track on Broadway, the stock market surged. This action is consistent with the start of an entirely new cycle of stock market speculation consistent with the titillating effects of Venus approaching her superior conjunction.[73]

7-Dec-1875. *dsa ASC square Venus.*
6-Apr-1876. *csa Venus square ASC.*

The impeachment trial of Secretary of War William Belknap appears a match to this set of directions. Belknap was charged with accepting illegal payments from individuals who received appointments as military post traders.[74]

Late 1875	Rumors of illegality began to surface
14-Jan-1876	Committee formed to investigate Belknap
2-Mar-1876	Belknap resigned as Secretary of War; impeachment ordered
30-Mar-1876	Judiciary Committee reported five articles of impeachment
3-Apr-1876	House passed impeachment charges; moved to Senate
5-Apr-1876	Chief Justice began Senate trial process.
1-Aug-1876	Belknap acquitted on impeachment charges by the Senate.

Belknap's impeachment trial matches delineation of Venus approaching her superior conjunction as the judgment of scandal (Venus-Sun superior conjunction) regarding consumer goods (Venus/Cancer) sold on military bases (Venus conjunct antiscion of Mars/Gemini; Venus also in bound of Mars).

25-Jun-1893. *dsa Venus sextile ASC.*
22-Nov-1893. *csa ASC sextile Venus.*

Consumerism and women's suffrage mark these 1893 directions. Falling during the Chicago World's Fair (*May 1 – October 31, 1893*), the first direction included construction of 'The Woman's Building,' a separate installation at the Chicago World's Fair which celebrated both the artistic skills of women and women as capable independent producers.[75] A meeting of the International Council of Women during the Fair demonstrated the growing power of the suffrage movement. Among the legacies of the fair was mass marketing of consumer goods. Marshall Field's exhibit was among the most popular. In addition, some of American's most famous consumer products were launched: Cream of Wheat, Shredded Wheat, Pabst Beer, Aunt Jemima syrup, and Juicy Fruit Gum.[76]

Ironically the opening of the sequence timed the ***June 27, 1893*** stock market crash ushering in an economic depression. This shows the weakness of Venus approaching the beams.

On ***November 16, 1893***, Susan B. Anthony was given a reception at the New York City Woman Suffrage League where she announced the start of a campaign to submit a petition of 1 million signatures in favor of women's suffrage.[77] This event matches the penchant of solar arcs for publicity.

6-Dec-1905. *dsa ASC sextile Venus.*
26-May-1906. *csa Venus sextile ASC.*

These directions are tied to publication of Upton Sinclair's muckraking exposé *The Jungle*, an indictment against unsanitary conditions in the meatpacking industry.

25-Dec-1904	Sinclair began to write *The Jungle*
Summer 1905	Sinclair finished writing *The Jungle*
Feb – Dec 1905	Published in weekly installments
28-Feb-1906	Book published by Doubleday, Page & Company.
9-Mar-1906	President Theodore Roosevelt indicated to Sinclair he would read *The Jungle*.
25-May-1906	Senate passed Meatpacking inspection bill.
4-Jun-1906	President Roosevelt released document describing poor conditions in meatpacking plants in order to facilitate passage of the Meatpacking bill.
1-Jul-1906	President Roosevelt signed the Meat Inspection Act and the Pure Food and Drug Act.

As a bizarre example for testing the **Solar Arc - Primary Direction Proposition**, consider Lithuania's Act of Independence was signed February 16, 1918 timed by Venus-Ascendant Direction #7. That direction was a sextile as are both December 1906 and May 1906 directions shown above. Now consider the opening scene of Upton Sinclair's Jungle featured a wedding feast of Lithuanian immigrants!

<u>15-Sep-1952</u>. *dsa Venus conj. ASC.*
<u>15-Apr-1953</u>. *csa ASC conj Venus.*

These directions correspond to key actions on school desegregation culminating with the Supreme Court's Brown vs. Board of Education decision.

18-Sep-1952	Supreme Court scheduled arguments for mid-October on school segregation.[78]
9-Dec-1952	*Brown v. Board of Education* argued
6-Apr-1953	Supreme Court reconvened after recess since March 16.[79]
8-Dec-1953	*Brown v. Board of Education* reargued.
17-May-1954	*Brown v. Board of Education* stated 'separate educational facilities are inherently unequal.'

The second direction covers the interval between ***February 11, 1953*** and ***June 13, 1953*** when the African American Baptist Minister Theodore Judson ("T.J.") Jemison sought desegregation of buses in Baton Rouge. Jemison's successful boycott was considered a model for subsequent nonviolent protests in Montgomery and elsewhere.[80]

<u>22-Dec-1964</u>. *dsa ASC conjunct Venus.*
<u>23-Jul-1965</u>. *csa Venus conj ASC.*

The first direction timed Martin Luther King's ***mid-December 1964*** decision to begin a voting rights campaign in Selma. The campaign officially started on January 2, 1965 which coincided with President Lyndon Johnson's January 4, 1965 'Great Society' address. The Voting Rights Act was passed by the House (August 3), the Senate (August 4), and signed by LBJ on ***August 6, 1965*** just after the last direction.

Jupiter-Ascendant Solar Arc Directions

<u>24-Dec-1785</u>. *dsa ASC opposed Jupiter.*
<u>27-Dec-1785</u>. *csa Jupiter opposed ASC.*

Most likely signifies events leading up to Shays' Rebellion (see Jupiter-Ascendant Direction #1) but needs more research to confirm.

<u>7-Sep-1829</u>. *dsa Jupiter trine ASC.*
<u>18-Oct-1829</u>. *csa ASC trine Jupiter.*

No events found.

<u>11-Apr-1848</u>. *dsa ASC trine Jupiter.*
<u>22-Jun-1848</u>. *csa Jupiter trine ASC.*

No events found.

<u>15-Jun-1860</u>. *dsa Jupiter square ASC.*
<u>14-Sep-1860</u>. *csa ASC square Jupiter.*

On ***June 20, 1860***, a certain Mrs. Hepburn borrowed $11,250 from Henry Griswsold payable on February 20, 1862. On February 25, 1862 Congress approved the issuance of $150 million in greenbacks, a form of currency which was not extant at the time of the original 1860 loan. Hepburn's attempt to pay off the loan in March 1864 with greenbacks was refused by Griswold. The case eventually made its way to the Supreme Court who in 1869 decided in favor of Griswold.[81] The decision was later reversed in *Knox v. Lee.* Both *Hepburn v. Griswold* and Shays' Rebellion concern debt repayment in a macroeconomic environment of inflation. By siding with Griswold, the Supreme Court favored the creditor class who could maintain their assets by requiring debt repayment with hard money.

<u>25-Sep-1878</u>. *dsa ASC square Jupiter.*
<u>29-Jan-1879</u>. *csa Jupiter square ASC.*

In the fall of 1878, the debate concerning greenback issuance came full circle when the resumption of specie payments on ***January 1, 1879*** approached. Despite passage of the Bland-Allison Act on February 28, 1878, a sop to inflationists for its inclusion of silver as a monetary unit of account, inflationists continued to agitate for inflation achievable through continued use of greenback currency. During ***September 1878***, President Hayes went on a western tour to convince greenbackers that specie resumption would strengthen the economy. Separately, President Hayes signed a Pension Arrears Act for disabled Union veterans on ***January 25, 1879***.

13-Sep-1890. *dsa Jupiter sextile ASC.*
6-Feb-1891. *csa ASC sextile Jupiter.*

The first direction timed the final events leading to passage of the McKinley tariff: *September 10, 1890*, Senate passed the trade reciprocity amendment; *September 27, 1890*, House passed the final bill; *October 1, 1890*, President Harrison signed the Tariff. How introduction of high tariffs resulting in higher prices paid by consumers is a delineation match to Jupiter/Cancer which favors consumer interests makes no apparent sense. Only when the McKinley tariff is considered jointly with the Sherman Anti-Trust Act passed *July 2, 1890* is the connection made. By limiting monopoly power whose side effects include higher prices to the detriment of consumers, the Sherman Anti-Trust Act is the better delineation match to Jupiter/Cancer. An *October 1, 1890* NYT editorial states that Sherman considered passage of the Sherman Anti-Trust Act necessary as a sop to the public in order to garner public support for the McKinley Tariff. Sherman apparently hoped that higher prices would attract new entrants to the ranks of producers and indirectly lower prices through competition.[82]

8-Sep-1908. *dsa ASC sextile Jupiter.*
2-Mar-1909. *csa Jupiter sextile ASC.*

On *September 10, 1908*, the U.S. Circuit Court for the Eastern District of Pennsylvania stuck down the commodity clause of the Hepburn Act.[83] The intent of the Hepburn act was to limit concentration of ownership in a single industry to 50%, a level which was violated by Pennsylvania coal and railroad companies whose ownership concentration was closer to 90%. Monitoring ownership concentration is one of the present day jurisdictions of the Federal Trade Commission, not yet in existence at the time of this direction. Why this Jupiter/Cancer direction timed the overturn of the Hepburn Act – an Act designed to disrupt a typical Saturn/Capricorn concentration of wealth – is not clear. Since Jupiter/Cancer fights concentration of wealth, the more logical fit would be *support* of the Hepburn Act. Saturn's signification as the Supreme Court (with Jupiter's application to Saturn by square aspect) clearly overpowered Jupiter for this event.

24-Dec-1949. *dsa Jupiter conj ASC.*
22-Jul-1950. *csa ASC conj. Jupiter.*

On **December 23, 1949**, Westinghouse Electric Corporation president Gwilym A. Price endorsed an income tax plan that would exempt ~20 million low income earners from any tax and would increase rates on highest income earners, both individuals and corporations.[84] This event raises the possibility that tax relief for the common people is another valid delineation for Jupiter/Cancer/8th.

On **December 25, 1949**, reports of Congressional plans to legislate retroactive income tax on life insurance companies for 1947-1948 were expected to be opposed by industry.[85] Here, the Jupiter/Cancer direction is better described by something it opposes: Saturn/Capricorn as a signature for accumulated capital owned by insurance companies.

On **July 20, 1950**, banking lobbyists urged passage of a bill to broaden the power of states to increase taxes for national banks.[86] This event is similar in spirit to Jupiter-Ascendant Direction #8 which harmed national banks by curtailing the expansion of national branch banking.

15-Sep-1967. *dsa ASC conj. Jupiter.*
15-Apr-1968. *csa Jupiter conj. ASC.*

On **September 1, 1967**, the U.S. Government raised insurance limits for individuals with savings accounts in banks and S&Ls from $10,000 to $15,000.[87] Note the NYT reported this event on September 14, 1967 within one day of the first direction.

On **April 11, 1968**, President Lyndon Johnson signed the Civil Rights Act of 1968. Also known as the Fair Housing Act, the thrust of the legislation was to prohibit discrimination in the sale, rental, and financing of housing based on race, religion, national origin, sex, (and as amended) handicap and family status. This event is a delineation match to Jupiter/Cancer/8th ruling the 4th as mortgage finance.

Notes

Abbreviations

ARM. *A Rectification Manual*, Regulus Astrology LLC, 2007.
NYT. *New York Times*, online article database; available from www.newyorktimes.com.

User's Guide

[1] Rumen Kolev can be reached through his website at www.babylonianastrology.com. Selected publications are available through www.astroamerica.com.

1. National Horoscopes in Mundane Astrology

[1] For Ptolemy's eclipse rule, see Claudius Ptolemy, *Tetrabiblos*, translated by J. M. Ashmand, New York: Astrology Classics, 2002, p. 53. One example supporting Ptolemy's logic is the solar eclipse of October 30, 1845 at 7SC26 falling in the Midheaven of both President James Polk and military leader Zachary Taylor. This eclipse, and subsequent transits of Mars to the eclipse degree, timed key incidents in the Mexican War including Taylor's election to the Presidency on November 7, 1847 one day after Mars transited the solar eclipse degree. Taylor was a general in the Mexican War and parlayed his battle victories into a successful Presidential bid. See *A Rectification Manual*, p. 328 for more details.
[2] Michael Baigent, Nicholas Campion, and Charles Harvey, *Mundane Astrology: An Introduction to the Astrology of Nations and Groups*, London: Harpers Collins Publishers, 1992, Chapter 4.
[3] Baigent, Campion, and Harvey, pp. 242-243.
[4] Charles Carter, *An Introduction to Political Astrology*, London, 1951.
[5] Baigent, Campion, and Harvey, pp. 17-111.
[6] Nicholas Campion, *The Book of World Horos*copes, Bournemouth: The Wessex Astrologer Ltd., 2004, pp. 2-29.
[7] Guido Bonatti, *Book of Astronomy,* translated by Benjamin Dykes, Minneapolis, Minn.: The Cazimi Press, 2007.
[8] Abū Ma'shar, *On Historical Astrology: The Book of Religions and Dynasties (On the Great Conjunctions)*, 2 Vols. Edited and Translated by Keiji Yamamoto and Charles Burnett. Leiden: E. J. Brill, 2000.
[9] David McCullough, *John Adams*, New York: Simon & Schuster, 2001.
[10] 'USA,' *Lois Rodden's Astrodatabank*; [article on-line]; available from http://astrodatabank.com/NM/USA.htm; accessed August 1, 2008.
[11] Campion, pp. 363-366. Also see Ed Kahout, *The Riddle of the Sibly Chart for American Independence: Masonic Astrology and the Fixed Square of the Zodiac*; [article on-line]; http://edkohout.com/mundane/sibly-1.html; accessed August 1, 2008.
[12] Campion, p 16.

[13] For an example of how transits are subjected to time lord procedures, see ARM, Chapter 13. In a case study of President Franklin Roosevelt, transits of Roosevelt's Ascendant Mercury ruler are subjected to time lord procedures including Directing by Triplicity, Abū Ma'shar's System of Distributors and Partners, Firdaria, the Lord of the Year, and the Lord of the Period.

[14] 'USA,' Lois Rodden's Astrodatabank; [article on-line]; available from http://astrodatabank.com/NM/USA.htm; accessed August 1, 2008. Event wording modified for this presentation.

[15] The Sibly USA National Horoscope is cast for July 4, 1776, 5:10 PM, LMT, Philadelphia, PA. There remains considerable debate over this figure. One often heard criticism is Sibly's calculation errors which yield alternative times of 11:50 AM and 4:50 PM. Then there is the argument made by Susan Manuel, 'Making Sense of Sibly', NCGR Journal, Spring 1994, Vol. 13 No. 1, pp. 35-40; that the Sibly figure was based on the Aries and Cancer ingresses for 1776 and modified by transits the day of July 4, 1776. For a discussion see Campion, pp. 363-366.

2. Revisiting the Sibly USA National Horoscope

[1] Campion, p. 365.

[2] CCAG; VIII.1; 241-242. Thanks to Demetra George for this reference.

[3] AMR, Chapter 15.

[4] In *The Thousands of Abū Ma'shar* (Warburg Institute, 1968), David Pingree presents a Firdaria sequence for mundane figures which is uniform for both diurnal and nocturnal figures. In my own testing, I have found application of diurnal and nocturnal variations of the Firdaria sequence used in natal astrology relevant to mundane applications. See AMR, Appendix B, pp. 369-417, for discussion and tests of natal Firdaria technique.

[5] 'Silent Cal and White House Christmas Traditions', *American Presidents Blog*; [article on-line]; available from http://www.american-presidents.org/2007/12/silent-cal-and-white-house-christmashtml; accessed August 1, 2008.

[6] It is not unreasonable to assume that JFK Jr. did not have full muscular control of his foot and ankle, freshly exposed from a cast. I suggest, and this is purely speculative, that an unexpected problem with his ankle contributed to the cause of JFK Jr.'s fatal plane crash.

[7] John F. Kennedy Jr., b. 25 November 1960, 12:22 AM, Washington D.C., ASC = 11VI57. Data: News report, A rated, www.astrodatank.com.

[8] Mars/Aquarius = fighting (Mars) against humanitarian ideals (Aquarius).

[9] This assumes the event is timed by the exact date Saturn transits the Moon. Events timed by transits can occur earlier when the transiting planet applies to the fixed natal planet.

[10] For definition of the primary direction sequence, see ARM, p. 132.

[11] ARM, pp. 282-283.

[12] Abū Ma'shar, *On Solar Revolutions* Part II, translated by Robert Schmidt, Cumberland, Md.: The Phaser Foundation, Inc., 1999, p. 12.

3. Divination and Rectification

[1] ARM, p. 303. Since making this initial observation, I am now under the opinion that it is connections made between *transiting* Mercury and *transiting* Moon to the natal figure which define the operative divination process.

[2] Geoffrey Cornelius, *The Moment of Astrology: Origins in Divination*, Bournemouth, U.K.: The Wessex Astrologer, Ltd, 2nd ed., 2003.

[3] Cornelius, p. 249.

[4] ARM, pp. 132-133.

[5] Cornelius, p. 250.
[6] Cornelius, pp. 82-83.
[7] AMR, pp. 291-292.
[8] Cornelius, pp. 26-31.
[9] Cornelius, p. 54.
[10] Cornelius, p. 67.
[11] Claudius Ptolemy, *Tetrabiblos*, translated by J. M. Ashmand, London, 1822, p. 123. Full quotation: "Moreover, should the Moon herself actually occupy the place of regulating the employment, and, after her conjunction, continue in course with Mercury, being at the same time in Taurus, Capricorn, or Cancer, she will then produce soothsayers, attendants on sacrifices, and diviners by the basin. If she be in Sagittarius or Pisces, she will make necromancers, and evokers of daemons: if in Virgo or Scorpio, magicians, astrologers, and oracular persons, possessing prescience: and, if in Libra, Aries, or Leo, she will produce fanatics interpreters of dreams, and makers of false vows and adjurations."
[12] Geoffrey Cornelius, 'Is Astrology Divination - and does it matter?'; [article on-line]; available from http://www.innerself.com/Astrology/divination.htm; accessed August 1, 2008.
[13] Ptolemy, p. 121.
[14] ARM, Chapter 15.
[15] Guido Bonatti, *Book of Astronomy*, translated by Benjamin Dykes, Minneapolis, Minn.: The Cazimi Press, 2007, p. 271. Bonatti lists combustion as the fourth of ten weaknesses of planets in the 6th consideration.
[16] Bonatti, p. 1325.

4. Abū Ma'shar's System of Distributors and Partners

[1] 'Zodiacal Releasing from Spirit,' Project Hindsight; [article on-line]; available from http://www.projecthindsight.com/products/releasing.html; accessed September 30, 2008.
[2] Robert Schmidt has chosen to translate the title for Treatise III in Abū Ma'shar's *On Solar Revolutions* as 'Concerning the Circumambulations of the Stars Taken in the Change-Overs. While I agree with Schmidt's choice of the words Distributors and Partners to explain the moving parts to this methodology, I believe some simplification is called for in the naming of the superstructure. I have chosen to name it *Abū Ma'shar's System of Distributors and Partners*.
[3] Abū Ma'shar, *On Solar Revolutions*, ed. and trans. by Robert Schmidt, Project Hindsight, 1999.
[4] I name the method whereby significators are moved through bounds by primary motion: *Directing through the Bounds*. Robert Zoller translates Bonatti's description of this method as *Directing by Terms*; Robert Schmidt translates Abū Ma'shar's description as *Circumambulation through the Bounds*. These names all refer to the same system.
[5] Ascendant, Midheaven, Moon, Sun, Part of Fortune, Prenatal Lunation.
[6] For definition of a planet's major years, translated by Ben Dykes as 'greater' years, see Bonatti, *Book of Astronomy*, Treatise 3: Planets, pp. 149-186. Major years are Saturn, 57; Jupiter, 79; Mars, 66; Venus, 82; Mercury, 76; Moon, 108; Sun, 120.
[7] ARM, Chapter 1.
[8] 'Dexter and Sinister,' *Glossary of Terms*, Skyscript.co.uk; [article on-line]; available from http://www.skyscript.co.uk/gl/dexter.html; accessed August 1, 2008.

5. Calculation: Distributors and Partners

[1] National Archives and Records Administration, Public domain image.
[2] Forthcoming: *Primary Directions: The Practice Manual*, Regulus Astrology LLC, 201X.
[3] For formulas, see Bob Makransky, *Primary Directions: A Primer of Calculation*, Occidental, CA..: Dear Brutus Press, 1988; [book on-line]; available from http://www.dearbrutus.com/; accessed August 1, 2008.

6. Distributor Results: Directing through the Bounds

[1] Bonatti, Treatise 8, Chapters 1-4, pp. 818-837.
[2] John Witherspoon, b. 15-Feb-1723. Natal Saturn 27SA20 falls in the bound of Mars/Sagittarius.
[3] Marie Kimball, *Jefferson, the Road to Glory: 1743 – 1776*. New York: Coward – McCann, 1943, p. 73.
[4] Wikipedia contributors, "Noah Webster," *Wikipedia, The Free Encyclopedia*; available from http://en.wikipedia.org/w/index.php?title=Noah_Webster&oldid=222411371; accessed August 8, 2008.
[5] Charles A. Beard, *An Economic Interpretation of the Constitution of the United States*, New York: The Free Press, 1913.
[6] Manilius, *Astronomica*, trans. G.P. Goold, Harvard University Press, 1977, p. 243.
[7] Peter L. Bernstein, *Wedding of the Waters: The Erie Canal and the Making of a Great Nation*, New York: W. W. Norton & Company, 2005, Chapters 2-3. Washington formed the Patowmack Company in 1785 as a vehicle to leverage his Potomac River landholdings by creating an East-West canal which would connect to the Potomac. Washington's interests in canal construction can be delineated through his Aquarius Ascendant; failure to complete, through Saturn/Aries (significator of obstructions) placed in the 3rd house of local transportation. For Washington's rectification see ARM, pp. 422-427.
[8] Henry Clay's American System had three components: a National Bank, tariffs, and internal improvements (canal and road construction). Tariffs were designed to protect nascent domestic manufacturers against foreign competition and to provide funding for internal improvements. The objective of canals and roads was to facilitate transportation of raw material and farm products throughout the nation as well as for export sale. A National Bank provided credit availability to support both agricultural and manufacturing sectors.
[9] John Lauritz Larson, *Internal Improvement: National Public Works and the Promise of Popular Government in the Early United States*, Chapel Hill, NC.: University of North Carolina Press, 2001, pp. 64-65.
[10] Calhoun's speech in support of the Bonus Bill of 1817 was vetoed by outgoing President James Madison on March 3, 1817 based on Madison's belief that the Constitution did not allow Congress to appropriate funds for internal improvements. Though Madison's veto (and James Monroe's later May 4, 1822 veto of internal improvements on similar grounds) reflect a disinterested Executive Branch, this lack of interest was more than made up for by States and private investors who funded the Erie Canal and other internal improvement projects.
[11] Harley J. McKee, 'Canvass White and Natural Cement, 1818-1834,' *Concrete International*, June 1979, pp. 39-43.
[12] Nobel E. Whitford, 'The Canals as a School of Engineering' in *History of the Canal System of the State of New York*, 1906, Chapter 24; [book on-line]; available from http://www.history.rochester.edu/canal/bib/whitford/old1906/index.htm; accessed October 20, 2008.
[13] Bernstein, p. 213.
[14] Larson, pp. 149-194.

[15] Josiah Holbrook, 'Society for Mutual Education' included in the *Memoir of Josiah Holbrook* and reprinted from *Barnard's American Journal of Education*, 1858, pp. 229-256; [article on-line]; available from http://www.assumption.edu/ahc/Lyceum%20Site/Holbrookslyceum.html; accessed September 1, 2008.

[16] J. C. Tumblin, 'The Holbrooks: Fountain Citians Who Made a Difference'; [article on-line]; available from http://www.fountaincitytnhistory.info/People22-TheHolbrooks.htm; accessed September 1, 2008.

[17] For an introduction to blackface performance, see Annemarie Bean, James V. Hatch, and Brooks McNamara, eds., *Inside the Minstrel Mask*, Wesleyan University Press, 1996.

[18] The other staple of minstrel shows was the song *Dixie*, developed much later and premiered by Bryant's Minstrels in New York City on April 4, 1859. For a speculative chart cast for *Dixie's* premiere at 9:00 PM, note the Moon-Mercury-Mars Taurus stellium disposed by Venus in Pisces. I give this example to demonstrate the connection between Venus/Pisces and minstrelsy. In performance, the chorus was the only section of the song not altered. The penultimate chorus lyric "In Dixie Land I'll take my stand to live and die in Dixie" is a delineation match to Venus/Pisces as sacrificial love. For further information see:
Wikipedia contributors, "Dixie (song)," *Wikipedia, The Free Encyclopedia*; [article on-line]; available from http://en.wikipedia.org/w/index.php?title=Dixie_(song)&oldid=232767353; accessed August 25, 2008.

[19] As reconstructed by historians including Eric Lott. See Eric Lott, *Love and Theft: Blackface Minstrelsy and the American Working Class*, Oxford University Press, 1993.

[20] See *The Juba Project* for this eyewitness account among other useful documentary material; available from http://www.utm.utoronto.ca/~sjohnson/juba/Microhistory/Eyewitness.html; accessed September 1, 2008.

[21] Bean, Match, and McNamara, p. 164.

[22] Winter's article is reprinted in Bean, Hatch, and McNamara, pp. 223-241.

[23] Eric Jay Dolin, *Leviathan: The History of Whaling in America*, New York: W. W. Norton & Company, 2007, pp. 205-211.

[24] Dolin, pp. 209-210.

[25] Dolin, p. 206.

[26] ARM, p. 449.

[27] Daniel Walker Howe, *What Hath God Wrought: The Transformation of America, 1815 - 1848*, Oxford University Press, 2007, p. 796.

[28] William H. McIlhany, *Evidence of a Master Conspiracy*, Individualist Research Foundation, 1992; [article on-line]; available from http://home.earthlink.net/~whm/download.txt; accessed August 1, 2008.

[29] John H. Martin, 'Saints, Sinners and Reformers: The Burned-Over District Re-Visited,' Chapter 12: Orson Squire Fowler; [article on-line], available from
http://www.crookedlakereview.com/books/saints_sinners/martin12.html;
accessed August 1, 2008. Fowler's natal Jupiter/Aries (b. 11-Oct-1809) recapitulates the bound planet/sign combination for the Distribution.

[30] Venus/Aries also signifies Stephen Douglas' greed for railroad investments as read through Abraham Lincoln's figure. See AMR, p. 16.

[31] Wikipedia contributors, "Uncle Tom's Cabin," *Wikipedia, The Free Encyclopedia*; http://en.wikipedia.org/w/index.php?title=Uncle_Tom%27s_Cabin&oldid=232578726
accessed August 21, 2008.

[32] David S. Reynolds, *Walt Whitman's America*, New York: Vintage Books, 1996, pp. 137-138.

[33] Buchanan's legalistic approach to the Kansas Constitutional Crisis is shown by Jupiter/Virgo in his natal figure, a placement amplified by the total solar eclipse of September 18, 1857. See AMR, p. 241

[34] Reynolds, p. 387.

[35] Gregory Eiselein, *Leaves of Grass: 1860 edition*, republished by The Walt Whitman Archive; [article on-line]; available from http://www.whitmanarchive.org/criticism/current/encyclopedia/entry_23.html; accessed October 10, 2008.

[36] Robert C. Kennedy, 'Ye Grand Ducal Ball at the Academy of Music (cartoon); complete HarpWeek Explanation', *HarpWeek*; [article on-line]; available from http://www.harpweek.com/09Cartoon/BrowseByDateCartoon.asp?Month=December&Date=16; accessed September 25, 2008.

[37] John Steele Gordon, 'To a Speculator Dying Young,' *American Heritage Magazine*, November 1992, Nol. 43, Issue 7; [article on-line]; available from http://www.americanheritage.com/articles/magazine/ah/1992/7/1992_7_18.shtml; accessed September 26, 2008.

[38] Ed Dinger, 'Company History: The Metropolitan Museum of Art,' International Directory of Company Histories, The Gale Group, Inc.; [article on-line]; available from http://www.answers.com/topic/metropolitan-museum-of-art; accessed September 25, 2008.

[39] Charter of the Metropolitan Museum of Art, State of New York, Laws of 1870, Chapter 197, passed April 13, 1870 and amended L. 1898, ch. 34; L. 1809, ch. 219.; [article on-line]; available from http://www.metmuseum.org/visitor/faq_hist.htm; accessed September 25, 2008.

[40] Werner Holzl and Andreas Reinstaller, *The Adoption and Enforcement of a Technological Regime: The Case of the First IT Regime*, Vienna University of Economics and Business Administration, Working Paper No. 12, September 2000, p. 7; [paper on-line]; available from http://www.wu-wien.ac.at/inst/vw1/gee/papers/gee!wp12.pdf; accessed August 1, 2008.

[41] Greg Gross, 'The Staff Breakup of McClure's Magazine,' Chapter 2; [article on-line]; available from http://tarbell.allegheny.edu/mctable.html; accessed June 18, 2008.

[42] Gross.

[43] John Steele Gordon, 'Woolworth's Cathedral,' *American Heritage Magazine*, July/August 1989, Vol. 50, No. 5.; [article on-line]; available from http://www.americanheritage.com/articles/magazine/ah/1989/5/1989_5_16.shtml; accessed September 30, 2008.

[44] Jean Maddern Pitrone, *F. W. Woolworth and the American Five and Dime*, Jefferson, NC.: McFarland & Company, Inc., 2003., p. 28.

[45] Pitrone, p. 21.

[46] Gross.

[47] Henry F. Pringle, *Theodore Roosevelt*, Harcourt, Brace and Company, 1931, p. 543.

[48] For visual documentation of the savagery of lynching, see the photo collection of James Allen at http://withoutsanctuary.org; accessed October 1, 2008.

[49] David J. Hanson, 'The Ku Klux Klan (KKK), Alcohol, & Prohibition'; [article on-line]; available from http://www2.potsdam.edu/hansondj/Controversies/1107362364.html; accessed June 24, 2008.

[50] Library of Congress, Prosperity and Thrift: The Coolidge Era and the Consumer Economy, 1921-1929, [reference on-line]; available from http://memory.loc.gov/ammem/coolhtml/coolhome.html; accessed October 20, 2008.

[51] NYT, 'Mae West Signs with Paramount,' October 1932, p. 18.

[52] Dairy Farmers of America, 'Get to Know Elsie the Cow'; [article on-line]; available from http://www.friendsofelsie.com/coop.asp?action=Elsie; accessed June 28, 2008.

[53] NYT, 'New Farm Group Formed in Senate,' April 2, 1939, p. 4.

[54] NYT, 'Farm Program: 1939 Model; An Analysis by Secretary Wallace,' April 2, 1939.

[55] Lawrence Lader, 'The Wallace Campaign of 1948,' *American Heritage Magazine*, Vol. 28, Issue 1, December 1976; [article on-line]; available from http://www.americanheritage.com/articles/magazine/ah/1976/1/1976_1_42.shtml; accessed July 8, 2008.

[56] NYT, 'Consumer Credit Urged by Banker,' June 7, 1939, p. 39.

[57] NYT, 'Bankers Name Speakers,' June 6, 1939, p. 39.

[58] Jay Mechling, *On My Honor: Boy Scouts and the Making of American Youth*, Chicago, IL.: The University of Chicago Press, 2001, p. 43.

[59] Wikipedia contributors, "Pledge of Allegiance," *Wikipedia, The Free Encyclopedia*, http://en.wikipedia.org/w/index.php?title=Pledge_of_Allegiance&oldid=225630935; accessed July 15, 2008.

[60] Mechling, pp. 42-46.

[61] ARM, pp. 40-41.

[62] Joseph Lanza, *The Cocktail: The Influence of Spirits on the American Psyche*, New York, St. Martin's Press, 1995, pp. 117-119.

[63] Susan Jeffords, *Hard Bodies: Hollywood Masculinity in the Reagan Era*, Rutgers University Press, 1994.

[64] NYT, 'The Media Business: Microsoft's Bold New Game Plan,' November 1, 1990.

[65] Peter Biskind, 'An American Family,' *Vanity Fair*, April 2007; [article on-line]; available from http://www.vanityfair.com/culture/features/2007/04/sopranos200704?currentPage=1; accessed July 15, 2008.

[66] Mark Scott, 'Brewer to Buy Remaining Stake in Grupo Modelo,' NYT, June 29, 2012; [article on-line]; https://dealbook.nytimes.com/2012/06/29/anheuser-busch-inbev-to-buy-remaining-stake-in-grupo-modelo-for-20-1-billion/?searchResultPosition=3; accessed April 18, 2021.

[67] Global Beer Trekking, 'Acquisitions and Mergers;' [reference on-line]; available from http://www.globalbeertrekking.com/acquisitions-and-mergers.html; accessed April 18, 2021.

[68] https://trends.google.com/trends/explore?date=all&geo=US&q=craft%20beer; accessed April 18, 2021.

[69] Statista, 'Average annual price of hops in the United States from 2010 to 2019;' https://www.statista.com/statistics/758004/average-annual-price-of-hops-in-the-us/; accessed April 18, 2021.

[70] Brewers Association, National Beer Sales & Production Data. available from https://www.brewersassociation.org/statistics-and-data/national-beer-stats/; accessed May 21, 2021.

[71] Christina Farr, 'Apple just hired the star of Stanford's digital health efforts,' CNBC, June 8, 2017; [article on-line]; available from https://www.cnbc.com/2017/06/08/apple-hires-sumbul-desai-stanford-digital-health-executive-director.html; accessed April 18, 2020.

[72] Michael Roberts, 'Tim Cook Pivots to Fitness,' Outside Magazine, Winter 2021, pp. 18-22.

[73] Gregory Wallace and Chandelis Duster, 'Trump administration announces plans to drill in Arctic National Wildlife Refuge,' August 17, 2020; [article on-line]; available from https://www.cnn.com/2020/08/17/politics/trump-arctic-wildlife-drilling/index.html; accessed April 18, 2021.

7. Participator Results: Ascendant Directions

[1] Abū Ma'shar, *On Historical Astrology: The Book of Religions and Dynasties (On the Great Conjunctions)*, 2 Vols. Edited and Translated by Keiji Yamamoto and Charles Burnett, Leiden: E.J. Brill, 2000.

[2] Guido Bonatti, *Book of Astronomy*, Translated by Benjamin Dykes, (Minneapolis, MN.: The Cazimi Press), 2007.

³ Bonatti, p. 933.
⁴ Mark Reisner, *Cadillac Desert: The American West and Its Disappearing Water*, New York: Viking Press, 1986.
⁵ Abū Ma'shar, p. 233.
⁶ Johannes Schoener, *On the Judgments of Nativities: Book I*, translated by Robert Hand, Reston, VA.: Arhat Publications, 2001, p. 175.
⁷ On May 17, 2007, World Bank President Paul Wolfowitz resigned after facing a series of ethics violations including favoritism towards his girlfriend and World Bank Senior Communications Officer Shaha Riza.
⁸ On October 25, 2008 the International Monetary Fund's Board announced results of an internal investigation which confirmed allegations made by board member Shakour Shaalan that Dominque Strauss-Kahn had an affair with IMF economist Piroska Nagy who later left her position with a severance package. The investigation concluded Strauss-Kahn's affair reflected an error in judgment but one which fell short of harassment, favoritism, or abuse of power. Strauss-Kahn was allowed to stay in his post.
⁹ Unless the planet is partile conjunct the Ascendant to the degree, minute, and second.

8. Partners: Moon

¹ Moon rules the 8th whole sign house by sign, the 6th whole sign house by exaltation, and the 5th quadrant house cusp by exaltation. Rulership by both sign and exaltation is identified for all planets in Chapters 8-15.
² Manilius, *Astronomica*, trans. G.P. Goold, Harvard University Press, 1977, p. 243.
³ Wikipedia contributors, "Molly Pitcher," *Wikipedia, The Free Encyclopedia*, http://en.wikipedia.org/w/index.php?title=Molly_Pitcher&oldid=214270685; accessed June 10, 2008.
⁴ Linda Grant De Pauw, *Cries and Lullabies: Women in War from Prehistory to the Present*, Norman, OK.: University of Oklahoma Press, 1998, p. 124.
⁵ ARM p. 365.
⁶ Wikipedia contributors, "Gilbert du Motier, marquis de La Fayette," *Wikipedia, The Free Encyclopedia*, http://en.wikipedia.org/w/index.php?title=Gilbert_du_Motier%2C_marquis_de_La_Fayette&oldid=217167172; accessed June 10, 2008.
⁷ Wikipedia contributors, "David Thompson (explorer)," *Wikipedia, The Free Encyclopedia*, http://en.wikipedia.org/w/index.php?title=David_Thompson_%28explorer%29&oldid=217623965 accessed June 10, 2008.
⁸ Start of construction for Erie Canal on July 4, 1817 timed by d. ASC trine Moon, lat=zero. Positions of Moon and Ascendant reversed as Significator and Promittor. Exact date match. Placidus under the Pole methodology.
⁹ Peter L. Bernstein, *Wedding of the Waters: The Erie Canal and the Making of a Great Nation*, New York: W. W. Norton & Company, 2005, p. 192.
¹⁰ Smithsonian Institution, 'The Will of James Smithson'; [article on-line]; available from http://www.sil.si.edu/Exhibitions/Smithson-to-Smithsonian/will.htm; accessed September 1, 2008.
¹¹ Smithsonian Institution, 'Will of the late James Smithson, Esq.'; [article on-line]; available from http://www.sil.si.edu/Exhibitions/Smithson-to-Smithsonian/new-amer.html; accessed September 1, 2008.
¹² Wikipedia contributors, Harriet Tubman," *Wikipedia, The Free Encyclopedia*, http://en.wikipedia.org/w/index.php?title=Harriet_Tubman&oldid=217312795; accessed June 10, 2008).

[13] Purchase of Panama Railroad Company assets by U.S. Government on April 23, 1904 timed by converse Ascendant sextile Moon, lat=zero, April 16, 1904; error of 7 days. Position of Moon and Ascendant reversed as significator and promittor. Placidus under the Pole methodology.

[14] Saturn is the killing planet for the Sun, computed according to rules presented in AMR, p. 62. Assumptions: Sun on the Ascendant, equal sign houses, and the Part of Death computed with the 8th cusp defined by equal sign houses.

[15] For more on the mythology concerning Mary Lincoln's alleged ride in the Pullman Palace Car's *Pioneer* car as part of her husband Abraham Lincoln's funeral cortege, see 'The Pullmans Palace Car Company'; [article on-line]; available from http://www.midcontinent.org/rollingstock/builders/pullman1.htm; accessed October 20, 2008.

[16] Note also that the title of the book 'Looking Backward' matches the sinister square aspect in this direction. Sinister aspects 'look back' against the diurnal movement of planets.

[17] James J. Kopp, 'Looking Backward at Edward Bellamy's Influence in Oregon, 1888-1936,' *Oregon Historical Quarterly*, Vol. 104, No. 1, Spring 2003; [article on-line]; available from http://www.historycooperative.org/journals/ohq/104.1/kopp.html; accessed August 3, 2008.

[18] NYT, 'Shipments for Abroad,' December 6, 1914, p. 6.

[19] NYT, 'Panama Agrees to Treaty,' December 9, 1914, p. 1.

[20] NYT, 'Foreign Warships Ignore Canal Laws,' December 14, 1914, page 1.

[21] NYT, 'Goethals Condemns Panama Agreement,' December 12, 1916, p. 7.

[22] Randall Davidson, '9XM Talking: The Early History of WHA Radio', PortalWisconsin.org; [article on-line]; available from http://www.portalwisconsin.org/9xm.cfm; accessed September 4, 2008.

[23] Wikipedia contributors, "Equal Rights Amendment," *Wikipedia, The Free Encyclopedia*, http://en.wikipedia.org/w/index.php?title=Equal_Rights_Amendment&oldid=217121959; accessed June 10, 2008.

[24] NYT, 'Women Office Holders have made big gains,' November 16, 1924, p. XX13.

[25] Wikipedia contributors, "Shirley Chisholm," *Wikipedia, The Free Encyclopedia*, http://en.wikipedia.org/w/index.php?title=Shirley_Chisholm&oldid=217924856; accessed June 10, 2008.

[26] NYT, 'House Passes Bill to Upset a Limit on U.S. Rights Law,' March 3, 1988.

[27] NYT, 'House and Senate Vote to Override Reagan on Rights,' March 23, 1988.

[28] NYT, 'House in '88 Rated Most Liberal in 40 Years,' January 25, 1989.

[29] NYT, 'Equal Rights Proposal is Revived in House,' January 4, 1989.

[30] George H. W. Bush, 1988 Republican National Convention Acceptance Address; [speech on-line]; available from http://www.americanrhetoric.com/speeches/georgehbush1988rnc.htm; accessed September 4, 2008.

[31] NYT, 'Crash on the New Jersey Transit,' February 19, 1996.

[32] NYT, 'As Rail Travel Declines, So Do Amtrak's Options,' January 17, 1998.

[33] NYT,' Feminists Gather to Affirm Relevancy of Their Movement.' February 3, 1996.

[34] NYT 'Author Revisits Gloria Steinem Milestones,' January 25, 1998.

9. Partners: Sun

[1] Thomas Paine, *The Rights of Man*, Chapter 5; [book on-line]; available from http://www.ushistory.org/paine/rights/index.htm; accessed May 4, 2008.

[2] *Chronological Table of Thomas Paine's Writings*, Thomas Paine National Historical Association; [reference on-line]; available from http://www.thomaspaine.org/chron.html; accessed May 4, 2008.

[3] Leonard Woolsey Bacon, History of American Christianity, Chapter XVI; [book on-line];

http://www.ccel.org/ccel/bacon_lw/history.ii.xvi.html; accessed May 5, 2008.

[4] Gerald N. Magliocca, 'The Cherokee Removal and the 14th Amendment,' *Duke Law Journal*, Vol. 53, No. 2, December 2003, p. 890.

[5] Brad Hursh, 'Emerson's Divinity School Address: Conditions and Reactions,' *Chrestomathy: Annual Review of Undergraduate Research at the College of Charleston*. Vol. 3, 2004; pp. 101-118.

[6] Martin Bickman, *Transcendental Ideas: Definitions; An Overview of American Transcendentalism*; [article on-line]; available from http://www.vcu.edu/engweb/transcendentalism/ideas/definitionbickman.html; accessed September 7, 2008.

[7] See National Parks Service, *Mormon Pioneer: Historic Resource Study*; [article on-line]; available from http://www.nps.gov/history/history/online_books/mopi/hrs6.htm; accessed September 7, 2008.

[8] 'Clara Barton'; [article on-line]; available from http://www.ilovethefingerlakes.com/history/famous-people-barton.htm; accessed September 7, 2008.

[9] United States Geological Survey, The Four Great Surveys of the West; [article on-line]; available from http://pubs.usgs.gov/circ/c1050/surveys.htm; accessed September 7, 2008.

[10] Robbie Fee-Thomson. Woman's Work for Woman in the Lord's Name: Lydia Lord Davis (1867-1952); [article on-line]; available from http://www.oberlin.edu/external/EOG/History322/LydiaLordDavis/Introduction.htm; accessed September 7, 2008.

[11] Ernest Grafe and Paul Horsted, Exploring with Custer, Golden Valley Press; [excerpt on-line]; available from http://www.custerstrail.com/; accessed September 7, 2008. See also http://www.nps.gov/archive/wica/History_of_the_Black_Hills.htm.

[12] 'Homestake Visitor Center'; [article on-line]; available from http://www.homestaketour.com/; accessed September 7, 2008.

[13] Vettius Valens, *Anthology*, Book 2, Chapter 21, trans. Robert Schmidt, Cumberland, MD.: Project Hindsight.

[14] Author Dan O'Brien's sympathetic portrayal of McGillycuddy is consistent with the outgoing caring delineation of Sun/Cancer. See *The Contract Surgeon*, The Lyons Press, 1999, and *The Indian Agent*, HarperTorch, 2005.

[15] Superannuated = incapacitated or disqualified for active duty by advanced age.

[16] NYT, 'Carnegie Millions for College Pension Fund,' April 28 1905, page 1.

[17] Franklin Roosevelt, *Democratic National Convention of 1932, Nomination Address*, Franklin & Eleanor Roosevelt Institute; [speech on-line]; available from http://www.feri.org/archives/speeches/jul0232.cfm; accessed September 7, 2008.

[18] For a biography, see *Francis A. Schaeffer: The Early Years*; [book on-line]; available from http://www.covenantseminary.edu/worldwide/en/CC578/CC578.asp; accessed September 7, 2008.

[19] NYT, 'Harvard Medical Center Set to Open This Week,' July 7, 1980, p. B11.

[20] NYT, 'Vincent Pulicano, Supported Hospices,' February 28, 1981.

[21] NYT, "Some Banks in Europe Suffer, Too," October 2, 2007.

10. Partners: Lunar Nodes

[1] For theory and examples behind the ability of the North Node to increase and the South Node to decrease, see AMR, pp. 228-229.

[2] Guido Bonatti, *Book of Astronomy*, translated by Benjamin Dykes, Minneapolis, Minn.: The Cazimi Press, 2007, p. 1326.

³ Vivian Robson, *The Fixed Stars & Constellations in Astrology*, 1923; reprint, New York: Astrology Classics, 2001, p. 209.

⁴ Relative to the Sun's position of 13CA22'03", Sirius' position was 12CA57'28" on November 11, 1918 for the WWI Armistice. On March 22, 1948 Sirius moved to 13CA22'03" conjunct the position of the Sun. This coincided with the communist takeover of Czechoslovakia during February 1948 and the suspicious suicide of Czechoslovakian Foreign Minister Jan Masaryk on March 10, 1948. Both of these events were catalysts for a reluctant Congress to approve funding for the Marshall Plan on March 31, 1948. Interpreting the Marshall Plan as the culmination of Sirius' precession towards the Sun is an interesting concept which requires further study.

⁵ Ptolemy assigns Gaul to Leo. Gaul is the location of modern day France and Belgium. With the capital of the European Union located in Brussels, Belgium, Leo has also worked well as a the sign for the European Union as a whole in recent years (author's finding).

⁶ ARM, pp. 234-236.

⁷ Eli Bimbaum, *The History of the Jewish People*, 1996-2006; [encyclopedia on-line], available from http://www.jewishhistory.org.il/history.php?startyear=1840&endyear=1849; accessed September 9, 2008.

⁸ John Melnick, *Army Chaplains & Spiritual care of soldiers during the Civil War: 1861-1865*; [article on-line]; available from http://www.angelfire.com/pa5/civilwarchaplain/; accessed September 9, 2008. For additional research, refer also to the National Civil War Chaplains Museum housed by Liberty University: http://chaplainsmuseum.org/; accessed September 9, 2008.

⁹ NYT, 'The Typical Volunteer; Unveiling of the Kearny Statue at Newark, Dec. 29, 1880, p. 1.

¹⁰ NYT, 'The Alaskan Boundary,' August 8, 1889, p. 2.

¹¹ NYT, 'Working for the Chinese; The Remarkable Career of the Rev. J. Crossett,' August 14, 1889, p. 2.

¹² NYT, p. 11.

¹³ NYT, 'Mgr. John J. Burke, Welfare Aide, Dies,' October 31, 1936, p. 19.

¹⁴ NYT, 'Princeton Student Wins Social Security Debate,' October 29, 1936, p. 17

¹⁵ NYT 'Roosevelt urges Guarding of Peace,' October 29, 1936, p. 21.

¹⁶ NYT 'L.J. Wilth, Dies,' June 8, 1955, p. 29.

¹⁷ NYT, 'Books and Authors,' p. 27.

¹⁸ NYT, 'Clarence E. Lovejoy, the Creator of College Guide, Dies at 79,' p. 42.

¹⁹ NYT, 'David Crawford, Ex-Head of U. of Hawaii, Dies at 84,' January 19, 1974, p. 34.

²⁰ NYT, 'The Video Dial Tone, Strangled,' August 31, 1992.

²¹ NYT 'Insurers to Share Shipwreck's Gold,' August 28, 1992.

²² George DeWan, 'Between Slavery and Freedom,' Newsday Inc.; [article on-line]; available from http://www.newsday.com/community/guide/lihistory/ny-past606,0,5538682.story; accessed September 9, 2008. See also David N. Gellman, *Emancipating New York: The Politics of Slavery and Freedom*, 1777-1827, LSU Press, 2006.

²³ A. P. van der Mei, 'Freedom of Movement for Indigents: A Comparative Analysis of American Constitutional Law and European Community Law,' *Arizona Journal of International and Comparative Law*, Vol. 19, No. 3, pp. 803-861; [article on-line]; available from http://www.law.arizona.edu/Journals/AJICL/AJICL2002/vol193/VanderMei.pdf; accessed September 9, 2008.

²⁴ NYT, 'Tammany Allies; The Startling Exposures of the Operations of the Canal Ring,' September 19, 1871, p. 2.

²⁵ NYT, 'Pacific Mail Company; Resignation of the President,' December 4, 1874, p. 5.

²⁶ NYT, 'Dr. F.D. Gamewell, Long A Missionary; Hero of Siege of Peking During Boxer Rebellion Dies at 92-- Served in China 49 Years,' August 8, 1950, p. 29.

27 NYT, 'Conferees Approve Social Security Bill,' August 2, 1950, p. 25.
28 NYT, 'Integration Bill Faces House Test,' May 20, 1962, p. 59.
29 NYT, '3 U.S. Missionaries Kidnapped by Vietcong in Raid on Hospital,' June 1, 1962, p. 6.
30 NYT, 'French Set a Date for 1st Satellite,' May 31, 1962, p. 4.
31 NYT, 'Reserve Obtains Supply of Pounds,' June 1, 1962, p. 33.
32 NYT, 'F.C.C. Repeals Net Neutrality Rules,' December 15, 2017, p. 1
33 NYT, 'Big Tech to Join Legal Fight Against Net Neutrality Repeal,' January 6, 2018, Section B, page 2.

11. Partners: Saturn

1 Using the five degree offset rule, when adding five degrees to Saturn's position, Saturn falls in the 10th house using Alchabitius house cusps. 14LI48 + 5 degrees = 19LI48.

2 Scholars have traced the first usage of the phrase back to 1836 by the writer Washington Irving. For further information, see Trivia-Library.com, http://www.trivia-library.com/b/origins-of-sayings-the-almighty-dollar.htm; accessed September 7, 2008.

3 NYT, 'US Exports Seen Key to World Fund,' December 20, 1946, p. 37.

4 ARM, pp. 656-657.

5 See ARM, pp. 654-657.

6 Alberto Alesina and Beatrice Weder, "Do Corrupt Governments Receive Less Foreign Aid?" American Economic Review 92 (4): September 2002, pp. 1126-1137.

7 Antal Fekete, The Dollar: An Agonizing Reappraisal - Gold Vanishing into Private Hoards, www.kitco.com, May 30, 2007; [article on-line]; available from http://www.kitco.com/ind/fekete/may302007.html; accessed September 7, 2007. The peak measure of U.S. gold reserves on September 21, 1949 was $24,690,998,991.

8 Mars/Gemini is also replicated in the natal figure of Franklin Roosevelt who served as the American President during most of World War II. See ARM, pp. 254-278 and 602-607.

9 The avoirdupois system defined one pound as sixteen ounces.

10 'A Historic Review of Weights and Measures in the United States,' Arizona Department of Weights & Measures, 2008; [article on-line]; available from http://www.azdwm.gov/Default.aspx?tabid=269; accessed September 7, 2008.

11 Ron Guth, *The History of the Early United States Mint - 1795*, Coinfacts.com; [article on-line]; available from http://www.coinfacts.com/mint_history/mint_history_1795/mint_records_1795.htm; accessed February 5, 2008.

12 Robert Sobel, *Panic on Wall Street*, New York: The MacMillan Company, 1968, Chapter 1.

13 Harry Ammon, *James Monroe: The Quest for National Identity*, Charlottesville: University of Virginia Press, 1971, pp. 466-467. After realizing the extent of their problems, the Bank of the United States took three actions to reduce lending on July 20, August 28, and October 30, 1818. Another deflationary event was the Federal government's need for $2 million in specie on October 21, 1818 to settle the Louisiana Purchase with the French Government.

14 Kathy Weiser, California Legends: The California Gold Rush, Legends of America, June 2008; [article on-line]; available from http://www.legendsofamerica.com/ca-goldrush.html; accessed September 7, 2008.

15 W.C. Mitchell, *A History of Greenbacks*, University of Chicago Press, 1903, p. 413.

16 NYT, 'Are Present High Prices Likely to be Maintained?' November 17, 1865.

17 NYT, 'The Report of the Confederate Bondholders' November 6, 1865, p. 4.

18 Charlie Cray and Lee Drutman, 'Corporations and Public Purpose'; [article on-line]; available from http://www.corporatepolicy.org/topics/public.htm; accessed September 7, 2008.

[19] *Santa Clara County v. Southern Pacific Railroad* was argued January 26-29, 1886 and decided May 10, 1886.

[20] NYT, 'New Banking Factors,' January 16, 1899, p. WFRQ1.

[21] Time, October 26, 1931. Quoted by Martin Armstrong in *The Greatest Bull Market In History*, Princeton Economic Institute, 1985, pp. 384-385.

[22] Harlan D. Unrau, 'The Evacuation and Relocation of Persons of Japanese Ancestry During World War II: A Historical Study of the Manzanar War Relocation Center', National Park Service, 1996; [article on-line]; available from http://www.nps.gov/archive/manz/hrs/hrs11.htm; accessed September 7, 2008.

[23] NYT 'Lowest Price in 16 Years', January 17, 1970, p. 52.

[24] NYT 'Monetary Discord,' January 8, 1970, p. 21.

[25] Martin Gansten, *Primary Directions: Astrology's Old Master Technique*, The Wessex Astrologer, 2009. See page 69 for a discussion of Bianchini's latitude adjustment. For this direction of Saturn, begin with Saturn's full latitude of 2deg31'1" or 2.5169 in decimal form. For trine aspects, the factor of -1/2 is multiplied. Result is -1.2585.

12. Partners: Mars

[1] Jerry Springer's natal figure (b. February 13, 1944) recapitulates Mars/Gemini found in the Regulus USA National Horoscope. Springer's Mars/Gemini = 11GE12.

[2] David E. Stannard, *American Holocaust: The Conquest of the New World*, Oxford University Press, 1992.

[3] Mentioned in his December 2, 1823 Monroe Doctrine speech.

[4] The 1824 Presidential election marked the last time Congress nominated Presidential candidates.

[5] David M. Pletcher, *The Diplomacy of Annexation: Texas, Oregon, and the Mexican War*, Columbia, MO.: University of Missouri Press, 1973.

[6] As a coincidence (?), note that 54-40 match the minutes and seconds for the Ascendant of the Regulus USA National Horoscope: 26SA54'50".

[7] Robert Sobel, *Panic on Wall Street*, New York: The Macmillan Company, 1968, p. 97.

[8] Dr. Odeen Ishmael, 'The Trail of Diplomacy: A Documentary History of the Guyana-Venezuela Border Issue,' 1998; [article on-line]; available from http://www.guyana.org/features/trail_diplomacy.html; accessed September 8, 2008.

[9] AMR, p. 557.

[10] Sobel, pp. 297-321.

[11] NYT, 'Racing the Real Test of Auto Development,' October 27, 1907, p. S1.

[12] NYT, 'Plans for Auto Race New York to Paris,' November 28, 1907, p. 1.

[13] NYT, 'Auto Race a Study in Public Schools,' March 17, 1908, p. 2.

[14] NYT, 'House Committee Studies Ways to Aid Railroads,' January 15, 1933, p. 6.

[15] NYT, 'Hoover Demands Revision to ease Bankruptcy Laws,' January 12, 1933, p. 1.

[16] NYT, 'Rail Pensions Held too Great Burden,' January 17, 1933, p. 27.

[17] NYT, 'Missouri Pacific put in Bankruptcy,' April 1, 1933, p. 23.

[18] NYT, 'President to Receive F. H. Prince's Plan for Consolidations of Country's Railroads,' March 31, 1933, p. 29.

[19] Wikipedia contributors, "MG Rover Group," *Wikipedia, The Free Encyclopedia*, http://en.wikipedia.org/w/index.php?title=MG_Rover_Group&oldid=237002870; accessed September 8, 2008.

[20] Allum Bokjhari, 'Antifail: Low Turnouts at Nationwide 'Refuse Fascism' Protests,' Breitbart, November 4, 2017 [article on-line]; available from

https://www.breitbart.com/politics/2017/11/04/antifail-low-turnouts-at-multi-city-antifa-apocalypse/; accessed April 16, 2021.

[21] Madison Park and Kyung Lah, 'Berkeley protests of Yiannopoulos caused $100,000 in damage,' CNN, February 2, 2017 [article on-line]; available from https://www.cnn.com/2017/02/01/us/milo-yiannopoulos-berkeley/index.html; accessed April 16, 2021.

[22] Doug Brown, '82nd Avenue of the Roses Parade Cancelled after Threats of Political Protests, Violence,' Portland Mercury, April 25, 2017 [article online]; available from https://www.portlandmercury.com/blogtown/2017/04/25/18973706/82nd-avenue-of-the-roses-parade-cancelled-after-threats-of-political-protests-violence; accessed April 16, 2021.

[23] https://en.wikipedia.org/wiki/Antifa:_The_Anti-Fascist_Handbook; accessed April 16, 2021.

13. Partners: Mercury

[1] Schoener states 'If the aforesaid places, namely, those of Mercury and of the Moon, apply to each other mutually, and there is concord between them, the soul will be made well ordered and harmonious.' Johannes Schoener, *Opusculum Astrologicum*, Translated and Edited by Robert Hand, Reston, Va.: Arhat Publications, 2001, p. 113. The implication is that for the opposite situation, e.g., no aspect between Mercury and the Moon, the soul will be in disarray.

[2] Ammon, pp. 460-461.

[3] Wikipedia contributors, "Seminole Wars," *Wikipedia, The Free Encyclopedia*, http://en.wikipedia.org/w/index.php?title=Seminole_Wars&oldid=234278129; accessed September 7, 2008.

[4] Joseph Rayback, *A History of American Labor*. The Macmillan Co., New York, 1959, p. 101.

[5] 'Resident Noncitizen Voting in California: A History', The Immigrant Voting Project; [book on-line]; available from http://www.immigrantvoting.org/statehistories/Californiahistory.html; accessed September 7, 2008.

[6] Gary Noy, ed., *Distant Horizon: Documents from the Nineteenth-Century American West*, Lincoln: University of Nebraska Press, 1999. As quoted by Ellen Baker, Columbia University History Department; [article on-line]; available from http://www.columbia.edu/itc/history/baker/w3630/edit/tex-caconv.html; accessed September 7, 2008).

[7] 'Uncle Tom's Cabin Study Guide,' BookRags.com; [article on-line]; available from http://www.bookrags.com/studyguide-uncletomscabin/intro.html; accessed September 7, 2008.

[8] Lincoln's statement on Stowe has been widely circulated but may not be accurate. For example, the PBS profile of Harriet Beecher Stowe comments 'These are the words legend attributed to Abraham Lincoln when he was introduced to Harriet Beecher Stowe in 1862.' Whether Lincoln actually made this statement is a question best left to Lincoln specialists. See Public Broadcasting Service, 'Harriet Beecher Stowe'; [article on-line]; available from http://www.pbs.org/wnet/ihas/poet/stowe.html; accessed October 20, 2008.

[9] NYT, 'Rebel Murder of Blacks,' January 5, 1863, p. 4.

[10] NYT, 'Affairs in Georgia, Condition of the Freedman,' July 16, 1867, p. 2.

[11] NYT, 'A Socialist Failure,' October 16, 1883, p. 4.

[12] Joseph Rayback, *A History of American Labor*. The Macmillan Co., New York, 1959, p. 172.

[13] NYT, 'The Brewers' Troubles,' May 4, 1888, p. 6.

[14] For another delineation example of Mars/Taurus as a raging bull, See Robert DeNiro, b. August 17, 1943, with Mars/Taurus in his natal figure a delineation match to his role in *Raging Bull*.

[15] NYT, 'Castle Garden Affairs,' April 8, 1890, p. 8.

[16] Janette Rainwater, 'The Central Intelligence Agency'; [article on-line]; available from http://www.janrainwater.com/htdocs/CIAp2.htm; accessed September 1, 2008.

14. Partners: Venus

[1] In my opinion, the latter phenomenon accounts for the popularity of breast enlargement surgery among American women. It also speaks to the role of Mae West, Jane Russell, and Dolly Parton in popular culture.

[2] Bruce Scofield, 'Quetzalcoatl and the Sexual Secrets of the Toltec Astrologers,' One Reed Publications; [article on-line]; available from http://www.onereed.com/articles/qvenus.html; accessed September 8, 2008.

[3] George L. Marshall, Jr., 'The Rise and Fall of the Newburgh Conspiracy: How General Washington and his Spectacles Saved the Republic,' *Early America Review*, Fall 1997; [article on-line]; available from http://www.earlyamerica.com/review/fall97/wshngton.html; accessed September 8, 2008.

[4] Adam Hochschild, 'Against All Odds,' *Mother Jones*, January/February 2004; [article on-line]; available from http://www.motherjones.com/news/feature/2004/01/12_403.html; accessed September 8, 2008.

[5] Wikipedia contributors, "Jump Jim Crow," *Wikipedia, The Free Encyclopedia*, http://en.wikipedia.org/w/index.php?title=Jump_Jim_Crow&oldid=223339216; accessed September 7, 2008.

[6] Wikipedia contributors, "Muncy Abolition Riot of 1842," *Wikipedia, The Free Encyclopedia*, http://en.wikipedia.org/w/index.php?title=Muncy_Abolition_Riot_of_1842&oldid=217311952; accessed September 8, 2008.

[7] Wikipedia contributors, "Pulaski Riot," *Wikipedia, The Free Encyclopedia*, http://en.wikipedia.org/w/index.php?title=Pulaski_Riot&oldid=193645559; accessed September 8, 2008.

[8] NYT, 'Difficulty in St. Augustine, Florida Between Blacks and Whites,' August 29, 1868.

[9] NYT, 'The Camilla Riot – An Unprovoked Massacre,' September 30, 1868, p. 1.

[10] NYT, 'The Rio in New Orleans,' September 28, 1868, p. 3.

[11] NYT, 'The Veto of the Marshals Bill,' June 16, 1880, p. 4.

[12] NYT, 'Bonanzas and 'Wildcats',' June 21, 1880, p. 3.

[13] NYT, 'Mining Swindles in Utah,' July 6, 1880, p. 3.

[14] NYT, 'Sixty-Day Crisis in Food Faces US, Asserts Hoover,' February 22, 1918, p. 1.

[15] Barbara Holden-Smith, 'Lynching, Federalism, and the Intersection of Race and Gender in the Progressive Era', *Yale Journal of Law and Feminism*, 1996; [article on-line]; available from http://www.soc.umn.edu/~samaha/cases/smith_lynching_feminism.html; accessed September 8, 2008.

[16] NYT, 'Harding Promises Justice to Negroes,' September 20, 1920, p. 2.

[17] See AMR, p. 175 for discussion of the connection between Thomas Jefferson and the 1802 Jupiter-Saturn conjunction in Virgo. For additional evidence of the Virgo-Latino connection, see AMR, pp. 484-485 for a discussion of Mars/Virgo in the nativity of President James Polk as a timer of agitation leading up to the Mexican War which secured Texas as an American territory.

[18] NYT, 'Business Diary: November 6-11,' November 13, 1994.

[19] Ibid.

15. Partners: Jupiter

[1] The significations of planets include class position within the ranks of society. Saturn signifies slaves and sorcerers; Jupiter, priests and magnates; Mars, warriors; Sun, leaders; Venus; artisans; Mercury, merchants; Moon, common people.

[2] Wikipedia contributors, "Aroostook War," *Wikipedia, The Free Encyclopedia*, http://en.wikipedia.org/w/index.php?title=Aroostook_War&oldid=229665573; accessed August 8, 2008.

[3] John Baker, 17 Jan 1796, 12:08:51 PM, LMT +04:39"35, Moscow, ME. Author's rectification.

[4] NYT, January 26, 1852, p. 2.

[5] NYT, February 28, 1852, p. 1.

[6] Bruce Champ, *The National Banking System: A Brief History*, Federal Reserve Bank of Cleveland, Working Paper 07-23, December 2007, pp. 11-12.

[7] NYT, August 3, 1870, p. 4.

[8] NYT, August 14, 1870, p. 7.

[9] NYT, 'Taxation of National Banks,' December 22, 1876, p. 4.

[10] NYT, 'Washington Alert to Aid Situation, 'August 1, 1914, p. 5.

[11] NYT, 'McAdoo Meets Bankers Here,' August 3, 1914, p. 3.

[12] NYT, 'Grants Billion Currency Issue' August 4, 1914, p. 4.

[13] NYT, 'To Pay Debts Abroad in Gold; Bankers Urge Washington to Permit Use of Banknotes in Reserves,' August 13, 1914, p. 5.

[14] NYT, 'The Federal Reserve Board,' August 15, 1914, p. 8.

[15] NYT, 'Restrict Branches State Bank Can Run' November 8, 1923, p. 21.

[16] NYT, 'States File Brief on Branch Banks,' November 9, 1923, p. 15.

[17] NYT, 'Dawes Makes Plea for National Banks,' December 15, 1923, p. 3.

[18] NYT, 'State Right to Bar Branch Bank Valid,' January 29, 1924, p. 23.

[19] NYT, 'A Job Easier Said Than Done for New Savings-Unit Owner,' February 20, 1989.

[20] NYT, 'Bank Closings Discriminate, Report Asserts,' January 30, 1989.

[21] AP, 'Hispanic Bank Finds Problems in Organizing,' February 19, 1989.

[22] Marc Winerman, 'The Origins of the FTC: Concentration, Cooperation, Control, and Competition,' *Antitrust Law Journal*, Vol. 71, 2003; [article on-line]; available from http://www.ftc.gov/ftc/history/docs/origins.pdf; accessed August 3, 2008.

Appendix C. Supplement: Directing through the Bounds

[1] Maxwell Bloomfield, 'John Elihu Hall, *'American National Biography*, Oxford University Press, 2000; [article on-line]; available from http://www.libarts.ucok.edu/history/faculty/roberson/course/1483/suppl/chpX/JohnElihuHall.htm; accessed September 1, 2008.

[2] Proposed rectification: 18-Mar-1782, 3:16:12 PM, LMT +05:29:31, Abbeville, South Carolina, 82w22'45, 34n10'41", ASC 22LE53'34".

[3] Evan Cornog, *The Birth of Empire: DeWitt Clinton and the American Experience, 1769-1828*, New York: Oxford University Press, 1998.

[4] Crawford's leading role in national politics as Senator (1807-1812), President pro tempore (1812-1813), Minister to France and Italy (1813-1815), Secretary of War (1815-1816), Secretary of the Treasury (1816-1815), and Presidential contender in national races held in 1816 and 1824 has been obscured by the absence of personal papers left to posterity which has hindered a definitive assessment by historians.

[5] Some reports of Crawford's illness say he suffered a negative reaction from an overdose of lobelia improperly administered by a physician. Under the arcus vitae methodology, his September 1823 illness was timed by d. Jupiter square Sun, lat=Jupiter; consistent with Sun as the hīlāj and Jupiter as the high scoring killing planet. Given Jupiter's signification as heart disease, these measurements favor Crawford suffered a stroke.

[6] Barbara L. Narendra, 'Benjamin Silliman and the Peabody Museum,' *Discovery*, Vol. 14, 1979, pp. 13-29; [article on-line]; available from http://www.peabody.yale.edu/archives/ypmbios/silliman.html; accessed September 30, 2008.

[7] 'Thomas Cole (1801-1848), The Dawn of the Hudson River School,' Hamilton Auction Galleries; [article on-line]; available from http://hamiltonauctiongalleries.com/Cole.htm; accessed September 30, 2008.

[8] Nathaniel Philbrick, *Sea of Glory: America's Voyage of Discovery*, New York: Penguin Books, 2003.

[9] Nathaniel Philbrick, 'A Voyage into Unchartered Waters: The Writing of Sea of Glory,' *Penguin Group*; [article on-line]; available from http://us.penguingroup.com/static/packages/us/maritime/seaofglory-story5.html. accessed September 30, 2008.

[10] For another example of this placement, see Rutherford Hayes, whose Jupiter/Gemini/12th signified financial aid to African Americans for university education. One recipient was W. E. B. Du Bois who attended Fisk and Harvard Universities and went on to help found the National Association for the Advancement of Colored People (NAACP).

[11] David S. Reynolds, *Walt Whitman's America*, New York: Random House, 1995, p. 422.

[12] Reynolds, p. 387.

[13] Reynolds, p. 413.

[14] Abraham Lincoln, 'General Order #38,' Documents on Wheels; [on-line]; available from http://lincolnconstitution.lincolnarchives.us/lincoln_constitution_burnside_order38.htm; accessed September 30, 2008.

[15] 'About the Morgan,' The Morgan Library & Museum'; [article on-line]; available from http://www.themorgan.org/about/historyMore.asp?id=6; accessed September 25, 2008.

[16] NYT, 'The Railroad Monopoly,' February 22, 1881, p. 1.

[17] NYT, 'His Majesty Jay Gould,' February 23, 1881, p. 4.

[18] As a signature for explosions, Mars/Taurus can be found in natal figures including Timothy McVeigh (b. 23-Apr-1968 and President Gerald Ford (b. 14-Jul-1913). Both McVeigh and Ford's military careers involved gunnery and ordnance.

[19] Charlotte Gray, *Reluctant Genius: The Passionate Life and Inventive Mind of Alexander Graham Bell,* Toronto: HarperCollins Publishers Ltd., 2006, p. 433.

[20] Kenneth P. Todd, Jr., *A Capsule History of the Bell System*, 1997; [article on-line]; available from http://www.porticus.org/bell/capsule_bell_system.html#Contents; accessed August 1, 2008.

[21] Jean Maddern Pitrone, Jefferson, NC.: McFarland & Company, Inc., 2003, p. 31. Photograph shows window display of mittens and gloves.

[22] First published by McClure's in serial form from November 1902 to October 1903, republished as 'The History of the Standard Oil Company' in November 1904.

[23] NYT, "The Scientific Management of the Dollar; That, Says Roger W. Babson, the Well Known Statistician, Will Be the Next Great Step in the Efficiency Movement, Section M, Page 6, October 6, 1912.

[24] Donald Warren, *Radio Priest: Charles Coughlin, The Father of Hate Radio.* New York: The Free Press, 1996, pp. 175-185.

[25] Shawn Levy, *Rat Pack Confidential*, New York: Broadway Books, 1998, pp. 29-30.

[26] Frank Sanello, *Stallone: A Rocky Life*, Mainstream Publishing, 1998, p. 79.

[27] Wikipedia contributors, "Big data," *Wikipedia, The Free Encyclopedia*, https://en.wikipedia.org/w/index.php?title=Big_data&oldid=1023360946 (accessed May 21, 2021).

[28] NYT, 'The Age of Big Data,' February 11, 2012, Section SR, p. 1.

Appendix D. Tests of Egyptian versus Ptolemaic Bounds

[1] ARM, Appendix A, pp. 357-367.

[2] Eaton's letters were published in the Philadelphia Observer in 1923 under the pseudonym 'Wyoming' and were reprinted in 1824 in pamphlet form. See Robert P. Hay, 'The Case for Andrew Jackson in 1824: Eaton's *Wyoming Letters*', *Tennessee Historical Quarterly*, Vol. XXIX, No. 2, Summer 1970, pp. 139-151.

[3] Pisces as a symbol for Christianity can be traced to Jesus of Nazarath whose birth followed a series Jupiter-Saturn conjunctions in Pisces during 7 BC.

[4] Nathanial Philbrick, *Sea of Glory: America's Voyage of Discovery, the U.S. Exploring Expedition, 1838-1842*, Viking, 2003, p. 81.

[5] Terry Burcin, *Commodore Perry's 1864 Japanese Expedition: How Whaling Influenced the Event that Revolutionized Japan*, Virginia Polytechnic Institute and State University, unpublished Masters dissertation, May 5, 2005; [dissertation on-line]; available from http://scholar.lib.vt.edu/theses/available/etd-05132005-131722/unrestricted/MAThesis.pdf; accessed October 20, 2008.

[6] Yonathan Eyal, *The Young America Movement and the Transformation of the Democratic Party: 1828 - 1861*, Cambridge University Press, 2007, pp. 95-96.

[7] Jean Strouse, *Morgan: American Financier*, New York: Random House, 1999, p. 143.

[8] Strouse, p. 160.

[9] *Railway Review*, January 29, 1887, p. 62.
Cited by Wikipedia contributors, "Gustavus Franklin Swift," *Wikipedia, The Free Encyclopedia*, http://en.wikipedia.org/w/index.php?title=Gustavus_Franklin_Swift&oldid=246419097; accessed October 21, 2008.

[10] Craig Phelan, *Grand Master Workman: Terence Powderly and the Knights of Labor*, Westport, CT.: Greenwood Press, 2000, Chapter 5.

[11] Phelan, pp. 174-175.

[12] The Anti-Saloon League of America was the most powerful lobbying group in support of prohibition.

[13] NYT, 'To Strengthen Dry Bill, Anti-Saloon Leader Proposes Change in Prohibition Movement,' March 28, 1917, p. 13.

[14] NYT, 'U.S. Leads World in Use of Cotton,' January 21, 1925, p. 29.

[15] This is another example which supports 'mean' calculation of the Lunar Nodes over the modern 'true' alternative calculation method. Computed for September 8, 1935, position of the mean Lunar South Node falls at 18CA56 falls in the bound of Mercury/Cancer which extends from 13CA00'00" to 18CA59'59" according to the Egyptian system. Position of the true Lunar South Node at 20CA34 does not. See ARM, Chapter 12, pp. 228-236 for further discussion of the mean versus true calculation debate.

[16] Conrad Black, *Franklin Delano Roosevelt: Champion of Freedom*, New York: Public Affairs, 2003, p. 220.

Appendix E. Solar Arc Directions

[1] John Quincy Adams, 'Letter on Amistad Africans,' New York Journal of Commerce, December 25, 1839; [letter on-line]; available from. http://www.amistadamerica.org/index.php?option=com_content&task=view&id=213&Itemid=100; accessed September 1, 2008.

[2] NYT, 'Wreck on the New York Centra,' August 29, 1900, p. 2.

[3] NYT, 'Riots a Result of Many Causes,' April 27, 1930, p. 135.

[4] NYT, 'Ohio is Divided on Prison Ethics,' May 11, 1930, p. 52.

[5] NYT, 'Gen. Brown Favors Taking Erie Canal,' May 6, 1930, p. 54.

[6] NYT, 'President Pledges Legal Aid on Rights,' July 3, 1958, p. 26.

[7] NYT, 'Civil Rights Unit Eyes New Fields,' October 15, 1959, p. 46.

[8] NYT, 'Ideas & Trends; High Court Gives Civil Rights Law A Broader Scope,' May 24, 1987.

[9] NYT, 'Princeton Clubs Told to Let in Women,' May 27, 1987.

[10] Wikipedia contributors, "Edward Fitzgerald Beale," *Wikipedia, The Free Encyclopedia*, http://en.wikipedia.org/w/index.php?title=Edward_Fitzgerald_Beale&oldid=215393428; accessed June 10, 2008.

[11] Wikipedia contributors, "Michael Owens (Medal of Honor)," *Wikipedia, The Free Encyclopedia*, +http://en.wikipedia.org/w/index.php?title=Michael_O+wens_%28Medal_of_Honor%29&oldid=193817162; accessed June 10, 2008.

[12] Wikipedia contributors, "United States expedition to Korea," *Wikipedia, The Free Encyclopedia*, http://en.wikipedia.org/w/index.php?title=United_States_expedition_to_Korea&oldid=217941702; accessed June 10, 2008.

[13] Wikipedia contributors, "E. S. Gosney," *Wikipedia, The Free Encyclopedia*, http://en.wikipedia.org/w/index.php?title=E._S._Gosney&oldid=205163836; accessed June 10, 2008.

[14] Mars/Virgo is the significator for abortion according to the author's research.

[15] David M. Damkaer, *A Century of Copepads: The U.S. Fisheries Steamer Albatross*, NOAA, Marine Fisheries Review, September 22, 1999.

[16] Kyle Enevoldsen, '120 Years Later, Historic Ship Found in Hawaii,' Internet Broadcasting, October 5, 2006; [article on-line]; available from http://www.wnbc.com/traffic/10009142/detail.html; accessed September 7, 2008.

[17] Henry Ford Peace Expedition; Records, 1915-1916, Records of Committee for Nonviolent Action, Swarthmore College Peace Collection; [reference on-line]; available from http://www.swarthmore.edu/Library/peace/DG001-025/dg018hford.htm; accessed September 7, 2008.

[18] Conrad Black, *Franklin Delano Roosevelt: Champion of Freedom*, New York: Public Affairs, 2003, p. 769.

[19] Black, p. 828.

[20] NYT, 'Spanish Galleon Believed Found,' July 20, 1975, p. 21.

[21] John Earnshaw, 'Thomas Muir (1765-1799), *Australian Dictionary of Biography Online Edition*; [dictionary on-line]; available from http://www.adb.online.anu.edu.au/biogs/A020231b.htm; accessed September 9, 2007.

[22] NYT, 'South America,' Lieut. Gilliss' Astronomical Expedition,' October 5, 1858, p. 5.

[23] NYT, 'The Nicaragua Canal; Outline of the French Project,' January 8, 1859, p. 2.

[24] NYT, 'General Telegraph News; News from the Isthmus,' May 24, 1880, p. 5.

[25] NYT, 'Miscellaneous City News; Arctic Exploration,' May 26, 1880, p. 3.

[26] NYT, 'Our South Polar Expedition Put Off,' April 24, 1910, p. 20.
[27] NYT, 'Wellman Off for Europe in his Airship America,' October 16, 1910, p. 1.
[28] NYT, 'Wellman Ovation at Atlantic City,' October 22, 1910, p. 16.
[29] NYT, 'To Watch Eclipse from a Seaplane Far above Clouds, Prof. Todd Heads Expedition that will Make Astronomical Experiment,' May 14, 1919, page 1.
[30] NYT, 'Victory Ship Here as Loan Goes Over,' May 11, 1919, p. 19.
[31] NYT, 'Byrd's Antarctic Ship Crashes Into Pier,' November 18, 1939, p.19.
[32] NYT, 'Byrd Party to Survey Vast Antarctic Domain,' November 19, 1939, p. E10.
[33] NYT, 'Red Cross Pioneer Honored at Dinner,' November 18, 1939, p. 6.
[34] NYT, 'Dr. J.I. Vance Dies; Noted Minister, 78,' November 25, 1939, p. 21.
[35] NYT, 'Salvation Army Asks War Funds of Public,' June 10, 1940, p. 7.
[36] NYT, 'War Aid is Speeded by Salvation Army,' June 15, 1940, p.18.
[37] NYT, 'Supreme Court Lifts Kennedy Ban on SST,' October 18, 1977, p. 77.
[38] NYT, 'A Growing Clamor for a Well-Fed World,' October 19, 1977, p. C1.
[39] NYT, 'Washington & Business; The U.S. Gold-Clause Legislation,' October 20, 1977, p. 87.
[40] NYT, 'Notes on People,' October 18, 1977, p. 22.
[41] NYT, 'Supreme Court Roundup,' May 16, 1978, p. 20.
[42] NYT, 'Partisan Dispute Over Plan to Reshape Social Security,' November 20, 1998.
[43] NYT, 'House Acts to Protect Social Security Surplus,' May 27, 1999.
[44] NYT, 'Affairs at the Capital,' August 20, 1887, p. 5.
[45] NYT, 'Steel Trust Plans to Conform to Law,' September 22, 1911, p. 1.
[46] NYT, 'New Exports Curb Urged,' April 12, 1941, p. 13.
[47] NYT, 'US and Canada Study Joint Task,' November 10, 1941, p. 6.
[48] NYT, 'US Exports Seen Key to World Fund,' December 20, 1946, p. 37.
[49] NYT, 'Martin Foresees New Central Bank on Global Basis,' September 15, 1970, p. 63.
[50] NYT, 'IMF Deal Cuts U.S. Gold Stock,' September 17, 1970, p. 69.
[51] NYT, 'Alarm is Sounded on Eurodollars,' April 19, 1971, p. 57.
[52] NYT, 'National Coin Week Starts Today,' April 18, 1971, p. D35.
[53] E. R. Lanier, 'Griffin Bell', The New Georgia Encyclopedia, October 20, 2003; [article on-line]; available from http://www.georgiaencyclopedia.org/nge/Article.jsp?id=h-1027; accessed September 7, 2007.
[54] NYT, 'Congress and Courts Try to Restore Balance,' July 14, 2006.
[55] Henry Adams. *History of the United States 1801-09. The First Administration of Thomas Jefferson*, Part II, Chapter 10; [book on-line]; http://en.wikisource.org/wiki/History_of_the_United_States_1801-09/The_First_Administration_of_Thomas_Jefferson/II:10; accessed September 7, 2008.
[56] Robert Higgs. *"Not Merely Perfidious but Ungrateful": The U.S. Takeover of West Florida*. The Independent Institute, Working Paper #55, March 14, 2005; [article on-line]; available from http://www.independent.org/publications/working_papers/article.asp?id=1478; accessed September 7, 2008.
[57] NYT, 'Protection to Emigrants. Message from the President,' May 15, 1872, p. 2.
[58] NYT, 'Insane Murderers,' September 11, 1872, p. 4.
[59] Allan R. Andrews, 'How yellow is today's journalism?' December 22, 1996; [article on-line]; available from http://www.toad.net/~andrews/yellow.html; accessed September 7, 2008.
[60] 'The World of 1898: The Spanish-American War,' Library of Congress; [article on-line]; available from http://www.loc.gov/rr/hispanic/1898/chronology.html;

accessed September 7, 2008.

[61] Jose Poncet, *The U.S. Ambassador to Spain: Stewart L. Woodford*, The Spanish American War Centennial Website; [article on-line]; available from http://www.spanamwar.com/Woodford.htm; accessed September 7, 2008.

[62] Douglas Linder, *The Sacco-Vanzetti Case: An Account*; [article on-line]; available from http://www.law.umkc.edu/faculty/projects/ftrials/SaccoV/chronology.html; accessed September 7, 2008.

[63] NYT, 'Quota Law Author Wants Door Closed,' March 29, 1927, p. 11.

[64] NYT, 'Alien Departures Exceeded Immigration in 1932,' August 18, 1932, p. 1.

[65] NYT, 'Soviet Says Testing by the U.S. In Space Renews Arms Race,' August 22, 1985, Section A, page 8.

[66] NYT, '1949 Test Linked to Radiation in Northwest' March 9, 1986, Section 1, page 35.

[67] Wikipedia contributors, "Gulf War," *Wikipedia, The Free Encyclopedia*, http://en.wikipedia.org/w/index.php?title=Gulf_War&oldid=236602192; accessed September 7, 2008.

[68] Diane Windham Shaw, 'Layfatette and Slavery,' *Lafayette Alumni News Magazine*, Winter 2007; [article on-line]; available from http://www.lafayette.edu/press/magazine/Jan07/slavery.html; accessed September 8, 2008.

[69] Robert Remini, *Andrew Jackson and the Course of American Freedom, 1822-1832*, New York: Harper & Row, 1981, p. 380.

[70] Ibid, p. 381.

[71] Herbert Clark, 'James Napier' in African-American Members of the Tennessee General Assembly, 1873-1995, Tennessee State University; [article on-line]; available from http://www.tnstate.edu/library/digital/napier.htm; accessed September 8, 2008.

[72] NYT, 'From the State Capital, The Anti-Gold Speculation Bill,' April 13, 1863, p. 1.

[73] NYT, Monetary Affairs, April 23, 1863, p. 4.

[74] 'The Impeach Trial of William Belknap,' in Hinds' Precedents, Volume III, Chapter LXXVII, section 2444, pp. 903-904; [book on-line]; available from http://frwebgate.access.gpo.gov/cgi-bin/getdoc.cgi?dbname=hinds_prec_vol_iii&docid=f:hinds_lxxvii.pdf; accessed September 8, 2008.

[75] NYT, 'In the Woman's Building,' June 25, 1893, p. 17.

[76] Julie K. Rose, 'The World's Columbian Exposition: Idea, Experience, Aftermath'; [article on-line]; available from http://xroads.virginia.edu/~MA96/WCE/title.html; accessed September 8, 2008.

[77] NYT, 'A Women's Aggressive Campaign,' November 17, 1893, p. 4.

[78] NYT, 'Court to Weigh Segregation,' September 19, 1952, p. 15.

[79] NYT, 'Race Rulings Due in Supreme Court,' April 6, 1953, p. 42.

[80] Wikipedia contributors, "T. J. Jemison," *Wikipedia, The Free Encyclopedia*, http://en.wikipedia.org/w/index.php?title=T._J._Jemison&oldid=231019460; accessed September 7, 2008.

[81] U. S. Supreme Court; Hepburn v. Griswold, *Justia.com*; [article on-line]; available from http://supreme.justia.com/us/75/603/case.html; accessed August 6, 2008.

[82] NYT, 'Mr. Sherman's Hopes and Fears,' October 1, 1890, p. 4.

[83] NYT, 'Roads may Retain Their Coal Mines,' September 11, 1908, p. 1.

[84] NYT, 'Income Tax Plan to Free 20,000,000; December 24, 1949, p. 20.

[85] NYT, 'Life Insurance Concerns to Fight U.S. Retroactive Income Tax Plan, December 25, 1949, p. F1.

[86] NYT, 'Bankers Urge Passage of Bill,' July 21, 1950, p. 30.

[87] NYT, 'Personal Finance: Insuring Savings,' September 14, 1967, p. 67.

LAUS DEO

NOTES

www.ingramcontent.com/pod-product-compliance
Lightning Source LLC
Chambersburg PA
CBHW030125240426
43672CB00005B/22